The Microwave Cook's Complete Companion

Also by Rosemary Dunn Stancil
and Lorela Nichols Wilkins
Published by Ballantine Books

SIMPLY SCRUMPTIOUS MICROWAVING
(with Mary Ann Feuchter Robinson)

KIDS' SIMPLY SCRUMPTIOUS MICROWAVING

The
Microwave Cook's Complete Companion

**ROSEMARY DUNN STANCIL
AND LORELA NICHOLS WILKINS**

FAWCETT COLUMBINE · NEW YORK

A Fawcett Columbine Book
Published by Ballantine Books
Copyright © 1990 by Kitchen Classics

Library of Congress Cataloging-in-Publication Data

Stancil, Rosemary Dunn.
    The microwave cook's complete companion / Rosemary Dunn Stancil
  and Lorela Nichols Wilkins.—1st ed.
      p. cm.
    ISBN 0-449-90409-1
    1. Microwave cookery. I. Wilkins, Lorela Nichols. II. Title.
TX832.S73 1990
641.5′882—dc20   89-90880
                                            CIP

EDITED BY JUDY KNIPE
ILLUSTRATIONS © 1990 BY LYNNE KOPCIK
BOOK DESIGN BY BARBARA MARKS

Manufactured in the United States of America

First Edition: April 1990

10 9 8 7 6 5 4 3 2 1

■

To our families
Frank, Jennifer, and Martin Stancil
Joe, Deirdre, and Darrick Wilkins
Your love and support give us
balance and creative energy.
We thank you.

■

CONTENTS

Foreword

We began using microwave ovens, professionally and at home, many years ago. In those pioneering microwave days, the only cookbooks available were the books that came with each oven. Published by the manufacturers, they were apparently based on the premise that anyone who wanted such a convenient appliance also wanted convenience food. The recipes relied heavily on mixes for everything from soups to mashed potatoes to cakes.

As working mothers, we were delighted with the speed and ease offered by the microwave, but as food professionals, we wanted to make tasty, nutritious food from scratch. We began developing our own microwave recipes, using fresh, seasonal ingredients and adapting some techniques used in conventional cooking. The result was *Simply Scrumptious Microwaving*, published in 1982, one of the first general cookbooks for the microwave oven, followed by *Kids' Simply Scrumptious Microwaving*, written for children to use.

We receive many encouraging letters asking for more microwave recipes and more information. One reader writes, "Of all the microwave cookbooks I have, I use your book every day. I love the way the foods are seasoned. Please let me know when you write another one." Well, here it is!

Both of us share the complex and busy lifestyles of many of our readers, with dual careers and active children. In our families, each member contributes in different ways, but we all help with food preparation. Our days begin with two or three different breakfast schedules and end with evening snacks for some, and for every meal the microwave oven is a part of the daily routine, helping to make life less hectic and run a bit smoother.

In our households, the holidays, birthdays, and anniversaries are celebrated with special meals, and like other families, we also entertain—sometimes casually and sometimes more formally. Whatever the occasion, the microwave plays a crucial role.

These recipes, all tested in our kitchens at home, are practical, healthy, and delicious. They range from simple dishes that kids enjoy making to traditional American favorites and sophisticated international recipes.

We believe that there are no magic formulas for cooking either conventionally or in the microwave. You must watch and taste food as it cooks in the microwave, and you must make decisions about it, just as you do in conventional cooking. Once you've mastered basic microwave techniques, experience will allow you to become innovative.

The Microwave Cook's Complete Companion was written for single people, couples, and busy families. Just as our mothers and grandmothers used earlier cookbooks to answer their culinary questions, we hope you will use this book as a complete resource for microwave cooking and that it will be just as helpful in answering your cooking and entertaining needs.

ROSEMARY DUNN STANCIL
LORELA NICHOLS WILKINS

The Microwave Cook's Complete Companion

About Microwaving

How a
Microwave Oven Works

The first microwave ovens were called radar ranges because they used the same type of energy that radar equipment does. The simplest radar devices transmit short, strong bursts of electromagnetic energy, many of which strike objects in the vicinity and are reflected back to the radar receiver. In the microwave oven these bursts of energy are contained in the oven cavity, where they bounce around. When the energy hits food, it is absorbed and heats the food.

Microwaves themselves are a form of electromagnetic energy of very high frequency, vibrating millions of times per second. These waves are similar to radio waves, which are around you all the time, waiting to be used by turning on your radio. The difference between radio waves and microwaves is the frequency and the length of the waves themselves. At 2450 megahertz, which is the most common frequency of home microwave ovens, the microwaves are 4.8 inches long, while radio waves can be several feet to several miles in length!

Microwaves are created in your oven by a special electronic oscillating tube called a *magnetron*. From the magnetron the energy travels through a hollow metal channel called a *waveguide*, which opens into the oven cavity, where the energy is dispersed by a *stirrer*, a fanlike deflector that distributes the energy as evenly as possible in the oven cavity. The energy then penetrates the food in the oven, where it is absorbed in varying degrees and heats the food.

Different foods have different absorption rates; those with the highest rates heat up hotter and faster. Fats and sugars heat up fastest of all. Water will take twice as long to heat as the same amount of fat in the microwave. When heating different kinds of food in the microwave, cold food will take longer to heat than the warmer food. That is the reason a piece of apple pie topped with a scoop of ice cream can be heated in the microwave for 15 to 20 seconds without melting the ice cream.

Basically, absorbed microwaves heat foods by making the molecules in the food vibrate billions of times per second. This vibration creates heat by the friction of the molecules rubbing against each other at this extremely high rate. The microwaves actually penetrate foods about 1½ inches; the heat generated at the surface is then carried to the center of the food by conduction, as in conventional cooking.

MICROWAVE FEATURES

Different makers of microwave ovens offer different features. Some ovens have *turntables* that move the food through the microwave field instead of depending on the stirrer to distribute the microwaves evenly. Ovens may have a *glass tray* that is either sealed in place or removable. This tray raises the food so that microwaves can be reflected into the bottom of the food and cook evenly.

Most microwave ovens have a *plastic panel* or *double glass door,* allowing you to see the food as it cooks. Sandwiched between the plastic panels or glass is a metal screen that keeps microwave energy contained in the oven cavity. Microwave ovens have at least two safety interlocks that prevent the oven from operating when the door is open.

Some ovens contain a *control* (or display) *panel* with a variety of features, such as on-and-off switches, a time-of-day clock, or operating controls. Other ovens have *mechanical controls* that may be pushbuttons, dials, or levers that can be set to control cooking time and power levels. It isn't possible to be as accurate when programming time on mechanical ovens, and they are harder to keep clean than electronic control panels.

Electronic control panels have many advantages. They operate by slight pressure from the operator's finger, they are easy to clean, and they allow greater cooking flexibility. It's easy to reheat one roll for 10 seconds, whereas on a mechanical oven you can't be as accurate because of the "play" in the controls.

Variable power automatically reduces the microwave energy received by food as the microwave cycles on and off. (When the microwave is set to cook at 50% power, the magnetron generates microwaves only half the time. When cooking on 100% power, the magnetron generates microwaves the entire time.) Variable power brings much more flexibility to microwave cooking since it allows you to choose the speed at which food cooks.

A *temperature probe* may come with your oven. This device can be attached to the microwave by a cable. The probe is inserted into the food to check the internal temperature while it cooks. When the food has reached the temperature set on the control panel, the panel will automatically turn off the oven or hold the food at that temperature.

A *browning element* is found in some microwaves. Mounted at the top of the oven, it is used to crisp food after it has been microwaved.

Moisture sensors are used to preprogram cooking time for different categories of food. As the food cooks and releases bursts of steam, the oven registers it, calculating the time needed to finish cooking. When the food is done, the microwave automatically beeps, and the oven turns off.

Braille overlays may be purchased from the oven manufacturers for visually impaired people. Often directions and recipes on cassette tapes are also available.

MICROWAVE OVEN SAFETY

All microwave ovens manufactured after October 1971 are required to meet radiation standards that are enforced by the Food and Drug Administration (FDA). Emissions standards are set by the Department of Health and Human Services (HHS), Center for Devices and Radiological Health in Washington, D.C. These standards set limits of radiation emission that are thousands of times lower than a level believed to have any possibility of being harmful to health.

GUIDELINES FOR SAFE MICROWAVE OVEN INSTALLATION AND OPERATION

- Follow the manufacturer's instructions concerning safe installation and use.
- For safe measure, have any microwave oven six years or older checked for leakage periodically by a qualified service technician.
- Never operate an oven when the door is bent, warped, or otherwise damaged.
- If you see that the seals around the door have visibly deteriorated, have a service technician replace them.
- Do not operate the oven when anything is caught in the door.
- Operate an oven only when food is in it.
- The United States Department of Agriculture (USDA) recommends that canning not be done in the microwave.
- Deep-frying foods in the microwave is not recommended because it is so difficult to control the temperature of the fat. "Pan-frying" in a microwave browning dish, however, is safe.
- Never use an extension cord with a microwave oven.
- Ovens designed for use in the United States are for 120 volt, 60 Hz current. If you move to a country with a different electrical current, you must use an oven that was designed for that current.

MICROWAVE OVEN COOKWARE

Our advice to microwave beginners is to start with what you already have in the kitchen, then add more microwavable equipment as you need it.

MATERIAL SUITABLE FOR MICROWAVE COOKWARE

A container used for microwave cooking should be nonporous, nonflammable, able to withstand the high temperatures reached during cooking, and made of a material that permits microwave energy to pass through it. It must be made of a material that is approved by the Food and Drug Administration (FDA) for safe contact with food. Heat-

POWER LEVELS

In this book, HIGH means 100% power. Other power levels are given in percentages, such as 70%, 50%, and so on.

Different manufacturers of microwave ovens assign different names to power levels. Check your owner's manual or the cookbook that came with your microwave to see the power designations for your oven.

MICROWAVE OVEN POWER LEVELS

POWER LEVEL	PERCENT OF POWER
HIGH	100%
MEDIUM HIGH	70%
MEDIUM	50%
MEDIUM LOW OR DEFROST	30%
LOW	10%

tempered glass, ceramic, china (no metal trim), pottery, glass-ceramics, ovenable paperboard, microwavable plastic, and paper are materials that can be used to cook in. Straw and wood containers and seashells can be used for reheating.

HEAT-TEMPERED GLASS

As you will see throughout this book, glass measures (made of heat-tempered glass) serve as our microwave saucepans for very good reasons:

1. They can withstand high temperatures.
2. The clear glass enables you to see the food while it is cooking.
3. The handles don't get hot (except when cooking sugar syrup for a prolonged time).
4. They are relatively inexpensive and widely available.
5. Sometimes ingredients can be measured right in the cooking container. We highly recommend using glass measures in all sizes for microwave cooking. The 2- and 2½-quart sizes are very handy for basic cooking. Smaller sizes are convenient for making sauces, and accommodating small amounts of food. Heat-tempered baking dishes are also useful in microwave cooking.

GLASS-CERAMIC

Glass-ceramic containers (such as Corning Ware®) are excellent microwave utensils. Because they can tolerate extreme temperature changes, they can go directly from freezer to microwave to dishwasher. They can also be used directly on the conventional rangetop for browning food, then put in the microwave for baking. (When doing this, protect the microwave oven floor from the heat of the dish with a microwavable mat, pad, or towel.)

CERAMIC, CHINA, POTTERY, AND STONEWARE

Dishes that do not contain a metal trim, metallic glaze, or metal in their composition are suitable for microwaving. If in doubt, perform the Microwave Dish Test explained on page 10. Cooking and serving in the same dish is very convenient. Dishes are often, but not always, labeled "For Microwave Use." Some imported pottery may contain lead; these dishes should *never* be used in contact with food—in the microwave or otherwise.

Dishes made of melamine absorb the microwaves and become very hot. They can crack, break, and even char. Do not use them. Metal trim on dishes can discolor, cause the dish to break, and cause arcing (page 9) in the oven.

PLASTIC

Plastics suitable for microwave cookware are usually either thermoset or thermoplastic. Use only plastic cookware specified by its manufacturer as microwavable. Plastic microwave utensils are lightweight and basically nonbreakable. Both of these characteristics offer real advantages in microwave cooking. Some plastic containers are attractively designed and can be used for serving as well as cooking.

Plastic storage containers, such as margarine or whipped topping containers or Tupperware® freezer containers, are usually made of polyethylene or polystyrene. Although microwaves can penetrate them, these containers cannot withstand high cooking temperatures. They become soft and distorted from the hot food and should not be used for microwave cooking.

Use plastic wrap that is designed for use in the microwave. (Not all plastic wrap is made from the same kind of plastic.)

PAPER

Some types of paper can be used for short-term cooking; for instance, several slices of bacon can cook on a paper plate or a paper towel. Paper containers are not used for long-term cooking. Avoid using paper with printed designs or made from recycled paper because it may contain impurities. Also the dyes or inks can be leached into the food.

"Ovenable" paper is a disposable product used for packaging heat-and-serve convenience foods, such as frozen dinners. In these products, the packaging is also the heating or cooking container. Ovenable paper is coated with heat-resistant plastic.

WOOD AND STRAW

Baskets and wooden bowls may be used in the microwave on a limited basis. For example, a basket of bread (covered with a paper napkin or cloth) can be reheated. Prolonged microwaving can cause wood to split or crack.

OVEN COOKING BAGS

Microwavable nylon oven cooking bags are very convenient to use for large items when an appropriate-size casserole is not available. They can also be handy lightweight storage and cooking containers that are convenient for entertaining or for transporting food. For example: Refrigerate prepared vegetables in a cooking bag. When you are ready to steam the vegetables, just before serving, simply place the cooking bag in the microwave and discard it after cooking. This technique is even more convenient when the vegetables are being taken to a potluck dinner and will be steamed after you get there. Do not use metal twist ties.

PARCHMENT

Cooking *en papillote* or cooking food wrapped in parchment paper lends itself well to microwaving. Always place the parchment-wrapped food over a dish to catch drips.

DISH SHAPE

Round or oval dishes allow food to cook more evenly than square ones. Rectangular dishes cook less well, but are used in some recipes. Containers should have rounded corners and straight, rather than slanted, sides.

METAL
IN THE MICROWAVE OVEN

Because microwaves will not pass through metal, containers made of metal cannot be used as microwave cookware. For the same reason, aluminum foil makes a good shield that can be placed over certain areas of food to prevent them from overcooking.

If metal touches metal when the microwave is on—for instance, when metal twists on food bags are folded over or when foil is crumpled or doubled over, or when dishes with metal trim are in the oven—arcing can occur. Arcing is an electrical discharge that produces a white spark, a loud, cracking sound, and heat that can damage the oven interior or cookware and can cause paper to ignite.

MICROWAVE DISH TEST

When you don't know whether a dish is microwavable or not, use this test. Place a glass measure containing ½ cup water in the microwave. Place the dish to be tested in the microwave, close to, but not touching, the water. Microwave on HIGH 1 minute. If the dish is cool or only slightly warm to the touch, the dish can be used for microwave cooking. The water should be very warm or hot. If the dish is hot, do not use it for microwave cooking because it would probably become too hot and break.

BASIC MICROWAVE EQUIPMENT

- 1- and 2-cup and 1- and 2-quart glass measures
- 1-, 2-, 3-, and 5-quart casseroles
- 2- and 3-quart shallow casseroles or baking dishes
- 8- and 9-inch round and square baking dishes
- 9- and 10-inch pie plates
- muffin dish

- fluted (Bundt) cake dish
- glass ring dish
- 6- or 7-inch soufflé dish
- custard cups of various sizes
- roasting rack
- bacon rack

MICROWAVE ACCESSORIES

A microwave accessory is an approved utensil or device that can be used to extend the capabilities of the oven to accomplish a task that it would otherwise be unable to do. Accessories are often expensive and whether you find them useful and worth the expense will be based on your preferences, needs, and cooking habits.

MICROWAVE BROWNER

Microwave browners are available in a variety of sizes and styles. Some are dishes and some are trays. The cooking surface of a microwave browner contains a dielectric substance that absorbs the microwave energy and causes the bottom of the dish or tray to become very hot, at which point food can be placed on it and seared or browned. Always follow manufacturer's instructions and never exceed the preheating time recommended.

MICROWAVE PIZZA PLATE

The plate operates on the same principle as a microwave browner: The hot surface browns and crisps the pizza crust while the microwaves heat the filling and melt the cheese.

MICROWAVE THERMOMETERS

Made especially for use in the microwave oven while it is in operation, a microwave thermometer is useful when an oven doesn't have a built-in probe or food sensor. Microwave candy thermometers, capable of reaching higher temperatures, are also available. A regular mercury cooking thermometer (meat or candy) cannot be used in food while it is microwaving.

CLAY POTS

A clay pot or "simmer pot" is a casserole made of very porous clay. The dish is soaked in water immediately before cooking. During cooking, the water absorbed by the clay cooks out, creating a lot of moist heat in the dish to "supersteam" the food. This accessory is handy for tenderizing tough cuts of meat and simmering foods that usually need long, slow cooking to blend flavors, such as stews, spaghetti sauce, and chili.

MICROWAVE POPCORN POPPERS

The microwave popcorn popper is basically a plastic, cone-shaped container. Because microwaves are attracted to moisture molecules, and there is not much moisture in popcorn, placing the kernels in a cone where they are concentrated or bunched together promotes popping. Usually, even with a microwave popcorn popper, there are a number of kernels that are left unpopped.

MICROWAVE COFFEEMAKERS

A microwave coffeemaker is usually a drip-type pot with a heat-activated valve that opens when the water in the holding area heats to a certain temperature, allowing the hot water to drip over the coffee grounds.

MICROWAVE TECHNIQUES

Many cooking skills are the same for both microwave and conventional cooking. Techniques specific to microwaving are easy to learn, and your proficiency will come with experience.

ARRANGEMENT OF FOOD

Unevenly shaped food cooks unevenly. To assure uniform cooking, arrange food with the thicker portions placed toward the outside of the dish, and the thinner parts toward the inside. Since microwaves cook from the outside in to a depth of about 2 inches, they will hit the food at the outer rim of the dish with somewhat greater force than the food in the center of the dish and both parts will be finished cooking at the same time. For example, place thicker meaty parts of chicken pieces toward the outside of the dish.

Arrange the tough stem ends of asparagus and broccoli toward the perimeter of the dish. Test for doneness during cooking and rearrange the food as necessary.

PIERCING FOOD

Use a sharp knife to pierce foods with thick skins, such as potatoes and acorn squash, so that steam can escape during cooking and the food will not burst. Pierce membranes of egg yolks with a toothpick or the point of a sharp knife.

STIRRING

Stirring facilitates even cooking. Since food placed around the perimeter of the dish cooks faster, stir toward the center. Most microwaved food requires stirring only once or twice, which is one of the advantages of microwave cooking.

ROTATING THE DISH

If your microwave cooks unevenly, rotate the dish a quarter- or half-turn during cooking. Follow manufacturer's instructions for best results.

SHIELDING

Aluminum foil is used to shield food to prevent it from overcooking. When cooking poultry, cover wings or the bottoms of legs with small pieces of foil; shield the thinner parts of whole fish and fillets. Shield the corners of square and the ends of oblong dishes to prevent the food in those parts of the dish from overcooking.

To prevent arcing, use only small amounts of foil and do not allow the foil to touch any other metal inside the oven.

Before using foil in your microwave, check the manufacturer's recommendations for shielding.

ELEVATING FOOD

In some ovens, a food such as an omelet or a cake will cook more evenly if the casserole in which it is being cooked is elevated, giving the microwaves more access to cook the bottom and center of the food. Place the casserole on another dish, such as a saucer, which will raise the casserole about ½ inch.

STANDING TIME

Many foods continue to cook by heat conduction after they are removed from the microwave. This period, called "standing time," must be allowed for in the microwaving time to prevent overcooking once the food is out of the oven. Check for doneness after the minimum amount of time recommended in the recipe and remember that most food will cook for another 1 to 5 minutes after the oven is turned off. At the low end of the standing time scale, smaller, less dense foods such as fish stop cooking quickly—almost immediately after they're removed from the microwave; at the high end is a large, dense beef roast or turkey, which continues to cook for 5 to 10 minutes.

FACTORS THAT AFFECT COOKING TIME

- Foods with high fat content heat more rapidly than those low in fat. Bacon, which is mostly fat, cooks very quickly and also browns. Large pieces of meat or poultry brown during cooking because they cook for a longer time than food such as hamburger patties or chicken pieces.
- Foods with a high concentration of sugar heat very quickly. For instance, if a slice of jelly roll is heated in the microwave, the jelly becomes hot much faster than the cake.
- Starting temperature: As in conventional cooking, add more cooking time when using chilled or frozen food.
- Shape, size, and density: A whole food, such as a potato, takes longer to cook than a sliced or cubed potato. Foods with a less compact texture, such as breads, cook more rapidly than dense foods like meat. It takes twice as long to cook a potato as an apple of the same size. Ground beef cooks faster than a roast or cut of beef of the same weight. If you were to heat a bowl of rice and then a bowl of mashed potatoes of the same size, the denser potatoes would take longer to heat.
- As volume increases, so does cooking time. As a guideline, increase time by about one-half when doubling a recipe. For example, if one pound of food cooks in 5 minutes, two pounds might require 7 to 8 minutes. Check doneness and increase time, if needed.
- Covering serves the same purpose in microwaving as it does in conventional cooking. It helps retain moisture, saves cooking time, ensures even cooking, helps tenderize, and prevents splattering. Usually, a casserole cover is sufficient. However, plastic coverings are especially good for some foods such as vegetables, rice, and pork (which should *always* be cooked tightly covered). Use loose covering—wax paper and paper towels—to prevent splattering when a tight covering is not needed. It is not necessary to vent plastic wrap, but remove it carefully from hot food.

- Line voltage: Electrical output varies from house to house and from place to place. Difference in line voltage affects cooking time. During times of peak electrical use, microwaved food will take slightly longer to cook. Other household appliances are affected also, but these fluctuations are more noticeable with the microwave because of the speed at which microwaved foods cook.

TIMING ADJUSTMENTS

The recipes in this book were developed and tested in ovens using 600 to 700 watts of energy. Check your oven's wattage and make adjustments for ovens using less wattage.

400 to 500 watt units: Add 30 seconds to every minute of cooking time.
500 to 600 watt units: Add 15 seconds to every minute of cooking time.

HIGH-ALTITUDE ADJUSTMENTS

Most foods cooked in the microwave behave the same way as in conventional cooking at a high altitude. However, use these guidelines for elevations of 3,500 feet and above:

- **Cakes and Breads** Use larger dishes and fill them half full. Use more liquid and cook longer. Elevate dishes to assure doneness on the bottom and center.
- **Candies** Reduce the doneness temperature of the candy by 2° F. for each 1,000 feet of elevation.
- **Fish and Vegetables** Longer cooking time is usually necessary. Test for doneness and cook accordingly.
- **Meats and Poultry** Longer cooking time is usually necessary. Check for doneness after cooking the length of time called for in a recipe and add additional cooking time as needed.

DEFROSTING

One of the great benefits of the microwave is being able to defrost foods at the last minute.

GUIDELINES FOR DEFROSTING

- Food defrosted at lower power settings requires less attention and is less likely to begin cooking before it thaws.
- If food has been frozen in a metal container, remove it and place on a microwavable dish before defrosting.
- To ensure more even defrosting and prevent moisture loss, cover food with wax paper.
- When defrosting food in boilable plastic, make a slash in the bag so steam can escape. Flex food in the bag during thawing so that heat is evenly distributed, allowing food to defrost more evenly and quickly.
- When defrosting meats that are on a Styrofoam tray, remove the meat from the tray as soon as the meat is soft. When the tray and paper become saturated with liquid, microwave energy is drawn away from the meat to the liquid, thus slowing the defrosting process.
- When defrosting ground meat, remove the meat from the outer edges as it defrosts to prevent it from beginning to cook.
- Drain liquid as it accumulates, since liquid absorbs energy, slowing the defrosting process.
- Shield parts of the food that are defrosting too quickly with aluminum foil (if you are permitted to use foil in your oven) so that the outside won't start to cook before the center has defrosted. This is usually necessary for larger cuts of meat.
- When defrosting is complete, the food may still be slightly icy. Run cold water over food such as meats, fish, or poultry to complete thawing.

REHEATING

The microwave is just as convenient for reheating as it is for defrosting. Obviously, the amount of food and its temperature when placed in the oven will have a direct bearing on the length of time needed to warm it up. Even so, the process seems miraculously fast and easy.

GUIDELINES FOR REHEATING

- Store leftovers in containers that can be put directly into the microwave.
- Cereals, pasta, and rice reheat well in the microwave and will taste freshly cooked. Cover tightly and reheat on HIGH.

- Eggs and casseroles containing eggs should be reheated at 50 to 70% power. Reheat a large casserole that cannot be stirred on 50% power so that the center will be warm without overcooking the outside.
- Meats reheat well in the microwave without losing texture or flavor. Arrange sliced meats in a circle on a plate, overlapping thinner pieces, and use 50 to 70% power. Do not reheat large cuts of meats because the outside will overcook before the center is warmed. Instead, cut the meat into serving pieces and place them in a circle on a plate. Microwave on 70% power until the center is warmed. Cover hot dogs, hamburgers, meat loaf, and sausage patties with wax paper and warm on HIGH, but watch carefully.
- It's easy to overcook vegetables that are being reheated, so use 70 to 80% power and watch closely. Stir if reheating a larger amount so that heat is equalized.

CONVERTING RECIPES

There are no fixed rules for converting conventional recipes to microwave cooking. However, when deciding whether to try a favorite recipe in the microwave oven, think about the basic cooking method and if it will translate easily and efficiently. If you have any doubts, turn to the chapter introductions in this book. The methods that are most suitable for the microwave are discussed in detail there.

GUIDELINES FOR CONVERTING RECIPES

- Select a microwave recipe similar to the conventional recipe you would like to prepare and use it as a guide. Both recipes should call for the same kinds of ingredients in similar proportions.
- Use a recipe that cooks best by moist heat. Recipes that call for a crisp, browned crust or dry surface should be cooked conventionally.
- Reduce the liquid in a conventional recipe about one-quarter because there is very little evaporation in microwave cooking.
- Use slightly less seasoning. Taste after cooking, then add extra seasoning, if desired.
- Cook in a dish similar to the one recommended for conventional cooking. However, use deep dishes for cooking cakes, soups, and milk sauces because these foods temporarily increase in volume during microwave cooking.
- Reduce the amount of cooking time by one-quarter to one-half of conventional time. Foods containing fat, sugar, and liquid will cook faster.
- Use the same test for doneness as recommended for conventional cooking. Test after the minimum time recommended.

COMBINATION COOKING

Although much of your cooking can be done using the microwave alone, you can enjoy even more benefits by using the microwave in combination with other conventional appliances, such as the conventional oven and range-top, and barbecue grill.

CONVENTIONAL OVEN

Meats, potatoes, breads, and pies can be partially cooked in the microwave to save cooking time and cleanup, then completed in the conventional oven, which will finish the cooking and crisp and brown the foods. Frozen uncooked fruit and pot pies can be defrosted in the microwave, then baked conventionally.

RANGETOP

Meats can be browned on the rangetop, then microwaved to complete cooking. Cook pasta on the rangetop while making sauce in the microwave.

BARBECUE GRILL

Nothing can duplicate the wonderful barbecued and smoked flavor of meat or poultry cooked over a grill. By using the microwave in combination with the grill, you can save as much as one-third to one-half the cooking time. While the coals are heating, cook the meat or poultry in the microwave, transfer it to the grill, and finish cooking. (See pages 170 and 199 to 200 for combination cooking of poultry and meat.)

DEEP-FAT FRYER

If you use the microwave to precook food that will later be deep-fried, the oil will not cool down when the food is added, which will reduce the deep-frying time. For example, you might microwave potatoes until almost done, cut them into quarters or eighths, and deep-fry for only a few minutes until golden brown.

TOASTER

Use the toaster to brown slices of bread, top with shredded cheese, and microwave 8 to 12 seconds for a quick sandwich. Defrost pancakes and waffles in the microwave, then crisp in the toaster.

Appetizers

The manner in which appetizers are presented sets the tone for the occasion. Elegantly served in grand style or casually offered in a comfortable, homey spirit, they create a happy anticipation of the evening to come.

The microwave oven is an especially welcome appliance in the early and final preparation steps of hors d'oeuvres and appetizers, many of which can be cooked completely ahead of time or at least to the point where they'll need only a last-minute reheating. This is particularly convenient to do in the microwave because no special attention is required to prevent sticking, scorching, or burning, leaving the host and hostess time to attend to guests or to other courses for the meal.

Dips and spreads can be heated or reheated in their serving dishes, as can hot canapés for up to 10 people. However, for larger gatherings, it's more efficient to reheat canapés in a conventional oven. The same is true for cooking anything that should be crisp or crusty, such as puff pastry or toast, where the radiant heat of a conventional oven will dry out any moisture on the surface of the food.

ANTIPASTO

A well-conceived antipasto offers such a variety of textures, colors, shapes, and flavors that it becomes a visual experience as well as a taste adventure. An antipasto can be as modest or as sumptuous as you like, running the gamut from a few salads and cold cuts served as a first course to a large assortment of dishes comprising a meal in itself.

Fortunately, all the cooking for an antipasto is done in advance, and a number of items can be purchased from a delicatessen or supermarket. Since the food is served at room temperature, you can leave yourself plenty of time to make a stunning presentation. Use one or two large platters and, for breads and salads, a few interesting bowls or baskets. Decorate the antipasto with fresh herbs, and serve a hearty wine.

Any of the following elements can be combined for antipasto:

- **Raw vegetables (crudités):** asparagus, carrots, celery hearts, Belgian endive, tomatoes, fennel, radishes, cucumbers, zucchini, carrots, scallions.
- **Blanched vegetables:** broccoli, cauliflower, green beans, asparagus. (See pages 243 and 244 for instructions for blanching vegetables in the microwave.)
- **Marinated raw and cooked vegetables and salads:** artichoke hearts; eggplant; mushrooms; red, green, and yellow bell peppers; green beans; garbanzos; zucchini; yellow squash; cauliflower; broccoli; carrots.
- **Olives, pickles, and relishes**
- **Fish and seafood:** marinated shrimp, canned tuna (imported from Italy, if available), drained anchovies, mussels, clams, and oysters.
- **Cold cuts:** prosciutto, mortadella, capicolla, soppressata, Genoa salami.
- **Hard-cooked eggs** (page 122).
- **Cheese:** mozzarella, provolone, fontina, Brie (even though it's not Italian).
- **Breads:** breadsticks, Italian and French breads, focaccia, toasted pitas.

ANTIPASTO PARTY

It's fun to plan an antipasto party using the microwave to make cooking easier than ever. Since all the dishes should be served at room temperature, you can make the food at your leisure over the course of two or three days.

Caponata (page 28)
Sweet Pepper Salad (page 31)
Steamed Artichokes with Garlic and Oil (page 251)
Mushrooms and Sweet Onions (page 27)
Marinated Cauliflower, Carrots, and Zucchini (page 30)
Italian-Style Rice Salad (page 107)
Shrimp Pasta Salad (page 109)
Italian Rum Cake (page 340)

CHILI CON QUESO

**MAKES
2 TO 3
CUPS;
15 TO 20
SERVINGS**

•

1 pound Velveeta cheese, cubed
1/4 cup milk
1/4 cup bottled picante sauce, or
more to taste

Chopped fresh coriander (cilantro)
to taste

Combine cheese, milk, and picante sauce in 1-quart measure and microwave on HIGH 3 to 5 minutes, or until cheese is melted. Stir until smooth. Add coriander and additional picante sauce to taste. Serve with tortilla chips or raw vegetables.

BLUE CHEESE BALL

4 ounces blue cheese
1 (8-ounce) package cream cheese
½ stick (¼ cup) unsalted butter
1 heaping tablespoon snipped fresh chives or finely chopped scallion tops

1 clove garlic, minced
¼ teaspoon freshly ground white pepper
1 (about 6 ounces) can pitted black olives, drained and chopped

MAKES
2 CUPS

∎

■ ■ ■ ■ ■ ■ ■ ■ ■ ■ ■

When crackers, chips, and popcorn absorb moisture, they become stale and lose their crispness. To freshen them, spread out 10 to 12 crackers or about 1 cup of chips or popcorn in a single layer on a paper towel and microwave at 70% power 1 to 2 minutes. Let stand 2 minutes to crisp.

■ ■ ■ ■ ■ ■ ■ ■ ■ ■ ■

Place blue cheese, cream cheese, and butter in 2-quart measure or bowl and microwave on HIGH 2 minutes to soften. Stir in chives, garlic, and pepper and blend well. Add black olives and stir into mixture, or reserve olives to decorate finished cheese ball.

Shape cheese mixture into a ball or press it into oiled 2-cup mold, wrap in plastic wrap, and chill. Serve with crackers.

Leftover blue cheese mix is good as sandwich filling or as stuffing for celery or cherry tomatoes.

WHITE GRAPES STUFFED WITH BLUE CHEESE MIX
Omit olives from Blue Cheese Ball recipe. Cut a slit in each grape and stuff with cheese mixture. Press cheese side of grapes into crushed toasted almonds.

CLASSIC FRENCH DIP

1 (8-ounce) package cream cheese
1 cup sour cream
2 teaspoons beef bouillon granules
1 clove garlic, minced
2 tablespoons chopped parsley
2 tablespoons snipped fresh chives

⅛ teaspoon dried crushed rosemary
⅛ teaspoon dried sage
Dash of hot pepper sauce, or more to taste

MAKES
2 CUPS

∎

Place cheese in 1-quart bowl and microwave on HIGH 1½ to 2 minutes to soften. Stir in sour cream, bouillon granules, garlic, parsley, chives, rosemary, sage, and hot pepper sauce to taste. Cover mixture and chill.

Serve as dip with raw vegetables, or corn or potato chips.

Liptauer Cheese

**MAKES
1½ CUPS**

•

Tastes best if made ahead of time to give flavors a chance to blend.

1 (8-ounce) package cream cheese
1 stick (½ cup) unsalted butter
2 anchovies, mashed, or 2 teaspoons anchovy paste
2 scallions, finely chopped
1 teaspoon capers, crushed
1 teaspoon paprika
Salt
Freshly ground black pepper
½ teaspoon caraway seeds (optional)
1 teaspoon Dijon mustard

Place cheese and butter in 2-quart bowl and microwave on HIGH 1 minute to soften. Add anchovies, scallions, capers, paprika, salt and pepper to taste, caraway seeds, and mustard and blend until smooth. Cover tightly and refrigerate for at least 1 day. Mixture will keep for up to 1 week, covered and in refrigerator. Serve with hearty bread or crackers.

Layered Cranberry Cheddar Spread

**MAKES
6 CUPS**

•

A festive appetizer for the holidays!

1 (8-ounce) package cream cheese
2 tablespoons sherry
1 cup heavy cream, lightly sweetened and whipped
1 (10-ounce) jar cranberry relish
3 cups grated sharp Cheddar cheese

Place cream cheese in 1-quart bowl and microwave on HIGH 1½ to 2 minutes to soften. Stir in sherry, then fold in whipped cream.

In 1½-quart clear glass dish, layer cranberry relish, Cheddar, and cream cheese mixture. Cover and chill. Serve spread with crackers or apple or pear wedges.

CHEESE PÂTÉ

3 (8-ounce) packages cream
    cheese
2 cups grated sharp Cheddar
    cheese
2 cloves garlic, minced
$^{1}/_{2}$ teaspoon curry powder
    (optional)

Salt
Freshly ground white pepper
$^{1}/_{4}$ cup mayonnaise (page 116)
$^{1}/_{2}$ teaspoon onion salt
$^{1}/_{2}$ to $^{2}/_{3}$ cup chutney
3 scallions, finely chopped

**MAKES
5 CUPS**

Place 2 packages of cream cheese in 2-quart bowl and microwave on HIGH 2 minutes to soften. Stir in Cheddar and garlic, curry powder, if desired, and salt and pepper to taste. Press mixture into oiled 9-inch springform pan or soufflé dish lined with plastic wrap. Cover tightly and chill.

Unmold cheese mixture on serving plate. Place remaining cream cheese in bowl and microwave on HIGH 1 to 2 minutes to soften. Stir in mayonnaise and onion salt and mix well. With spatula, frost side of pâté with cream cheese–mayonnaise mixture, bringing enough cream cheese up over top edge of pâté to make ½-inch lip. (For a more elaborate presentation, pack cream cheese mixture into pastry bag or pastry tube, decorate sides of pâté with vertical designs, and make shell border around top edge.)

Spread chutney over top of pâté and sprinkle with scallions. Serve with crackers.

Use an eggplant as a vase for flowers, fresh herbs, or vegetable garnishes on skewers. Cut a slice off the bottom of the eggplant, allowing it to stand upright. Cut an inch or so from the stem end and scoop out the flesh with a melon baller or paring knife, leaving a ¾-inch shell.

NACHOS

36 tortilla chips
1½ cups grated Monterey Jack or
    sharp Cheddar cheese

$^{1}/_{3}$ cup sliced olives or chopped
    jalapeño peppers or green
    chilies

**MAKES
36 PIECES**

Spread chips on 12-inch plate in single layer. Sprinkle with cheese, then with olives, jalapeños, or chilies. Microwave on HIGH 1 to 2 minutes, or until cheese melts. Serve at once.

CHEDDAR CHEESE FONDUE

MAKES
1½ CUPS

1 (10½-ounce) can condensed
    Cheddar cheese soup
1½ cups grated Cheddar cheese
½ teaspoon dried oregano
2 tablespoons catsup

1 clove garlic, minced
¼ teaspoon freshly ground white
    pepper
½ loaf French or Italian bread,
    cut into 1½-inch cubes

Place cheese soup, grated cheese, oregano, catsup, garlic, and white pepper in 1-quart casserole. Microwave on 70% power 4 to 5 minutes, stirring, or until cheese melts. Serve in a fondue pot and use bread cubes for dunking.

SWISS FONDUE

MAKES
3 CUPS

2 cups dry white wine
2 cloves garlic, minced
1 pound Swiss cheese, grated
3 tablespoons kirschwasser
½ teaspoon paprika

Pinch of freshly grated nutmeg
Salt
Freshly ground white pepper
1 (1-pound) loaf French or Italian
    bread, cut into 1½-inch cubes

When reheating deep-fried appetizers in the microwave, use a browning dish or place the fried food on a microwave baking rack or paper towel to prevent it from becoming soggy.

Put wine and garlic in microwavable fondue pot or 1-quart measure and microwave on HIGH 4 to 6 minutes, or until just boiling. Stir in cheese gradually. Microwave on 70% power 3 to 6 minutes, or until cheese melts.

Stir in kirschwasser, paprika, nutmeg, and salt and pepper to taste. Pour mixture into fondue pot, if necessary, and keep warm while serving with bread. If fondue becomes too thick while serving, stir in a little warmed wine.

To reheat leftover fondue, microwave on 70% power 2 to 3 minutes, stirring several times.

MOLDED EGG SALAD

2 to 3 slices bacon
6 hard-cooked eggs (page 122),
    chopped
3 tablespoons mayonnaise
2 tablespoons minced onion
2 tablespoons finely chopped
    olives

1 teaspoon capers, crushed
1/2 teaspoon curry powder
1 teaspoon mustard
1/2 teaspoon white horseradish
Salt
Freshly ground black pepper

**MAKES
1½ CUPS**

Place bacon strips on plate or paper towel and microwave on HIGH 2 to 3 minutes, or until cooked and crisp. Let bacon cool, then crumble it into mixing bowl. Add chopped eggs, mayonnaise, onion, olives, capers, curry powder, mustard, horseradish, and salt and pepper to taste and combine well.

Oil 1½-cup bowl and spoon in egg mixture, pressing it down compactly. Cover with plastic wrap and chill. Unmold egg salad on plate and serve with crackers or party rye bread.

MUSHROOMS AND SWEET ONIONS

1 pound medium mushrooms,
    cleaned and stemmed
1 medium sweet onion, thinly
    sliced
2 tablespoons snipped fresh chives
1/2 cup extra-virgin olive oil

2 tablespoons dry white wine
1/4 cup fresh lemon juice
1/4 teaspoon dried rosemary
3 cloves garlic, minced
Salt
Freshly ground white pepper

**MAKES
4 CUPS**

Place mushrooms in 2-quart measure, cover, and microwave on HIGH 4 to 5 minutes. Drain mushrooms and add onion, chives, oil, wine, lemon juice, rosemary, garlic, and salt and pepper to taste. Toss to coat mushrooms and onions with dressing, cover, and chill several hours or overnight.

Serve as part of antipasto platter (page 24) or use as vegetable side dish.

HOT BROCCOLI DIP

**MAKES
5 CUPS**

Leftover broccoli dip is good thinned with a little milk and served as a sauce over chicken or pasta.

1 onion, minced
1 (10-ounce) package frozen chopped broccoli
2 (10½-ounce) cans condensed cream of chicken soup
2 cloves garlic, minced

3 cups grated Monterey Jack cheese
2 (4-ounce) cans chopped green chilies
½ teaspoon ground coriander
Freshly ground white pepper

Place onion in 2-quart measure, cover with plastic wrap, and microwave on HIGH 3 to 4 minutes, or until tender.

Place broccoli in a dish and microwave on HIGH 5 minutes to defrost and cook. Drain well.

Add broccoli, soup, garlic, cheese, chilies, coriander, and pepper to taste to onions. Microwave on HIGH 4 to 6 minutes, stirring several times, or until cheese is melted and ingredients are blended. Serve hot with tostadas, corn chips, or vegetables.

CAPONATA

**MAKES
ABOUT 6 CUPS**

This delicious vegetable stew is part of the traditional Italian antipasto (page 21). Caponata is a good topping for hamburgers or hot dogs, or serve it as a salad or side dish with meats.

1 medium eggplant, peeled and cut into 1-inch cubes
4 teaspoons salt plus salt to taste
2 large tomatoes, peeled, seeded, and chopped
1 green bell pepper, cut into 1-inch cubes
1 zucchini, cut into 1-inch cubes
1 medium onion, thinly sliced

2 tablespoons capers, crushed
1 bay leaf
¼ cup sliced pitted green olives
2 tablespoons extra-virgin olive oil
2 tablespoons balsamic or red wine vinegar
Pinch of sugar
Freshly ground black pepper

Place eggplant in large bowl and sprinkle with 4 teaspoons of salt. Weight down with a plate and let stand for at least 30 minutes. (Salt will draw liquid and bitterness from eggplant.)

Drain eggplant, pat dry, and place in 2-quart measure with tomatoes, bell pepper, zucchini, onion, capers, bay leaf, olives, oil, vinegar, sugar, and salt and pepper to taste. Cover with plastic wrap and microwave on HIGH 5 minutes, then on 50% power 12 to 15 minutes, or until vegetables are tender and flavors are blended.

Caponata can be stored in a tightly covered container in refrigerator for 1 week. Bring to room temperature before serving.

FRESH ONION RELISH

2 cups chopped onions
2 teaspoons sugar
2 tablespoons cider vinegar
1/3 cup mayonnaise (page 116)

1/4 teaspoon freshly ground white
*   pepper*
2/3 cup chopped cucumber
*   (optional)*

MAKES
1½ CUPS

■

Light and tasty.

Place onions in 1-quart measure, cover, and microwave on HIGH 2 to 4 minutes, or until tender-crisp. Drain onions, stir in sugar and vinegar, and let stand 5 minutes.

Stir in mayonnaise, pepper, and, if desired, cucumber. Cover relish and chill up to 3 days.

Serve with crackers or use as sandwich spread.

HOT ONION DIP

2 cups chopped mild onions
1 cup freshly grated Parmesan
*   cheese*
1 cup mayonnaise (page 116)

1 teaspoon Worcestershire sauce
1/2 teaspoon freshly ground white
*   pepper*

MAKES
3 CUPS

■

Combine all ingredients in 2-quart bowl, cover, and microwave on HIGH 5 to 6 minutes, or until onions are tender, stirring several times.

Pour mixture into shallow 1-quart casserole or pie plate and microwave, uncovered, on 50% power 5 to 7 minutes, or until bubbly. Spread may also be browned in preheated conventional broiler. Serve hot with melba toast or crackers.

MARINATED CAULIFLOWER, CARROTS, AND ZUCCHINI

8 SERVINGS

.

Serve alone or in combination with other antipasti.

1 pound carrots, cut into 3-inch sticks
2 to 3 tablespoons water
1 medium cauliflower, cut into small flowerets
2 medium zucchini, cut into 3-inch sticks
1 cup extra-virgin olive oil

1 cup red wine vinegar
3 cloves garlic, minced
1/2 cup freshly grated Parmesan cheese
1/2 teaspoon salt
1 teaspoon freshly ground black pepper
1 teaspoon dried basil

Place carrots in 1-quart casserole, add water, and cover. Microwave on HIGH 7 to 9 minutes, or until tender.

Place cauliflower in large casserole, cover, and microwave on HIGH 4 to 7 minutes, or until tender-crisp, being very careful not to overcook it. Add carrots and raw zucchini and set aside.

In small bowl, combine oil, vinegar, garlic, cheese, salt, pepper, and basil. Pour over vegetables and toss to coat. Cover and let stand several hours or overnight.

SPINACH BALL

MAKES 3 CUPS

.

2 (10-ounce) packages frozen chopped spinach
4 scallions, chopped

1 cup mayonnaise (page 116)
Salt
Freshly ground black pepper

Place spinach in 2-quart bowl and microwave on HIGH 4 minutes. Break up spinach with fork and drain off liquid. Microwave on HIGH 2 minutes longer. Turn spinach into sieve and press out all liquid with back of spoon.

Place spinach in bowl, add scallions, mayonnaise, and salt and pepper to taste, and mix well. Form into a ball, wrap in plastic wrap, and chill. Serve with crackers.

SWEET PEPPER SALAD

2 red bell peppers, cut into
    1/2-inch-wide vertical strips
2 green bell peppers, cut into
    1/2-inch-wide vertical strips
2 yellow bell peppers, cut into
    1/2-inch-wide vertical strips

1 medium onion, sliced vertically
2 or 3 cloves garlic, minced
1/4 cup extra-virgin olive oil
Salt
Freshly ground black pepper

**MAKES
4 CUPS**

▪

Use red, green, and yellow bell peppers for a colorful antipasto.

Combine bell peppers, onion, garlic, oil, and salt and pepper to taste in 2-quart measure and stir to coat vegetables with oil. Cover with plastic wrap and microwave on HIGH 4 to 7 minutes, or until peppers are tender-crisp.

Peppers will keep, well covered and refrigerated, for several days, but bring to room temperature before serving. To take chill off, microwave on 30% power 2 to 3 minutes.

SWEET PEPPER AND MUSHROOM SALAD
Add 2 cups sliced mushrooms and 3 tablespoons red wine vinegar to peppers and onion before cooking. Just before serving, add 1/3 cup freshly grated Parmesan cheese and toss to mix.

SMOKED ALMONDS

2 tablespoons vegetable oil
Several drops of liquid smoke
1/4 teaspoon garlic powder
1/4 teaspoon onion powder

1/4 teaspoon paprika
Salt
1 cup blanched whole almonds
    (page 441)

**MAKES
1 CUP**

▪

Combine oil, liquid smoke, garlic powder, onion powder, paprika, and salt to taste in glass pie plate. Add nuts and stir to coat with seasoning. Spread nuts evenly in pie plate and microwave on HIGH 5 to 8 minutes, or until nuts are toasted. Stir every 2 minutes and watch closely after first 5 minutes. Let stand 5 to 10 minutes to crisp.

Store in tightly covered container for up to 1 week.

HONEY-ROASTED PEANUTS

**MAKES
1 CUP**

·

A delicious snack!

1 cup shelled raw Spanish
  peanuts
2 tablespoons honey

2 tablespoons sugar
Pinch of salt

Spread nuts evenly in glass pie plate and microwave on HIGH 3 minutes. Stir. Drizzle honey over nuts and microwave on HIGH 2 to 3 minutes longer, or until peanuts look and smell cooked. Stir during cooking and watch closely; do not overcook.

Sprinkle sugar and salt over nuts and stir to coat. Let nuts stand to cool and crisp. Store in airtight container.

CANDIED NUTS
Instead of honey, use 2 tablespoons light corn syrup blended with several drops food coloring, if desired.

SWEET WALNUTS

**MAKES
1 CUP**

·

Walnuts were hailed by the ancient Romans as the gift of Jupiter.

1 cup walnut halves
¼ cup crème de cacao
½ cup sifted confectioners' sugar

1½ tablespoons instant coffee
  powder, pressed through sieve
  to make a fine powder

Place nuts in small bowl or plastic bag, add crème de cacao, and toss to coat nuts with liqueur. Spread nuts evenly in glass pie plate and microwave on HIGH 5 to 8 minutes, or until nuts begin to crisp and give off pleasant, toasted aroma. Stir every 2 minutes and watch closely after first 5 minutes to prevent burning.

In plastic sandwich bag, combine sugar and coffee powder. Add nuts and shake in sugar mixture. Spread nuts on pie plate again and let stand to cool. Store in airtight container.

SEASONED WALNUTS

2 tablespoons vegetable oil
1 teaspoon seasoned salt
1/8 teaspoon garlic powder

Pinch of cayenne pepper
1 1/2 cups walnut halves

**MAKES
1½ CUPS**

In small bowl, combine oil, seasoned salt, garlic powder, and cayenne. Add nuts and stir to coat. Spread nuts evenly in glass pie plate and microwave on HIGH 5 to 6 minutes, stirring every 2 minutes. Let nuts stand 5 to 10 minutes to crisp. Store in tightly covered container.

Walnuts are rich in phosphorus and an excellent source of iron and vitamin B.

NUTTY NOODLES

1/2 stick (1/4 cup) unsalted butter
4 teaspoons soy sauce
1/2 teaspoon hot pepper sauce
1/4 teaspoon garlic powder

1/2 teaspoon seasoned salt
1 (12-ounce) can chow mein
    noodles
1 cup roasted peanuts

**MAKES
3 TO 4 CUPS**

In pie plate, microwave butter on HIGH 30 to 45 seconds until melted. Stir in soy sauce, hot pepper sauce, garlic powder, and seasoned salt. Add noodles and toss to coat. Spread noodles evenly in pie plate and microwave on HIGH 3 minutes. Stir well and spread out evenly again. Microwave on HIGH 3 to 4 minutes longer. Let stand 10 minutes to cool and crisp. Stir in nuts. Store mixture in airtight container.

Trays and bowls made of wood or straw may be used for reheating appetizers since they are in the microwave for only a short time.

CLAMS CASINO

4 TO 6 SERVINGS

■

A classic first course for an Italian meal. In this recipe, the microwave is used to steam open the clams and cook the topping. The dish is then finished in a conventional broiler, which will brown the top.

▪ ▪ ▪ ▪ ▪ ▪ ▪ ▪ ▪ ▪

Seashells make handsome and unusual containers for seafood appetizers. If your shells come directly from the beach, wash them, soak in chlorine bleach for 5 minutes, then soak in one or two changes of fresh water.

▪ ▪ ▪ ▪ ▪ ▪ ▪ ▪ ▪ ▪

24 littleneck or cherrystone clams
4 slices bacon
2 scallions, cut into 1-inch pieces
½ stalk celery, cut into 1-inch pieces
¼ small green bell pepper, cut into 1-inch squares

½ stick (¼ cup) unsalted butter
1 teaspoon fresh lemon juice
Rock salt
¼ cup fine dry bread crumbs
1 tablespoon chopped parsley
Lemon wedges

Scrub clams under cold running water. Arrange 12 clams on 10-inch glass pie plate, hinged edges to outside of plate. Cover tightly with plastic wrap and microwave on HIGH 4 minutes, or until clams open. Remove open clams and continue microwaving closed clams up to 1 minute more. Discard any clams that do not open. Repeat with 12 remaining clams.

Place bacon in small bowl and microwave on HIGH 1 to 2 minutes to blanch. Drain bacon and pat dry.

Place bacon, scallions, celery, bell pepper, butter, and lemon juice in food processor fitted with steel blade and process until mixture is finely chopped and well combined. Place mixture in small bowl, cover with plastic wrap, and microwave on HIGH 5 minutes, or until vegetables are tender and bacon is cooked but still soft.

Spread ½-inch layer of rock salt in pie plate or conventional ovenproof dish. Discard half the clam shells and loosen clams in bottom shells. Place clams on bed of rock salt and spoon bacon mixture over them. Sprinkle with bread crumbs and parsley. Dish may be prepared ahead to this point, covered with plastic wrap, and kept in refrigerator for up to 4 hours.

Preheat conventional broiler.

Remove plastic wrap from clams and broil 3 to 4 inches from heating element 2 to 4 minutes, or until clams are thoroughly heated and topping is browned. Serve at once with lemon wedges.

CLAMS IN GARLIC BUTTER
Substitute Garlic Butter (page 82) for bacon mixture.

CLAM DIP

1 (8-ounce) package cream cheese
1 (10½-ounce) can minced clams
1 tablespoon snipped fresh chives
¼ teaspoon freshly ground white
    pepper

½ teaspoon salt
Dash of fresh lime juice
Dash of hot pepper sauce

MAKES

1½ CUPS

▪

In 1-quart measure, microwave cream cheese on 70% power 1 to 2 minutes to soften.

Drain clams, reserving liquid. Add clams, chives, white pepper, and salt to cream cheese. Stir in lime juice and hot pepper sauce to taste. Add 1 to 2 tablespoons reserved clam juice to thin dip to desired consistency. Cover and chill.

Serve with chips or raw vegetables.

CHAFING DISH CRAB

2 (6½-ounce) cans crabmeat,
    drained
2 (8-ounce) packages cream
    cheese

1½ sticks (¾ cup) unsalted butter
Freshly ground white pepper

MAKES

3 CUPS

▪

Delicious!

Place crabmeat, cheese, butter, and pepper to taste in 2-quart measure or chafing dish liner and microwave on 70% power 5 to 8 minutes, or until thoroughly heated. Stir several times during cooking. Transfer to a hot chafing dish and serve with toast points, melba toast, or crackers.

SALMON·STUFFED MUSHROOMS

12 TO 15 SERVINGS

∎

A good low-calorie treat.

1 (15-ounce) can salmon, drained
12 to 15 large mushrooms
Mayonnaise (page 116)
Capers

2 or 3 hard-cooked eggs (page 122), chopped
Sprigs of fresh dill

Remove skin and bones from salmon and flake fish. Wipe mushrooms with damp paper towel, remove stems, and reserve stems for another use. Stuff mushroom caps loosely with salmon. Place caps in a circle on large plate and microwave on HIGH 3 to 5 minutes, or until very hot.

Immediately decorate mushrooms with a dollop of mayonnaise, a few capers, chopped eggs, and sprigs of dill, and serve hot. Omit mayonnaise and eggs to reduce cholesterol.

ARTICHOKE SEAFOOD DIP

MAKES 1 QUART

∎

½ cup chopped onion
½ cup chopped celery
1 (14-ounce) can artichoke hearts, drained and chopped
1 cup mayonnaise (page 116)

6 ounces fresh crabmeat, picked over, or chopped shrimp
1 cup freshly grated Parmesan cheese
½ teaspoon freshly ground white pepper

Place onion and celery in bowl, cover, and microwave on HIGH 2 minutes, or until vegetables are tender. Add artichoke hearts, mayonnaise, crabmeat, cheese, and pepper and stir well. Spread in 1-quart casserole, cover, and microwave on HIGH 2 minutes. Stir and microwave on 70% power 3 to 4 minutes longer. Serve hot with melba toast or crackers.

SHRIMP PARFAIT

DRESSING

*1 cup fresh spinach leaves,
    washed and drained*
2 cups mayonnaise (page 116)
1 avocado, cut into chunks
2 tablespoons chopped parsley
1 tablespoon snipped fresh chives

1 teaspoon capers, crushed
*1 tablespoon minced fresh
    tarragon*
1 teaspoon snipped fresh dill
1 tablespoon fresh lemon juice

1 pound medium shrimp, in shells
3 cups shredded lettuce
*2 or 3 hard-cooked eggs (page
    122), sliced*
8 to 12 cherry tomatoes, sliced

1 avocado, thinly sliced
8 to 12 pitted black olives, sliced
*1 cucumber, peeled and thinly
    sliced*
8 thin slices of lemon

8 SERVINGS

•

This makes an elegant first course and an equally delicious summer luncheon dish.

To prepare dressing, place spinach in small bowl, cover with plastic wrap, and microwave on HIGH 1 minute to wilt. Place spinach, mayonnaise, avocado chunks, parsley, chives, capers, tarragon, dill, and lemon juice in blender or food processor and puree. Dressing may be prepared 2 or 3 days in advance and kept, tightly covered, in refrigerator.

Place shrimp around edge of glass pie plate, leaving center of plate empty. Cover with plastic wrap and microwave on HIGH 3 to 5 minutes, or until shrimp turn pink. Do not overcook. Uncover immediately and allow to cool. Peel, devein, and chill shrimp.

To assemble in parfait glasses, glass compotes, or salad bowls, layer shrimp, lettuce, eggs, tomatoes, avocado slices, olives, and cucumber, spooning dressing between each layer. Decorate with lemon slices. If serving salad as part of buffet meal, layer ingredients in glass trifle dish or very large brandy snifter.

Fish, poultry, and vegetable salads make good canapé fillings. They should, however, be more strongly seasoned when served in bite-size portions.

BARBECUED SHRIMP

4 TO 6 SERVINGS

▪

1 cup Barbecue Sauce (page 86)
3 tablespoons fresh lemon juice
1 tablespoon Worcestershire sauce

1 pound large or jumbo shrimp, peeled and deveined

In a bowl, combine barbecue sauce, lemon juice, and Worcestershire sauce. Stir to mix, add shrimp, and toss to coat shrimp with sauce. Cover and refrigerate for several hours.

Remove shrimp from sauce, reserving sauce, and place shrimp on glass pie plate, pushing them to sides of dish so that center of plate is empty. Cover with plastic wrap and microwave on HIGH 3 to 5 minutes, or until shrimp are cooked.

While shrimp are cooking, transfer sauce to microwavable serving bowl. Microwave sauce on HIGH 30 to 45 seconds, or until hot. Serve as a dip for shrimp.

CHICKEN CHEESE BALL

MAKES 4-CUP BALL

▪

Leftovers make a great sandwich spread

2 (8-ounce) packages cream cheese
2 cups chopped cooked chicken (page 167)
1/3 cup chopped scallions
3/4 cup chopped celery
2 tablespoons chopped parsley
1/4 teaspoon garlic salt

1/2 teaspoon curry powder
1/4 teaspoon salt
1/2 teaspoon freshly ground white pepper
1/2 to 1 cup chopped pecans, walnuts, or almonds, toasted (page 441)

Place cheese in 2-quart bowl or measure and microwave on HIGH 1 1/2 to 2 minutes, or until softened. Stir in chicken, scallions, celery, parsley, garlic salt, curry powder, salt, and pepper.

Shape mixture into ball and roll in toasted nuts. Serve with crackers or apple slices.

To prepare ahead, shape mixture into a ball, but do not roll in nuts. Refrigerate for several days or freeze for several weeks. To serve, thaw ball and roll in toasted nuts.

PINEAPPLE PÂTÉ MOLD

1 recipe Chicken Liver Pâté (page 40), chilled
1 cup mayonnaise (page 116)
1 tablespoon unflavored gelatin

2 teaspoons mustard
½ cup drained stuffed green olives, sliced

10 TO 15 SERVINGS

•

A distinctive presentation for a very special occasion.

Place tightly covered 1-pint jar (a mayonnaise jar would serve very well) upright on serving plate. Spread jar with pâté, forming it into a pineapple shape. Mold can be prepared ahead to this point, covered with foil, and frozen. Defrost in refrigerator.

Just before serving, prepare mayonnaise-mustard coating: Place mayonnaise in 2-cup measure, sprinkle gelatin over mayonnaise, and let stand 5 minutes to soften gelatin. Microwave mixture on 50% power 2 to 3 minutes, or until gelatin is dissolved. Blend in mustard.

Spread coating over pâté. If coating begins to congeal, microwave it at 50% power 15 seconds or longer to soften. Score coating and place an olive slice within each diamond to resemble a pineapple eye. Place a fresh or artificial pineapple top on top of jar lid.

Serve "pineapple" at once, or cover it with plastic wrap that has been sprayed with vegetable spray and refrigerate for 2 to 3 days.

CHICKEN LIVER PÂTÉ

**MAKES
2 CUPS**

1 pound chicken livers
Pinch of cayenne pepper
2 sticks (1 cup) unsalted butter
½ teaspoon freshly grated nutmeg
2 teaspoons dry mustard
¼ teaspoon ground cloves

2 tablespoons grated onion
¼ teaspoon anchovy paste
Salt
Freshly ground white pepper
1 tablespoon brandy (optional)

Foods that taste best served at room temperature may be taken from the refrigerator and microwaved instantly to room temperature. A low power level—10 to 30% power—is best for taking the chill off food without heating it.

Trim fat and membranes from chicken livers and prick them with fork. Place livers in 2-quart bowl or measure, cover with plastic wrap, and microwave on 50% power 8 to 10 minutes, stirring several times during cooking. Drain liquid from bowl and let livers stand 2 to 3 minutes.

Place livers, cayenne, butter, nutmeg, mustard, cloves, onion, anchovy paste, salt and pepper to taste, and, if desired, brandy in food processor fitted with steel blade and process until smooth. Taste pâté for seasoning and turn into 2-cup crock. Cover tightly and store in refrigerator up to 3 days.

Serve pâté at room temperature with fresh toast or crackers.

SWEET AND SOUR MEATBALLS

**MAKES
ABOUT
36 MEATBALLS**

1 pound lean ground pork
1 (8-ounce) can water chestnuts,
    drained and minced
5 scallions, finely chopped
½ cup dry bread crumbs

1 tablespoon soy sauce
1 large egg
Pinch of salt
Bottled sweet and sour sauce,
    heated

In mixing bowl, place pork, water chestnuts, scallions, bread crumbs, soy sauce, egg, and salt and mix until well blended. Form mixture into balls 1 inch in diameter. Place meatballs in a circle on microwavable plate and microwave on HIGH 4 minutes. Drain drippings from plate, turn meatballs over, and microwave again on HIGH 6 to 10 minutes, or until no longer pink.

Transfer meatballs to fondue pot or chafing dish and pour sweet and sour sauce over them. Keep meatballs hot while serving.

SAUSAGE·STUFFED MUSHROOMS

8 ounces mild breakfast or Italian
   sausage
1 (8-ounce) package cream cheese

1/2 teaspoon garlic salt
Freshly ground black pepper
12 large mushrooms

12 SERVINGS

•

Break up sausage and place in 2-quart glass measure. Microwave on HIGH 2½ to 3 minutes, or until cooked. Drain off fat. Add cheese, garlic salt, and pepper to taste, and microwave on HIGH 2 minutes longer. Mix well and adjust seasonings if necessary.

Wipe mushrooms with damp paper towel, remove stems, and reserve stems for another use. Mound sausage mixture in mushroom caps and arrange caps in circle on glass pie plate. Microwave on HIGH 5 to 8 minutes, or until mushrooms are cooked and stuffing is very hot.

PEPPERED BEEF ROULADE

2 (8-ounce) packages cream
   cheese
1/2 teaspoon garlic powder
3 scallions, finely chopped
1 (2½-ounce) jar dried beef, finely
   chopped

1/2 cup finely chopped green bell
   pepper
2 teaspoons freshly ground black
   pepper
1/3 cup finely chopped walnuts or
   pecans

**MAKES
A 3-CUP
ROLL**

•

Place cheese in 2-quart bowl and microwave on HIGH 2 to 3 minutes, or until softened. Add garlic powder and scallion and blend until smooth.

Spread mixture on 10-inch square sheet of plastic wrap. Sprinkle dried beef and bell pepper evenly over cream cheese. Combine black pepper and nuts and sprinkle half the mixture over bell pepper. Chill. When cold lift up edge of plastic sheet and roll cheese into a pinwheel. Sprinkle remaining pepper-nut mixture evenly over outside of roll. Serve with crackers.

SPICY MEXICAN FONDUE

**MAKES
4 TO 5 CUPS**

■

Serve with tortilla chips
or fresh vegetables.

1 pound lean ground beef
1 pound Velveeta cheese, cut into
    2-inch cubes
1 (15-ounce) can tomato sauce
1 (4-ounce) can green chilies

2 teaspoons Worcestershire sauce
1 large clove garlic, minced
1 teaspoon chili powder
Hot pepper sauce

Place beef in 2-quart measure and microwave on HIGH 4 to 6 minutes. Drain off liquid and stir in cheese, tomato sauce, chilies, Worcestershire sauce, garlic, and chili powder. Microwave on 70% power 5 to 8 minutes, or until hot and bubbly. Stir in hot pepper sauce to taste.

Transfer mixture to fondue pot or chafing dish and keep hot while serving.

Freeze leftovers and reheat later to serve as dip or topping for baked potatoes.

Soups

As a first course, entrée, or even dessert, soup is always a dependable menu choice, offering the benefits of flavor, nutrition, and economy.

Soup and the microwave oven are made for each other. In the absence of direct heat, frequent stirring to prevent the soup from sticking to the pot is unnecessary. Of course, soup cooks faster in the microwave than on top of the conventional stove, and with equally delicious results.

Generally, soup is cooked, covered, in a container at least twice the volume of the ingredients, so that the mixture will not boil over.

Some, such as vegetable soups, are cooked on HIGH only, since a large amount of liquid cooks more slowly in the microwave. Other soups, such as Cheddar Cheese Chowder, begin cooking on HIGH; when they have reached a boil, they're simmered on 50% to 70% power.

Many soups, especially those with a broth base, can be made in concentrated form. At the beginning only half the liquid is cooked with meat, vegetables, and seasonings, and when the vegetables or meat are tender, the remaining liquid is added. This method shortens overall microwave cooking time.

STOCK

Flavorful homemade stock has so many uses—in soups, sauces, stews, and pot roasts of the widest possible variety, and as a poaching medium for vegetables and grains—that it is almost indispensable.

Fortunately, nothing could be easier than stock made in the microwave. Many of the classic stock recipes, written for conventional rangetop cooking, call for simmering the stock for four and sometimes five hours. The same results can be achieved in the microwave in less than half the time. Once you've begun using homemade stock, you'll always want to have some on hand.

REDUCING STOCK

To intensify its flavor or to cook it down to a concentrated form, stock can be reduced, uncovered, on HIGH in the microwave. However, if the stock is to be reduced greatly, cooking it, uncovered, on top of a conventional range is the most efficient method.

REMOVING FAT

To degrease stock or other soup, allow it to cool to room temperature, uncovered, then chill it. The fat will rise to the top and form a layer—hard in the case of beef and veal, somewhat softer for chicken fat. With a spatula or large spoon, lift off the fat and discard it. Any grease remaining on the surface of the soup can be blotted off with paper towels.

CLARIFYING STOCK

Strained, degreased stock is satisfactory for most uses. But when a crystal-clear stock is needed—for consommé or sparkling jellied aspic, for instance—the stock must be clarified.

Chill the stock before you begin. To clarify 1 quart of stock, allow 1 egg white, stiffly beaten, and 1 egg shell, crushed. Pour stock into a 2- to 2½-quart casserole or measure, then beat in egg white and crushed shell with a wire whisk. Microwave, uncovered, on HIGH 6 to 10 minutes, or just until mixture foams up, whisking every minute. Let stock stand, undisturbed, for at least 1 hour, or until it has reached room temperature.

TYPES OF SOUP

BISQUE *A thick cream soup usually made with a stock base, pureed seafood, and vegetables.*

BOUILLON *The French word for stock.*

BROTH *See Stock.*

CHOWDER *A hearty, thick soup, sometimes made with a milk and stock base. The main ingredient can be a vegetable, such as corn, or fish or shellfish.*

CONSOMMÉ *Beef or chicken stock that has been clarified. (See above for clarifying stock.) Consommé Madrilène has tomatoes added and is usually served chilled. Jellied consommé is very rich stock that has been made with enough meat bones to jell the stock naturally, or with unflavored gelatin added after the stock has been clarified.*

GUMBO *A thick Southern soup from Louisiana made with seafood, poultry, or pork, and containing tomatoes and spices. Gumbo is thickened with either okra or filé powder (ground sassafras).*

POTAGE *The French word for soup. It has come to mean a thick, creamed vegetable soup.*

STOCK *A clear soup made by simmering poultry, meat, bones, or seafood with vegetables and seasonings in water.*

Line a sieve with 3 or 4 layers of well-rinsed and wrung-out cheesecloth. Ladle broth and coagulated egg whites into sieve, taking care not to disturb the sediment at the bottom of the stock container. Do not press liquid through the sieve; simply allow stock to drain through, undisturbed. Refrigerate stock, covered.

STORING STOCK

Stock can be kept in the refrigerator, tightly covered, for several days. After that, it must be boiled every day, cooled to room temperature, covered, and then refrigerated again.

Stock freezes well; just divide it among containers of the most useful sizes and freeze for up to 2 months. Stock frozen in ice cube trays can be removed from the trays and transferred to plastic freezer bags.

BEEF STOCK

MAKES

3 QUARTS

▪

To enrich the color and flavor, brown the bones and beef convention-ally, then cook the soup in the microwave.

3 to 5 pounds beef bones
    (including some marrow
    bones)
2 pounds boneless chuck roast,
    cut into 1½-inch cubes
2 to 3 tablespoons vegetable oil
3 quarts water
1 large onion, chopped

2 carrots, sliced
1 turnip, sliced
2 stalks celery, sliced
3 or 4 bay leaves
Several sprigs of parsley
1 teaspoon dried thyme leaves
2 or 3 whole cloves
8 peppercorns

Ask your butcher to split or break beef bones into 2-inch pieces. To brown bones and chuck on rangetop, place in heavy Dutch oven with vegetable oil, place over high heat, and brown them, turning pieces often with tongs. To brown meat and bones in conventional oven broiler, preheat broiler. Arrange bones and chuck in broiler pan and broil 6 inches from heat source about 10 minutes per side, checking often to see that bones have not burned.

Transfer browned meat and bones to 5-quart casserole and add water, onion, carrots, turnip, celery, bay leaves, parsley, thyme, cloves, salt, and peppercorns. Cover and microwave on HIGH 15 minutes. Skim foam as it rises to surface. Stir stock and microwave on 50% power 1½ hours, skimming foam as necessary.

Strain stock into a bowl, reserving beef for another use and discarding remaining solids. Cool stock to room temperature, chill, then remove hardened layer of fat from top. Freeze stock in conveniently sized containers.

CHICKEN STOCK

2 pounds chicken parts (necks
    and leftover carcasses
    included)
1 onion
1 clove garlic
2 carrots, sliced

1 stalk celery, cut into chunks
2 or 3 sprigs of parsley
1 bay leaf
½ teaspoon dried thyme leaves
3 quarts water

**MAKES
3 QUARTS**

■

Place chicken, onion, garlic, carrots, celery, parsley, bay leaf, thyme, and water in 5-quart casserole and cover with container cover or plastic wrap. Microwave on HIGH 15 minutes, then skim any foam that has risen to surface. Microwave on 50% power 45 minutes, skimming foam as necessary.

Remove any usable chicken meat and reserve for another purpose. Break up carcasses and return to stock. Cover and microwave on 50% power 45 minutes longer.

Strain stock, discarding solids, and cool to room temperature. Chill stock, lift off and discard fat congealed on surface, and freeze stock in conveniently sized containers.

HAM STOCK
Substitute a 3- to 4-pound ham bone for the chicken.

STOCKPOT:
Keep a plastic bag or other container in the freezer to accumulate meat and bones for stock. Do not include liver or other organ meats. Lamb has a strong, distinctive flavor and should not be combined with other meats for making an all-purpose stock.

CANTONESE CHICKEN STOCK

2½ pounds bony chicken pieces,
    such as backs and necks
2 quarts water
2 tablespoons dry sherry

1 (2-inch) piece fresh ginger,
    peeled and cut in half
3 scallions, root ends trimmed
8 black peppercorns

**MAKES
2 QUARTS**

■

Fresh ginger and scallions impart an Oriental flavor.

Place chicken, water, sherry, ginger, scallions, and peppercorns in deep 3-quart casserole and microwave, uncovered, on HIGH 20 to 25 minutes. Skim foam from surface, cover casserole, and microwave on 30% power 1 to 1½ hours. Strain stock and cool to room temperature. Chill stock, then lift off and discard fat congealed on surface. Freeze stock in 1- or 2-cup containers.

COURT BOUILLON

**MAKES
5 CUPS**

Use this vegetable stock in soups and sauces and as a poaching liquid for fish.

2 carrots, diced
2 stalks celery, chopped
2 onions, sliced
1 bay leaf
3 sprigs of parsley
1 teaspoon dried thyme leaves

2 whole cloves
8 whole peppercorns
1 quart water
1 cup white wine

Place carrots, celery, onions, bay leaf, parsley, thyme, cloves, peppercorns, water, and wine in 3-quart container and cover with plastic wrap. Microwave on HIGH 10 to 15 minutes, or until boiling. Stir, cover again, and microwave on 50% power 30 to 40 minutes. Strain stock, cool to room temperature, and freeze in 1- or 2-cup containers.

FISH STOCK

**MAKES
3 QUARTS**

The bones and skin of white-fleshed fish are best for stock.

4 to 5 pounds fish carcasses, heads, and skin
2 carrots, chopped
2 stalks celery, chopped
4 onions, chopped
½ cup parsley, chopped
1 teaspoon dried thyme leaves

6 bay leaves
3 or 4 whole cloves
1½ tablespoons salt
15 black peppercorns
3 quarts hot water
2 cups dry white wine

Rinse fish carcasses, heads, and skin and place in 5-quart container with carrots, celery, onions, parsley, thyme, bay leaves, cloves, salt, peppercorns, and hot water. Microwave, covered, on HIGH 15 minutes, or until mixture boils. Skim surface and stir in wine. Microwave, covered, on 50% power 1 hour. Skim foam as it rises to surface. Strain stock, cool to room temperature, and freeze in 2-cup and/or 1-quart containers.

ASPARAGUS AND MUSHROOM SOUP

1 pound asparagus, trimmed and cut into 1-inch pieces
8 ounces mushrooms, sliced (reserve a few slices for garnish)
1 onion, chopped
4 stalks celery, chopped
2 leeks, white part only, thinly sliced

½ stick (¼ cup) unsalted butter
½ cup olive oil
⅔ cup all-purpose flour
6 cups Chicken Stock (page 47) or canned chicken broth
1 cup half-and-half
1 large tomato, peeled, seeded, and chopped (optional)

6 TO 8 SERVINGS

The roux gives this soup a deep, rich flavor.

Place asparagus and sliced mushrooms in bowl large enough to hold them, cover with plastic wrap, and microwave on HIGH 5 minutes, or until tender-crisp. Set aside.

In another bowl, combine onion, celery, and leeks. Cover with plastic wrap and microwave on HIGH 5 to 6 minutes, or until tender. Transfer onion mixture to food processor fitted with steel blade, puree, and reserve.

Place butter and oil in 3-quart container and microwave on HIGH 1 minute, or until butter is melted. Stir in flour and microwave on HIGH 8 to 12 minutes, stirring several times, or until roux is browned. Check roux after 8 minutes, and watch carefully. If black specks appear, it means roux has burned and will taste bitter; discard mixture and start over.

Stir vegetable puree into roux, then blend in stock. Microwave on HIGH 10 to 15 minutes, or until soup is hot and has thickened. Add half-and-half, asparagus and mushrooms, and, if desired, tomato, and microwave 2 to 3 minutes more to heat soup.

Serve soup in heated bowls, and garnish with reserved raw mushroom slices.

Garnish adds interest to a bowl of soup. Consider using croutons; thinly sliced lemon, lime, or orange; crumbled French fried onions; sliced or cubed tomatoes, avocado, cucumber, onion, radishes, or other raw vegetables; julienne strips of cooked vegetables; a dollop of yogurt or sour cream; chopped pistachio or pine nuts; fresh herbs; or crumbled crisp bacon.

BLACK BEAN SOUP

6 TO 8 SERVINGS

■

This soup looks beautiful, and tastes even better, decorated with chopped scallion greens, sour cream, or thinly sliced lemon. Or use any combination of these three.

½ cup chopped salt pork, or 4 slices bacon, chopped
2 onions, sliced
1 stalk celery, thinly sliced
1 or 2 green bell peppers, chopped
2 or 3 cloves garlic, minced
1 tablespoon fresh lemon juice
3 tablespoons extra-virgin olive oil

1 teaspoon ground cumin
2 teaspoons dried oregano
½ teaspoon dry mustard
1 quart Chicken Stock (page 47) or canned chicken broth
2 (15-ounce) cans black beans, undrained
2 cups cooked rice (page 289)

Place salt pork in 3-quart measure or container and microwave on HIGH 2 to 3 minutes. Add onions, celery, peppers, and garlic. Cover and microwave on HIGH 3 to 4 minutes, or until vegetables are tender.

Add lemon juice, olive oil, cumin, oregano, mustard, stock, and beans and stir until well mixed. Microwave, covered, on HIGH 15 minutes, then on 50% power 20 minutes. If you prefer a thicker soup, puree 1 cup soup in blender and stir back into bean mixture.

Place mound of hot rice in each heated soup bowl and pour soup over rice. Decorate with garnish of your choice and serve at once.

SENATE BEAN SOUP

8 SERVINGS

■

An adaptation of the soup served in the U.S. Senate dining room.

1 large potato, peeled and diced
1 carrot, sliced
1 stalk celery, sliced
½ cup chopped green bell pepper
1 onion, chopped
1 bay leaf
4 whole cloves
1 cup water

2 chicken bouillon cubes
1 cup cooked ham, diced
2 (16-ounce) cans white lima beans, undrained
3 cups Chicken Stock (page 47) or canned chicken broth
Salt
Freshly ground black pepper

Place potato, carrot, celery, bell pepper, onion, bay leaf, cloves, water, and bouillon cubes in 3-quart casserole. Cover and microwave on HIGH 8 to 10 minutes, or until vegetables are tender.

Add ham, beans, and stock. Cover and microwave on HIGH 10 minutes, then on 50% power 15 to 20 minutes. Add salt and pepper to taste.

BROCCOLI CHEESE CHOWDER

½ stick (¼ cup) unsalted butter
1 onion, thinly sliced
1 carrot, finely chopped
1 stalk celery, finely chopped
1 clove garlic, minced
¼ cup all-purpose flour
2 cups Chicken Stock (page 47),
  Ham Stock (page 47), or
  canned chicken broth
2 (10-ounce) packages frozen
  chopped broccoli

1 large potato, cooked (page 248),
  peeled, and diced
2 cups milk or half-and-half
¼ teaspoon curry powder
Pinch of baking soda
Salt
Freshly ground white pepper
1 cup grated Cheddar or Swiss
  cheese

10 TO 12 SERVINGS

•

Soups are great to take along on picnics. Transport soup in vacuum bottles to keep it hot or cold.

Place butter, onion, carrot, celery, and garlic in 3-quart casserole and microwave, covered, on HIGH 4 minutes, or until vegetables are tender. Stir in flour, then stir in stock and microwave, uncovered, on HIGH 5 minutes, or until thickened.

To defrost broccoli, remove printed wrapper, puncture carton in several places, and microwave on HIGH 5 minutes. Stir broccoli into stock mixture. Add potato, milk, curry powder, soda, and salt and pepper to taste. Microwave on HIGH 5 to 8 minutes. Stir in cheese and microwave 1 minute longer, or until cheese has melted and soup is very hot. Serve at once.

VARIATIONS
- For a heartier chowder, add diced leftover ham or chicken.
- Instead of broccoli, use equal amount of cooked cauliflower, zucchini, spinach, or asparagus.

HEARTY CORN CHOWDER

6 TO 8 SERVINGS

▪

Filling enough for a one-dish meal.

1/4 cup bacon drippings
1 stalk celery, chopped
1 onion, chopped
1 clove garlic, minced
1/2 green bell pepper, chopped
1 bay leaf
1/4 cup all-purpose flour
2 potatoes, cooked (page 248), peeled, and cut into small dice
2 cups corn kernels, fresh or frozen and defrosted

8 ounces smoked sausage, cut into bite-size pieces
3 cups milk or half-and-half, or 2 cups Chicken Stock (page 47) or canned chicken broth and 1 cup milk
1 teaspoon chili powder
1 teaspoon salt
1/2 teaspoon freshly ground white pepper

Place bacon drippings, celery, onion, garlic, bell pepper, and bay leaf in 3-quart casserole and microwave, covered, on HIGH 4 minutes, or until vegetables are tender. Stir in flour.

Add potatoes, corn, sausage, milk, chili powder, salt, and pepper. Microwave on HIGH 12 to 15 minutes, or until thickened. Serve with a green salad and crusty French or Italian bread.

VARIATIONS
Ham or chicken may be substituted for sausage, or meat may be omitted altogether.

EGG DROP SOUP

4 SERVINGS

▪

1 quart Cantonese Chicken Stock (page 47)
1 scallion, sliced diagonally
1 teaspoon soy sauce

2 tablespoons cornstarch blended with 3 tablespoons cold water
1 egg, beaten with 1 tablespoon cold water

Place stock and scallion in 2-quart measure and microwave on HIGH 6 to 8 minutes, or until boiling. Stir in soy sauce and cornstarch mixture. Microwave on HIGH 2 to 3 minutes longer, or until soup is boiling and slightly thickened.

Slowly drizzle beaten egg mixture into hot soup, stirring constantly, and serve at once.

GAZPACHO

1 (12-ounce) can tomato-vegetable
juice
1 beef bouillon cube
1 (12-ounce) can tomato juice
3 large tomatoes, cut into 1/2-inch
dice
3 cucumbers, peeled, seeded, and
cut into 1/2-inch dice
1 stalk celery, chopped
1/2 Vidalia or other sweet onion,
finely chopped
1 carrot, chopped
1/2 red bell pepper, chopped
1/2 green bell pepper, chopped

1 or 2 radishes, chopped
(optional)
1 clove garlic, minced
1 teaspoon seasoned salt
3 tablespoons balsamic vinegar or
other red wine vinegar
1/3 cup extra-virgin olive oil
(optional)
Salt
Freshly ground black pepper
Hot pepper sauce

**6 TO 8
SERVINGS**

■

A low-cal treat! Serve in
a wineglass with a
sprig of fresh basil or a
lime wedge. A dish of
Spanish peasant origin,
gazpacho has long
been enjoyed in France,
Portugal, and Italy as
well. European gazpa-
cho usually contains
soaked bread or bread
crumbs; the American
versions generally do
not. Gazpacho keeps in
the refrigerator 4 or 5
days and is good for a
snack, light lunch or
dinner treat. Chopping
all the vegetables with
12 ounces tomato-veg-
etable juice in a food
processor or blender
makes the preparation
quick and easy.

In 2-quart measure, microwave 1 cup of the tomato-vegetable juice and bouillon cube on HIGH 2 to 3 minutes, or until boiling. Stir to dissolve bouillon cube. In a bowl or pitcher, combine hot juice with remaining tomato-vegetable juice and remaining ingredients. Chill for several hours.

MINESTRONE

15 TO 18
SERVINGS

■

Serve with freshly
grated Parmesan
cheese and Italian
bread.

¹/₄ cup elbow macaroni
¹/₂ cup water
4 ounces salt pork or bacon,
 chopped
1 clove garlic, minced
Pinch of dried sage
Pinch of dried oregano
2 stalks celery, sliced
2 medium onions, sliced vertically
1 turnip, chopped
2 cups coarsely chopped carrots
2 parsnips, sliced (optional)
1 quart shredded cabbage
1 (29-ounce) can tomatoes,
 undrained

¹/₂ cup chopped parsley
1 tablespoon fresh basil, or 1
 teaspoon dried
¹/₄ teaspoon dried rosemary
6 cups Beef Stock (page 46) or
 canned beef broth
1 (15-ounce) can kidney or navy
 beans, drained
2 cups spinach leaves, well
 washed
Worcestershire sauce
Salt
Freshly ground black pepper

Place macaroni, water, salt pork, garlic, sage, and oregano in deep 5-quart casserole. Cover and microwave on HIGH 3 minutes, or until boiling. Stir, then reduce power to 50% and microwave 5 to 8 minutes, or until liquid is absorbed. Reserve.

In 2-quart measure, place celery, onions, turnip, carrots, and, if desired, parsnips. Cover with plastic wrap and microwave on HIGH 7 to 10 minutes, or until carrots are tender-crisp. Transfer vegetables to casserole with macaroni mixture.

Add cabbage, tomatoes, parsley, basil, rosemary, and stock to casserole and stir to blend all ingredients. Microwave, covered, on HIGH 15 minutes. Stir, then reduce power to 50% and cook 20 minutes longer.

Add beans and spinach and microwave, covered, on 50% power 5 to 10 minutes. Season to taste with Worcestershire, salt, and pepper.

**A BOUQUET
GARNI**
is a little bundle of
herbs, usually bay leaf,
thyme, and parsley,
tied in a cheesecloth
bag and added to sea-
son soup, sauces, and
other foods.

MUSHROOM-BARLEY SOUP

½ stick (¼ cup) unsalted butter
1 onion, thinly sliced
1 small carrot, thinly sliced
1 pound mushrooms, sliced
2 cloves garlic, minced
1 bay leaf
½ cup pearl barley
6½ cups Beef Stock (page 46) or
  Chicken Stock (page 47), or
  canned beef or chicken broth

½ to 1 teaspoon salt
1 potato, peeled, cooked, and diced
Freshly ground black pepper
½ to ¾ cup plain low-fat yogurt
  (optional)
2 to 3 tablespoons snipped fresh
  dill (optional)

6 TO 8 SERVINGS

■

In 3- to 4-quart measure, combine butter, onion, carrot, mushrooms, garlic, bay leaf, barley, and 1½ cups of the stock. Microwave, covered, on HIGH for 10 minutes, then on 50% power 30 minutes, or until barley is tender.

Add remaining stock, salt, and potato. Microwave on HIGH 10 minutes, then on 50% power 15 to 20 minutes, or until thoroughly heated. Add pepper to taste. Serve in heated bowls, garnished with a dollop of yogurt and dill, if desired.

HUNGARIAN MUSHROOM SOUP

6 TO 8 SERVINGS

■

Delicious flavor! Serve as a first course or a light main dish.

1 stick (1/2 cup) unsalted butter
1 large onion, chopped
1 tablespoon fresh lemon juice
1 tablespoon tamari or soy sauce
2 teaspoons Hungarian paprika
1/2 teaspoon chopped fresh dill
6 tablespoons all-purpose flour
1 pound mushrooms, sliced
3 cups Chicken Stock (page 47) or
 canned chicken broth

2 cups half-and-half or milk
2/3 cup sour cream or plain lowfat
 yogurt
1/2 teaspoon sugar
Salt
Freshly ground black pepper
2 tablespoons chopped parsley or
 garlic croutons

In 3-quart casserole, place butter, onion, lemon juice, tamari, paprika, and dill, cover, and microwave on HIGH for 3 minutes. Stir in flour and mushrooms, cover, and microwave on HIGH 4 to 5 minutes, or until mushrooms are tender.

Add stock and half-and-half and stir. Microwave, covered, on HIGH 10 minutes, then on 50% power 10 minutes. Stir in sour cream and sugar and season to taste with salt and pepper.

Serve in heated soup bowls and garnish with parsley or garlic croutons.

FRENCH ONION SOUP

½ stick (¼ cup) unsalted butter
3 to 4 medium onions, thinly
sliced
1 clove garlic, minced
1 tablespoon all-purpose flour
2 (10½-ounce) cans condensed
beef broth
1½ cups water
1 cup dry white wine or water
1 bay leaf

1 teaspoon Worcestershire sauce
¼ teaspoon dried thyme
Salt
Freshly ground white pepper
4 to 6 (1-inch-thick) slices toasted
French bread
½ cup freshly grated Parmesan
cheese
1 to 2 cups grated Gruyère or
Swiss cheese

4 TO 6 SERVINGS

Place butter in large, heavy skillet. On rangetop, over moderately low heat, melt butter, then add onions and garlic and cook, stirring often, until onions are rich brown color, about 15 to 20 minutes.

Transfer onions to 2½-quart microwavable casserole, stir in flour, then add ½ cup of the broth and stir. Add remaining broth, water, wine, bay leaf, Worcestershire, and thyme and microwave on HIGH 8 to 10 minutes. Add salt and pepper to taste.

Preheat conventional broiler.

Ladle soup into ovenproof bowls, topping each with a slice of toasted bread. Sprinkle each bowl generously with Parmesan and Gruyère. Place under broiler and broil until cheese is melted and slightly browned, about 4 to 5 minutes. Serve at once.

LOW-CALORIE FRENCH ONION SOUP

Omit butter. Place onions in dish large enough to hold them, cover with plastic wrap, and microwave on HIGH 5 to 6 minutes, or until onions are steamed. Stir in flour and proceed with recipe.

SOUP POT:

Keep a covered container in the freezer in which leftover food can be accumulated to make soup. Strong vegetables such as turnips and cabbage should not be included. Leftover green beans lose their firm texture. When enough leftovers have accumulated for a "pot" of soup, defrost the Soup Pot and add stock, seasonings, and additional meat and vegetables as desired.

POTATO CHOWDER

4 TO 6 SERVINGS

■

This is an American version of the famous French *Soupe Bonne Femme*, which uses whites of leeks in addition to onion and calls for water instead of stock. On either side of the Atlantic the soup is the basis for a seemingly infinite number of variations, a few of which follow the main recipe. This is a comforting soup, simple to prepare and perfect for cold weather.

½ cup chopped celery
2 cups chopped onion
3 or 4 large potatoes, peeled and sliced
⅓ cup unsalted butter
1 quart Chicken Stock (page 47) or canned chicken broth

2 cups half-and-half or milk
Salt
Freshly ground black pepper
Snipped fresh chives
Freshly grated Parmesan, Cheddar, or Gruyère cheese (optional)

Place celery, onion, potatoes, and butter in 3-quart casserole. Cover and microwave on HIGH 10 to 14 minutes, or until vegetables are tender. Transfer vegetables to food processor fitted with steel blade, add 2 cups stock, and process to achieve texture desired.

Return mixture to casserole, add remaining stock and half-and-half, and microwave, uncovered, on 70% power 6 to 8 minutes, or until hot but not boiling. Add salt, pepper, and chives to taste. Serve at once, sprinkled with grated cheese, if desired.

ARUGULA BISQUE

Add 1 clove garlic, minced, 1 tablespoon finely chopped parsley, and ¼ cup or more finely chopped arugula (rocket) leaves to potato mixture before microwaving. Omit grated cheese and garnish each bowl with roughly chopped arugula leaves.

COUNTRY CHOWDER

Add 1 red bell pepper, chopped, and 1 star anise (available in Oriental food shops) to the celery, onion, and potatoes. Remove star anise, then process only long enough to break up potatoes. To finished soup, stir in 8 ounces grated Monterey Jack cheese and ½ cup ham cut into short julienne strips. Stir to melt cheese and thin, if necessary, with more hot half-and-half or milk.

SALMON BISQUE

Coarsely chop vegetables and 2 cups broth in food processor. Add 1 (7-ounce) can of salmon, undrained but with skin and bones removed, 1 teaspoon paprika, a pinch of snipped fresh dill, and 1 tablespoon sherry, if desired, and stir before final microwaving.

VICHYSSOISE

To celery, onion, and potato mixture, add 1 pinch dried thyme leaves, 1 dash cayenne pepper, and 1 bay leaf. Cook as directed. Remove bay leaf before transferring mixture to food processor. Puree until smooth. Continue with recipe and, after final cooking, ladle ½ cup soup into 1 beaten egg yolk, stirring constantly. Slowly stir egg yolk mixture back into soup and microwave on 70% power 3 to 5 minutes longer to thicken soup. Cool to room temperature, then chill. Serve in chilled soup bowls, decorated with chopped parsley or snipped chives.

SORREL AND ROSEMARY SOUP

2 cups chopped sorrel leaves
2 tablespoons unsalted butter
3 cups Chicken Stock (page 47) or
    canned chicken broth
¼ teaspoon dried rosemary
½ cup heavy cream

2 egg yolks, beaten
1 cup fine egg noodles or angel
    hair pasta, cooked according
    to package instructions
    (optional)

**4 TO 6
SERVINGS**

▪

A lovely spring soup.
Serve it hot or cold.

Place sorrel and butter in 2-quart measure and microwave, covered, on HIGH 3 minutes, or until sorrel is wilted. Add stock and rosemary and microwave on HIGH 6 to 8 minutes longer. Stir in cream. Ladle ½ cup of soup mixture into beaten eggs, stirring constantly, then stir egg mixture back into soup. Microwave on 70% power 3 to 5 minutes, or until soup thickens; do not allow soup to boil. Strain, add cooked noodles, if desired, and serve at once.

CREAM OF TOMATO SOUP

6 TO 8 SERVINGS

•

3 tablespoons olive oil
3 tablespoons unsalted butter
3 tablespoons chopped onion
1 tablespoon chopped fresh basil
   or 1 teaspoon dried
2 tablespoons all-purpose flour
3 cups coarsely chopped peeled
   and seeded tomatoes

2 teaspoons chicken bouillon
   granules
3 cups half-and-half or milk
2 tablespoons catsup
Salt
Freshly ground black pepper

Place olive oil, butter, onion, basil, and flour in 2-quart measure and microwave, covered, on HIGH 3 minutes. Stir in tomatoes and bouillon granules and microwave on HIGH 3 minutes.

    Stir in half-and-half and catsup, season to taste with salt and pepper, and microwave on HIGH 5 minutes, or until soup is thick and very hot; be careful not to let soup boil. Serve at once.

SPICY TOMATO SOUP

8 TO 10 SERVINGS

•

The flavor of this soup will improve if it's made a day ahead. Served cold, it makes a wonderful start for a summer party.

3 tablespoons unsalted butter
2 onions, chopped
1/2 cup finely chopped celery
2 cloves garlic, minced
1-inch piece fresh ginger, peeled
   and thinly sliced or grated
1 bay leaf
1/4 teaspoon ground cumin

Pinch of ground allspice
6 cups Chicken Stock (page 47) or
   canned chicken broth
3 pounds tomatoes, peeled, seeded,
   and chopped, or 2 (28-ounce)
   cans tomatoes, undrained
2 pinches saffron threads

ONE OR TWO OF THE FOLLOWING GARNISHES

Plain low-fat yogurt, mixed with
   garlic salt to taste (optional)
Minced fresh ginger (optional)

Chopped fresh or canned green
   chilies (optional)

In 3-quart casserole, combine butter, onions, celery, garlic, ginger, bay leaf, cumin, and allspice. Microwave, covered, on HIGH 5 minutes, or until vegetables are tender.

Stir in 3 cups of stock and tomatoes and microwave on HIGH 10 minutes. Stir in saffron threads and microwave at 50% power 15 minutes longer. Add remaining broth and, if serving hot, microwave on HIGH 8 to 10 minutes, or until boiling.

Serve soup hot or cold, garnished with yogurt, ginger, or chilies, if desired.

BASQUE VEGETABLE SOUP

2 carrots, sliced
1 potato, peeled and cut into ½-inch dice
1 turnip, peeled and cut into ½-inch dice
1 onion, chopped
2 leeks, white part only, sliced
1 clove garlic, minced
1 cup shredded cabbage
3 cups chopped cooked chicken (optional)
1 (1-pound) can tomatoes, undrained

1 (15-ounce) can white navy beans, undrained
6 cups Chicken Stock (page 47) or canned chicken broth
1 teaspoon dried thyme
1 tablespoon chopped parsley
2 bay leaves
Salt
Freshly ground black pepper
Hot pepper sauce

8 TO 10 SERVINGS

Place carrots in 5-quart casserole, pushing them to sides of dish. Place potato, turnip, onion, leeks, garlic, and cabbage in center. Cover and microwave on HIGH 15 minutes, or until vegetables are tender-crisp. Stir.

Add chicken, if desired, tomatoes, beans, stock, thyme, parsley, bay leaves, and salt, pepper, and hot pepper sauce to taste. Cover and microwave on HIGH 15 minutes, then on 50% power 20 minutes. Serve with crusty bread.

WILD RICE SOUP

8 SERVINGS

▪

A good first course or luncheon entrée.

1 (6-ounce) package mixed long-grain and wild rice
2 tablespoons unsalted butter
1 stalk celery, thinly sliced
1 small onion, thinly sliced
1 cup sliced mushrooms
1 carrot, chopped

1 quart Chicken Stock (page 47) or canned chicken broth
$1/2$ cup milk or half-and-half
$1/4$ teaspoon dried marjoram
$1/4$ teaspoon dried basil
Salt
Freshly ground black pepper

In 3-quart casserole, cook rice according to package microwave directions. In separate bowl, combine butter, celery, onion, mushrooms, and carrot. Microwave, covered, on HIGH 5 minutes, or until vegetables are tender. Add vegetables to rice. Stir in stock, milk, marjoram, basil, and salt and pepper to taste. Microwave on HIGH 10 minutes, then on 50% power for 10 minutes.

ITALIAN SAUSAGE SOUP
Add 8 ounces Italian sausage, cooked and crumbled, with the stock and milk.

CHEDDAR CHEESE SOUP

8 SERVINGS

▪

4 stalks celery, thinly sliced
2 carrots, thinly sliced
2 medium onions, thinly sliced
$1/4$ cup slivered red bell pepper or 2 tablespoons chopped pimiento
$1 1/2$ quarts Chicken Stock (page 47) or canned chicken broth

1 stick ($1/2$ cup) unsalted butter
$2/3$ cup all-purpose flour
12 ounces Tillamook or other sharp Cheddar cheese, grated
Pinch of baking soda
Salt
Freshly ground white pepper

ONE OR TWO OF THE FOLLOWING GARNISHES
2 or 3 slices bacon, cooked and crumbled
2 tomatoes, peeled, seeded, and cut into $1/4$-inch dice

3 tablespoons minced green chilies
$1/4$ cup snipped fresh chives

In 3-quart bowl, combine celery, carrots, onions, and bell pepper. Microwave, covered, on HIGH 5 to 8 minutes, or until vegetables are tender-crisp. Add stock and microwave, covered, on HIGH 8 minutes. Strain, reserving stock and vegetables separately.

In 3-quart casserole, microwave the butter on HIGH 1 to 1½ minutes to melt. Stir in flour and microwave on HIGH 10 to 15 minutes to make a light brown roux. Stir in reserved hot stock, then add reserved vegetables. Microwave on 50% power 10 minutes, or until thickened. Add cheese and stir until melted. Add baking soda and salt and pepper to taste. Decorate soup with optional garnishes and serve at once.

CHEESEBURGER SOUP

1 pound lean ground beef
1 onion, chopped
1 stalk celery, sliced
3 tablespoons chopped green bell
    pepper
¼ cup all-purpose flour
1 quart milk
1 tablespoon beef bouillon
    granules

2 potatoes, cooked (page 248),
    peeled, and diced
1 cup grated sharp Cheddar
    cheese
Salt
Garlic salt
Freshly ground black pepper
3 tablespoons chopped parsley or
    ¾ cup croutons

4 TO 6 SERVINGS

Quick, easy, and a special favorite of kids.

Crumble beef into 3-quart casserole and microwave on HIGH 5 minutes. Drain off fat. Add onion, celery, and bell pepper, cover, and microwave on HIGH 5 minutes, or until meat is browned and vegetables are tender.

Stir in flour, then blend in milk, bouillon granules, and potatoes. Microwave on HIGH 6 to 10 minutes, or until thickened. Stir in cheese and salt, garlic salt, and pepper to taste. Microwave on HIGH 1 minute longer, or until very hot. Serve at once in heated bowls, sprinkled with parsley or croutons.

CHINESE SOUP

4 TO 6
SERVINGS

■

This is a light, flavorful soup you can invent anew each time you make it, simply by varying the combinations of ingredients.

1 quart Chinese Chicken Stock (page 47)

½ CUP OF 3 OR 4 OF THE FOLLOWING:

shredded cooked chicken
shredded cooked pork
shredded cooked beef
medium shrimp, shelled and deveined
bay scallops or sliced sea scallops
coarsely shredded carrot
thinly sliced celery
thinly shredded lo bok *(Chinese turnip)*

finely shredded cabbage
snow peas, strings removed and diagonally sliced
diagonally sliced scallions
sliced mushrooms
sliced water chestnuts
sliced bamboo shoots
bean sprouts
½-inch cubes firm tofu
fine egg noodles

Place stock in 2-quart casserole, add 3 or 4 suggested ingredients, and microwave on HIGH 5 to 10 minutes, or long enough to cook raw seafood but not to overcook vegetables, which should remain quite crisp.

CHICKEN AND RICE SOUP

6 TO 8
SERVINGS

■

1 (3-pound) frying chicken, cut into 8 pieces
1 onion, chopped
2 celery stalks, with tops, sliced
¼ cup chopped parsley
1 teaspoon salt

½ teaspoon freshly ground black pepper
7 cups water
¾ cup rice
2 teaspoons chicken bouillon granules

In deep 4-quart casserole, combine chicken, onion, celery, parsley, salt, pepper, and 1 quart of water. Microwave, covered, on HIGH 25 minutes.

Remove chicken from stock and reserve. Adjust soup seasoning and add rice, bouillon granules, and remaining 3 cups water. Microwave, covered, on HIGH 10 to 12 minutes. Stir and microwave on 50% power 10 to 15 minutes, or until rice is cooked.

While soup is cooking, remove and discard chicken skin and bones. Cut meat into ½-inch dice and add to soup. Thin soup with additional water if too thick. Microwave on HIGH 3 to 4 minutes, or until soup comes to a boil.

CHICKEN NOODLE SOUP

Substitute 4 to 6 ounces noodles for rice and cook as directed.

MULLIGATAWNY

1 pound chicken breasts, bone in
3 cups Chicken Stock (page 47) or
*   canned chicken broth*
2 tomatoes, peeled, seeded, and
*   chopped*
½ cup carrot, cut into 2-inch
*   strips*
½ cup celery, cut into 2-inch
*   strips*
½ cup sliced onion
1 leek, white part only, finely
*   chopped*

2 tablespoons unsalted butter
2 tablespoons all-purpose flour
¼ cup cooked rice
2 cloves garlic, minced
½ teaspoon curry powder
⅛ teaspoon ground coriander
⅛ teaspoon grated fresh ginger
Salt
Freshly ground white pepper

6 FIRST-
COURSE
SERVINGS; 3
OR 4 MAIN-
COURSE
SERVINGS

▪

A curried chicken soup from India, very appealing as a first or a main course. Use less chicken if you intend to serve the soup as a first course.

Place chicken and stock in shallow 1½-quart casserole, cover tightly, and microwave on HIGH 6 to 8 minutes, or until chicken is cooked. Strain broth into 2-quart casserole. Remove and discard skin and bones from chicken. Cut meat into ½-inch dice, add to broth, and reserve.

Combine tomatoes, carrot, celery, onion, leek, and butter in 1-quart measure, cover with plastic wrap, and microwave on HIGH 4 to 7 minutes, or until carrots are tender. Stir in flour and transfer mixture to casserole with broth and chicken. Stir in rice, garlic, curry powder, coriander, and ginger. Microwave on HIGH 5 minutes, then on 50% power 10 to 15 minutes. Add salt and pepper to taste.

FRENCH PEASANT SOUP

**MAKES
5 QUARTS**

•

Great for serving a crowd on a cold day. Accompany with crusty French bread and a hearty red wine.

2 tablespoons olive oil
8 ounces boneless beef or veal
    scallops, cut into 1-inch strips
1 clove garlic, minced
½ cup chopped onion
½ cup chopped celery
½ cup chopped green bell pepper
½ cup chopped spinach
1 potato, peeled and cut into
    ½-inch dice
1 turnip, peeled and cut into
    ½-inch dice
1 carrot, cut into ½-inch dice

4 ounces pepperoni, thinly sliced
2 cups cooked pasta shells
3 quarts Beef Stock (page 46) or
    canned beef broth
1 (1-pound) can tomatoes,
    undrained
½ cup fresh or frozen green peas
2 tablespoons chopped fresh basil
    or 1 teaspoon dried
Salt
Freshly ground black pepper
Hot pepper sauce

Pour olive oil into medium skillet, place over moderate heat on conventional rangetop, and heat. Add beef and garlic and sauté until meat is browned on both sides. Reserve.

Place onion, celery, bell pepper, spinach, potato, turnip, carrot, and pepperoni in 5-quart casserole. Microwave, covered, on HIGH 10 to 12 minutes, or until vegetables are tender-crisp.

Add beef mixture, pasta shells, stock, tomatoes, peas, and basil, and microwave, covered, on HIGH 15 to 20 minutes, or until soup is boiling. Stir, add salt, pepper, and hot pepper sauce to taste, and simmer, covered, on 50% power 30 to 40 minutes to blend flavors and finish cooking.

WESTERN CHILI SOUP

1 pound lean ground beef
1 small onion, chopped
1 clove garlic, minced
1 tablespoon beef bouillon granules
1 (1-pound) can kidney beans, undrained

1 (1-pound) can tomatoes, undrained
2 cups cooked elbow macaroni
2 cups water
1/2 teaspoon salt
1 tablespoon chili powder
1 tablespoon vinegar

6 TO 8 SERVINGS

·

Place beef, onion, and garlic in 3-quart casserole and microwave on HIGH 5 minutes. Stir in bouillon granules, beans, tomatoes, macaroni, water, salt, chili powder, and vinegar. Break up tomatoes with a fork. Microwave, covered, on HIGH 10 minutes, then on 50% power for 10 to 15 minutes. Serve with tortilla chips.

SCOTCH BROTH

1 pound lean boneless lamb, cut into thin bite-size pieces
1 onion, chopped
1/2 cup carrots, diced (1/4-inch pieces)
1/4 cup celery, diced (1/4-inch pieces)
1/4 cup turnip, diced (1/4-inch pieces)

1 bay leaf
2 whole cloves
2 or 3 sprigs parsley
1/4 cup pearl barley
1 quart water
1 tablespoon Scotch whisky (optional)
Salt
Freshly ground black pepper

4 TO 6 SERVINGS

·

A light Scottish soup that features the flavor of lamb.

Place lamb, onion, carrots, celery, turnip, bay leaf, cloves, and parsley in 2½-quart casserole and microwave, covered, on HIGH 5 to 10 minutes, or until vegetables are tender.

Add barley and water and microwave, covered, on HIGH 10 minutes, then on 50% power 15 minutes. Add Scotch, if desired, and season with salt and pepper to taste.

SAUSAGE AND WILD RICE SOUP

8 SERVINGS

•

A fireside favorite on a
blustery day!

4 ounces wild rice
2 quarts Chicken Stock (page 47)
   or canned chicken broth
1/2 stick (1/4 cup) unsalted butter
1/4 cup vegetable or olive oil
1/2 cup all-purpose flour
1/2 red bell pepper, chopped

1 onion, thinly sliced
2 stalks celery, thinly sliced
8 ounces Polish sausage
   (kielbasa), skin removed, and
   cut into thin strips
Salt
Freshly ground black pepper

Place rice and 2 cups of stock in 3-quart casserole. Cover and microwave on HIGH 10 minutes, then on 50% power 10 to 15 minutes. Rice should burst open and be very tender.

To prepare roux, combine butter, oil, and flour in 1-quart bowl and microwave, uncovered, on HIGH 10 to 12 minutes, or until mixture is caramel colored, stirring several times during cooking. Stir roux into rice mixture and add remaining stock.

Combine bell pepper, onion, celery, and sausage in 1-quart measure, cover, and microwave on HIGH 6 to 7 minutes, or until vegetables are tender-crisp. Add vegetables to rice mixture, cover, and microwave on HIGH 10 to 15 minutes, or until very hot. Add salt and pepper to taste.

CATCH·OF·THE·DAY CHOWDER

**4 TO 6
SERVINGS**

•

2 tablespoons bacon drippings
2 tablespoons all-purpose flour
1 cup chopped onion
1/2 cup chopped red or green bell
   pepper
3 medium potatoes, peeled and
   cut into 1/2-inch dice
1 (1-pound) can whole tomatoes,
   undrained
2 1/2 cups water
2 cloves garlic, minced

1 bay leaf
2 teaspoons sugar
1 teaspoon dried basil
1 tablespoon Worcestershire sauce
Dash of hot pepper sauce
1 teaspoon salt
1 teaspoon freshly ground black
   pepper
1 pound skinless fish fillets, cut
   into bite-size pieces

To make roux, combine bacon drippings and flour in 4-quart casserole and microwave, uncovered, on HIGH 3 to 5 minutes, or until mixture is light brown. Add onion, bell pepper, and potatoes, cover with plastic wrap, and microwave on HIGH 8 to 10 minutes. Stir midway through cooking.

Add tomatoes, water, garlic, bay leaf, sugar, basil, Worcestershire, hot pepper sauce, salt, and pepper. Break up tomatoes with fork or wooden spoon. Microwave, covered, on 50% power 5 to 7 minutes. Add fish and cook on HIGH 5 to 8 minutes, or until fish flakes easily. Adjust seasoning, if necessary.

MEDITERRANEAN CREAM OF MUSSEL SOUP

1 onion, sliced
2 scallions, chopped
1 stalk celery, thinly sliced
½ stick (¼ cup) unsalted butter
1 cup dry white wine
1 (28-ounce) can tomatoes, undrained
Pinch of saffron threads

2 teaspoons chicken bouillon granules
1 to 2 pounds mussels, well scrubbed and debearded
1 quart half-and-half or milk
Salt
Freshly ground white pepper
1 to 2 tablespoons chopped parsley

6 TO 8 SERVINGS

■

This is a microwave version of Billi Bi.

In 3-quart casserole, combine onion, scallions, celery, and butter. Microwave, covered, on HIGH 5 minutes, or until vegetables are tender. Add wine, tomatoes, saffron, bouillon granules, and mussels. Break up tomatoes with fork or wooden spoon and mix ingredients well. Cover and microwave mixture on HIGH 10 minutes, or until mussels have opened.

Stir in half-and-half and salt and pepper to taste. Cover again and microwave on 70% power 5 to 10 minutes, or until soup is very hot; do not let boil. Discard any mussels that have not opened. Sprinkle soup with parsley and serve.

NEW ENGLAND CLAM CHOWDER

4 TO 6 SERVINGS

■

1 (1-inch) cube salt pork, chopped
2 tablespoons unsalted butter
1 onion, sliced
1 stalk celery, chopped
1 potato, peeled and cubed
1 bay leaf
1/2 teaspoon dried thyme

1 cup water or clam juice
1 or 2 (7-ounce) cans minced
    clams, undrained
3 cups milk or half-and-half
Salt
Freshly ground white pepper

Place salt pork in 3-quart casserole and microwave on HIGH 2 to 3 minutes. Stir in butter, onion, celery, potato, bay leaf, thyme, and water. Microwave, covered, on HIGH 5 to 6 minutes, or until vegetables are tender.

Add clams, milk, and salt and pepper to taste. Microwave on 70% power 5 minutes, or until soup is very hot, but not boiling. Serve at once in heated soup bowls.

OYSTER STEW

Substitute 1 pint shucked oysters for clams, adding them when soup is almost at a boil, and microwave, covered, 1 to 2 minutes on 70% power. Oysters are cooked when their edges begin to curl. Sprinkle with paprika, if desired, float a few small dabs of unsalted butter on top, and serve at once with oyster crackers.

IMPERIAL CRAB SOUP

4 TO 6 SERVINGS

■

Serve as a first course or an entrée for a light supper.

1/2 cup chopped onion
1 stick (1/2 cup) unsalted butter
3 tablespoons all-purpose flour
12 to 16 ounces fresh crabmeat,
    picked over
1 teaspoon salt
1/2 teaspoon freshly ground white
    pepper

1 quart milk or Chicken Stock
    (page 47)
1 cup half-and-half
1/4 cup Scotch whisky
2 to 3 tablespoons chopped
    parsley

Place onion and butter in 2½-quart casserole and microwave on HIGH 3 to 4 minutes, or until onion is tender-crisp. Stir in flour and microwave on HIGH 2 minutes longer. Stir in crabmeat, salt, pepper, and milk. Microwave on HIGH 5 to 10 minutes, or until soup is thickened. Stir in half-and-half and Scotch and microwave on HIGH 2 to 3 minutes to heat through; do not allow to boil. Sprinkle with parsley and serve from casserole.

SPANISH SEAFOOD SOUP

1 (7-ounce) package paella, saffron, or Spanish rice mix
1 onion, sliced
1 teaspoon capers, crushed
3 tablespoons olive oil
5 black or green olives, sliced
1 (28-ounce) can tomatoes, undrained
3 cloves garlic, minced
1 small green bell pepper, cut into ¼-inch dice
3 bay leaves
2 quarts Chicken Stock (page 47) or canned chicken broth

1 cup dry white wine
½ cup fresh or frozen green peas
1 cup asparagus, sliced (1-inch pieces)
8 to 10 mushrooms, sliced
8 ounces shrimp, peeled and deveined
1 cup chopped or shredded chicken breast meat
1 pound mussels or littleneck clams, well scrubbed (and mussels debearded)
Salt
Freshly ground black pepper

10 TO 12 SERVINGS

•

This interesting combination of seafood and vegetables makes a delicious main course for an informal meal. The soup may be made early in the day and reheated at serving time.

Combine rice mix, onion, capers, oil, olives, tomatoes, garlic, bell pepper, bay leaves, and 2 cups of the chicken stock. Break up tomatoes with fork or wooden spoon. Microwave, covered, on HIGH 10 minutes, then on 50% power 30 minutes.

Stir in 1 quart chicken stock, then add wine, peas, asparagus, mushrooms, shrimp, and chicken. Microwave, covered, on HIGH 15 minutes, then on 50% power 30 to 40 minutes. Add the remaining stock and mussels and salt and pepper to taste. Microwave, covered, on 50% power 15 minutes, or until mussels have opened. Discard any mussels that have not opened.

Serve hot with crusty bread and a green salad.

GUMBO

This Cajun specialty, which is halfway between a soup and a stew, probably gets its name from its origin. The African word for okra, which is a common ingredient, is *guin-gombo*, and the Choctaw word for sassafras, another common ingredient, is *kombo*. This recipe, if prepared conventionally, requires over three hours of cooking. The same delicious flavor can be achieved in one hour using the microwave.

Filé powder, which gives gumbo its characteristic flavor and consistency, is made of ground sassafras. Always add filé after the gumbo has stopped cooking, otherwise the texture will become stringy and the gumbo will taste bitter.

¹/₄ cup vegetable oil
¹/₄ cup all-purpose flour
2 stalks celery, diced
1 onion, chopped
1 green bell pepper, chopped
2 cloves garlic, minced
2 bay leaves
4 cups fresh or frozen okra, sliced
*1 pound shrimp, peeled and
    deveined*
*2 (1-pound) cans tomatoes,
    undrained*

*3 to 4 cups Chicken Stock (page
    47) or canned chicken broth*
¹/₂ teaspoon ground allspice
1 tablespoon Worcestershire sauce
¹/₂ teaspoon dried thyme
Salt
Freshly ground black pepper
Hot pepper sauce
¹/₂ teaspoon filé powder
Hot cooked rice

To prepare roux, combine oil and flour in 3-quart casserole. Microwave, uncovered, on HIGH 4 to 8 minutes, or until roux is caramel colored, stirring several times during cooking. If black spots appear, roux is burned; discard mixture and start over again.

Stir in celery, onion, bell pepper, garlic, and bay leaves. Microwave, covered, on HIGH 10 minutes, or until vegetables are tender. Add okra, shrimp, tomatoes, stock, allspice, Worcestershire sauce, and thyme. Break up tomatoes with fork or wooden spoon and stir ingredients to mix well. Microwave, covered, on HIGH 15 minutes, then reduce power to 50% and cook 15 to 20 minutes. Season to taste with salt, pepper, and hot pepper sauce.

To serve, pour into a heated soup tureen. Sprinkle with filé powder and stir. Carefully mound rice in one end of tureen so that guests can serve themselves individually. Pass additional filé powder.

VARIATIONS

Oysters, crabmeat, or boneless chicken may be used instead of shrimp, or try a combination of seafood and chicken.

Sauces

In the past, sauces were often used to mask stale or tasteless food. Now, fresh foods are available almost year round, and sauces enhance the foods they're served with, adding flavor, color, and moisture.

In the microwave, you can achieve smooth, silky sauces without constant stirring or worry over burned pot bottoms. In conventional cooking, scorching is the number one problem in sauce preparation; but because there is no heat source with the microwave, there is no possibility of scorching.

Sauces that are thickened with flour, cornstarch, or arrowroot adapt easily to microwaving. The ingredients should be well blended before cooking and stirred to prevent lumps. Whisking with a wire whisk helps to smooth sauces after cooking. The food processor or blender can usually salvage a sauce, even when it has been totally neglected during cooking.

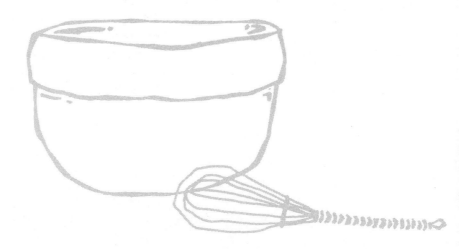

THICKENING AGENTS FOR SAUCES

FLOUR *Makes an opaque sauce and is used in more robust sauces that need not be translucent. Do not use bread flour because the higher gluten content will produce a stringy sauce. All-purpose flour is called for in all our sauce recipes.*

CORNSTARCH *Makes a smooth, shiny, translucent sauce and is used in Oriental cooking and in fruit sauces. Always dissolve cornstarch in a small amount of cold liquid, or mix it with sugar, before adding to hot liquid. Boil the sauce for less than 3 min-utes after cornstarch is added; otherwise, the sauce will thin out.*

ARROWROOT *Makes a clear, shiny sauce and is used primarily in dessert sauces. Like cornstarch, arrow-root should be mixed with cold liquid before it is added to hot liquid. To pre-vent the sauce from thinning, do not boil it once the arrowroot is added.*

POTATO FLOUR *Makes a clear sauce and can be substituted as a thickener for flour or cornstarch, espe-cially for people with allergies.*

THICKENING POWER FOR 1 CUP OF LIQUID

SAUCE	FLOUR	CORNSTARCH	ARROWROOT	POTATO
Thin	1 tablespoon	1½ teaspoons	1 rounded teaspoon	1½ teaspoons
Medium	2 tablespoons	1 tablespoon	2 rounded teaspoons	1 tablespoon
Thick	3 tablespoons	1½ tablespoons	1 rounded tablespoon	1½ tablespoons

BASIC BROWN SAUCE

MAKES
1½ CUPS

•

This sauce can transform leftover meat into an elegant entrée.

1 cup dry red wine
1 (10½-ounce) can beef broth
3 tablespoons unsalted butter
1 medium onion, finely chopped
½ teaspoon dried thyme

½ bay leaf
1 tablespoon parsley, chopped
3 tablespoons all-purpose flour
Salt
Freshly ground black pepper

Pour wine and beef broth into conventional 2-quart saucepan, place on rangetop over high heat, and bring to a rapid boil. Boil mixture, uncovered, until reduced by one-third.

Meanwhile, place butter in 1-quart microwavable dish and microwave on HIGH 3 minutes, or until butter begins to brown. Add onion, thyme, bay leaf, and parsley, cover with plastic wrap, and microwave on HIGH 4 minutes, or until onion is tender. Stir in flour and microwave, uncovered, on HIGH 1 to 1½ minutes, or until flour is cooked.

Stir hot reduced broth into flour mixture and microwave on HIGH 2 to 3 minutes, or until sauce is thickened. Remove bay leaf, strain mixture if smooth sauce is desired, and season with salt and pepper to taste. Strained sauce will keep, tightly covered, in refrigerator up to 3 weeks.

BASIC WHITE SAUCE (BÉCHAMEL)

MAKES
1 CUP

•

This recipe is for a medium sauce. For a thin sauce, use 1 tablespoon flour, and for a thick sauce, use 3 tablespoons flour.

2 tablespoons salted or unsalted
    butter
2 tablespoons all-purpose flour

1 cup milk
Salt

Place butter and flour in 1-quart measure and microwave on HIGH 45 to 60 seconds. Stir until smooth, then gradually add milk, stirring to blend. Microwave on HIGH 2½ to 3½ minutes, or until thickened, stirring several times. Add salt to taste and whisk until smooth.

CHEESE SAUCE
Add ½ to 1 cup grated Cheddar cheese, ¼ teaspoon dry mustard, and

⅛ teaspoon freshly ground white pepper to finished sauce. Stir until cheese is melted.

DILL SAUCE

Stir 2 teaspoons snipped fresh dill or ½ teaspoon dried dill and 1 tablespoon fresh lemon juice into finished sauce.

MORNAY SAUCE

Add ⅓ cup freshly grated Parmesan cheese or ½ cup grated Swiss cheese to finished sauce. Stir until cheese is melted.

MUSHROOM CREAM SAUCE

Add 1 cup steamed sliced mushrooms (see Braised Mushrooms, page 262), ½ teaspoon Worchestershire sauce, and ⅛ teaspoon freshly ground white pepper to finished sauce. Stir to blend.

Many fruit and vegetable sauces freeze well. Keep them on hand and defrost them in the microwave for immediate use. However, starch- and egg-thickened sauces separate when frozen.

INSTANT WHITE SAUCE MIX

2 sticks (1 cup) salted or unsalted
   butter
1 cup all-purpose flour

2 teaspoons salt
½ teaspoon freshly ground white
   pepper

ENOUGH TO MAKE 8 CUPS WHITE SAUCE

Very convenient to have on hand.

In 1-quart measure, soften butter on 50% power 30 to 60 seconds. Add flour, salt, and pepper, blend well, and form into 8 balls, about 3 tablespoons each. Freeze on a tray, then store in plastic bags.

To make white sauce, combine 1 cup milk and 1 frozen ball of sauce mix in 2-cup measure. Cook on HIGH 2 to 4 minutes, or until thick, stirring several times.

Velouté Sauce

**MAKES
1½ CUPS**

•

Velouté is a white sauce made with chicken stock rather than milk. Use with poultry, fish, and vegetable dishes.

¹⁄₃ cup unsalted butter
¹⁄₃ cup all-purpose flour
2 cups Chicken Stock (page 47), canned chicken broth, or Fish Stock (page 48)

Salt
Freshly ground white pepper

Place butter and flour in 1-quart measure and microwave on HIGH 1 to 1½ minutes, or until butter melts. Stir until mixture is smooth. Gradually whisk in stock, stirring to blend. Microwave on HIGH 5 to 6 minutes, or until sauce is thickened. Add salt and pepper to taste.

Cucumber-Lemon Sauce

**MAKES
1¾ CUPS**

•

Serve with veal, fish, or chicken.

2 medium cucumbers, peeled, seeded, and diced (about 2 cups)
1 cup water
½ teaspoon salt
3 tablespoons unsalted butter
3 tablespoons all-purpose flour

½ cup Chicken Stock (page 47) or canned chicken broth
1 teaspoon grated lemon zest
2 tablespoons fresh lemon juice
½ cup sour cream
Salt
Freshly ground white pepper

Place cucumbers, water, and salt in 1-quart bowl, and microwave, covered, on HIGH 5 minutes. Drain, then cover and microwave on HIGH 3 minutes longer. Reserve.

Place butter in 1-quart measure and microwave on HIGH 1 minute, or until melted. Stir in flour, then whisk in stock. Add cucumbers and microwave on HIGH 6 to 10 minutes, or until thickened. Whisk in lemon zest, lemon juice, and sour cream. Add salt and pepper to taste. Sauce can be made in advance and reheated on 50% power 3 to 4 minutes.

HORSERADISH AND ALMOND SAUCE

3 tablespoons unsalted butter
5 tablespoons all-purpose flour
1½ cups Chicken Stock (page 47)
   or canned chicken broth

2 to 3 teaspoons prepared white
   horseradish
½ teaspoon salt
½ teaspoon almond extract
3 tablespoons sour cream

MAKES
1½ CUPS

•

Great with roast beef.
Serve warm or at room
temperature.

Place butter in 1-quart measure and microwave on HIGH 1 minute, or until melted. Blend in flour, then add stock, whisking until smooth. Stir in horseradish, salt, and almond extract. Microwave on HIGH 5 to 7 minutes, or until thickened. Whisk in sour cream.

PARMESAN CHEESE SAUCE

1 tablespoon unsalted butter
1 tablespoon all-purpose flour
¼ teaspoon freshly ground white
   pepper
¼ teaspoon dry mustard

¼ teaspoon paprika
1 cup milk
⅓ cup freshly grated Parmesan
   cheese

MAKES
1 CUP

•

Wonderful served over
steamed vegetables.
For a mock Pasta Carbonara, stir crisp,
crumbled bacon into
the sauce and serve
over fettucini.

Place butter in 2-cup measure and microwave on HIGH 1 minute to melt. Stir in flour, pepper, mustard, and paprika, then whisk in milk. Microwave on 70% power 3 to 4 minutes, or until thickened. Stir in cheese. Serve hot.

ROUX

MAKES
⅓ CUP

■

Roux is an essential thickener for Cajun gumbos, stews, and bisques, and is used in many other sauces as well. It is made of equal parts of fat and flour that are browned to develop a deep, rich, distinctive flavor.

French roux (below) is made with butter instead of oil. It too can be kept almost indefinitely in the refrigerator. French roux takes less time to cook in the microwave than the version made with oil because butter browns faster.

¼ cup vegetable oil   *¼ cup all-purpose flour*

Pour oil into a casserole and microwave on HIGH 2 minutes. Stir in flour and microwave, uncovered, on HIGH 4 to 8 minutes, or until mixture is as brown as you want it to be, stirring several times. If black specks appear in mixture during cooking, the roux has burned and should be discarded. Simply start over and watch more carefully. You can reduce the power level to 50% and cook the roux longer, if you prefer.

If the recipe calls for light brown roux, it should be the color of peanut butter. Generally, a light roux is used with beef and pork to give the sauce a nutty, toasted flavor. Dark brown roux is a much deeper color and is used as rich flavoring for chicken, rabbit, veal, and *etouffée*, a form of Cajun stew.

In terms of thickening power, the browner the flour (and the roux), the less thickening power it has. The following chart will give you an idea of how much of each kind of roux to use to thicken 1 cup of liquid.

ROUX	THIN SAUCE	MEDIUM SAUCE	THICK SAUCE
White	1 tablespoon	2 tablespoons	3 tablespoons
Medium brown	1½ tablespoons	3 tablespoons	4 tablespoons
Dark	2 tablespoons	4 tablespoons	6 tablespoons

Cooked roux can be kept indefinitely, refrigerated in a covered container, ready for use in sauces and soups. The roux will separate during storage, but it can be reemulsified simply by stirring.

FRENCH ROUX

MAKES
¾ CUP

■

1 stick (½ cup) unsalted butter   *½ cup all-purpose flour*

Place butter in 1-quart casserole and microwave on HIGH 4 minutes. Stir in flour and microwave on HIGH 3 minutes to achieve a medium-brown roux.

CLARIFIED BUTTER

2 sticks (1 cup) unsalted or salted butter

Place butter in 2-cup measure. Microwave on 30% power 4 to 5 minutes, without stirring, or until butter is melted. Do not let butter boil.

Let butter cool to room temperature, then carefully skim off clear layer on top or pour it into a bowl. Discard sediment at bottom of measure or, if you used salted butter, serve it over vegetables.

Clarified butter can be stored, tightly covered, for up to 1 month in refrigerator.

■

Use clarified butter in recipes where butter must be heated to a high temperature without browning or burning. It is especially good to use to sauté delicately flavored food and for making sauces.

TIGER BUTTER

1 pound (4 sticks) unsalted butter
1 teaspoon Worcestershire sauce
2 teaspoons fresh lemon juice
1 tablespoon chopped parsley
1 tablespoon snipped fresh chives
1 teaspoon snipped fresh dill or ¼ teaspoon dried

1 clove garlic, minced
1 teaspoon seasoned salt
¼ teaspoon freshly ground black pepper
1 teaspoon paprika

■

This herbed butter perks up the flavor of steaks, corn on the cob, and other vegetables. It's also a good spread for bread. Cut the recipe in half, if you like.

Place butter in 1-quart measure and microwave on 20% power 2 minutes, or until softened. Add Worcestershire, lemon juice, parsley, chives, dill, garlic, salt, pepper, and paprika and whisk to combine ingredients thoroughly. Transfer to storage container, cover tightly, and store in refrigerator, or freeze in ice cube trays, then store in plastic bags.

GARLIC BUTTER

MAKES
½ CUP

1 stick (½ cup) unsalted butter
3 cloves garlic, minced

Salt
Freshly ground black pepper

Place butter in 2-cup measure and microwave on HIGH 45 seconds, or until softened. Stir in garlic and salt and pepper to taste. Store, tightly wrapped, in refrigerator.

BROWNED BUTTER

MAKES
1 CUP

2 sticks (1 cup) unsalted butter
1 tablespoon chopped fresh herbs
    (dill, basil, parsley, chives, or
    tarragon)

1 tablespoon fresh lemon juice
    (optional)

Place butter in 2-cup measure and microwave on HIGH 4 to 6 minutes, or until golden brown, stirring once or twice. Skim foam. Add herbs and, if desired, lemon juice. Serve with fish, poultry, or vegetables.

HERB BUTTER

MAKES
1 CUP

Serve with homemade bread or fresh vegetables.

2 sticks (1 cup) salted or unsalted
    butter (no substitute)
1 tablespoon finely chopped onion
1 tablespoon chopped parsley

1 clove garlic, minced
1 teaspoon snipped fresh chives
¼ teaspoon freshly ground white
    pepper

In 2-cup measure, soften butter on 30% power 30 to 40 seconds. Add onion, parsley, garlic, chives, and white pepper and stir until well blended. Store in tightly covered container in refrigerator up to 1 week.

HOLLANDAISE SAUCES

Hollandaise, a smooth, rich, yellow sauce, is an essential element of Eggs Benedict and a sublime topping for vegetables.

Basic Hollandaise is a mixture of egg yolks and lemon juice to which hot melted butter is added. The eggs absorb and hold the fat in a thick emulsion.

Obviously, because of its high caloric and cholesterol content, Hollandaise often is replaced by a simple mixture of melted butter and lemon juice. But for those occasions when a special treat is in order, Hollandaise can fill the bill.

It's easy to cook Hollandaise in the microwave and easier still to reheat the sauce if it has been prepared ahead of time, even after it's been refrigerated for several days or frozen for 1 to 2 weeks.

- **To reheat** ¾ cup of Hollandaise, cover with plastic wrap and microwave at 10 to 30% power for 2 to 3 minutes, or until warm.
- **To defrost** 2 or 3 tablespoons of frozen Hollandaise, cover and microwave on 20% power 1 minute, checking after 30 seconds.

Even the best cooks have occasional lapses. If the hollandaise is:

- **Too thick:** Beat in a little warm water.
- **Too thin:** Place 1 tablespoon sauce in another bowl, add 1 egg yolk, and whisk until the mixture is thickened. Slowly whisk in the remaining sauce. Microwave on 50% power 1 minute, whisking the sauce after 30 seconds.
- **Curdled:** Add 1 tablespoon of cold water and beat with a wire whisk. If the reemulsified sauce is not completely smooth, some of the irregular texture can be masked by the addition of chopped herbs.

HOLLANDAISE SAUCE

MAKES
¾ CUP

■

1 stick (½ cup) unsalted butter
1 tablespoon water
1 tablespoon fresh lemon juice
2 egg yolks

Salt
Freshly ground white pepper
Hot pepper sauce (optional)

Place butter in 1-cup measure and microwave on HIGH 1 to 2 minutes, or until melted and bubbly. Stir in water and lemon juice.

Place egg yolks in 2-cup measure. Using small whisk, beat yolks, then gradually add hot butter mixture, beating constantly. Microwave on 50% power 45 to 60 seconds, or until sauce is thickened, whisking briskly 2 or 3 times during cooking. Add salt and pepper to taste. For a livelier flavor, stir in 2 or 3 drops hot pepper sauce.

THICK HOLLANDAISE
Increase number of egg yolks to 3 or 4.

For a quick, delicious sauce, combine half sour cream or yogurt and half mayonnaise with any of the following: crisp bacon, blue cheese, grated cheese, capers, fresh herbs, mustard, minced garlic, fresh lemon juice or grated zest, pimiento, chives, chutney, horseradish, peeled, seeded, and chopped tomatoes and cucumbers or other pureed or chopped fresh or cooked vegetables.

STABILIZED HOLLANDAISE
If you plan to keep sauce on the table for a while, or to refrigerate and reheat it, Hollandaise Sauce can be stabilized in one of two ways:
1. Stir 1 teaspoon of cornstarch into lemon juice before adding it to melted butter.
2. Beat 1 to 2 tablespoons Basic White Sauce (page 76) into finished Hollandaise.

HORSERADISH HOLLANDAISE
Add 1 teaspoon white horseradish to finished sauce. Good served with beef.

MALTAISE SAUCE
Instead of water, use 3 tablespoons fresh orange juice. Reduce lemon juice to 2 teaspoons. Stir 2 to 3 teaspoons finely grated orange zest into finished sauce. This is the classic sauce for steamed asparagus or broccoli.

MOUSSELINE SAUCE
Fold ¼ to ½ cup whipped cream or 1 stiffly beaten egg white into finished sauce. This more ethereal version of Hollandaise is good served with eggs, fish, asparagus, broccoli, or cauliflower.

MUSTARD HOLLANDAISE

Add 1 tablespoon Dijon mustard to finished sauce. Serve with ham, fish, chicken, or egg dishes.

BÉARNAISE SAUCE

2 tablespoons white wine vinegar
2 tablespoons dry white vermouth
2 tablespoons minced shallots
1 tablespoon finely chopped fresh
    tarragon, or 1 teaspoon dried

1 stick (½ cup) unsalted butter,
    cut into chunks
3 egg yolks
Salt
Freshly ground white pepper

MAKES

¾ CUP

■

While Hollandaise is flavored simply with lemon juice, Béarnaise has a spicier, more robust flavor. Serve it with eggs, fish, grilled filet mignon, and vegetables.

Combine vinegar, vermouth, shallots, and tarragon in small bowl. Microwave on HIGH 1 to 2 minutes, or until mixture is reduced to 3 tablespoons. Add butter and microwave on HIGH 1 to 2 minutes longer, or until butter is melted and mixture is hot and bubbly.

In 2-cup measure, beat egg yolks with small whisk, then slowly whisk in butter mixture. Microwave on 50% power 1 to 1½ minutes, or until thickened, whisking briskly every 30 seconds. Add salt and pepper to taste.

BROCCOLI PESTO

3½ cups broccoli flowerets
⅓ cup fresh basil leaves
3 tablespoons pine nuts
1 teaspoon minced garlic

¼ teaspoon salt
½ cup extra-virgin olive oil
½ cup freshly grated Parmesan
    cheese

MAKES

1 CUP

■

Delicious served with hot vermicelli.

Wash broccoli and place in 1-quart casserole, cover with plastic wrap, and microwave on HIGH 3 to 4 minutes, or until tender. Place broccoli, basil, pine nuts, garlic, salt, and oil in food processor or blender. Process until mixture is smooth. Add Parmesan cheese and process several seconds.

BARBECUE SAUCE

**MAKES
3½ CUPS**

Wonderful on shrimp, pork, or chicken. Fresh ginger is the secret zinger in this tasty sauce.

1 cup cider vinegar
1 cup catsup
½ cup vegetable oil
⅓ cup Worcestershire sauce
¾ cup, packed, brown sugar
1 tablespoon grated fresh ginger

1 teaspoon minced garlic
2 tablespoons dry mustard
Juice of 1 lemon
2 tablespoons liquid smoke
Salt
Freshly ground black pepper

In 1½- to 2-quart bowl, combine vinegar, catsup, oil, Worcestershire, sugar, ginger, garlic, mustard, lemon juice, liquid smoke, and salt and pepper to taste. Stir to mix well. Microwave on HIGH 5 to 7 minutes, or until boiling. Stir, then microwave on 30% power 5 to 8 minutes, or until flavors are blended. Store, tightly covered, in refrigerator for up to 1 month.

MUSTARD BARBECUE SAUCE

**MAKES
1¼ CUPS**

1 stick (½ cup) unsalted butter,
    cut into chunks
¼ cup cider vinegar
⅓ cup water
3 tablespoons sugar
¼ cup mustard

2 teaspoons freshly ground black
    pepper
1 tablespoon Worcestershire sauce
½ teaspoon cayenne pepper
    (optional)

In 2-cup measure, combine butter, vinegar, water, sugar, mustard, black pepper, Worcestershire, and, if desired, cayenne. Microwave on HIGH 1 to 2 minutes. Stir to blend.

Serve at room temperature with barbecued pork or chicken or use as a basting sauce during grilling.

DIJON MUSTARD GLAZE

½ cup Dijon mustard
2 teaspoons dry mustard
½ cup, packed, light brown sugar

3 tablespoons red wine vinegar
¼ cup salad oil

MAKES
1½ CUPS

▪

Use as a glaze for ham or corned beef.

In 2-cup bowl or measure, combine Dijon and dry mustards, sugar, vinegar, and oil and beat well. Microwave on HIGH 1 minute. Spread on cooked ham or corned beef and microwave at 50% power 5 to 10 minutes, or bake in preheated conventional oven at 350° F. 15 to 20 minutes.

DRIED FRUIT SAUCE

1 cup dried pitted fruit (apricots, peaches, pears, or prunes)

Water
Fruit juice, rum, or other spirits

MAKES
ABOUT
1 CUP

▪

Use as a glaze for roast fresh pork or ham.

▪ ▪ ▪ ▪ ▪ ▪ ▪ ▪ ▪ ▪ ▪

Unsweetened fruit purée, made by processing very ripe soft fruit in a food processor or blender, is good served over ice cream, puddings, chicken, or ham.

▪ ▪ ▪ ▪ ▪ ▪ ▪ ▪ ▪ ▪ ▪

OPTIONAL FLAVORINGS (USE ONE OR SEVERAL)
1 cinnamon stick
½ vanilla bean
2 or 3 slices lemon or orange, with rind

1 (½-inch) piece fresh peeled ginger, sliced
Sprig of fresh mint

Place fruit in 2-cup measure, add cold water to cover and any optional flavorings desired. Cover with plastic wrap and microwave on HIGH 5 minutes, or until fruit is tender. Let mixture stand 3 to 4 minutes.

Remove cinnamon stick, vanilla bean, lemon or orange slices, fresh ginger, or mint and transfer mixture to blender or food processor fitted with steel blade. Puree fruit, adding more water, fruit juice, or rum to thin sauce to consistency desired.

GREEK LEMON SAUCE

**MAKES
1 CUP**

Serve over pilaf, fish, stuffed artichokes, chicken, or Greek *dolmades* (stuffed grape leaves).

1½ teaspoons cornstarch
¾ cup Chicken Stock (page 47) or
    canned chicken broth
1 egg yolk

3 tablespoons fresh lemon juice
Salt
Freshly ground white pepper

Place cornstarch in 1-cup measure, stir in stock, and mix well. Microwave on HIGH 2 minutes, or until hot. Place egg yolk in 1-quart measure and beat with whisk. Add lemon juice, then stir in broth mixture, whisking constantly. Add salt and pepper to taste and microwave on 70% power 1 to 2 minutes, or until thickened, but do not let boil or egg yolk will curdle. Serve at once.

MAYONNAISE VERTE

**MAKES
1½ CUPS**

A complement for fish, eggs, or a cold meat tray.

½ cup spinach leaves, well
    washed
2 tablespoons chopped scallions
1 (3-ounce) package cream cheese
    (optional)

1 cup mayonnaise (page 116)
½ cup watercress leaves
2 tablespoons chopped parsley
1 teaspoon dried tarragon
1 teaspoon capers, crushed

Place spinach and scallions in 2-cup bowl or measure, cover with plastic wrap, and microwave on HIGH 1 to 1½ minutes, or until wilted. Let stand 1 minute, then drain and cool.

Place cream cheese, if using, in small dish and microwave on HIGH 30 to 45 seconds to soften. In food processor or blender, place spinach mixture, mayonnaise, watercress, parsley, tarragon, capers, and, if desired, softened cream cheese. Process until mixture is smoothly pureed. Store mayonnaise, tightly covered, in refrigerator for up to 1 week.

MUSHROOM SAUCE

¹/₃ cup unsalted butter
¹/₃ cup extra-virgin olive oil
3 cloves garlic, minced
1 pound fresh mushrooms, sliced
¹/₄ teaspoon dried oregano

¹/₄ cup chopped parsley
¹/₃ cup red wine
Salt
Freshly ground black pepper

**MAKES
3 CUPS**

■

A quick light sauce to serve over pasta, poultry, or pork.

Place butter, oil, garlic, and mushrooms in 2-quart measure, and microwave, covered, on HIGH 3 to 5 minutes. Stir in oregano, parsley, and wine. Microwave on HIGH 2 to 3 minutes, or until very hot. Add salt and pepper to taste.

MUSHROOM-TUNA SAUCE FOR PASTA

1 onion, sliced vertically
¹/₂ stick (¹/₄ cup) unsalted butter
1 (10-ounce) can condensed cream of mushroom soup
1 (14-ounce) can evaporated milk
¹/₂ cup freshly grated Parmesan cheese
1 (4-ounce) jar pimientos, drained and chopped
1 cup frozen small early peas (optional)

1 (5-ounce) can whole or sliced mushrooms, drained (optional)
1 to 2 tablespoons dry sherry (optional)
1 tablespoon chopped parsley
3 tablespoons fresh lemon juice
Salt
Freshly ground black pepper
1 (6-ounce) can water- or oil-packed tuna, undrained and flaked

**MAKES
5 TO 6 CUPS**

■

■■■■■■■■■■■
Leftover vegetables and meats may be pureed in a food processor or blender and mixed with milk and seasonings to make a sauce.
■■■■■■■■■■■

Place onion and butter in 2-quart measure, cover, and microwave on HIGH 3 minutes. Stir in mushroom soup, evaporated milk, Parmesan, pimientos—and, if desired, peas, mushrooms, and sherry—parsley, lemon juice, and salt and pepper to taste. Gently stir in tuna and its juices, cover, and microwave on HIGH 5 to 8 minutes, or until very hot. Serve over hot fettucine.

SALSA

**MAKES
3 CUPS**

Serve with tortilla chips or as a sauce, heated or at room temperature, with fish, steak, chicken, hamburgers, or hot dogs.

1 large mild onion, chopped
1 red or green bell pepper, chopped
1 clove garlic, minced
1 tablespoon red wine vinegar
1 tablespoon extra-virgin olive oil
1 teaspoon salt
1 (28-ounce) can tomatoes,
    drained and chopped

1 (4-ounce) can green chilies,
    drained and chopped
1/4 cup minced fresh coriander
    (cilantro)
1 teaspoon fresh lime juice
Pinch of ground cloves

Place onion, bell pepper, and garlic in 2-quart measure and microwave on HIGH 3 minutes. Add vinegar, oil, salt, tomatoes, chilies, coriander, lime juice, and cloves. Cover and chill.

TOMATO-BASIL SAUCE

**MAKES
4½ CUPS**

A classic light tomato sauce, especially good made with fresh ingredients. Serve over 1 pound of pasta with freshly grated Parmesan cheese.

3 tablespoons extra-virgin olive oil
1 medium onion, chopped
2 cloves garlic, minced
1 (28-ounce) can tomatoes,
    undrained, chopped, or 1
    pound fresh tomatoes, peeled
    and chopped

3 tablespoons chopped fresh basil,
    or 1 teaspoon dried
1 teaspoon dried oregano
2 teaspoons sugar
Salt
Freshly ground black pepper

Place oil and onion in 2-quart measure and microwave on HIGH 2 to 3 minutes, or until onion is tender-crisp. Add garlic, tomatoes, basil, oregano, sugar, and salt and pepper to taste. Stir to mix well. Cover and microwave on HIGH 10 minutes.

VARIATIONS
Add cooked chicken, ham, or fresh pork just before serving.

VINEGAR MINT SAUCE

¹/₄ cup vinegar
2 tablespoons sugar

2 tablespoons water
¹/₂ cup chopped fresh mint leaves

Combine vinegar, sugar, water, and mint in 1-quart measure. Microwave on HIGH 3 minutes. Let stand 10 to 15 minutes before serving.

Serve with lamb.

TUNA AND TOMATO SAUCE

3 cloves garlic, minced
¹/₂ cup extra-virgin olive oil
1 pound tomatoes, peeled and chopped, or 1 (16-ounce) can tomatoes, undrained, chopped
Salt

Freshly ground black pepper
1 (6¹/₂-ounce) can tuna, drained and flaked
1 tablespoon chopped fresh basil, or 1 teaspoon dried
1 teaspoon dried oregano

**6
FIRST-COURSE
SERVINGS**

In 2-quart casserole, combine garlic, oil, tomatoes, and salt and pepper to taste, bearing in mind that tuna is already salty. Microwave, covered, on HIGH 5 minutes. Stir in tuna, basil, and oregano and microwave, covered, on 50% power 2 minutes, or until tuna is very hot. Do not allow sauce to boil. Serve over hot pasta at once.

This recipe makes enough sauce for 10 ounces of spaghetti, cooked *al dente* according to package instructions. Be sure that the sauce and pasta are ready at the same time because neither improves with sitting around. Italians never serve grated Parmesan with fish sauces, but if you feel that something is missing, and it's cheese, by all means serve a bowl of it on the side.

Salads

In ancient Greece, salad was considered food for the gods, and in Shakespearean times it was regarded as a source of youth. Today we have an equally high esteem for salad, which, in its many guises, brings fresh textures and good nutrition to our diets.

In the making of salads, the microwave is most useful for cooking potatoes and steaming other fresh vegetables until they are just tender-crisp but still beautifully colored; defrosting frozen fruit and vegetables; softening cream cheese; toasting nuts and seeds; and cooking bacon, shrimp, fish, chicken, and meats quickly and easily.

Salad dressings made in the microwave do not stick or scorch and need not be stirred constantly while cooking.

SALAD OILS

The choice of oil for a salad dressing depends on whether a flavorless or flavored oil is required and what considerations are given to cholesterol and saturated fat content.

For salad dressings and other cooking as well, try to use polyunsaturated and mono-unsaturated fats, which can help lower total blood cholesterol. Polyunsaturated fats are found in vegetable oils, such as corn, soy, sunflower, sesame, cottonseed, and safflower oils. They are liquid at room temperature and are contained in most salad oils and dressings. However, read ingredient labels carefully. The word *hydrogenated* on a label means that the liquid (unsaturated) fat has been converted to a saturated one in the manufacturing process.

Monounsaturated fats, such as olive oil, canola oil, and the oil found in avocados and in many nuts, are liquid at room temperature but solidify when chilled. Research indicates that these oils may be helpful in reducing bad (LDL-) cholesterol in the blood.

A bottle of salad oil may be labeled NO CHOLESTEROL, meaning that it contains no saturated *animal* fat. But, if it contains saturated *vegetable* fats, such as coconut or palm oil, it is just as unhealthful, because all saturated fats tend to raise blood cholesterol. Saturated fats are easy to recognize since they are solid at room temperature.

A flavorless oil should be used when the distinctive flavors of other ingredients are highlighted. Among the flavorless oils, corn and sunflower oils are good choices.

Flavored oils widely used in salads are peanut oil, which has only a faint peanut taste, and, most glorious of all, olive oil. Extra-virgin olive oil, from the first pressing, has the purest flavor. Good olive oil should never taste heavy or strong.

Walnut and hazelnut oils add refinement to salads but taste too strong to be used alone.

VINEGARS AND CITRUS JUICES

Very sour vinegars include white vinegar, which is flavorless and very tart, and apple cider vinegar, which has a mild, fruity flavor.

Wine and fruit vinegars, such as those made with raspberries and blueberries, are more delicately flavored and considerably less acidic than cider or white vinegar. Herbed vinegars, often containing tarragon or basil, add subtle flavor to salad.

Lemon juice is often used in seafood salads and in those originating in the Middle East and Greece. Lime juice, not as tart as lemon, is also used for seafood and in Mexican dishes.

TO UNMOLD GELATIN SALADS

1. Loosen the edge of the gelatin from the top of the mold with the tip of a spatula or a knife.

2. Rub the outside of the mold with a towel that has been dipped in hot water and wrung out, or run very warm tap water over the outside of the mold, taking care not to melt the gelatin.

3. Shake the mold gently to see that the gelatin is not sticking to the sides of the mold.

4. Moisten the surface of the serving plate (so you can slide the salad into place if it is not unmolded in the center of the plate), then invert the plate over the top of the mold and quickly invert the mold over the plate.

ARTICHOKE-RICE SALAD

1 (8-ounce) package chicken-
    flavored rice
2 tablespoons extra-virgin olive oil
¼ cup finely chopped scallions
¼ cup sliced pitted green olives
1 (14-ounce) can artichoke hearts,
    drained and quartered

1 (8-ounce) can water chestnuts,
    drained and sliced
1 tablespoon cider vinegar
½ cup mayonnaise (page 116)
¼ teaspoon curry powder
¼ teaspoon snipped fresh dill

6 TO 8 SERVINGS

■

Use this salad to stuff tomatoes or as an accompaniment to chicken or shrimp.

Cook rice in microwave according to package instructions. Transfer rice to bowl, sprinkle with olive oil, and stir gently. Add scallions, olives, artichoke hearts, water chestnuts, vinegar, mayonnaise, curry powder, and dill and toss gently. Serve chilled.

ASPARAGUS AND EGG MOUSSE

6 SERVINGS

▪

A good choice for brunch—serve it with ham and fruit.

2 envelopes unflavored gelatin
¼ cup cold water
1 (10¾-ounce) can condensed cream of asparagus soup
½ teaspoon salt
2 tablespoons catsup
¼ cup mayonnaise (page 116)

2 cups asparagus, sliced (1-inch pieces)
4 hard-cooked eggs (page 122), coarsely chopped
1 cup heavy cream
Lettuce leaves

Sprinkle gelatin over water in cup or small bowl and let stand 5 minutes. Place soup in 2-quart measure and microwave on HIGH 2 to 3 minutes, or until hot. Add gelatin mixture and stir until gelatin is dissolved. Stir in salt, catsup, and mayonnaise.

Place asparagus in 2-cup measure, cover with plastic wrap, and microwave on HIGH 2 to 4 minutes, or until tender-crisp. Stir asparagus and chopped eggs into soup mixture, cover with plastic wrap, and chill until cool but not set.

Whip cream and fold into gelatin mixture. Transfer mousse to lightly oiled 1½-quart mold, cover with plastic wrap, and chill until set. Unmold mousse onto bed of lettuce.

BROCCOLI MOLD

5 OR 6 SERVINGS

▪

1 (10¾-ounce) can beef consommé
1 envelope unflavored gelatin
2 tablespoons fresh lemon juice
1 tablespoon vinegar
⅔ cup mayonnaise (page 116)
3 hard-cooked eggs (page 122), chopped or sliced
1 (10-ounce) package frozen chopped broccoli, defrosted and blanched according to package instructions

Garlic salt
Dash of Worcestershire sauce
Dash of hot pepper sauce
Lettuce leaves
¾ cup Curry Mayonnaise (page 116; optional)

Pour ¼ cup of the consommé into cup or small bowl. Sprinkle gelatin over consommé and let stand 5 minutes. In 2-quart measure, microwave remaining consommé on HIGH 2 to 3 minutes, or until boiling. Add lemon juice, vinegar, and gelatin mixture, stirring until gelatin is dissolved. Let mixture cool almost to room temperature, then beat in mayonnaise thoroughly. Chill until mixture thickens, but do not allow to set.

Stir in chopped eggs, broccoli, garlic salt to taste, Worcestershire, and hot pepper sauce. Transfer mixture to lightly oiled 1½-quart mold, cover with plastic wrap, and chill until set. Unmold onto bed of lettuce and serve with Curry Mayonnaise, if desired.

■ ■ ■ ■ ■ ■ ■ ■ ■ ■ ■ ■ ■

Torn lettuce edges will not darken as quickly as cut edges. Always tear greens that are being prepared ahead of time.

■ ■ ■ ■ ■ ■ ■ ■ ■ ■ ■

CAESAR SALAD

1 large egg
¼ cup extra-virgin olive oil
1 clove garlic, minced
¼ teaspoon salt
1 tablespoon fresh lemon juice
1 teaspoon dry mustard

1 head romaine lettuce, washed
    and torn in pieces
¼ cup freshly grated Parmesan
    cheese
1 cup croutons
Freshly ground black pepper

8 SERVINGS

■

An adaptation of Alex Caesar Cardini's Romaine Salad. This wonderful creation was presented at his Mexico City restaurant in the 1920s.

Place egg, olive oil, garlic, salt, lemon juice, and dry mustard in 2-cup measure and beat with wire whisk until all ingredients are mixed. Microwave mixture on 70% power 1 to 1½ minutes, whisking every 30 seconds. (Dressing can be prepared 1 or 2 days ahead of time, covered tightly, and refrigerated.)

In salad bowl, toss together romaine, Parmesan, and croutons. Add dressing and toss again. Grind black pepper over salad and gently mix in. Serve at once.

CUCUMBER MOUSSE

8 SERVINGS

2 envelopes unflavored gelatin
¼ cup water
1 (8-ounce) package cream cheese
2 cups pared, grated, and drained
    cucumbers (remove seeds if
    they are large)
⅓ cup finely chopped scallions

2 tablespoons finely chopped
    parsley
1 cup mayonnaise (page 116)
1 tablespoon fresh lemon juice
½ teaspoon salt
Dash of hot pepper sauce
2 or 3 drops green food coloring
    (optional)

Sprinkle gelatin over water in cup or small bowl and let stand 5 minutes. Microwave softened gelatin on 50% power 30 to 45 seconds, or until melted.

Place cream cheese in 2-quart measure and microwave on HIGH 1 minute to soften. Stir gelatin into cheese and mix well. Add cucumbers, scallions, parsley, mayonnaise, lemon juice, salt, hot pepper sauce, and if desired, food coloring.

Transfer mixture to lightly oiled 5-cup mold, cover with plastic wrap, and chill until set. Unmold onto serving plate.

GERMAN COLESLAW

8 SERVINGS

1 cup sugar
1 cup cider vinegar
¾ cup salad oil
1 teaspoon celery salt
1 teaspoon dry mustard
1 large head cabbage, finely
    shredded

1 large onion, thinly sliced
1 green or red bell pepper, thinly
    sliced
Salt
Freshly ground white pepper

In 1-quart bowl, combine sugar, vinegar, oil, celery salt, and mustard and microwave on HIGH 3 to 4 minutes, or until boiling.

While dressing heats, place cabbage, onion, and bell pepper in large mixing bowl. Pour boiling dressing over vegetables and toss to mix well. Add salt and pepper to taste. Cover with plastic wrap and refrigerate for at least 1 day and up to 1 week.

FROZEN SLAW

1 head cabbage, shredded
1 teaspoon salt
1 onion, finely chopped
1 carrot, grated
1 green bell pepper, chopped

1 red bell pepper, chopped
1 cup cider vinegar
1½ cups sugar
1 teaspoon celery seeds
2 teaspoons dry mustard

10 SERVINGS

A zesty sweet-sour flavor! Portions may be defrosted and served as needed.

Put cabbage in 2-quart storage container, sprinkle with salt, and let stand 30 minutes. Drain well, pressing out all liquid. Add onion, carrot, and bell peppers.

In 1-quart measure, combine vinegar, sugar, celery seeds, and dry mustard. Microwave on HIGH 3 to 4 minutes, or until mixture boils. Stir to completely dissolve sugar. Let stand until lukewarm, then pour over cabbage mixture.

Freeze slaw, covered, in one large container or in smaller portions for up to 2 months. To serve, defrost by microwaving at 30% power until defrosted. Serve chilled. Salad may be refrozen several times without loss of flavor.

VARIATION
Drain slaw and stir in mayonnaise or yogurt to bind.

GREEN PEA SALAD

1 hard-cooked egg (page 122), chopped
1 (10-ounce) package frozen green peas, defrosted
1 cup coarsely grated Cheddar cheese

1 cup chopped celery
¼ cup chopped pitted green olives
3 scallions, finely chopped
¼ cup mayonnaise (page 116)
Salt
Freshly ground black pepper

6 TO 8 SERVINGS

In mixing bowl, place chopped egg, peas, cheese, celery, olives, and scallions and mix well. Add mayonnaise and salt and pepper to taste and combine gently. Chill.

Marinated Garden Salad

10 TO 12 SERVINGS

▪

Delicious and perfect for a cookout! Prepare one day ahead.

▪ ▪ ▪ ▪ ▪ ▪ ▪ ▪ ▪ ▪ ▪

Leftover steamed tender-crisp vegetables, such as broccoli, cauliflower, zucchini, asparagus, carrots, or mushrooms, can be marinated for an hour or two in vinaigrette (page 114) and tossed with mixed greens and additional dressing, if needed.

▪ ▪ ▪ ▪ ▪ ▪ ▪ ▪ ▪ ▪ ▪

MARINADE
¾ cup extra-virgin olive oil
⅓ cup wine vinegar
2 tablespoons sugar

2 teaspoons salt
1 teaspoon freshly ground black pepper

SALAD
3 medium carrots, sliced
3 tablespoons water
1 (10-ounce) package frozen green peas, defrosted
2 (15½-ounce) cans green beans, drained

1 mild onion, sliced
1 cup chopped celery
½ cup sliced black olives
⅔ cup mayonnaise (page 116; optional)

To make marinade, combine oil, vinegar, sugar, salt, and pepper in a bowl and whisk together. Reserve.

Place carrots and water in small bowl, cover with plastic wrap, and microwave on HIGH 3 to 4 minutes, or until tender-crisp. Drain carrots and place in 2-quart container.

Add peas to carrots along with green beans, onion, and marinade. Toss to mix well, cover with plastic wrap, and refrigerate overnight.

Drain salad well and stir in celery, black olives, and, if desired, mayonnaise. Serve cold.

A Salad for all Seasons

8 TO 10 SERVINGS

▪

A versatile and delicious marinated salad, handy to keep in the refrigerator for quick suppers, especially when family members eat at different times.

1 pound asparagus
1 (14-ounce) can artichoke hearts, drained and quartered
8 ounces mushrooms, sliced
1 mild onion, thinly sliced

1 (14-ounce) can hearts of palm, drained and sliced (optional)
1 package Italian dressing mix, prepared

Place asparagus in 2-quart casserole, cover, and microwave on HIGH 3 to 3½ minutes to blanch. Drain and return to casserole, add artichoke hearts, mushrooms, onion, hearts of palm, and salad dressing, and toss to mix well. Cover and refrigerate at least several hours and up to 3 days.

Serving options:

1. Arrange marinated vegetables over mixed salad greens and add sliced hard-cooked egg (page 122), sliced cucumber, tomato, olives, and any other garnish that seems appropriate. Add more dressing, if desired.

2. Toss marinated vegetables with cooked pasta or rice and drizzle with additional dressing, if desired. For a one-dish meal, add chunks of cooked chicken or strips of ham.

MARINATED VEGETABLE SALAD

¹/₂ medium head cauliflower, cut into flowerets
¹/₂ bunch broccoli, cut into flowerets
4 large carrots, cut into thick julienne strips
³/₄ cup water
2 zucchini, sliced
1 pint cherry tomatoes, halved
4 large stalks celery, sliced diagonally
1 (8-ounce) jar pickled baby corn, drained

1 cup extra-virgin olive oil
¹/₂ cup white wine vinegar
1 teaspoon sugar
1 teaspoon dried thyme
1 teaspoon dried marjoram
1 teaspoon dried basil
2 teaspoons salt
1 teaspoon freshly ground black pepper
1 small clove garlic
1 bay leaf

12 TO 15 SERVINGS

•

A very colorful salad for the buffet table.

Place cauliflower, broccoli, and carrots in 2-quart measure with ¼ cup of the water. Cover and microwave on HIGH 5 to 7 minutes to soften vegetables slightly. Drain and add zucchini, tomatoes, celery, and corn.

In small bowl, whisk together olive oil, vinegar, remaining water, sugar, thyme, marjoram, basil, salt, pepper, garlic, and bay leaf. Pour over salad.

Cover with plastic wrap and refrigerate several hours, tossing occasionally. Before serving, drain vegetables, reserving dressing to serve over mixed salad greens, if desired. Discard garlic and bay leaf.

MEXICAN CHEF'S SALAD

6 TO 8
SERVINGS

•

A beautifully composed salad.

1 (4-ounce) can green chilies, undrained

1/3 cup chopped fresh coriander (cilantro)

2 cloves garlic, minced

1 tablespoon chili powder

1/2 teaspoon ground cumin

2/3 cup extra-virgin olive oil

1/4 cup fresh lime juice

4 chicken breasts, cooked (page 169), boned, and cut into strips

1 (16-ounce) can kidney beans, drained

1 head iceberg or other lettuce

3 tomatoes, cut into wedges

1 cucumber, peeled and sliced

10 to 15 pitted black olives

1 mild onion, sliced

1 green or red bell pepper, sliced

1 avocado, sliced

2 hard-cooked eggs (cooked conventionally), peeled and quartered

1 1/2 cups grated Monterey Jack or Cheddar cheese

1/3 cup milk

1 to 1 1/2 cups sour cream mixed with 1/4 cup snipped fresh chives, or Blue Cheese Vinaigrette (page 114)

To separate the leaves from a head of iceberg lettuce, cut out the stem. Hold the head, cut side up, under a stream of running water, gently pulling the leaves apart to allow the water to flow between them and forcing them farther apart. Carefully pull the leaves off the head and drain them well.

In mixing bowl combine chilies, coriander, garlic, chili powder, cumin, olive oil, and lime juice. Add chicken and kidney beans, toss to mix, and cover with plastic wrap. Let marinate several hours or overnight.

On individual serving plates or large serving platter, arrange lettuce, tomatoes, cucumber, olives, onion, bell pepper, avocado, eggs, and chicken mixture, including marinade.

Just before serving, place cheese and milk in small bowl and microwave on 50% power 1 to 3 minutes, or until cheese is melted. Stir until smooth and creamy and immediately drizzle over salad. Pass the sour-cream-and-chive mixture or Blue Cheese Vinaigrette separately. Serve with tortilla chips.

SALADE NIÇOISE

2 pounds small new potatoes
½ cup water
1 pound green beans, trimmed
1 (14-ounce) can artichoke hearts,
    drained
1 large mild onion, sliced
1 recipe Garlic Dressing (page
    115)
1 pound small cherry tomatoes
1 cup oil-cured black olives

6 hard-cooked eggs (page 122),
    sliced
1 green bell pepper, sliced
1 red bell pepper, sliced
1 (2-ounce) can rolled anchovies,
    drained (optional)
2 (6-ounce) cans tuna, drained
    and chunked
1 tablespoon capers
Mixed salad greens

**8 TO 10
SERVINGS**

■

This is a delightful one-dish meal for a hot day.

Scrub potatoes. Cut smaller ones in half and larger ones into quarters. Arrange in 2-quart casserole, add ¼ cup water, and cover. Microwave on HIGH 8 to 12 minutes, or until tender. Drain, transfer to large mixing bowl, and keep warm.

Place green beans and remaining ¼ cup water in 2-quart casserole, cover, and microwave on HIGH 5 to 10 minutes, or until tender-crisp. Drain and transfer to mixing bowl with potatoes. Add artichoke hearts, onion, and 1 cup dressing. Toss gently to coat vegetables, cover with plastic wrap, and chill mixture for 2 to 3 hours, or up to 2 days.

To serve, line platter or large shallow bowl with salad greens. Drain marinated vegetables, reserving dressing, and place vegetables in center of platter. Arrange onion, tomatoes, olives, eggs, bell peppers, anchovies if desired, tuna, and capers around and over vegetables. Drizzle reserved dressing over salad and pass remaining dressing in sauceboat. Serve wtih crusty French or Italian bread.

▪ ▪ ▪ ▪ ▪ ▪ ▪ ▪ ▪ ▪ ▪

Radicchio or red Italian chicory grows in small, compact heads of deep red leaves with white veins. Rosa di Treviso comes in longer, looser heads. Both varieties enhance a mixed salad and look beautiful as a bed for other salads.

▪ ▪ ▪ ▪ ▪ ▪ ▪ ▪ ▪ ▪ ▪

Spinach Salad

4 TO 6

SERVINGS

■

The flowers of many plants are edible and can be used effectively in tossed salads or as garnish. It is equally true, however, that some plants and their flowers are poisonous. The following flowers may be eaten without any ill effects if you know they have not been treated with harmful herbicides or insecticides: apple blossoms, blueberry flowers, borage, calendula petals, chive blossoms, hollyhocks, nasturtiums, rose petals, and zucchini blossoms. If flowers have thick centers, use only the petals.

SALAD

1 bunch spinach (12 ounces)
8 ounces lean bacon, cooked (page 227) and coarsely crumbled
1 (8-ounce) can water chestnuts, drained and cut into slivers

1 red onion, thinly sliced
3 hard-cooked eggs (page 122), grated or sliced (optional)

DRESSING

1/3 cup salad oil
1/3 cup extra-virgin olive oil
2 tablespoons red wine vinegar
2 tablespoons fresh lemon juice
2 teaspoons chopped fresh basil, or 3/4 teaspoon dried
1 tablespoon finely chopped parsley

1 bay leaf
1/4 teaspoon sugar
3/4 teaspoon salt
1/4 teaspoon freshly ground black pepper

Cut off and discard spinach stems, wash leaves well, and dry with paper towels or in salad spinner. Place leaves in salad bowl, cover with plastic wrap, and chill.

In bowl, whisk together salad and olive oils, vinegar, lemon juice, basil, parsley, bay leaf, sugar, salt, and pepper. Let dressing stand at least 30 minutes to blend flavors.

Add crumbled bacon, water chestnuts, and onion to spinach. Pour dressing over salad and toss gently. Sprinkle with grated eggs, if desired, and serve at once.

POTATO SALAD

6 medium red new potatoes,
  cooked (page 248)
6 medium tomatoes, sliced
2 red or green bell peppers, sliced
2 medium mild onions, sliced
2 cucumbers, peeled and sliced
4 hard-cooked eggs (page 122),
  sliced

1/4 cup salad oil or extra-virgin
  olive oil
1/2 cup white wine vinegar
2 or 3 cloves garlic, minced
1 teaspoon paprika
Salt
Freshly ground black pepper

6 TO 8 SERVINGS

Potatoes absorb flavors best while they are still hot, so peel, slice, and dress them immediately after cooking. If the potatoes have cooled before the dressing can be added, put them into a bowl, cover, and microwave on HIGH until hot.

While potatoes are still warm, peel and slice them.
   In wide shallow serving bowl, alternate layers of potatoes, tomatoes, bell peppers, onions, cucumbers, and sliced eggs. In small bowl, whisk together oil, vinegar, garlic, paprika, and salt and pepper to taste. Pour dressing over vegetables, cover bowl with plastic wrap, and chill.

POTATO SALAD WITH SOUR CREAM

6 medium all-purpose potatoes,
  cooked (page 248)
1 cup mayonnaise (page 116)
3/4 cup sour cream
1 teaspoon prepared white
  horseradish
8 scallions, chopped

1/3 cup finely chopped parsley
1 teaspoon salt
1/2 teaspoon freshly ground black
  pepper
1 cucumber, peeled and very
  thinly sliced
3 stalks celery, thinly sliced

6 TO 8 SERVINGS

While potatoes cook, prepare dressing: In bowl, whisk together mayonnaise, sour cream, horseradish, scallions, parsley, salt, and pepper.
   Peel potatoes, if you wish, and slice while still warm. In serving bowl, make alternate layers of warm potatoes, dressing, cucumber, and celery. Cover with plastic wrap and chill.

GERMAN POTATO SALAD

6 TO 8 SERVINGS

•

A perfectly delicious salad.

5 medium all-purpose potatoes (about 2½ pounds), cooked (page 248)
⅓ cup extra-virgin olive oil
⅓ cup salad oil
⅓ cup cider vinegar
1 cup Chicken Stock (page 47) or canned chicken broth

5 or 6 scallions, chopped
2 or 3 small cucumbers, peeled and very thinly sliced (optional)
Salt
Freshly ground black pepper
3 slices bacon, cooked (page 227) and crumbled

Let potatoes stand until just cool enough to handle, then peel and slice them. Keep potatoes warm.

To make dressing, in small bowl, whisk together olive oil, salad oil, vinegar, and stock. Microwave on HIGH 5 to 7 minutes, or just until boiling. Keep dressing very hot.

In serving bowl, make alternate layers of warm potatoes, scallions, and, if desired, cucumbers, drizzling potato layers heavily with dressing and adding salt and pepper to taste. Top with crumbled bacon and serve warm or at room temperature.

SUMMER RICE AND VEGETABLE SALAD

4 TO 6 SERVINGS

•

1 cup long-grain rice, cooked in 2-quart casserole (page 289)
1 cup broccoli flowerets
1 to 2 tablespoons water
⅔ cup mayonnaise (page 116)
1 tablespoon fresh lemon juice
1 teaspoon curry powder
Salt
Freshly ground white pepper

½ cup chopped onion
½ cup chopped green bell pepper
1 cup tomatoes, diced (½-inch pieces)
1 cup thinly sliced mushrooms
1 cup chopped celery
1 cup chopped pitted black olives (optional)

ncover cooked rice and cool slightly.

In 2-cup measure, combine broccoli and water, cover with plastic wrap, and microwave on HIGH 1½ to 2 minutes to blanch just until slightly softened. Drain.

In small bowl, whisk together mayonnaise, lemon juice, curry powder, and salt and pepper to taste. Stir dressing into warm rice, then add broccoli, onion, bell pepper, tomatoes, mushrooms, celery, and, if desired, olives. Toss gently, cover, and chill before serving.

ITALIAN·STYLE RICE SALAD

1 cup long-grain rice, cooked in 2-quart measure (page 289)
⅓ cup extra-virgin olive oil
2 tablespoons red or white wine vinegar
½ teaspoon dry mustard
¼ teaspoon paprika
3 tablespoons chopped fresh basil, or 1 teaspoon dried

½ cup chopped green bell pepper
½ cup chopped celery
½ cup chopped scallions
½ cup sliced pitted black olives
Salt
Freshly ground white pepper
Lettuce or spinach leaves
2 or 3 tomatoes, cut into wedges

6 TO 8 SERVINGS

∙

Especially good on a hot summer day.

∙∙∙∙∙∙∙∙∙∙∙

Romaine, also known as Cos lettuce, was discovered by the ancient Romans on the Greek island of Kos, where it still grows abundantly. The lettuce was so widely used in Rome that travelers identified it by the city's name.

∙∙∙∙∙∙∙∙∙∙∙

hile rice is cooking, in small bowl whisk together oil, vinegar, mustard, paprika, and basil. Stir dressing into hot cooked rice, cover container, and chill.

When rice is cold, gently stir in bell pepper, celery, scallions, olives, and salt and pepper to taste.

On platter or in shallow serving bowl, make a bed of lettuce or spinach leaves and spoon salad in center. Garnish with tomatoes.

SEAFOOD SALAD

10 TO 12 SERVINGS

This salad is terrific for filling lettuce cups, hollowed-out tomatoes, and avocado halves.

1 pound shrimp, steamed (page 155), peeled, and deveined
8 ounces fresh crabmeat, picked over
1 cup chopped or shredded cooked chicken breast (page 169)
2 cups thinly sliced celery
1/2 cup thinly sliced scallions
1/2 cup thinly sliced peeled cucumber

1 to 2 cups cherry tomatoes, halved
2/3 cup sour cream
2/3 cup mayonnaise (page 116)
1 tablespoon fresh lemon juice
1 to 2 teaspoons dried tarragon
1 teaspoon fines herbes (available at specialty foods stores)
1/2 teaspoon salt, or to taste
1/4 teaspoon freshly ground white pepper

Place shrimp in mixing bowl and chill. Add crabmeat, chicken, celery, scallions, cucumber, and tomatoes and toss gently.

In small bowl, whisk together sour cream, mayonnaise, lemon juice, tarragon, *fines herbes*, salt, and pepper. Add dressing to shrimp mixture and toss gently to mix. Cover bowl and chill salad.

TUNA SALAD

6 TO 8 SERVINGS

Serve on a bed of lettuce, in a tomato cup or in a sandwich.

2 hard-cooked eggs (page 122), chopped
2 (6 1/2-ounce) cans tuna, drained and flaked
1/2 cup chopped mild onion
1/2 cup sliced olives
1/2 cup chopped pecans
1 cup chopped celery

1 unpeeled apple, cored and chopped
1/2 cup mayonnaise (page 116)
1/4 teaspoon dried dill
1 tablespoon Worcestershire sauce
1 teaspoon mustard
2 teaspoons capers, crushed
Salt
Freshly ground white pepper

In salad bowl, combine eggs, tuna, onion, olives, pecans, celery, and apple.

In small bowl, combine mayonnaise, dill, Worcestershire, mustard, capers, and salt and pepper to taste and mix well. Add dressing to tuna mixture and toss gently to mix. Chill before serving.

SHRIMP PASTA SALAD

**12 TO 14
SERVINGS**

■

Serve as a main course
or as a side dish—it's
a winner either way!

DRESSING

*1/2 cup chopped fresh basil or
    parsley*
2 teaspoons minced garlic
1 tablespoon salt
*1 teaspoon freshly ground white
    pepper*

*3 tablespoons fresh thyme leaves,
    or 1 1/2 teaspoon dried*
1 cup extra-virgin olive oil
1 cup salad oil
2/3 cup wine vinegar

SALAD

8 ounces pasta
*1 pound shrimp, steamed (page
    155), peeled, and deveined*
*1 (8 1/2-ounce) can bamboo shoots,
    drained*
*1 (14-ounce) can artichoke hearts,
    drained and quartered*
*1 (14-ounce) can hearts of palm,
    drained and sliced*

*8 ounces mushrooms, caps only,
    sliced*
*1 cucumber, peeled and thinly
    sliced*
1 stalk celery, thinly sliced
1 pint small cherry tomatoes
1 cup pitted black olives (optional)

To make dressing, in small bowl combine basil, garlic, salt, pepper, thyme, olive oil, salad oil, and vinegar. Reserve.

To make salad, cook pasta on rangetop according to package instructions. Drain pasta, then plunge into bowl of cold water to stop cooking. Drain again and place in large mixing bowl. Add shrimp, bamboo shoots, artichoke hearts, hearts of palm, mushrooms, cucumber, celery, tomatoes, and, if desired, olives.

Add dressing and toss salad. Cover tightly and marinate overnight in refrigerator, where salad will keep for 2 days.

Summer Chicken Salad

2 TO 4
SERVINGS

Light and cool on a hot summer evening.

In an emergency, underripe avocados can be "ripened" or softened to a usable texture by microwaving them on HIGH 45 seconds to 1 minute. Cool before using. Of course, the taste will not be as fully developed as that of a naturally ripened avocado.

SALAD

2 chicken breasts (about 1 pound), cooked (page 169)
Lettuce leaves
1 ounce ham, thinly sliced
1 ounce Swiss or Monterey Jack cheese, cut into strips

1 large navel orange, peeled and sliced
1 medium avocado, sliced
1/4 cup sliced black olives
Melon slices (optional)

DRESSING

1/3 cup mayonnaise (page 116)
1/3 cup sour cream
1 tablespoon vinegar
1 tablespoon fresh lemon juice

1 to 2 tablespoons finely minced onion
1/4 teaspoon dry mustard
1/4 teaspoon garlic salt

When chicken is cool enough to handle, remove skin and bones and cut flesh into strips.

In small bowl, whisk together mayonnaise, sour cream, vinegar, lemon juice, onion, mustard, and garlic salt. Transfer dressing to sauceboat and reserve.

Arrange lettuce leaves on a platter and place chicken on them. Roll up ham slices and arrange over lettuce with cheese, orange, avocado, olives, and, if desired, melon. Serve dressing separately.

Chicken Salad

4 SERVINGS

Great for sandwiches or a salad plate.

2 chicken breast halves (about 1 pound), cooked (page 169)
1/4 cup chopped onion
1 cup chopped celery
1/4 cup sliced pitted green olives (optional)

2/3 to 1 cup mayonnaise (page 116)
2 tablespoons fresh lemon juice
1/2 teaspoon salt
1/4 teaspoon freshly ground white pepper

When chicken is cool enough to handle, remove and discard skin and bones and cut meat into 1/2-inch dice. Place chicken in mixing bowl, add onion, celery, and, if desired, olives, and toss to mix. In a small bowl, whisk together mayonnaise, lemon juice, salt, and pepper. Add dressing to chicken mixture and toss gently until ingredients are well blended. Chill before serving.

HAM SALAD

Substitute 3 cups chopped ham for chicken. Add 2 teaspoons Dijon mustard and 2 to 3 tablespoons snipped fresh dill to dressing.

CLASSIC COBB SALAD

DRESSING

3 tablespoons snipped chives
3 tablespoons chopped fresh basil
    (optional)
1 teaspoon dry mustard
1 tablespoon sugar

1 teaspoon Worcestershire sauce
¾ cup extra-virgin olive oil
¼ cup wine vinegar
¼ cup dry white wine

SALAD

4 chicken breast halves (about 1
    pound), cooked (page 169)
2 ounces Roquefort or blue
    cheese, crumbled
Salad greens
4 hard-cooked eggs (page 122),
    sliced

1 avocado, sliced (coat with fresh
    lemon juice if preparing in
    advance)
2 tomatoes, cut into wedges
½ cup pitted black olives
4 slices bacon, cooked (page 227)
    and crumbled

4 SERVINGS

∎

This is a modern version of the salad created in 1936 by Robert Cobb for his Hollywood restaurant. It's delicious served with a loaf of crusty sourdough bread and a bottle of chilled wine.

To make dressing, in large mixing bowl, whisk together chives, basil, if desired, mustard, sugar, Worcestershire, oil, vinegar, and white wine.

When chicken is cool enough to handle, remove skin and bones and cut flesh into strips. Add chicken to bowl with dressing, stir in Roquefort, and cover. Allow chicken to marinate in refrigerator at least 4 hours and preferably overnight.

Distribute salad greens on individual serving plates. Drain chicken, reserving marinade, and arrange over greens. Garnish salad with eggs, avocado, tomatoes, olives, and bacon. Pass marinade separately as a sauce.

Avocados are "nutrient dense," a great source of vitamin A and potassium. They also contain monounsaturated fats. Half an average avocado has about 200 calories.

HOT TURKEY SALAD

6 TO 8 SERVINGS

1 cup chopped onion
2 cups chopped celery
2 cups chopped cooked turkey
1 (8-ounce) can water chestnuts, drained and chopped or sliced
1 cup sliced mushrooms
1 cup green peas
1 cup mayonnaise (page 116)
2 tablespoons fresh lemon juice
½ teaspoon salt

¼ teaspoon freshly ground black pepper
¼ teaspoon poultry seasoning
½ cup slivered almonds, toasted (page 441)
1 cup crushed Ritz crackers
½ cup grated Cheddar or Swiss cheese
¼ teaspoon paprika

In 2-quart measure or bowl, place onion and celery, cover with plastic wrap, and microwave on HIGH 4 minutes. Add turkey, water chestnuts, mushrooms, peas, mayonnaise, lemon juice, salt, pepper, and poultry seasoning and mix well. Spread mixture in 2-quart casserole, cover with plastic wrap, and microwave on HIGH 5 minutes.

Sprinkle almonds, crushed crackers, and cheese over top and dust with paprika. Microwave, uncovered, on 70% power 8 to 12 minutes, or until hot and bubbly. Serve at once.

BEEF TACO SALAD

6 TO 8 SERVINGS

Another great one-dish meal!

1 pound lean ground beef
1 large onion, cut into strips
1 clove garlic, minced
1 green bell pepper, chopped
1 teaspoon chili powder
1 (4-ounce) can green chilies, drained
1 cup sour cream
1 head iceberg lettuce, shredded

3 tomatoes, chopped
2 scallions, chopped
1 cup sliced mushrooms (optional)
1 cup pitted black olives (optional)
1 (8-ounce) package corn chips
1 cup grated Cheddar cheese
Bottled taco sauce

Place beef, onion, garlic, and bell pepper in 2-quart measure and stir to mix. Cover with plastic wrap and microwave on

HIGH 5 to 6 minutes, or until meat is cooked. Drain mixture and stir in chili powder, chilies, and sour cream. Cover with plastic wrap and reserve.

In salad bowl, place lettuce, tomatoes, scallions, and, if desired, mushroom and olives, and toss gently to mix. If preparing ahead, cover with plastic wrap and store in refrigerator for up to 4 hours.

To serve, reheat meat mixture: Microwave on 70% power 2 to 3 minutes, just until mixture is warm. Spread meat over greens and tomatoes and sprinkle with corn chips and cheese. Serve with separate bowl of taco sauce.

CHICKEN TACO SALAD

Omit beef. Microwave onion, garlic, and bell pepper, covered, on HIGH 3 to 4 minutes, or until tender-crisp. Stir in 2 cups cooked chopped chicken with sour cream mixture and proceed with recipe.

CRANBERRY SALAD MOLD

1 cup ground raw cranberries or
   1 (16-ounce) can whole
   cranberry sauce
1 cup chopped unpeeled apples
1 cup sugar
1 cup hot water
1 (3-ounce) package lemon-
   flavored gelatin

1 cup pineapple juice or syrup
   from crushed pineapple
1/2 cup seedless or Tokay grapes,
   halved and seeded
1/4 cup broken walnuts or pecans
1 (8-ounce) can crushed pineapple
Lettuce leaves

6 SERVINGS

A Thanksgiving holiday special.

To prevent cut fruit, such as peaches, pears, apples, and bananas, from turning brown, coat the cut edge with lemon juice or another source of ascorbic acid.

In mixing bowl, combine cranberries, apples, and sugar and let stand. In 2-quart measure, microwave water on HIGH 2 to 3 minutes, then add gelatin and stir until dissolved. Add pineapple juice and chill until partially set.

Stir in cranberry mixture, grapes, nuts, and pineapple. Chill until set. Unmold on crisp lettuce.

VINAIGRETTE

MAKES
ABOUT
1 CUP

■

This is the basic dress-
ing for greens or mari-
nated vegetables.

3 tablespoons wine vinegar
¼ teaspoon dry mustard
¼ teaspoon salt
¾ cup extra-virgin olive oil
¼ teaspoon dried herbs or
    2 tablespoons minced fresh
    herbs (chives, tarragon, basil,
    or thyme)

½ teaspoon coarsely ground black
    pepper

▪ ▪ ▪ ▪ ▪ ▪ ▪ ▪ ▪ ▪ ▪
Allow about ½ cup
vinaigrette-type dress-
ing or ¾ cup creamy
dressing for every 2
quarts of salad
greens.
▪ ▪ ▪ ▪ ▪ ▪ ▪ ▪ ▪ ▪ ▪

In blender or food processor, combine vinegar, mustard, and salt. With motor running, slowly add oil in a steady stream. Pour into storage container and add herbs and pepper.

BLUE CHEESE VINAIGRETTE
Add 1 teaspoon snipped fresh chives and 1 clove garlic, minced, to vinegar mixture before blending. Add oil (you can substitute salad oil for olive oil) as directed. Transfer to storage container. Omit herbs and stir in 2 tablespoons crumbled blue cheese, or to taste, and 2 tablespoons heavy cream, if a richer dressing is desired.

DIJON MUSTARD DRESSING

MAKES
1¼ CUPS

■

This subtly piquant
dressing is delicious
with mixed salad
greens or with this
favorite combination:
hearts of palm, toma-
toes, and sweet Vidalia
onions over a bed of
lettuce.

1½ teaspoons salt
1½ teaspoons sugar
1 teaspoon coarsely ground black
    pepper
¼ teaspoon dried tarragon
1 tablespoon chopped parsley

1 tablespoon Dijon mustard
1 clove garlic, crushed
½ cup extra-virgin olive oil
¼ cup white wine vinegar
5 tablespoons heavy cream
2 large eggs, beaten

In 1-quart measure, whisk together salt, sugar, pepper, tarragon, parsley, mustard, garlic, oil, vinegar, and cream. Microwave on HIGH 1½ to 2 minutes. Beat 2 to 3 tablespoons of hot oil mixture into eggs. Add egg mixture back to hot oil mixture, beating constantly. Microwave on 50% power 2 minutes, or until thickened, stirring once during cooking. Chill dressing.

GARLIC DRESSING

1 or 2 cloves garlic
1 small onion
1/2 cup wine vinegar
2 to 4 tablespoons sugar

1 teaspoon dry mustard
1/2 teaspoon salt
1 1/2 cups extra-virgin olive oil or
  salad oil

**MAKES
2 CUPS**

▪

A good basic dressing and marinade.

Place garlic, onion, vinegar, sugar to taste, mustard, and salt in blender or food processor, and process until mixture is pureed. With motor running, slowly add oil.

THOUSAND ISLAND DRESSING

After processing in blender, add 1/4 cup bottled chili sauce, 2 tablespoons heavy cream or sour cream, 2 tablespoons finely chopped celery, and 2 tablespoons finely chopped green bell pepper.

CREAMY
BLUE CHEESE DRESSING

1 cup mayonnaise (not
  homemade)
1 cup sour cream
1 clove garlic, minced

1 tablespoon fresh lemon juice
2 ounces blue cheese, crumbled
Salt
Freshly ground white pepper

**MAKES
2 CUPS**

▪

A blue cheese lover's dream!

In bowl, place mayonnaise, sour cream, garlic, lemon juice, cheese, and salt and pepper to taste and stir to combine. Store in refrigerator in tightly covered container for up to 2 weeks.

MAYONNAISE

**MAKES
1½ CUPS**

■

Fresh mayonnaise is a delicious alternative to the bottled kind and takes no time at all to make in the food processor.

2 egg yolks
1 teaspoon dry mustard
½ teaspoon salt
1 teaspoon sugar
¼ cup wine vinegar or fresh
    lemon juice

1½ cups extra-virgin olive oil or
    vegetable oil, or a
    combination
Freshly ground white or black
    pepper

Place egg yolks, mustard, salt, sugar, and vinegar in bowl of food processor fitted with steel blade and process until smooth. With motor running, pour oil slowly through feed tube. Add pepper to taste, then pulse to blend in.

Store in tightly covered container in refrigerator for up to 3 days.

NO-CHOLESTEROL MAYONNAISE

Substitute egg whites for egg yolks. Add drops of hot pepper sauce or chopped herbs with other seasonings to pick up flavor.

CURRY MAYONNAISE

Add 1 teaspoon curry powder with other seasonings.

SAFFRON MAYONNAISE

Add several threads of saffron, crushed, with other seasonings. Good with seafood.

SESAME MAYONNAISE

Substitute ¼ to ⅓ cup Oriental sesame oil for olive or vegetable oil. Good with chicken.

CRUNCHY SALAD TOPPING

3 tablespoons unsalted butter
2 teaspoons Worcestershire sauce
Dash of hot pepper sauce

1 teaspoon curry powder
1 teaspoon garlic salt
1 (16-ounce) can Chinese noodles

**MAKES
2 CUPS**

Terrific with tossed greens!

Place butter in glass pie plate and microwave on HIGH 30 to 45 seconds. Stir in Worcestershire, hot pepper sauce, curry powder, and garlic salt. Add noodles and stir to coat with butter mixture.

Spread noodles evenly in pie plate and microwave on HIGH 4 to 6 minutes, stirring several times during cooking. Let stand to cool. Noodles will become crisp during standing time. Store in sealed container.

MINTED LIME CREAM

1 (8-ounce) package cream cheese
½ cup sugar
1 cup, loosely packed, mint leaves

¼ cup fresh lime juice
½ teaspoon anise seeds

**MAKES
1½ CUPS**

Delicious with fresh fruit—especially peaches, blueberries, and melon.

In 2-cup measure, microwave cream cheese on HIGH 45 to 60 seconds to soften. Stir in sugar.

In blender or food processor, process mint, lime juice, and anise seeds until mint is finely chopped. Add cream cheese mixture and process until smooth. Chill dressing and serve over fresh fruit as a salad or dessert.

FLUFFY MINTED CREAM
Blend 1 cup whipped topping or sweetened whipped cream into finished Minted Lime Cream.

Eggs and Cheese

Eggs and cheese, both delicate foods, are delicious when cooked in the microwave provided they are treated with tenderness and respect.

Eggs

Eggs can be successfully poached, baked (shirred), fried, and hard-cooked in the microwave. They can also be used with excellent results in combination with other foods—in custards, for instance (although not in soufflés, which must be baked conventionally). Only a few rules need be followed.

The first rule is: Never microwave an egg in its shell, except in a microwave egg cooker. Rapid steam buildup inside the shell might cause the egg to burst.

Before baking, frying, or poaching eggs, gently pierce the yolks to prevent them from bursting, once again because of steam buildup. Simply puncture the yolks in several places with a toothpick, a fork, or the point of a sharp knife. This will *not* cause the yolks to bleed.

Standing time, during which the eggs finish cooking, is important for eggs cooked in the microwave, as it is for conventional rangetop cooking. The eggs should remain covered while they stand to keep in the steam.

COOKING TEMPERATURES

The correct temperature is crucial to cooking eggs in the microwave. Too high a temperature or overcooking will produce a rubbery egg.

To bake, fry, or hard-cook eggs, cover the eggs and use MEDIUM power.

To poach and scramble eggs, or to cook omelets, cover and use HIGH power.

BUYING AND STORING EGGS

When purchasing eggs, check the carton label for grade and size. Grade is a guide to the quality and appearance of the eggs. The classifications are: USDA Grade AA, USDA Grade A, and USDA Grade B. A lower grade does not indicate that the eggs are of lower nutritional value. For example, an egg examined under a light in the grading process may show a blood spot, lowering the grade but not the nutritive value.

If egg appearance and egg white volume is important (in making meringue shells, for instance), select Grade AA or Grade A eggs, which contain a high portion of white and do not spread as much as lower-grade eggs.

For eggs that will be beaten into other ingredients (meat loaf or quiche), lower-grade eggs might very well be a better buy and will perform just as well as the higher-grade eggs.

All recipes in this book call for large eggs.

Store eggs in the refrigerator and, if possible, keep them in their original carton to prevent the yolk from moving off center. The carton also prevents the absorption of odors from the refrigerator. For best flavor and quality, use eggs within one week of purchase, although those that have been stored for several weeks may be combined with other ingredients with no loss of flavor or nutrition.

Eggs may be stored in the refrigerator for three to four weeks after the expiration date on the carton. However, during this time the egg white may spread, and the yolk may flatten, so these eggs are best used for baking.

Leftover egg whites may be stored, in a tightly covered container, in the refrigerator for up to 3 days, and in the freezer for as long as 30 days. Leftover yolks should be covered with a thin layer of cold water and can be kept, well covered, in the refrigerator for 3 days. Pour off water before using.

Cheese

Cheese, one of our most versatile foods, works very well in microwave sauces, fondue, cheesecakes, sandwich fillings, quiches, and casseroles.

Like eggs, cheese and cheese products are high-protein food and for that reason also require a low cooking temperature. However, this is not an absolute rule. The power level will depend on the amount of food being cooked, the ingredients with which the cheese is combined, and the characteristics of the particular cheese used in the recipe. Follow guidelines in individual recipes.

HARD-COOKED EGGS

Hard-cooking eggs in the microwave takes much less time than cooking them conventionally: Depending on the number of eggs you're cooking, it can take from one-seventh to one-half the time. Another advantage is that, because the egg is cooked in a custard cup or muffin pan, there are no cracked shells leaking egg white into the cooking water, and there is no need to peel the cooked egg.

Of course, microwave hard-cooked eggs are not oval like those cooked conventionally because they take on the shape of the vessel in which they cook, so it's best to use them in egg salads or in other recipes calling for chopped eggs.

TIMETABLE FOR HARD-COOKED EGGS	
LARGE EGGS	**COOKING TIME ON 50% POWER**
1	1½ to 1¾ minutes
2	3 to 4 minutes
4	4 to 5 minutes
6	5 to 6 minutes

Butter or oil a microwave muffin pan or individual custard cups. Break 1 egg into each muffin form or cup and pierce the yolk quickly with a toothpick or the point of a small sharp knife. Cover tightly with plastic wrap. If using custard cups, arrange them in a circle and microwave according to the chart above.

Allow eggs to stand, covered, at least 5 minutes before unmolding.

POACHED EGGS

Eggs poached in the microwave take less time to cook than those prepared conventionally; otherwise, the process is very similar. Use individual custard cups, as instructed below, or cook up to 4 eggs in a single casserole, as in the recipe for Eggs Benedict, which follows.

TIMETABLE FOR POACHED EGGS	
LARGE EGGS	**COOKING TIME ON HIGH**
1	45 seconds to 1½ minutes
2	1 to 1½ minutes
4	2½ to 3½ minutes
6	3½ to 4½ minutes

Measure 2 tablespoons of water and ¼ teaspoon vinegar into each 6-ounce cup. Cover cup(s) tightly with plastic wrap and microwave on HIGH until water boils.

Break an egg into each cup and prick yolk with a toothpick or knife point. Cover tightly with plastic wrap and microwave according to the chart above, or until most of the white is opaque. Let egg(s) stand, covered, in water 2 to 3 minutes, or until white is set. Pour off water and remove eggs with a slotted spoon.

EGGS BENEDICT

2 TO 4 SERVINGS

■

In this recipe, four eggs are poached together in the same casserole. Vinegar is used to help the whites coagulate, producing a more compact egg.

■ ■ ■ ■ ■ ■ ■ ■ ■ ■ ■

When frying or poaching an egg, gently pierce the yolk to break the surface membrane. This will prevent the possibility of the egg yolk bursting.

■ ■ ■ ■ ■ ■ ■ ■ ■ ■ ■

2 English muffins, split and toasted

4 slices Canadian bacon or ham, warmed 2 minutes in microwave

1 recipe Hollandaise Sauce (page 84)

2 cups hot water

4 large eggs

1 teaspoon cider or white vinegar

Place English muffins, cut side up, in 12 × 7½-inch casserole. Place 1 slice Canadian bacon on each muffin half and set aside. Keep warm in a conventional oven preheated to 200° F.

Prepare Hollandaise Sauce and reserve.

To poach eggs, pour hot water into 1-quart casserole, cover with plastic wrap, and microwave on HIGH 4 to 5 minutes, or until water boils. Meanwhile, break eggs into individual saucers, or use 2 saucers and break 2 eggs into each one. When water boils, add vinegar and, using spoon, stir until liquid is swirling. Slip eggs into swirling water, pierce yolks, and cover with plastic wrap. Microwave on HIGH 2 to 3 minutes, or until whites are set. While eggs cook, prepare a bed of 2 or 3 layers of paper towels.

Remove 1 egg from water with slotted spoon and gently deposit it, yolk side up, on towels. Repeat with remaining eggs. Very gently blot tops of eggs with paper towel and, with slotted spoon, carefully scoop up each egg and deposit on top of an English muffin half. Cover casserole with plastic wrap and microwave on HIGH 1 to 2 minutes, or until heated. Do not overcook eggs. Let eggs stand, covered, 2 to 3 minutes.

With a slotted spoon, place eggs on bacon. Place muffins on serving plates, spoon Hollandaise Sauce over eggs, and serve at once.

SHIRRED EGGS

2 teaspoons unsalted butter
2 large eggs
1 to 2 teaspoons chopped fresh
herbs (optional)

1 to 2 tablespoons cooked sliced
mushrooms (optional)

2 SERVINGS

■

Shirred eggs are wonderful prepared in the microwave. They are very much like poached eggs, but, since they are cooked in butter rather than water, they taste more luxurious.

Place 1 teaspoon butter in each of two 6-ounce custard cups and microwave on HIGH 30 to 40 seconds, or until melted. Break 1 egg into each cup, pierce yolk gently with toothpick, fork, or knife point, and cover tightly with plastic wrap. Microwave at 70% power 1½ to 2 minutes, or until whites are almost set.

Let stand, covered, for 2 to 3 minutes to complete cooking. Serve in cups, sprinkled with herbs and mushrooms, if desired, or run thin-bladed knife around perimeter of cups to loosen eggs, then unmold.

BACON AND EGG

2 slices bacon

1 large egg

1 SERVING

■

The all-time American favorite.

■ ■ ■ ■ ■ ■ ■ ■ ■ ■ ■

It's easy to separate the slices in a pound of bacon by heating the entire package for 20 to 30 seconds on HIGH.

■ ■ ■ ■ ■ ■ ■ ■ ■ ■ ■

Place bacon in 9-inch pie plate or casserole, cover with a paper towel, and microwave on HIGH 2 to 3 minutes. Remove bacon, leaving drippings in plate, and drain on paper towel.

Crack egg into plate with hot drippings, gently pierce yolk with toothpick or fork, and cover tightly with plastic wrap. Cook on 80% power 50 to 60 seconds. Let egg set 1 to 2 minutes and serve with bacon.

SCRAMBLED EGGS

Eggs scrambled in the microwave are fluffier and have more volume than eggs scrambled conventionally. It's also convenient to cook and serve the eggs from the same dish. For a quick cleanup, scramble an egg in a Styrofoam cup.

TIMETABLE FOR SCRAMBLED EGGS			
LARGE EGGS	**BUTTER**	**MILK OR WATER**	**COOKING TIME ON HIGH**
1	1 teaspoon	1 tablespoon	40 to 60 seconds
2	2 teaspoons	2 tablespoons	1¼ to 1¾ minutes
4	1 tablespoon	3 tablespoons	2 to 3 minutes
6	2 tablespoons	¼ cup	3½ to 4½ minutes

Place butter in casserole, custard cup, or glass measure. Cook on HIGH 30 to 60 seconds, or until butter melts.

Add eggs and liquid and stir with fork to mix. Cover with plastic wrap and cook on HIGH half the recommended cooking time.

Stir eggs, pushing cooked portion to center of dish. Cover again and microwave on HIGH for remaining cooking time, stirring 2 or 3 times additionally if cooking more than 4 eggs. Eggs are done when they look set but are still soft and moist.

Allow to stand, covered, 3 to 4 minutes longer or until eggs are set to your taste, before serving.

OMELET FILLINGS

There are so many good omelet fillings that entire books have been devoted to the subject. We list here a few of our favorites which might inspire you to create some of your own. Our only caution is that the filling should never be so insistent that it overwhelms the flavor of the eggs.

Except for the cheeses, each of the savory fillings that follows should be heated in the microwave for a minute or two while the omelet sets. About ½ cup of savory filling will be enough to fill one Basic Omelet (page 128).

SAVORY OMELET FILLINGS
- Grated Cheddar, mozzarella, Swiss, or any other firm cheese.
- Cream, cottage, or ricotta cheeses, mixed with fresh herbs, if you like.
- Sautéed sliced mushrooms, green bell pepper, and onion.
- Ham-Mushroom Duxelles (page 262).
- Cooked vegetables, such as broccoli flowerets, 1-inch pieces of asparagus, or zucchini.
- Creamed vegetables, such as chopped spinach or mushrooms.
- Salsa or other fresh-tasting tomato-based sauces.
- Sliced cooked potatoes sautéed with sliced onions.
- Sour cream and red caviar.

SWEET OMELET FILLINGS
- 2 to 3 tablespoons jam, jelly, apple butter, or preserves topped with 2 to 3 tablespoons softened cream cheese or ricotta.
- Sautéed sliced apples sprinkled with cinnamon and sugar.
- Sliced fruit, stewed with spices and drained. Spike with ½ teaspoon fruit liqueur or *eau de vie*.
- Any combination of fresh berries, whole or sliced, and cottage cheese thinned with a bit of yogurt (using all yogurt would make too thin a filling).

BASIC OMELET

1 SERVING

•

Straining the hard bits of albumen out of the beaten eggs will make the omelet silkier. To prepare a tender, easy-to-roll omelet, cover the dish tightly with plastic wrap. No stirring is necessary.

1 tablespoon unsalted butter
2 large eggs
2 tablespoons water
Salt

Freshly ground black or white
  pepper
Omelet filling (page 127)

Place butter in 9-inch pie plate and microwave on HIGH 30 to 45 seconds to melt. In small bowl, place eggs, water, and salt and pepper to taste and beat 40 to 50 strokes with wire whisk. Pour (or strain) egg mixture into pie plate and cover tightly with plastic wrap.

Microwave on HIGH 2 to 3 minutes, or until center is almost set. Let stand, covered, 2 minutes before spreading filling over top. To remove eggs from dish, gently lift and fold with rubber spatula, then turn out on plate seam side down.

HERBED OMELET
After eggs are strained into pie plate, stir in 1 tablespoon finely chopped herbs: Tarragon, basil, parsley, chives (or scallion tops), and chervil are all good choices.

BASQUE OMELET

6 TO 8 SERVINGS

•

A light main dish with a mild flavor. Serve with a salad, a fresh vegetable, and hearty bread.

1 tablespoon extra-virgin olive oil
1 cup chopped green bell pepper
1 cup chopped onion
1 clove garlic, minced
1/2 teaspoon dried oregano
4 tomatoes, peeled, seeded, and
  cut in strips
1 cup 1/4-inch strips ham

1/4 teaspoon salt
1/4 teaspoon freshly ground black
  pepper
8 large eggs, beaten
2 tablespoons unsalted butter
3 tablespoons chopped parsley
2 tablespoons freshly grated
  Parmesan cheese

Place olive oil, bell pepper, onion, garlic, and oregano in 2-quart measure, cover with plastic wrap, and microwave on HIGH 4 minutes, or until vegetables are tender-crisp. Stir in tomatoes and ham, cover, and set aside.

Add salt and pepper to eggs. Place butter in 9-inch pie plate and microwave on HIGH 30 seconds to melt. Pour eggs into pie plate, cover with plastic wrap, and microwave on HIGH 2 minutes. Gently stir the cooked outer edges to center, pushing the uncooked center portion to outer edge of plate. Cover again and cook on 70% power 2 to 5 minutes longer, or until eggs are almost set. Let stand, covered, 2 to 3 minutes.

Heat vegetable mixture, covered, on HIGH 2 to 3 minutes, or until hot. Spread over eggs, then sprinkle with parsley and Parmesan. Serve immediately.

SPICY BASQUE OMELET

For zestier flavor, add ¼ teaspoon dry mustard and 1 teaspoon vinegar to vegetable mixture. Add ½ cup grated sharp Cheddar, Swiss, or mozzarella cheese to beaten eggs. Omit Parmesan.

> Do not microwave eggs in the shell because steam builds up, causing the egg to burst. Do not reheat whole boiled eggs for the same reason.

VEGETABLE CUSTARD

1 pound zucchini or yellow
    summer squash, grated
1½ teaspoons salt
2 cups grated Monterey Jack
    cheese
⅓ cup freshly grated Parmesan
    cheese

½ cup half-and-half
3 large eggs, beaten
½ cup chopped scallions
½ teaspoon dried dill
½ teaspoon freshly ground white
    pepper

4 TO 6 SERVINGS

Place zucchini in colander, sprinkle with salt, and toss to mix. Put colander in sink and let zucchini stand 10 to 15 minutes to draw out excess liquid. Drain vegetable and pat dry.

Place Monterey Jack and Parmesan cheeses, half-and-half, eggs, scallions, dill, and pepper in 2-quart bowl and blend well. Add zucchini and toss to coat with egg mixture. Cover tightly with plastic wrap and microwave on HIGH 5 minutes, then stir.

Pour custard into 10-inch glass pie plate or porcelain quiche pan with fluted sides. Cover custard tightly with plastic wrap and microwave on 70% power 10 to 15 minutes, or until set. Serve warm.

SALMON QUICHE

6 TO 8 SERVINGS

WHOLE WHEAT CRUST

1 cup whole wheat flour

²/₃ cup grated sharp Cheddar cheese

¹/₄ cup chopped walnuts, pecans, or sesame seeds

¹/₂ teaspoon paprika

¹/₂ teaspoon freshly ground white pepper

6 tablespoons vegetable oil

FILLING

1 (15¹/₂-ounce) can salmon, drained

3 large eggs, beaten

1 cup plain low-fat yogurt or sour cream

2 tablespoons mayonnaise

¹/₂ cup grated sharp Cheddar cheese

¹/₄ cup grated onion

2 tablespoons chopped parsley

¹/₂ teaspoon freshly ground white pepper

To make crust, oil 10-inch pie plate. In mixing bowl, combine flour, cheese, nuts, paprika, pepper, and oil. Mix well with fork until dough holds together, then transfer to pie plate, pressing dough evenly around plate to form crust. Microwave on 70% power 7 to 9 minutes, or until cooked and dry. Place pie plate on rack and let crust cool.

Prepare filling while crust cooks and cools. Remove skin and bones from salmon and place fish in 1-quart casserole. Add eggs, yogurt, mayonnaise, cheese, onion, parsley, and pepper and stir to combine well. Microwave on HIGH 5 to 7 minutes, or until mixture begins to set around edges, stirring once during cooking.

Pour filling into shell and microwave on 70% power 4 to 7 minutes, or until filling is set. Serve warm.

Reheat egg dishes for a minimum amount of time at 50 to 70% power to reduce the possibility of the eggs toughening.

SHRIMP AND CORN CUSTARD

3 large eggs, beaten
2 cups fresh corn, sliced off cob
3 tablespoons unsalted butter
2 tablespoons all-purpose flour
1/2 cup milk or half-and-half

1 cup fresh steamed shrimp (page 155), peeled
1 teaspoon Worcestershire sauce
Salt
Freshly ground white pepper

4 SERVINGS

▪

A modern-day version of a recipe that originated in the American colonies. Make it with *fresh* shrimp.

In 2-quart measure, combine the eggs, corn, butter, flour, milk, shrimp, Worcestershire, and salt and pepper to taste. Cover with plastic wrap and microwave on HIGH 5 minutes, stirring once.

Pour filling into buttered 9-inch pie plate, cover with plastic wrap and microwave on 70% power 7 to 10 minutes, or until set. Serve custard warm.

CHEESY GRITS

1 quart milk
1 1/2 sticks (3/4 cup) unsalted butter
1 cup quick-cooking (not instant) grits
1 1/2 cups grated Gruyère or Swiss cheese

1 teaspoon salt
1/4 teaspoon freshly ground white pepper

4 SERVINGS

▪

A delicious brunch dish that can be partially cooked in the microwave the night before, then finished the next day in the conventional oven.

Place milk, 1 stick of butter, and grits in 2-quart measure and microwave on HIGH 9 to 12 minutes, or until grits are cooked and thickened, stirring several times. Stir in cheese, salt, and pepper and combine well. Pour mixture into 13 × 9-inch baking dish, cover, and refrigerate overnight.

Preheat conventional oven to 400° F. Butter a 1 1/2-quart casserole.

Place remaining 1/4 cup butter in 1-cup measure and microwave on HIGH 1 minute to melt. Cut grits into squares and place in casserole in overlapping layers. Pour melted butter over grits and bake in preheated conventional oven 10 to 15 minutes, or until brown. Serve at once.

GREEN CHILI CUSTARD

4 TO 6 SERVINGS

6 large eggs, beaten
2 cups grated Monterey Jack
   cheese
1 (4-ounce) can green chilies,
   drained and chopped

1 cup evaporated milk or half-
   and-half
1/4 cup all-purpose flour
1/2 teaspoon baking powder
1 teaspoon salt

In mixing bowl, combine eggs, cheese, chilies, milk, flour, baking powder, and salt and whisk well to blend. Pour into 9-inch square dish and microwave on HIGH 2 minutes. Stir, pushing outside portions to center.

Cover with plastic wrap and microwave on 50% power 8 to 12 minutes, or just until mixture is set. Serve with Salsa (page 90), taco sauce, or picante sauce.

BAKED MACARONI AND CHEESE

4 TO 6 SERVINGS

2 cups elbow macaroni
2 cups hot tap water
1/2 stick (1/4 cup) unsalted butter,
   cut into chunks
1/2 teaspoon salt
1/4 teaspoon freshly ground white
   pepper

1/4 teaspoon dry mustard
1 (14-ounce) can evaporated milk
3 large eggs
1 pound sharp Cheddar cheese
Paprika

Combine macaroni and water in 2-quart measure, cover tightly with plastic wrap, and microwave on HIGH 5 minutes. Stir, then cover tightly again and microwave on 50% power 4 to 6 minutes. The liquid will be absorbed. Add butter, salt, pepper, and mustard and stir until butter is melted and ingredients are well blended.

Place the milk and eggs in mixer bowl and beat well. Pour over macaroni and stir.

Cut 12 ounces of cheese into 1-inch cubes and stir into macaroni mixture. Cover tightly with plastic wrap and microwave on HIGH 5 minutes, then stir. Pour mixture into 2-quart casserole and microwave on 70% power 10 to 12 minutes, stirring after 5 minutes.

Meanwhile, grate remaining cheese. Sprinkle grated cheese over macaroni and let stand 2 to 3 minutes to melt. Sprinkle lightly with paprika before serving.

VARIATIONS

When adding cubed Cheddar, stir in any or all of the following: ¼ cup finely chopped onions or scallions; 1 (4-ounce) jar pimiento, drained and chopped; ¼ cup finely chopped green bell pepper; 1 (4-ounce) can sliced mushrooms, drained.

When using grated cheese as a topping for a casserole, add during the last few minutes of cooking time or standing time. Cheese becomes rubbery and toughens if cooked too long at too high a temperature.

MEXICAN "LASAGNA"

1 pound lean ground beef	1 cup cottage cheese
½ cup chopped onion	1 cup sour cream
1 teaspoon minced garlic	1 (4-ounce) can chopped green
1 (1¼-ounce) package taco	chilies, drained
seasoning	1 (7-ounce) package tortilla chips
1 (16-ounce) can tomato sauce	8 ounces sharp Cheddar cheese,
	grated

5 TO 6 SERVINGS

Enjoy this wonderful blend of Mexican flavors.

Combine beef, onion, and garlic in 1½-quart casserole, cover, and microwave on HIGH 5 to 6 minutes. Stir mixture and drain off fat. Stir in taco seasoning and tomato sauce, mixing well, and microwave, covered, on HIGH 4 to 5 minutes.

Combine cottage cheese, sour cream, and chilies in mixing bowl and stir to blend.

In 2-quart casserole, layer half of following ingredients: tortilla chips, beef mixture, Cheddar cheese, cottage cheese mixture. Repeat, beginning with beef mixture. Top with remaining tortilla chips. Microwave "lasagna" on 70% power 10 to 15 minutes, or until hot and bubbly. Serve at once.

EGG AND CHEESE PUFF

6 TO 8 SERVINGS

•

½ cup chopped scallions
6 slices white bread
8 ounces sharp Cheddar cheese, grated
2½ cups milk
4 large eggs

1 teaspoon dry mustard
1 teaspoon Worcestershire sauce
½ teaspoon salt
½ teaspoon freshly ground white pepper

Place scallions in 1-cup measure, cover with plastic wrap, and microwave on HIGH 2 minutes, or until softened. Reserve.

Place 3 slices bread in bottom of 1½-quart casserole and sprinkle over them half each of Cheddar cheese and cooked scallions. Repeat with remaining bread, cheese, and scallions.

In mixing bowl, place milk, eggs, mustard, Worcestershire, salt, and pepper and beat to blend well. Pour mixture over bread and cheese, cover tightly with plastic wrap, and refrigerate overnight.

Place covered casserole in microwave and cook on HIGH 3 minutes, then on 50% power 15 to 20 minutes, or until custard is set.

VEGETABLE STRATA

4 TO 6 SERVINGS

•

2 cups chopped raw broccoli or 1 (10-ounce) package frozen broccoli
½ cup chopped scallions
½ cup chopped celery
4 slices white bread

2 cups grated Cheddar cheese
5 large eggs, beaten
2 tablespoons milk
½ teaspoon freshly ground white pepper

Place broccoli, scallions, and celery in small bowl, cover with plastic wrap, and microwave on HIGH 4 to 6 minutes, or until vegetables are tender-crisp. Drain off liquid.

Place 2 slices bread in bottom of 1-quart casserole and sprinkle with half the Cheddar cheese and half the vegetable mixture. Repeat with remaining bread, cheese, and vegetables.

Combine beaten eggs, milk, and pepper and beat. Pour mixture over bread and cheese and cover tightly with plastic wrap. Strata can be refrigerated overnight at this point, if desired.

Place covered casserole in microwave and cook on HIGH 3 minutes, then at 50% power 12 to 15 minutes, or until center of strata is set. Let stand, covered, 5 to 10 minutes.

To produce fluffier scrambled eggs, stir frequently.

CRABMEAT STRATA

2 cups unseasoned croutons
1 1/2 cups grated Gruyère or Swiss cheese
8 ounces fresh crabmeat, picked over
3 or 4 scallions, chopped

1 1/2 cups milk
4 large eggs, beaten
1 teaspoon dry mustard
1/2 teaspoon freshly ground white pepper
1 tablespoon dry sherry

6 SERVINGS

This is an easy brunch dish. The variation gives instructions for advance preparation.

Spread 1 cup croutons in bottom of 1½-quart casserole. Layer cheese and crabmeat alternately over croutons and set aside.

In 1-quart measure, combine scallions, milk, eggs, mustard, pepper, and sherry and beat until well mixed. Microwave, covered, on HIGH 5 minutes, stirring once. Pour custard over crabmeat mixture. Cover and cook on 70% power 7 to 10 minutes, or until center is set. Let stand, covered, 5 to 10 minutes, then sprinkle with remaining croutons and serve.

VARIATION

Do not microwave milk-and-egg mixture; instead, pour it into casserole over crabmeat mixture, cover dish with plastic wrap, and refrigerate for up to 24 hours. Microwave, covered, on HIGH 5 minutes, then gently stir partially set custard from the outer edges of casserole toward center. Cover again and microwave on 70% power for 12 to 18 minutes, or until set in center. Let strata stand, covered, about 5 minutes before serving.

WELSH RAREBIT

4 SERVINGS

•

A Welshman is credited with serving this melted cheese dish as a quick supper for an unexpected guest.

2 tablespoons unsalted butter
4 teaspoons cornstarch
2 teaspoons Worcestershire sauce
1/2 teaspoon freshly ground white
    pepper
2 teaspoons mustard

1 (12-ounce) can light beer
1 pound sharp New York Cheddar
    cheese, grated
1 large egg, beaten
4 English muffins, split and
    toasted

Place butter in 2-quart casserole and microwave on HIGH 1 minute to melt. Stir in cornstarch, Worcestershire, pepper, mustard, and beer and blend well. Microwave on HIGH 4 to 5 minutes, or until boiling. Add cheese and stir until melted.

Beat 2 tablespoons cheese mixture into beaten egg, then gradually add egg mixture to cheese, stirring constantly. Microwave on HIGH 1 minute.

Arrange English muffins on plates and pour rarebit over them. Serve at once.

VARIATION

Place cooked ham or bacon slices on muffins before topping with rarebit.

Fish and Shellfish

There is almost universal agreement that microwaving can produce the best fish and seafood you have ever eaten. Whether poached, steamed, or baked, fish cooked in the microwave is delicate, moist, and tender.

Begin by buying fish and seafood that smell fresh and don't have a strong fishy odor. Whole fish should have clear eyes, rosy gills, and scales that cling to the skin. The flesh must be firm and translucent.

Frozen fish and seafood packages should be frozen solid and show no sign of freezer burn or having been refrozen. Do not buy a package with water frozen on the bottom. Thaw frozen fish and seafood completely before cooking (see the timetable on page 140).

COOKING BASICS
FOR FISH AND SHELLFISH

Once it is cooked, fish—especially fillets—flakes easily, so it's best to cook and serve from the same dish, microwaving the fish immediately before serving.

PREPARATION AND SEASONING

Blot the fish or seafood dry with paper towels. Melt butter, if called for in the recipe, and add fish, turning to coat it on all sides with the butter. Add other seasonings and wine, lemon juice, or vinegar.

ARRANGEMENT OF FISH

Arrange fish fillets so that the thicker portions are placed around the perimeter of the baking dish, with the thinner parts overlapping in the center of the dish. Place crawfish, lobster tails, scallops, shrimp, and squid in a circle within the perimeter, leaving the center of the dish empty.

COVERING DISH

Fish are steamed and poached in the microwave using the same technique. For poaching, however, a little liquid is used—lemon juice and butter, for instance. The fish is then covered with plastic wrap and steamed in the liquid.

For steaming, the fish is cooked covered with a dampened paper towel and microwaved without any added liquid.

If the fish is coated with a heavy sauce before cooking, often the dish need not be covered because the sauce will hold the moisture and prevent the fish from becoming too dry.

COOKING TEMPERATURE

Because fish has a high moisture content, it can be cooked on HIGH and still retain its delicious natural flavor. However, fish can overcook very quickly, thin fillets in particular, so watch carefully during the last minutes of cooking. If the center flakes easily when lifted with a fork, the fish is done.

STANDING TIME

After microwaving, thinner cuts of fish need only 2 to 3 minutes of standing time. Take them directly from the microwave to the table, by which time they will have finished cooking.

Allow thicker cuts of fish to stand, covered, 4 to 5 minutes to complete cooking.

It is difficult to reheat fish without drying it out.

TIPS FOR COOKING THICK CUTS OF FISH

Fatty fish are usually darker in color and have a stronger flavor than lean fish. For a milder flavor, season the fish with lemon juice or wine vinegar. Butter is delicious, but not a necessary addition, especially if cholesterol is a consideration. Use fresh herbs and freshly ground pepper to augment flavor.

Thick fillets and steaks cook more evenly when tightly wrapped; turn the fish over halfway through cooking.

TIMETABLE FOR COOKING FISH

FISH	POWER LEVEL	MINUTES PER POUND	STANDING TIME
Fish fillets	HIGH	4 to 6	2 to 3 minutes
Whole fish	HIGH	4½ to 6	5 minutes
Fish steaks (1 inch)	HIGH	4½ to 5	5 minutes, or until fish flakes

DEFROSTING FISH AND SEAFOOD

To defrost a whole fish, unwrap it and place on a microwavable roasting track or in a baking dish. Microwave the fish for half the recommended cooking time (see below). Turn the fish over and shield with aluminum foil any parts of it that have cooked too quickly. Cook for the remaining time.

Microwave all frozen fish, either whole or fillets, at 30% power according to the times given in the chart below. If any part of the fish begins to cook, shield it with a small piece of foil (if permitted in your oven). To prevent the fish from cooking in its own juices, drain it as water collects during defrosting.

Allow the fish to stand, covered, 4 to 5 minutes after defrosting, then rinse under cold running water to complete thawing. Always separate fillets gently under cold running water; do not break them apart.

TIMETABLE FOR DEFROSTING FISH AND SEAFOOD

FISH OR SEAFOOD	PACKAGE WEIGHT	MINUTES AT 30% POWER
Whole fish	1½ to 2 pounds	13 to 15
Fish fillets	1 pound	12 to 14
Salmon steaks	1 pound	5 to 7
Scallops	12 ounces	3 to 4
Shrimp	1 pound	4 to 6
Lobster tails	1 pound	9 to 12
	8 ounces	5 to 7

POACHED FRESH FISH FILLETS

1 pound fresh fish fillets, cut ¹/₂
*   inch thick*
1 tablespoon fresh lemon juice

Chopped fresh herbs (dill, parsley,
*   chervil, or basil)*
1 lemon, thinly sliced

3 OR 4
SERVINGS

■

In 2-quart casserole, arrange fish fillets with thicker portion toward outside of dish. Sprinkle with lemon juice and cover with plastic wrap. Cook on HIGH 3 to 5 minutes, or until fish flakes easily.

Garnish with herbs and lemon slices and serve immediately.

This master recipe produces a truly elegant low-calorie, low-cholesterol dish that is extremely easy to prepare. The poached fillets are light fare served by themselves. For a heartier meal, serve fillets with Salsa (page 90).

FISH FILLETS FLORENTINE

2 (10-ounce) packages frozen
*   chopped spinach, defrosted*
*   and well drained*
¹/₄ cup finely chopped onions
1 tablespoon fresh lemon juice
1 pound sole (or other white fish)
*   fillets*

¹/₃ cup freshly grated Parmesan
*   cheese*
¹/₂ stick (¹/₄ cup) unsalted butter,
*   melted (optional)*
Salt
Freshly ground black pepper

4 SERVINGS

■

. . . .
When serving fish as a main course, cook any vegetable dishes first and keep them warm while cooking the fish in the microwave. Fish cools off rapidly and is easy to overcook, so plan to serve the moment it is taken from the oven.
. . . .

Place spinach in 2-quart round casserole, add onions and lemon juice, and mix well. Spread mixture evenly in bottom of dish. Arrange fish over spinach, with thicker edges around perimeter of dish and thinner parts overlapping toward center.

Cover tightly with plastic wrap and microwave on HIGH 4 to 5 minutes. Sprinkle fish with Parmesan and, if desired, melted butter, then add salt and pepper to taste. Cover again and microwave on HIGH 3 to 6 minutes, or until fish flakes easily. Let stand, covered, 2 to 3 minutes and serve at once.

POACHED FLOUNDER FILLETS

4 SERVINGS

▪

Simple and delicious.

1 pound flounder fillets
1 tablespoon fresh lemon juice
2 tablespoons mayonnaise
1/3 cup chopped scallions

Salt
Freshly ground white pepper
Paprika

▪ ▪ ▪ ▪ ▪ ▪ ▪ ▪ ▪ ▪ ▪

Test fish for doneness by inserting a fork into the thickest part and twisting gently. If the fish flakes and looks opaque, it is done. Fish that needs to cook longer will look translucent. Since fish cooks so quickly, check for doneness often.

▪ ▪ ▪ ▪ ▪ ▪ ▪ ▪ ▪ ▪ ▪

Place flounder in shallow 2-quart casserole with thicker edges of fillets around perimeter of dish. In small bowl, combine lemon juice, mayonnaise, scallions, and salt and pepper to taste and mix well. Spread mayonnaise mixture evenly over fillets.

Cover casserole with plastic wrap and microwave on HIGH 3 to 4 minutes. Rearrange fillets, placing undercooked parts around perimeter of dish. Cover again and microwave on HIGH 1 to 2 minutes, or until fish flakes easily. Let stand, covered, 2 to 3 minutes, then sprinkle with paprika and serve.

SAUCED FLOUNDER

4 SERVINGS

▪

A quick and easy supper dish.

1 pound flounder fillets
1 (8-ounce) can spaghetti sauce
  with mushrooms
3 tablespoons chopped fresh basil,
  or 1 teaspoon dried

3 tablespoons chopped onions
4 ounces mozzarella cheese, thinly
  sliced
1 cup mushrooms, sliced

Place flounder fillets in shallow 2-quart casserole with thicker edges around perimeter of dish. In small bowl, combine spaghetti sauce, basil, and onions. Pour sauce over fillets. Cover with plastic wrap and microwave on HIGH 5 to 7 minutes. Spread mozzarella and mushroom slices over fish, cover, and microwave on HIGH 4 to 5 minutes longer. Let stand 2 to 3 minutes, covered, before serving.

SIMPLY ELEGANT FLOUNDER

4 cups cooked rice (page 289)
2 pounds frozen flounder fillets,
    defrosted (page 140)
3/4 cup plain low-fat yogurt or sour
    cream
1 (10³/4-ounce) can condensed
    cream of shrimp soup
1 teaspoon minced garlic
1/4 teaspoon freshly grated nutmeg

1/2 teaspoon salt
1/2 teaspoon freshly ground white
3 to 4 tablespoons chopped
    parsley
1/2 teaspoon paprika
1/2 cup slivered, blanched almonds,
    toasted (page 441)

8 SERVINGS

This dish tastes good when it's been assembled the day before and then cooked just before serving. You can save a lot of calories by using yogurt instead of sour cream, although the flavor is a little tarter.

Spread rice evenly in a 3-inch-high, 3-quart casserole. Cut flounder fillets into serving portions. Arrange fillets over rice, with thickest edges around perimeter of dish and thinner parts overlapping toward center.

In mixing bowl, combine yogurt, soup, garlic, nutmeg, salt, and pepper and stir to blend well. Pour mixture evenly over fish and sprinkle with parsley and paprika. Cover tightly with plastic wrap and refrigerate overnight, if desired.

Microwave on HIGH 5 minutes if the dish is cooked immediately and 10 to 12 minutes if dish has been refrigerated. Cook on 70% power 12 to 15 minutes longer, or until fish flakes easily. Let stand, covered, 5 minutes before serving. Sprinkle almonds over fish and serve at once.

HALIBUT WITH VEGETABLES

6 TO 8 SERVINGS

▪

A subtle blend of halibut and squash makes a tasty dish that can be prepared for cooking early in the day.

2 pounds halibut fillets
1/2 teaspoon paprika
1/2 teaspoon freshly ground white
   pepper
1 medium yellow summer squash,
   thinly sliced

1 medium zucchini, thinly sliced
6 scallions, cut into 1-inch pieces
1 tablespoon fresh lemon juice

Place halibut in 13 × 9-inch oblong casserole, skin side down and thicker edges of fillets around perimeter of dish and thinner parts overlapping, if necessary. Cover with wax paper and microwave on HIGH 6 minutes.

Turn fillets over and rearrange if necessary. Sprinkle with paprika and pepper, then spread yellow squash, zucchini, and scallions evenly over fish. Sprinkle with lemon juice, cover with plastic wrap, and cook on HIGH 5 to 8 minutes, or until fish flakes easily. Let stand, covered, 5 minutes before serving.

STEAMED SALMON

3 OR 4 SERVINGS

▪

A delicious combination of flavors!

4 salmon steaks (about 1 pound)
1/4 cup dry white wine
Freshly ground black pepper

1 onion, thinly sliced
1 lemon, thinly sliced

Arrange salmon steaks in single layer in shallow 2-quart casserole, thinner parts pointing toward center of casserole. Pour wine over steaks, sprinkle with pepper, and layer onion and lemon over fish. Cover with wax paper and microwave on HIGH 6 to 8 minutes, or until salmon flakes easily.

Serve salmon hot or cold with Cucumber-Dill Sauce.

CUCUMBER-DILL SAUCE

1 medium cucumber, peeled,
  seeded, and thinly sliced
2 tablespoons mayonnaise
1/2 cup sour cream or plain low-fat
  yogurt
2 teaspoons fresh lemon juice

1 teaspoon snipped fresh dill, or
  1/4 teaspoon dried
Salt
Freshly ground white pepper

4 SERVINGS

■

Combine all ingredients in bowl and chill for at least 1 hour, allowing flavors to blend. Serve with poached salmon.

SALMON LOAF

1 (15 1/2-ounce) can salmon,
  drained
1 medium onion, chopped
1 medium green or red bell pepper,
  chopped
1/3 cup milk

1/2 cup fresh bread crumbs
3 large eggs, well beaten
1 cup grated sharp Cheddar
  cheese
1/2 teaspoon freshly ground black
  pepper

**4 TO 6
SERVINGS**

■

A quick and tasty main dish.

Remove skin and bones from salmon, flake fish, and set aside. Place onion and bell pepper in 1-quart casserole, cover with plastic wrap, and microwave on HIGH 3 to 5 minutes, or until vegetables are tender-crisp. Add milk, bread crumbs, eggs, cheese, and black pepper and stir to combine well. Add flaked salmon and mix gently.

Pour mixture into deep, straight-sided 1-quart casserole or soufflé dish, cover, and cook on 70% power 10 to 15 minutes. Stir mixture, and cook on 70% power 5 to 7 minutes longer, or until mixture is set. Allow dish to stand, covered, 5 minutes before serving.

BAKED SHAD ROE

4 SERVINGS

1 pound shad roe
½ cup milk (or enough to cover
    roe)

Lemon pepper
½ cup fine fresh bread crumbs
½ stick (¼ cup) unsalted butter

Remove connective tissue from roe and place in bowl. Add milk, cover tightly, and refrigerate for 8 hours to remove fishy odor and improve flavor.

Remove roe from milk, sprinkle with lemon pepper, and roll in bread crumbs.

In 1-quart casserole, melt butter on HIGH 2 to 3 minutes or until very hot. Place roe in butter, cover loosely, and cook on 70% power 7 to 10 minutes, turning roe over once.

BAKED RED SNAPPER

4 SERVINGS

You may also use tile-fish, black sea bass, or another mild-flavored fish.

1 (3-pound) red snapper, cleaned
    and scaled
2 tablespoons extra-virgin olive oil
½ cup chopped scallions
½ cup chopped red bell pepper
½ cup chopped green bell pepper
1 large tomato, peeled, seeded, and
    chopped

2 tablespoons chopped fresh
    thyme
2 tablespoons chopped fresh basil
6 pitted black olives, sliced
Salt
Freshly ground black pepper

Cook whole fish on a microwavable rack or grill to prevent it from becoming watery.

Place fish on rack in 12 × 9-inch casserole. Combine olive oil, scallions, and bell peppers in small bowl. Cover tightly with plastic wrap and cook on HIGH 2 to 3 minutes, or until tender-crisp. Combine with chopped tomato, thyme, basil, olives, and salt and pepper to taste. Stuff cavity of fish with vegetable mixture, cover dish, and microwave on HIGH 4½ to 6 minutes per pound. Let stand, covered, 5 minutes before serving.

SQUID AND FRESH TOMATO SAUCE FOR PASTA

2 teaspoons minced garlic
1 medium onion, chopped
1/4 cup extra-virgin olive oil
1/4 cup chopped fresh basil
Salt

Freshly ground black pepper
1 pound plum tomatoes, peeled
   and chopped
1 pound cleaned squid, cut into
   1/2-inch pieces

4 SERVINGS

■

Combine garlic, onion, oil, basil, and salt and pepper to taste in a 2-quart casserole. Cover tightly with plastic wrap and cook on HIGH 3 to 4 minutes, or until tender-crisp, stirring once. Add tomatoes and cook on HIGH 4 to 5 minutes, or until boiling, stirring once.

Add squid and cover tightly with plastic wrap. Cook on HIGH 3 to 5 minutes, or until hot and bubbly. Stir and cover again. Cook on 50% power 2 to 3 minutes. Serve with pasta and crusty bread.

POACHED FROG LEGS

1 pound frog legs
1/4 cup milk
1/4 cup dry white wine
1/2 teaspoon salt
1/4 teaspoon freshly ground white
   pepper

1/4 cup minced parsley
2 tablespoons unsalted butter,
   melted

2 SERVINGS

■

Frog legs are delicate and should be treated simply.

Place frog legs in 1 1/2-quart casserole with thicker parts around perimeter of dish. Add milk and wine and sprinkle with salt, pepper, and parsley. Cover and microwave on HIGH 6 to 8 minutes or until tender.

Let stand, covered, 5 minutes. Remove from broth and drizzle with melted butter.

BARBECUED TUNA

2 SERVINGS

•

This dish is low in cholesterol and offers variety to special diets.

1 (6½-ounce) can water-packed tuna, drained and flaked
⅓ cup Barbecue Sauce (page 86)

2 hamburger buns, split and toasted

Combine tuna and barbecue sauce in 1-quart dish. Microwave on 50% power 3 to 4 minutes, or until hot and bubbly. Serve on warmed buns immediately. (Do not prepare ahead. Barbecued tuna will have a fishy flavor if it is refrigerated before it is eaten.)

POACHED MOUNTAIN TROUT

2 SERVINGS

•

Trout is wonderful served with Dill Caper Sauce.

2 whole trout (6 to 8 ounces each), cleaned
2 tablespoons red wine vinegar

2 tablespoons water
2 bay leaves
Salt

Place trout in 8-inch square casserole with thickest parts next to outside of dish. Sprinkle with vinegar, water, and bay leaves. Cover loosely with wax paper and microwave on HIGH 5 minutes. Turn fish over, cover again, and microwave on HIGH 4 to 6 minutes, or until fish flakes easily. Let stand, covered, 2 to 3 minutes. Sprinkle with salt to taste.

DILL CAPER SAUCE

MAKES ABOUT ⅔ CUP

•

Prepare at least several hours before serving time so flavors can blend.

½ cup mayonnaise (page 116)
1 teaspoon capers, crushed
1 teaspoon snipped fresh dill

2 tablespoons fresh lemon juice
Dash of hot pepper sauce

Combine mayonnaise, capers, dill, lemon juice, and hot pepper sauce in bowl. Cover with plastic wrap and refrigerate 2 to 3 hours before serving.

STEAMED CLAMS IN THE SHELL

⅓ cup water
1 tablespoon fresh lemon juice

8 littleneck clams, well scrubbed
under cold running water

1 OR 2 SERVINGS

■

Prepare them simply and enjoy the wonderful flavor of the sea.

Combine water and lemon juice in 2-quart casserole. Arrange clams in a circle in casserole, cover, and cook on HIGH 5 to 6 minutes, or until shells open. Let stand, covered, 5 minutes before serving. Discard any clams that do not open.

LINGUINE WITH CLAM SAUCE

1 pound linguine, preferably
imported from Italy
1 star anise
¼ cup extra-virgin olive oil
2 cloves garlic, minced
3 scallions, chopped
½ teaspoon freshly ground black
pepper

1 teaspoon dried oregano
1 tablespoon chopped parsley
½ cup dry white wine
1 large tomato, chopped
24 littleneck clams, well scrubbed
under running water

4 TO 6 SERVINGS

■

The secret ingredient in this otherwise traditional recipe is the star anise cooked with the linguine, which gives the dish an exotic overtone. Star anise is available at Oriental food stores and at some gourmet food shops. Serve as a first course or light supper.

Prepare and measure ingredients before beginning to cook.
Cook linguine and star anise conventionally in boiling water, following package instructions, until pasta is *al dente*.

While pasta cooks, prepare sauce. In 2-quart casserole combine oil, garlic, and scallions and microwave, uncovered, on HIGH 3 minutes, until tender-crisp. Add pepper, oregano, parsley, wine, tomato, and clams. Stir to mix, then push hinged sides of clams toward edge of casserole. Cover tightly with plastic wrap and microwave on HIGH 5 to 7 minutes, or until clams open, stirring halfway through cooking. Discard any unopened clams.

Strain linguine and transfer to large deep bowl or to individual wide soup bowls. Ladle clams and sauce over linguine and serve at once in heated bowls.

BAKED AVOCADO WITH CRAB

6 SERVINGS

1 cup Basic White Sauce (page 76)

½ teaspoon freshly ground white pepper

1 teaspoon Worcestershire sauce

1 tablespoon dry sherry

1 (6-ounce) can crabmeat, drained and flaked

3 avocados, halved and pitted

½ cup grated sharp Cheddar cheese

Combine White Sauce with pepper, Worcestershire, sherry, and crabmeat in mixing bowl, stirring to blend. Spoon mixture into avocado halves and place in a shallow 2-quart casserole. Sprinkle with cheese. Microwave on 70% power 8 to 10 minutes, or until heated through.

DEVILED CRAB

4 OR 5 SERVINGS

1 medium onion, chopped

1 medium green or red bell pepper, chopped

½ cup chopped celery

1 pound fresh crabmeat, picked over

½ cup fresh bread crumbs

½ teaspoon freshly ground white pepper

1 tablespoon mustard

1 tablespoon catsup

1 tablespoon mayonnaise

When freezing crabmeat, cover with milk first to retain a fresh flavor.

In small bowl, combine onion, bell pepper, and celery, cover with plastic wrap, and microwave on HIGH 3 to 5 minutes, or until tender-crisp. Add crabmeat, bread crumbs, pepper, mustard, catsup, and mayonnaise and mix well.

Divide mixture among 4 3- to 4-inch ramekins or scallop shells and microwave, uncovered, on 70% power 5 to 7 minutes, or until hot and bubbly.

STEAMED CRABS

12 live blue crabs
3 tablespoons crab boil mix

1 tablespoon vinegar or fresh
  lemon juice

**2 OR 3
SERVINGS**

Put crabs, crab boil, and vinegar in deep 3- to 4-quart casserole and cover tightly with plastic wrap. Microwave on HIGH 6 to 7½ minutes. Rearrange crabs in casserole, moving uncooked portions to edge of dish, cover again, and microwave on HIGH 6 to 7½ minutes longer. Serve at once with lemon wedges and melted butter or Salsa (page 90).

Serve hot or cold, plain or with a sauce.

STEAMED LOBSTER

1 (1½-pound) live lobster (claws
  pegged)
½ cup water

1 teaspoon salt
Browned Butter (page 82)
Lemon wedges

2 SERVINGS

Combine lobster, water, and salt in deep 4-quart casserole. Cover tightly with plastic wrap and microwave on HIGH 9 to 12 minutes, or until shell turns red. Let stand, covered, several minutes, then serve with browned butter and lemon wedges.

Cooking two live lobsters in the microwave would take much longer than it does on top of the range, but cooking only one is ideal—no waiting around for the water to boil, no huge pot to clean up. Cooked in this simplest of ways, a lobster needs no further embellishment than browned butter and lemon wedges.

CLASSIC MUSSELS IN WHITE WINE

2 FIRST-COURSE SERVINGS

.

2 pounds mussels, well scrubbed
  and debearded
½ cup chopped celery
2 carrots, diced
1 medium onion, chopped
1 teaspoon minced garlic
½ teaspoon dried thyme

1 bay leaf
½ cup dry white wine
2 tablespoons chopped parsley
½ cup heavy cream
Salt
Freshly ground black pepper

In a 2-quart casserole, combine mussels, celery, carrots, onion, garlic, thyme, bay leaf, and white wine. Cover tightly with plastic wrap and microwave on HIGH 7 to 8 minutes, or until mussels open.

Transfer mussels to deep serving dish. Strain liquid into 2-cup measure through two layers of rinsed cheesecloth. Taste broth, then add parsley, cream, and salt and pepper to taste. Microwave on HIGH 1 minute to heat through and pour over mussels. Serve at once with crusty bread.

SCALLOPED OYSTERS

5 OR 6 SERVINGS

.

1 stick (½ cup) unsalted butter
½ cup half-and-half or light
  cream
¼ cup oyster liquor
½ teaspoon salt
¼ teaspoon freshly ground black
  pepper

½ teaspoon Worcestershire sauce
2 cups coarse saltine or butter
  cracker crumbs
12 oysters, shucked

In a 4-cup measure, melt butter on HIGH 45 to 60 seconds. Add half-and-half, oyster liquor, salt, pepper, and Worcestershire and microwave on HIGH 2 to 3 minutes, or until boiling.

Layer cracker crumbs and oysters in 2-quart casserole. Pour hot butter mixture on top. Cover and cook on 70% power 7 to 10 minutes, or until hot and bubbly. Let stand, covered, 5 minutes before serving.

COQUILLES SAINT-JACQUES

1 teaspoon minced garlic
2 tablespoons fresh lemon juice
1 pound scallops, washed and
    drained
1 pound boneless, skinless
    chicken breasts or tenders, cut
    into scallop-size pieces
1/2 cup chopped onion
1/2 cup chopped celery
2 cups sliced mushrooms (about 8
    ounces), or 1 (3-ounce) can
    sliced mushrooms, drained

1/2 stick (1/4 cup) unsalted butter or
    margarine
1/4 cup all-purpose flour
1/2 teaspoon freshly ground white
    pepper
1 cup light cream
1/2 cup milk
1 cup grated Gruyère cheese
1/3 cup dry white wine
3 tablespoons chopped parsley

8 SERVINGS

▪

This interesting version of the famous French specialty includes chicken as well as scallops in a Mornay sauce —a white sauce with cheese. An excellent main course for a special occasion, serve it with Perfect Rice (page 289) and follow with a salad of mixed greens and julienned cooked beets tossed with a lemon and dill vinaigrette.

In 2-quart dish, combine garlic, lemon juice, scallops, and chicken. Toss to coat scallops and chicken with liquid. Cover dish and refrigerate for at least 1 hour and up to 24 hours.

Place covered dish in microwave and cook on HIGH 4 to 6 minutes. Stir, cover again, and microwave on HIGH 3 to 5 minutes longer, or until scallops and chicken are completely cooked. Let dish stand, covered, while preparing vegetables and Mornay sauce.

Place onion and celery in 1-quart bowl, cover with plastic wrap, and microwave on HIGH 2 to 3 minutes. Add mushrooms, cover again, and microwave on HIGH 2 to 3 minutes longer, or until tender-crisp. Drain vegetables and stir into scallop-chicken mixture.

Place butter, flour, and pepper in 1-quart casserole and microwave on HIGH 1 to 1½ minutes, or until butter is melted. Stir roux, then add cream and milk and stir to blend well. Microwave, uncovered, 2 to 4 minutes, or until sauce is thickened, stirring once during cooking. Add cheese, wine, and parsley and stir until cheese melts. Stir cheese sauce into scallop-vegetable mixture.

Dish can be prepared a day in advance, covered, and kept in refrigerator. To reheat, place covered casserole in microwave and cook at 70% power 12 to 15 minutes, or until hot and bubbly. Serve at once.

STEAMED SCALLOPS

**2 OR 3
SERVINGS**

.

Scallops are an almost perfect protein. But best of all, they require very little advance preparation before cooking. These sweet, nutty mollusks can be fully enjoyed when they are steamed by themselves or with just a little lemon juice.

1 pound bay or sea scallops

1 lemon, thinly sliced, or 2 tablespoons fresh lemon juice (optional)

Arrange scallops in a circle around perimeter of 9-inch glass pie plate, leaving the center of plate empty. Spread lemon slices over scallops or sprinkle with lemon juice, if desired. Cover plate tightly with plastic wrap and microwave on 50 to 70% power 3 to 6 minutes for bay scallops and 4 to 7 minutes for sea scallops. Rearrange scallops once during cooking. Allow to stand, covered, 3 minutes before serving.

SCALLOPS PROVENÇALE

**2 OR 3
SERVINGS**

.

The two kinds of scallops most widely available are bay scallops, about ½ inch in diameter, and sea scallops, from 1 to 1½ inches in diameter. Steaming or poaching is the simplest way to cook scallops; just take care not to overcook them.

1 pound sea scallops
2 tablespoons fresh lemon juice
3 tablespoons unsalted butter
½ teaspoon minced garlic

2 tablespoons dry vermouth
¼ teaspoon salt
¼ teaspoon freshly ground white pepper

Combine scallops and lemon juice in shallow 2-quart casserole and allow to stand at room temperature 15 minutes. This will have the effect of "cooking" the scallops slightly. Drain scallops, pat dry, and return to casserole. Add butter, garlic, vermouth, salt, and pepper and stir to mix. Push scallops into a circle around perimeter of casserole.

Cover casserole tightly with plastic wrap and microwave on 70% power 4 to 5 minutes. Stir, cover again, and microwave on 70% power 2 to 3 minutes longer. Scallops will be opaque when cooked. Let stand, covered, 2 to 3 minutes before serving.

STEAMED SHRIMP

1 pound shrimp
1 lemon, thinly sliced, or 2
    tablespoons fresh lemon juice
    (optional)

Packaged seafood seasoning
    (optional)
Browned Butter (page 82)

**2 OR 3
SERVINGS**

▪

Shrimp steamed or
poached in the micro-
wave taste better and
stay juicier when
they're cooked in their
shells. Watch them
carefully so they don't
overcook.

Arrange shrimp in circle around perimeter of 9-inch pie plate or shallow casserole. Distribute lemon slices over shrimp or sprinkle with lemon juice and seafood seasoning to taste, if desired. Cover tightly with plastic wrap and microwave on HIGH 3 to 6 minutes, stirring once to rearrange shrimp. Shrimp are cooked when they turn pink. Uncover to prevent overcooking. Serve with browned butter.

CURRIED SHRIMP

2 pounds shrimp, peeled and
    deveined
1/2 cup chopped scallions
1 (10¾-ounce) can condensed
    cream of shrimp soup

1 cup sour cream or yogurt
1 teaspoon curry powder, or to
    taste
Salt
Freshly ground white pepper

6 SERVINGS

▪

Enjoy this easily made
curry served over Per-
fect Rice (page 289)
and accompanied by
condiments such as
raisins, chopped green
bell pepper, and
toasted almonds.

Place shrimp and scallions in 2-quart casserole, cover tightly, and microwave on HIGH 5 to 6 minutes, or until shrimp are pink, stirring several times during cooking.

Add soup, sour cream, curry powder, and salt and pepper to taste and stir to blend ingredients. Cover again and microwave at 70% power 5 to 8 minutes, or until hot and bubbly, stirring several times.

SHRIMP ETOUFFÉE

4 TO 6 SERVINGS

■

Simply scrumptious served over Perfect Rice (page 289).

1 large onion, chopped
1 large red or green bell pepper, chopped
2 stalks celery, chopped
6 to 8 garlic cloves, minced

2 pounds shrimp, peeled and deveined
1/4 cup chopped parsley
1/2 cup chopped scallion tops
Salt
Cayenne pepper

Place onion, bell pepper, celery, and garlic in 2-quart casserole. Cover and microwave on HIGH 4 to 5 minutes.

Add shrimp to casserole, arranging them around edge of dish. Cover again and microwave on HIGH 5 to 8 minutes, or until shrimp are pink, checking after 5 minutes. Stir in parsley, scallion tops, and salt and cayenne to taste.

LOW-COUNTRY SHRIMP BOIL

6 TO 8 SERVINGS

■

A modern-day version of a summertime meal that was prepared in the 1800s along any seacoast, when corn was plentiful, the sausage was in the smokehouse, and the shrimp were running. This recipe was often used to serve large crowds on the lawn.

4 cups sliced onions
4 ears corn, husked and broken into 3-inch pieces
2 tablespoons packaged seafood seasoning (Old Bay Seafood Seasoning preferred)

1 pound Polish sausage (kielbasa), cut into 1-inch pieces
2 pounds shrimp or crawfish, rinsed
Garlic salt
Freshly ground black pepper
Hot pepper sauce

Place onions, corn, and seafood seasoning in 4-quart casserole or microwave-safe clay pot, cover, and microwave on HIGH 7 to 9 minutes, or until onions are tender-crisp.

Add sausage, shrimp, and garlic salt, black pepper, and hot pepper sauce to taste and stir to mix. Cover again and microwave on HIGH 7 to 10 minutes longer, or until shrimp are pink and cooked, stirring once or twice. Serve with coleslaw and crusty bread.

JAMBALAYA

2 teaspoons minced garlic
1 cup chopped scallions
2 cups chopped onions
1 cup chopped celery
¼ cup olive oil or bacon drippings
1 (16-ounce) can tomatoes, chopped, undrained
1 (16-ounce) can tomato sauce
3 tablespoons chopped parsley
1 teaspoon dried basil
1 teaspoon dried thyme
1 tablespoon sugar
½ teaspoon freshly ground white pepper

1 teaspoon freshly ground black pepper
Salt
1 pound boneless, skinless chicken breasts, cooked (page 169) and cut into bite-size pieces
2 pounds raw shrimp, peeled and deveined
1 pound smoked sausage, cut into ½-inch pieces

10 TO 12 SERVINGS

■

A spicy well-known Creole dish that contains shrimp or other shellfish, pork sausage or ham, and chicken, all cooked in a tomato-based sauce with green pepper, onions, herbs, and spices. This dish is better if prepared several hours before serving time or even the day before. Serve over Perfect Rice (page 289).

In 4-quart casserole, combine garlic, scallions, onions, celery, and olive oil. Cover and microwave on HIGH 4 to 7 minutes, or until vegetables are tender-crisp.

Stir in tomatoes, tomato sauce, parsley, basil, thyme, sugar, white and black pepper, and salt to taste. Cover again and microwave on HIGH 8 to 12 minutes, or until boiling. Stir sauce, taste, and adjust seasonings. Cover again and microwave mixture on 30% power 15 to 20 minutes.

Add chicken, shrimp, and sausage and stir well. Cover and microwave on 50% power for 10 to 15 minutes, or until shrimp are pink.

SHRIMP AND ANGEL HAIR PASTA WITH GARLIC-BASIL SAUCE

4 TO 6 SERVINGS

▪

¼ cup extra-virgin olive oil
1 tablespoon unsalted butter or margarine
3 cloves garlic, minced
1 medium onion, finely chopped
½ cup fresh basil, chopped
½ cup parsley, chopped
1 pound large shrimp, peeled and deveined

2 cups heavy cream
½ teaspoon freshly ground white pepper
Salt
1 pound angel hair pasta, cooked conventionally and drained
Freshly grated Parmesan cheese

Combine oil, butter, garlic, and onion in 2-quart casserole. Cover and microwave on HIGH 3 to 4 minutes. Stir in basil, parsley, and shrimp. Cover again and cook on HIGH 3 to 4 minutes or until shrimp turn pink.

Remove shrimp with slotted spoon and set aside. Add cream, white pepper, and salt to taste. Cover and microwave on 70% power 5 to 6 minutes.

Combine sauce with just-cooked and drained pasta. Sprinkle with Parmesan cheese and arrange shrimp on top.

SHRIMP MOSCA

4 SERVINGS

▪

Serve when good food takes precedence over formality! Provide hand towels or a generous supply of napkins.

⅓ cup olive oil or unsalted butter
2 teaspoons minced garlic
1½ teaspoons freshly ground black pepper

2 teaspoons dried oregano
2 teaspoons dried rosemary
2 pounds large shrimp

In 2-quart casserole, combine oil, garlic, black pepper, oregano, and rosemary. Microwave on HIGH 2 to 3 minutes. Add shrimp and stir to coat with garlic mixture. Push shrimp to side of dish, leaving center empty. Cover and cook on HIGH 5 to 7 minutes, or until shrimp are pink and opaque. Let stand, covered, for 2 to 3 minutes.

SHRIMP PILAU

1½ cups basmati *or long-grain* rice

3 cups water

1 teaspoon salt

2 large onions, chopped

2 or 3 cloves garlic, minced

2 bay leaves

1 teaspoon black mustard seeds (available at Oriental food shops)

5 whole cloves

10 black peppercorns

½ stick (¼ cup) unsalted butter or vegetable oil

4 large tomatoes, chopped, or 1 (16-ounce) can tomatoes, drained

½ teaspoon ground coriander

½ teaspoon ground cumin

½ teaspoon curry powder

½ teaspoon cayenne pepper

1½ pounds medium shrimp

1 (10-ounce) package frozen peas, defrosted

1 cup sliced blanched almonds, toasted (page 441)

6 SERVINGS

·

If you enjoy spicy Indian food, this will become a favorite.

Place rice in 2-quart casserole with water and salt, cover, and microwave on HIGH 8 minutes; reduce power to 50% and cook 12 minutes longer. Keep rice warm.

In another 2-quart casserole, combine onions, garlic, bay leaves, mustard seeds, cloves, peppercorns, and butter. Cover and microwave on HIGH 4 to 6 minutes, or until onions are tender-crisp. Stir in tomatoes, coriander, cumin, curry powder, and cayenne. Cover again and microwave on HIGH 4 to 5 minutes, or until hot.

Stir in shrimp, cover tightly, and microwave on HIGH 4 to 5 minutes, or until shrimp turn pink. Add peas and cook on HIGH 1 to 2 minutes, or until peas are heated through. Remove whole cloves and peppercorns.

Spread rice on heated platter, then mound shrimp mixture over rice. Sprinkle with almonds and serve at once.

To open fresh clams and oysters, soak them in cold water for 3 to 4 hours. Arrange 5 or 6 oysters or clams in a circle in a casserole. Cover tightly with plastic wrap and microwave on HIGH 45 seconds to 1 minute or until the shells open. Remove each shellfish as it opens and continue cooking any unopened shellfish for 15-second intervals. Discard unopened oysters or clams.

Stir-Fry Shrimp with Fried Rice

4 TO 6 SERVINGS

•

¼ cup vegetable oil
2 large eggs, beaten
1 to 1½ cups chopped scallions
3 or 4 cloves garlic, minced
½ teaspoon freshly ground white pepper

1 pound shrimp, peeled and deveined
1 (8-ounce) can sliced water chestnuts, drained
5 to 6 cups cooked rice (page 289), chilled
⅓ cup low-sodium soy sauce

Place 1 tablespoon oil in 2-quart casserole and microwave on HIGH 1 minute. Pour in eggs and cook on HIGH 1 minute. Stir and cook on HIGH 30 to 45 seconds longer, or until eggs appear dry. Transfer eggs to another dish and reserve.

Add remaining oil to same casserole along with scallions, garlic, pepper, and shrimp, arranging shrimp in a circle around perimeter of dish. Microwave, covered, 4 to 6 minutes, or until shrimp turn pink. Stir, then add water chestnuts, rice, and soy sauce and stir again to mix well. Microwave on HIGH 3 to 5 minutes, or until hot. Stir in scrambled eggs and serve at once.

VARIATION

Substitute leftover thinly sliced cooked meat such as chicken breast, ham, turkey, or beef for the shrimp.

Spicy Shrimp

4 SERVINGS

•

A natural prepared in the microwave. Enjoy with a green salad and crusty bread.

1 tablespoon unsalted butter or oil
1 pound shrimp, peeled and deveined
1 tablespoon grated fresh ginger
2 tablespoons chopped scallions

1 tablespoon chopped red or green bell pepper
1 tablespoon dry white wine
2 tablespoons catsup
Cayenne pepper

Place butter, shrimp, ginger, scallions, and bell pepper in shallow 2-quart casserole, arranging shrimp in a circle around perimeter of dish. Cover with plastic wrap and microwave on HIGH 2 to 3 minutes. Stir and add wine, catsup, and cayenne pepper. Cover again and cook on HIGH 1 to 2 minutes, or until shrimp are pink.

SHRIMP PRIMAVERA

1/2 cup unsalted butter or margarine
3 tablespoons all-purpose flour
1/2 cup chopped scallions
1 cup chopped fresh basil, or 2 teaspoons dried
3 or 4 cloves garlic, minced
1 teaspoon freshly ground white pepper
1 1/2 cups heavy cream
1 1/2 cups freshly grated Parmesan cheese
Milk for thinning sauce

3 cups cooked chicken breast (page 169), cut into bite-size pieces
1 pound shrimp, steamed (page 155) and peeled
1 pound fettucine or linguine, cooked conventionally al dente *and drained*
2 cups each 3 to 4 vegetables of choice: fresh asparagus, cauliflowerets, sliced zucchini, yellow squash, carrots, mushrooms, and others

8 SERVINGS

•

A beautiful company dish that can be partially prepared before guests arrive—just cook the vegetables at the last minute. Serve with crusty bread, fresh fruit, and a good white wine.

In 4-quart casserole, combine butter, flour, scallions, basil, garlic, and white pepper. Cover and cook on HIGH 3 to 4 minutes, stirring once. Add cream and microwave on 70% power 4 to 6 minutes. Stir in cheese and thin with milk if needed.

Stir cooked chicken pieces and half the shrimp into cream sauce and set aside.

While fettucine cooks, arrange vegetables on a platter, denser ones close to perimeter, cover with plastic wrap, and microwave on HIGH 8 to 12 minutes.

Drain fettucine and toss with cream sauce, then pour onto a large platter. Arrange vegetables on top and garnish with remaining shrimp. Serve at once.

Fresh Seafood Medley

1 medium onion, chopped
1 teaspoon minced garlic
1 tablespoon chopped parsley
1/2 teaspoon salt
1/2 teaspoon freshly ground white
    pepper
2 teaspoons Worcestershire sauce
1 cup mayonnaise (page 116)
1/2 to 3/4 cup freshly grated
    Parmesan cheese

1 cup heavy cream
1 (14-ounce) can artichoke hearts,
    drained and chopped
1 cup fresh crabmeat, picked over
1 cup (about 8 ounces) shrimp,
    peeled and deveined
4 hard-cooked eggs (page 122),
    sliced
1 cup toasted fresh bread crumbs

Combine onion and garlic in 1-quart measure, cover with plastic wrap, and microwave on HIGH 3 to 4 minutes, or until vegetables are tender-crisp. Stir in parsley, salt, pepper, Worcestershire and mayonnaise and blend sauce well. Add Parmesan and heavy cream and stir again. Reserve sauce.

In 2-quart casserole, make single layers as follows: artichokes, crabmeat, shrimp, and eggs. Spread sauce over eggs. Cover casserole tightly with plastic wrap and microwave on HIGH 5 minutes. Stir gently, bringing ingredients around perimeter to inside of casserole. Cover again and cook on 70% power 12 to 15 minutes, or until shrimp turn pink. Carefully uncover and sprinkle bread crumbs on top. Let casserole stand, covered, for 3 to 4 minutes before serving.

Poultry

From early recorded history, poultry has been a favorite meat. It is an ideal choice for microwaving because it is naturally juicy and tender. Poultry is one of the most economical and best sources of protein and is also lower in calories and cholesterol than many meats. Because it is so versatile, it can be served as an elegant entrée at a dinner party or as an everyday dish for a family meal.

Proper microwave cooking produces tender meat with a delicate flavor, which combines well with other foods and spices in a wide variety of dishes. No matter which way you choose to microwave poultry, you will always be happy with the results if the following guidelines are used.

PURCHASING POULTRY

When buying chicken, select plump broilers weighing 2½ pounds or more. All poultry should be smooth-skinned and have light-colored flesh. Do not buy prepackaged fresh poultry that is sitting in a pool of its juices. Fresh poultry is quite perishable and should be used the day it is purchased, or the next day at the latest. If longer storage is required, freeze the poultry.

When buying frozen poultry, be sure the package is intact. Torn or open packages can cause freezer burn and result in loss of flavor.

COOKING POULTRY

To help prevent salmonella poisoning: Before cooking *any* poultry, scrub skin with a vegetable brush in hot water to remove the oily film and wash away harmful bacteria. Wash cavity of whole birds under warm running water. Rinse off skinless poultry under warm water. Pat meat dry with paper towels. Wash all utensils and work surface before letting other food touch them.

Be sure poultry is completely cooked and that the juices run clear. If juices are still pink, continue cooking.

When cooking poultry with a "pop-out" doneness indicator, it may be left in the meat, but it will not indicate doneness. Also the metal clips that hold the drumsticks in place need not be removed.

COOKING WHOLE BIRDS

Place the bird, breast side down, on a microwave baking rack set in a shallow casserole. (For smaller poultry, a saucer turned upside down may be used in place of a rack.) If you want the bird to taste roasted, not boiled or steamed, do not let it stand in its own juices.

Parts such as wings or legs often cook faster than the rest, just as in conventional cooking. If the use of foil is permitted in your oven, shield these areas by covering them with small pieces of foil to prevent overcooking. (See Shielding, page 12.)

Because microwave energy is attracted to the fat in drippings, you may need to drain off the juices several times during cooking, which will also reduce cooking time. Drape wax paper loosely over the bird to prevent the juices from splattering.

DEFROSTING POULTRY IN THE MICROWAVE

1. Leave poultry in the original wrapping and place it in a casserole to catch any liquid.
2. Begin defrosting whole poultry with the breast side up. Turn a turkey or chicken over midway through defrosting.
3. Poultry should still be icy in the center when it is removed from the microwave. Complete the thawing by immersing the bird in cold water. Poultry should be completely thawed before cooking so it will cook evenly.
4. Remove giblets from the cavity of whole poultry before cooking and reserve them for another use.

TIMETABLE FOR DEFROSTING POULTRY

POULTRY	50% POWER (MINUTES/POUND)	30% POWER (MINUTES/POUND)
Whole chicken	4 to 6	5 to 9
Chicken quarters	5 to 6	6 to 9
Chicken pieces	3 to 5	5 to 9
Chicken breast, boneless	6 to 8	9 to 13
Capon	5 to 6	9 to 12
Cornish hens	5 to 7	9 to 12
Duck	5 to 6	9 to 12
Turkey, whole	4 to 6	6 to 8
Turkey, half	4 to 6	6 to 8
Turkey, pieces	4 to 6	7 to 9
Turkey cutlets	6 to 8	10 to 12

BROWNING

A whole turkey, chicken, or duck will brown naturally without a glaze. If you prefer a rich, darker color, brush the bird with a bottled glaze, or make your own using equal amounts of browning bouquet sauce and butter. First, dry the bird with a paper towel, then *rub* the mixture into the skin. (Brushing the glaze on can cause streaking.)

After the bird is out of the microwave, allow the meat to stand to finish cooking. Chicken should stand 5 minutes, and turkey 15 minutes. The poultry will be easier to carve after standing.

Poultry is cooked when the juices run clear. The meat will be fork tender, with no pinkness showing after standing time.

CARVING WHOLE POULTRY

Proper carving produces attractive, uniform slices.

Begin by pulling the drumstick away from the body of the bird. Cut through the meat between the thigh and backbone, using the tip of the knife to disjoint the leg. Slice the meat from the leg, holding the leg vertically and cutting parallel to the bone. Slice the thigh meat parallel to the bone.

To carve the white meat, first make a deep horizontal cut into the breast close to the wing. At this point, remove the wing if desired by slicing vertically between the wing and the body. Using straight, even strokes, cut thin slices across the grain from the top of the breast down to the horizontal cut.

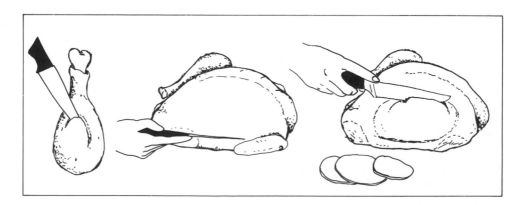

WHOLE CHICKEN

Wash and dry a 3- to 3½-pound chicken. If wings are to be left in place during carving, fold wing tips behind back. Place chicken breast side down on baking rack or inverted saucer placed in casserole. Cover loosely with wax paper to prevent splattering. Microwave on HIGH 7 to 10 minutes per pound. Turn bird breast side up halfway through cooking and drain fat. Remove bird from oven and let stand 5 minutes as meat continues to cook. (As in conventional cooking, meat continues to cook after it is removed from oven.)

When chicken is done, juices will run clear with no hint of pink, leg will move freely in socket, and meat thermometer inserted into breast will register 170° F.

If a crisp skin is preferred, place cooked chicken in preheated 500° F. conventional oven 6 to 8 minutes.

> To close the cavity of whole poultry, use wooden picks to secure. Tie the legs together with a cotton or nylon string.

WHOLE TURKEY

Whole turkey should be no larger than 10 to 14 pounds. There should be at least 2 to 3 inches of space between turkey and microwave oven wall.

Wash and dry bird and, if wings are to be left in place during carving, fold wing tips behind back. Place turkey breast side down on baking rack set in dish to catch drippings. Microwave turkey on HIGH 10 minutes.

Reduce power to 50% and microwave 12 to 15 minutes per pound. Halfway through cooking time, turn turkey breast side up and drain fat, then continue cooking. Remove bird from oven, tent with foil, and let stand 10 to 15 minutes to finish cooking and to firm up so it will be easier to carve.

Turkey is done when juices run clear with no hint of pink, leg moves freely in socket, and a thermometer stuck into thigh or breast registers 170° F.

If crisp skin is preferred, place cooked turkey in preheated 500° F. conventional oven 6 to 8 minutes.

> **COOKED POULTRY**
> Leftover cooked chicken or turkey should be regarded as an opportunity to easily create dishes that are speedy and convenient, as many recipes in this chapter attest.

WHOLE CAPON, CORNISH GAME HENS, DUCKLING, AND PHEASANT

Cook on a baking rack set in a casserole to catch drippings. After microwaving, tent the bird with foil and let stand 5 to 10 minutes. For capon, follow carving instructions on page 166. Use kitchen shears to cut game hen, duckling, and pheasant into quarters.

CAPON

Cook a whole capon weighing 6 to 7 pounds on HIGH 4 minutes per pound, breast side down. Turn capon breast side up and cook on 70% power 3 to 4 minutes per pound, or until a meat thermometer registers 180° F.

CORNISH GAME HEN

Microwave 1 or 2 whole hens, breast side down, on HIGH 8 to 9 minutes per pound. Halfway through cooking time, turn hen(s) over breast side up.

DUCKLING

Cook a whole duck weighing 4 to 5 pounds on HIGH 10 minutes. Drain and microwave on 70% power 6 to 8 minutes per pound. After first half of cooking time, turn duck over breast side up. Cook until juices run clear and meat is no longer pink near the bone.

PHEASANT

Cook a whole pheasant weighing 2 to 3 pounds on 70% power 8 to 9 minutes per pound or until 180° F. is reached on a meat thermometer and the juices run clear.

NOTE:

A hen (or stewing chicken) requires long, slow cooking whether cooked conventionally or in the microwave. We prefer cooking it conventionally because there is no real time saving. Hens are best used in stews and soups.

COOKING CHICKEN PARTS

Place chicken pieces in casserole with thicker parts placed next to outside edge of dish. Overlap thinner portions. Cover and microwave on HIGH 7 to 10 minutes per pound. Let stand 5 minutes before serving.

TIMETABLE FOR COOKING INDIVIDUAL CHICKEN PIECES

NUMBER OF PIECES (BREAST, LEG, OR THIGH)	MINUTES ON HIGH POWER
1	3 to 5
2	6 to 7
3	8 to 9
4	9 to 11
1 quarter	8 to 9

BONELESS CHICKEN BREASTS

Place chicken breasts in casserole and cover with a layer on top of thin lemon slices and fresh herbs, if desired. Cover and microwave on HIGH 5 to 7 minutes, rearranging once halfway through cooking. Allow to stand, covered, 5 minutes before using.

(One pound of boneless chicken breasts yields 2 cups cubed cooked chicken.)

COOKING A TURKEY BREAST

Place 4½- to 5-pound turkey breast, skin side down, in 2-quart shallow casserole. Microwave uncovered on HIGH 5 minutes. Reduce power to 50% and microwave 11 to 15 minutes per pound. Turn the breast skin side up halfway through cooking time. After removing from microwave, cover loosely with foil and allow to stand for 15 minutes.

BARBECUED WHOLE CHICKEN

4 TO 6 SERVINGS

•

To achieve a wonderful smoky barbecue flavor, first cook the poultry in the microwave, then finish up on the barbecue grill. This combination of cooking procedures saves time and energy and produces moist, tender meat with a crisp browned skin.

1 (2½- to 3½-pound) chicken　　　*1 cup Barbecue Sauce (page 86) or bottled barbecue sauce*

Preheat a charcoal or gas outdoor grill.

Place chicken, breast side down, in 10-inch casserole and microwave on HIGH 5 minutes. Turn bird breast side up and cook on 70% power 10 minutes.

Transfer bird to foil roasting pan, brush generously with barbecue sauce, and place on grill over hot coals. Cover grill and cook chicken 18 to 20 minutes, or until juices run clear and meat near bone is no longer pink. Brush again with sauce 5 minutes before end of cooking time.

BARBECUED CHICKEN PARTS

4 TO 6 SERVINGS

•

1 (2½- to 3½-pound) chicken, cut into 8 serving pieces, skin removed (optional)　　　*1 cup Barbecue Sauce (page 86) or bottled barbecue sauce*

Preheat a charcoal or gas outdoor grill.

Place chicken in 12 × 8-inch casserole, arranging pieces bony sides down and thicker parts toward outside of dish. Cover loosely with wax paper and microwave on HIGH 10 to 15 minutes, turning and rearranging pieces halfway through cooking time.

Brush chicken with barbecue sauce and place on grill, skin sides down. Grill 15 to 20 minutes, or until juices run clear and meat is no longer pink near bone. Brush again with sauce 5 minutes before end of cooking time.

GRILLED TURKEY

1 (12- to 14-pound) turkey

*1 recipe Barbecue Sauce (page 86)
or bottled barbecue sauce*

1 recipe Barbecue Sauce (page 86)

**14 TO 16
SERVINGS**

Preheat a charcoal or gas grill.
Place turkey, breast side down, in 12 × 8-inch glass baking dish and microwave on HIGH 10 minutes. Cook on 50% power 25 minutes longer. Turn bird breast side up and continue cooking on 50% power 25 to 30 minutes.

Transfer turkey to foil roasting pan, brush generously with barbecue sauce, and place on grill over hot coals. Cover grill and cook 35 to 45 minutes, or until juices run clear and meat near bone is no longer pink. Brush with sauce several times during last 20 minutes of cooking time.

Soak mesquite or hickory chips in water for 30 to 40 minutes and place them on the coals just before putting the meat on the grill.

STEWED CHICKEN

1 onion, cut into wedges
1 (2½- to 3-pound) chicken
2 or 3 cloves garlic, sliced
½ cup water
½ cup white wine
1 chicken bouillon cube

1 teaspoon dried basil
1 teaspoon dried marjoram
1 teaspoon dried rosemary
1 teaspoon salt
*½ to 1 teaspoon freshly ground
black or white pepper*

**4 TO 6
SERVINGS**

Wine and herbs impart a wonderful flavor. Good served with buttered egg noodles.

Put onion wedges in chicken cavity. Slip garlic slices under breast and thigh skin. Place chicken, breast side down, in deep 4-quart casserole or microwavable clay pot.

Pour water and wine into 2-cup measure, add bouillon cube, and microwave on HIGH 2 minutes, or until liquid is hot. Stir until bouillon cube is dissolved, add basil, marjoram, rosemary, salt, and pepper, and pour mixture over chicken.

Cover casserole and microwave on HIGH 15 minutes. Turn chicken breast side up and baste. Cover again and microwave on HIGH 15 to 20 minutes longer, or until meat is no longer pink near bone and juices run clear.

CHICKEN AND WILD RICE SUPREME

8 SERVINGS

·

You can cook and assemble this dish a day ahead, then reheat just before serving. It's a good choice for a casual dinner party.

1 (2½- to 3-pound) chicken
½ teaspoon salt
½ teaspoon curry powder
1 onion, cut into quarters
2 or 3 cloves garlic, peeled
2 or 3 celery tops
½ cup water
½ cup dry sherry

1 (6-ounce) package long-grain and wild rice with seasonings
1 cup sour cream
½ stick (¼ cup) unsalted butter, melted
8 ounces mushrooms, sliced
½ teaspoon freshly ground white pepper

Place chicken, breast side down, in deep 3- or 4-quart casserole. Sprinkle with salt and curry powder. Tuck onion, garlic, and celery around chicken and pour water and sherry over all. Cover tightly and microwave on HIGH 15 minutes. Turn chicken over, cover again, and microwave on HIGH 15 to 20 minutes longer, or until chicken is cooked. Thigh bone should move easily in socket and thigh juices will run clear. Let chicken stand, covered, 5 minutes to complete cooking. Remove chicken from stock and let cool. Strain and reserve stock, discarding vegetables.

When chicken is cool enough to handle, remove and discard skin, bones, and cartilage. Cut meat into bite-size pieces and reserve.

Cook rice following package instructions, using reserved chicken broth with water added as liquid. Transfer rice to a 2-quart casserole, then fold reserved chicken, sour cream, butter, mushrooms, and pepper into hot rice.

Cover casserole tightly with plastic wrap and microwave on HIGH 10 minutes. Stir rice mixture gently, cover again, and microwave on 70% power 10 to 15 minutes longer, or until hot throughout.

CHICKEN PAPRIKA

3 slices bacon
1 cup chopped onions
1 cup all-purpose flour
1 teaspoon paprika
1 teaspoon salt

GRAVY

2 tablespoons all-purpose flour
$^1/_2$ teaspoon paprika
$^1/_2$ teaspoon salt
$^1/_4$ to $^1/_2$ teaspoon freshly ground
   white pepper

1 teaspoon freshly ground white
   pepper
1 (2$^1/_2$- to 3-pound) chicken, cut
   into 8 pieces and skin
   removed

$^1/_2$ cup sour cream
$^1/_2$ cup milk
1 cup Chicken Stock (page 47) or
   canned chicken broth

4 TO 6 SERVINGS

One of the national dishes of Hungary. Serve over plain wide egg noodles or Poppy Seed Noodles (page 285).

Put bacon in shallow 2-quart casserole, cover with plastic wrap, and microwave on HIGH 3 to 4 minutes. Drain bacon on paper towels. Add onions to drippings in casserole, cover, and microwave on HIGH 4 to 5 minutes.

In shallow bowl or on piece of wax paper, combine flour, paprika, salt, and pepper. Dredge chicken pieces in flour mixture, then place in casserole with onions, arranging pieces so that thicker parts are close to perimeter of dish. Spoon some bacon drippings and onions over chicken, cover dish, and microwave on HIGH 15 to 18 minutes, or until chicken is cooked and juices run clear.

To make gravy, remove chicken from casserole with slotted spoon. Stir in flour, paprika, salt, and pepper, then add sour cream, milk, and stock, blending well. Microwave, uncovered, on HIGH 3 minutes. Stir and cook on 70% power 3 to 4 minutes, or until gravy is slightly thickened.

Return chicken to casserole and spoon gravy over it. Cook on 50% power 5 minutes, or until chicken is reheated. Crumble bacon and sprinkle over chicken.

CHICKEN AND DUMPLINGS

4 TO 6 SERVINGS

■

The ultimate in comfort food.

1 (2½- to 3-pound) chicken, cut
    into 8 pieces, or 2½ to 3
    pounds chicken parts
1 onion, chopped
3 carrots, sliced
3 stalks celery, with leaves, sliced
3 tablespoons chopped parsley
½ teaspoon dried rosemary

½ teaspoon dried thyme leaves
1 teaspoon salt
½ teaspoon freshly ground white
    pepper
1 cup water
1 (10-ounce) package frozen snow
    peas or green peas

DUMPLINGS

2 cups all-purpose flour
½ stick (¼ cup) cold unsalted
    butter, cut into 1-inch pieces
1 tablespoon baking powder
1 tablespoon chopped parsley

2 teaspoons chopped fresh sage
    leaves, or ¼ teaspoon dried
½ teaspoon salt
½ teaspoon freshly ground white
    pepper
¾ cup milk

A good way to salt chicken and improve its flavor is to soak the bird in salted water in the refrigerator for several hours before cooking or overnight. Use a ratio of 1 teaspoon of salt to 1½ cups of water. This is one of the secrets of making wonderful Southern fried chicken.

Place chicken in deep 3-quart casserole and add onion, carrots, celery, parsley, rosemary, thyme, salt, and pepper. Pour water over chicken and cover casserole tightly with plastic wrap. Microwave on HIGH 20 minutes. Rearrange chicken in casserole, cover again, and microwave on HIGH 10 to 15 minutes longer, or until chicken is cooked. Remove chicken from casserole, reserving broth and vegetables. When chicken is cool, remove skin and bones, cut meat into bite-size pieces, and reserve.

While chicken cools, prepare dumplings in food processor or bowl. If using processor, place flour and baking powder in processor bowl and pulse several times. Add butter, parsley, sage, salt, and pepper and pulse 5 or 6 times, or until butter is cut into size of small peas. Remove processor cover and pour milk in circle on top of flour mixture. Replace cover and quickly pulse mixture until it just holds together.

If making dumplings by hand, combine flour and baking powder in bowl, add butter and cut in with pastry blender or two knives. Stir in herbs and seasonings, then add milk, stirring with a fork, until mixture is just combined.

Measure reserved chicken broth and vegetables and add enough water to make 1 quart. Pour liquid into casserole in which chicken cooked, and microwave on HIGH 4 to 5 minutes, or until boiling. Drop heaping teaspoons of dumpling mixture into broth, cover with casserole lid or plastic wrap, and microwave on HIGH 10 to 14 minutes. Do not uncover for the first 10 minutes of cooking. Add snow peas and chicken pieces, cover again, and let stand 5 minutes, or until chicken is very hot and snow peas are tender-crisp.

CHICKEN CURRY

1 (3- to 3½-pound) chicken, cut
    into 8 pieces and skin
    removed
2 cups chopped onions
¼ cup clarified butter (page 81)
1 teaspoon salt
½ teaspoon freshly ground black
    pepper
1 teaspoon grated fresh ginger or
    ½ teaspoon ground ginger
½ teaspoon cayenne pepper

Pinch of saffron threads
2 teaspoons coriander seeds
1 cup plain low-fat yogurt
1 recipe Palau (page 293)
1 cup sliced blanched almonds,
    toasted (page 441)
1 cup raisins
½ cup chopped scallions
    (optional)
½ cup chopped green bell pepper
    (optional)

**4 TO 6
SERVINGS**

The spices and condiments in this curry combine for an intriguing blend of textures and flavors. The curry is first cooked in the microwave and then finished in a conventional oven.

Preheat conventional oven to 400° F.

In shallow 3-quart casserole that can be used in both microwave and conventional ovens, arrange chicken pieces with meatier parts near perimeter of dish. Cover with plastic wrap and microwave on HIGH 12 to 14 minutes.

Combine onions, butter, salt, black pepper, ginger, cayenne, saffron, and coriander seeds in 2-cup measure, cover with plastic wrap, and microwave on HIGH 4 to 5 minutes, or until butter is bubbling and permeated with flavor of spices.

Stir yogurt into spice mixture and pour over chicken, turning pieces over to coat with sauce. Bake, uncovered, on top rack of preheated conventional oven for 20 to 25 minutes, or until browned. While chicken cooks, prepare Palau.

To serve, spoon Palau on platter, arrange chicken on top and pour sauce over chicken. Sprinkle with toasted almonds, raisins, and, if desired, scallions and bell pepper.

CHICKEN TERIYAKI

4 TO 6 SERVINGS

■

This dish can be partially prepared the day before. This is an excellent recipe to finish cooking on the grill.

2 tablespoons vegetable oil
1/4 cup soy sauce
2 tablespoons dry white wine
3 or 4 cloves garlic, minced
1 onion, chopped
1 tablespoon brown sugar

1 teaspoon chili powder
1/2 teaspoon ground ginger
1 (2 1/2- to 3-pound) chicken, cut into 8 pieces and skin removed

To prepare marinade, place oil, soy sauce, wine, garlic, onion, sugar, chili powder, and ginger in blender or food processor and process until onion is pureed. Place chicken in bowl and add marinade, turning pieces to coat. Cover and refrigerate at least 1 hour or as long as 24 hours.

If planning to finish cooking chicken on grill, prepare it, or preheat a conventional broiler.

Remove chicken from marinade, reserving marinade, and arrange in shallow 2-quart casserole, placing thicker parts close to perimeter of dish. Cover and microwave on HIGH 8 to 10 minutes. Baste with marinade, turn chicken over, and baste again. If chicken will be finished on grill, arrange pieces over coals or under broiler, and cook until juices run clear. If you prefer to finish chicken in microwave, cover and microwave on 70% power 10 to 12 minutes, or until chicken is cooked and juices run clear.

CHICKEN CACCIATORE

4 SERVINGS

■

Delicious and low-calorie, too!

1 (16-ounce) can stewed tomatoes, undrained
1 large green bell pepper, chopped
1 medium onion, chopped
2 or 3 cloves garlic, minced
2 cups sliced mushrooms
1 tablespoon chopped parsley
1 teaspoon dried basil

1/4 teaspoon dried thyme
1 teaspoon salt
1/4 teaspoon freshly ground black pepper
1 1/2 pounds boneless, skinless chicken breasts, cut into bite-size pieces

In shallow 2-quart casserole, combine tomatoes, bell pepper, onion, garlic, mushrooms, parsley, basil, thyme, salt, and black pepper and stir to blend well. Cover and microwave on HIGH 4 to 6 minutes, or until tender.

Uncover and stir in chicken pieces. Cover again and microwave on 70% power 10 to 15 minutes, or until chicken is cooked, stirring after 6 or 7 minutes. Serve over rice or noodles.

CHICKEN·BROCCOLI COMBO

1 pound boneless, skinless
   chicken breasts, cut into
   1-inch pieces
½ teaspoon Oriental sesame oil
2 tablespoons vegetable oil
1 tablespoon soy sauce
1 tablespoon fresh lemon juice

1 to 2 teaspoons minced garlic
½ teaspoon freshly ground white
   pepper
4 cups fresh broccoli flowerets
3 tablespoons sesame seeds,
   toasted (page 441)

**4 TO 6
SERVINGS**

Simple, quick, and delicious! Serve with Perfect Rice (page 289).

In 3-quart casserole, combine chicken, sesame oil, vegetable oil, soy sauce, lemon juice, garlic, and pepper and mix well to coat chicken. Let marinate 20 minutes.

Cover and microwave chicken mixture on HIGH 8 to 11 minutes or until chicken is cooked, stirring several times. Set aside.

Place broccoli in 1½-quart casserole. Cover and microwave on HIGH 4 to 6 minutes or until tender-crisp. Toss broccoli with chicken. Sprinkle with sesame seeds and serve at once.

CHICKEN PARMIGIANO REGGIANO

4 SERVINGS

This dish receives its name from Reggio in Italy, where Parmesan —supreme among Italian cheeses—is produced. Enjoy this low-fat hard cheese freshly grated whenever possible.

1 tablespoon olive oil
½ cup finely chopped onion
1 (8-ounce) can tomato sauce
1 teaspoon dried basil
2 or 3 cloves garlic, minced
½ teaspoon salt
½ teaspoon freshly ground black pepper

1 teaspoon sugar
4 boneless, skinless chicken breast halves
1 large egg
¾ cup fine dry bread crumbs
1 cup shredded mozzarella cheese
¼ cup freshly grated Parmesan cheese

Place oil and onions in 2-cup measure, cover, and microwave on HIGH 2 to 3 minutes, or until onions are tender. Stir in tomato sauce, basil, garlic, salt, pepper, and sugar.

Place chicken between two sheets of wax paper and pound with mallet or flat side of heavy knife until ¼ inch thick. Roll up breasts from long side.

In shallow dish, beat egg. On piece of wax paper, spread bread crumbs. Dip chicken in egg, coating all over, then roll in crumbs. Place in a circle around edge of 10-inch round casserole. Top with tomato mixture, cover loosely with wax paper, and microwave on HIGH 5 minutes. Reduce power to 50% and cook 10 to 12 minutes, turning rolls over once. Sprinkle with mozzarella and Parmesan. Cover again and let stand for 5 minutes.

LEMON CHICKEN

4 SERVINGS

Tastes best if the chicken is marinated overnight in the refrigerator.

4 chicken breast halves, skin removed
1 tablespoon olive or vegetable oil
1 tablespoon soy sauce
2 tablespoons water
2 tablespoons fresh lemon juice

2 or 3 cloves garlic, minced
1 teaspoon grated lemon zest
¼ teaspoon red pepper flakes
2 teaspoons cornstarch
1 pound spinach leaves, well washed and chopped

Place chicken breasts in 2-quart freezer bag or shallow dish. In cup, combine oil, soy sauce, water, lemon juice, garlic, lemon zest, red pepper, and cornstarch and mix well. Pour marinade over chicken, cover with plastic wrap, and refrigerate at least 30 minutes or overnight, turning several times.

Drain chicken and place in 10-inch casserole with thicker parts close to perimeter of dish. Pour marinade into 2-cup measure and set aside. Cover chicken and microwave on HIGH 10 to 14 minutes, turning pieces after first 7 minutes. Let stand, covered. Cook marinade on HIGH 3 to 4 minutes, stirring several times.

Arrange chopped raw spinach on a platter. Place chicken on spinach and pour marinade on top.

Skin poultry products before microwaving so that the flavors of herbs and spices or marinade will be absorbed.

CHICKEN KIEV

2 tablespoons unsalted butter
2 tablespoons chopped parsley, snipped fresh chives, or chopped fresh tarragon
1 teaspoon minced garlic
¼ teaspoon freshly ground white pepper

4 boneless, skinless chicken breast halves
1 large egg
1 cup cracker crumbs
⅓ cup freshly grated Parmesan cheese
1 teaspoon paprika

4 SERVINGS

Place butter in cup and microwave on 30% power 20 to 30 seconds to soften. Stir in parsley, garlic, and pepper. Reserve.

Place chicken between two pieces of wax paper or in plastic bag and pound with mallet or flat side of heavy knife until ¼ inch thick.

Divide seasoned butter among chicken breasts, spreading to cover completely. Roll up chicken from narrow ends.

In shallow dish, beat egg. On piece of wax paper, combine crumbs, Parmesan, and paprika, mixing well. Dip chicken in egg, coating all over, then roll in crumb mixture. Shake off excess crumbs and place chicken rolls in a circle around edge of shallow 2-quart casserole. Microwave, uncovered, on HIGH 8 to 12 minutes, or until chicken is cooked and juices run clear.

Do not attempt to deep-fry poultry in the microwave; the oil will reach a very high temperature and could result in a fire.

CAJUN CHICKEN

4 TO 6 SERVINGS

A dish made famous in the bayou country of Louisiana. Cajun cooking reflects the cuisines of Spain, France, and the American Indians—mixed with the magic seasonings brought over by African cooks.

4 chicken breast halves, skin removed
1/2 teaspoon cayenne pepper
1 teaspoon salt
1/2 teaspoon freshly ground black pepper
2 tablespoons vegetable oil
2 large onions, chopped

2 teaspoons minced garlic
1 large green bell pepper, cut into thin julienne strips
8 ounces smoked sausage, cut into 1-inch pieces
1/2 cup chopped parsley
1/2 cup chopped scallions with tops

Arrange chicken in 3-quart casserole with thickest portions close to perimeter of dish. Sprinkle with cayenne, salt, and black pepper. Cover and microwave on HIGH 6 to 8 minutes.

In a mixing bowl, combine oil, onions, garlic, bell pepper, smoked sausage, and parsley. Spread mixture over chicken. Cover and microwave on HIGH 7 to 9 minutes, or until chicken is cooked.

Sprinkle with scallions and serve on a bed of fluffy rice.

CHICKEN-HAM PINWHEELS

4 SERVINGS

A pretty company dish —good served over noodles or rice.

4 boneless, skinless chicken breast halves
4 thin slices cooked ham
4 slices Swiss cheese
1 cup medium Basic White Sauce (page 76)

1/4 cup dry white wine
1 cup sliced mushrooms
Paprika
1/2 cup chopped fresh basil or parsley

Place chicken breasts between two pieces of wax paper and flatten with a rolling pin. Remove top piece of wax paper and place ham and then cheese slices on chicken. Roll up breasts from narrow ends and secure with wooden toothpicks.

Place chicken rolls in a circle around edge of shallow 2-quart casserole. Combine white sauce, wine, and mushrooms, mixing well, and pour over chicken. Cover casserole and microwave on 70% power 12 to 16 minutes, or until chicken is cooked. Rearrange chicken after 8 minutes of cooking. Sprinkle with paprika and basil and serve.

CHICKEN CANTONESE

1 pound boneless, skinless
    chicken breasts, cut into
    1-inch pieces
2 tablespoons vegetable oil
1 cup sliced mushrooms
1 cup sliced red or green bell
    pepper
1 cup sliced onion

1 teaspoon minced garlic
1 teaspoon paprika
1 teaspoon salt
1/2 teaspoon red pepper flakes
2 tablespoons cornstarch
2 tablespoons soy sauce
2 cups fresh tomato wedges

4 TO 6 SERVINGS

Place chicken pieces and oil in shallow 2-quart dish. Cover and microwave on HIGH 3 to 5 minutes. Add mushrooms, bell pepper, onion, garlic, paprika, salt, and red pepper flakes. Cover and microwave on HIGH 3 to 5 minutes, or until chicken is cooked through and vegetables are tender-crisp. Toss to mix.

Combine cornstarch with soy sauce and add to casserole. Cook on HIGH 2 to 4 minutes or more, until sauce thickens. Add tomato wedges, cover, and let stand 5 minutes. Serve with rice or noodles.

CURRIED CHICKEN PITAS

4 boneless, skinless chicken breast
    halves, cut into 1/2-inch
    chunks
1 medium onion, chopped
1/2 teaspoon salt
1/2 teaspoon freshly ground white
    pepper
1 teaspoon curry powder

1/3 cup mayonnaise (page 116)
1 tablespoon fresh lemon juice
1/2 cup chopped celery
1/3 cup golden raisins
1 tomato, peeled and chopped
2 cups chopped iceberg lettuce
4 pita breads, slit open

4 SERVINGS

A quick and easy dish for picnics and informal entertaining.

Place chicken and onion in 2-quart casserole, cover, and microwave on HIGH 9 to 12 minutes. Cool to room temperature. Add salt, pepper, and curry powder and stir to mix. Add mayonnaise, lemon juice, celery, raisins, tomato, and lettuce and toss to combine well.

Fill pita breads with curried chicken mixture and serve.

CHICKEN SCAMPI

4 SERVINGS

Scrumptious served with a green salad and crusty bread! Quick too!

1/3 cup unsalted butter
1 pound boneless, skinless chicken breasts, cut into bite-size pieces
1 to 2 teaspoons minced garlic
3 tablespoons finely chopped parsley

1/4 teaspoon paprika
1/4 cup chopped scallions
1/4 cup dry sherry
1/4 cup fresh lemon juice
Salt
Freshly ground black pepper

In 2-quart casserole, microwave butter on HIGH 1 minute to melt. Add chicken, garlic, parsley, paprika, scallions, sherry, lemon juice, and salt and pepper to taste. Cover and microwave on HIGH 5 minutes. Stir well, cover, and microwave on 50% power 3 to 5 minutes. Let stand, covered, 5 minutes, to blend flavors.

SHRIMP SCAMPI

Substitute 1 pound medium shrimp, peeled and deveined, for chicken and cook 2½ to 3½ minutes, or until pink.

CHICKEN-TOMATO BAKE

6 SERVINGS

Serve over hot noodles for a different and delicious main dish.

1/2 stick (1/4 cup) unsalted butter
6 boneless, skinless chicken breast halves
1 medium onion, thinly sliced
1 teaspoon minced garlic
2 tablespoons all-purpose flour
Salt
Freshly ground black pepper

1 to 2 tablespoons chopped fresh basil, or 1 teaspoon dried
1 (16-ounce) can tomatoes, drained and chopped
1/2 cup sour cream or plain low-fat yogurt
1/2 cup freshly grated Parmesan cheese

In a shallow 2-quart casserole, microwave butter on HIGH 1 minute to melt. Add chicken, placing thicker portions next to perimeter of dish. Microwave on HIGH 9 to 12 minutes or until juices run clear.

Remove chicken, arrange on platter, and keep warm. Stir onion, garlic, flour, salt, pepper, and basil into hot liquid. Cover and microwave on HIGH 3 to 5 minutes. Add chopped tomatoes, then stir in sour cream and Parmesan. Microwave on 70% power for 3 to 5 minutes, or until very hot but not boiling. Pour over chicken and serve at once.

CHICKEN STROGANOFF

5 chicken breast halves, skin
   removed
2 medium onions, chopped
3 tablespoons chopped parsley
   plus chopped parsley for
   garnish
1/2 teaspoon freshly ground black
   pepper
2/3 cup water
1/2 stick (1/4 cup) unsalted butter

1 tablespoon all-purpose flour
1/2 cup sour cream or plain low-fat
   yogurt
1 1/2 tablespoons Dijon mustard
Salt
1/2 teaspoon freshly ground white
   pepper
2 cups sliced mushrooms
Cooked rice (page 289)

**6 TO 8
SERVINGS**

■

This dish offers a delicious blend of seasonings and is perfect to serve at a small dinner party.

Place chicken in 3-quart casserole with thickest parts close to perimeter of dish. Sprinkle with half of chopped onion, 3 tablespoons chopped parsley, and black pepper. Add water, cover, and microwave on HIGH 13 to 16 minutes, or until chicken is cooked.

Set chicken aside to cool in broth. When cool, bone chicken and cut into chunks. Measure broth and add enough water to equal 1 cup.

Place butter and remaining chopped onion in 13 × 9-inch dish and microwave on HIGH 2 to 3 minutes. Stir in flour, then broth mixture. Add chicken, sour cream, mustard, salt to taste, and pepper. Cover and microwave on 70% power 4 to 8 minutes, or until mixture is very hot. Let stand, covered, while mushrooms cook.

Place mushrooms in 2-cup measure, microwave on HIGH 2 to 3 minutes, and drain.

Spoon hot cooked rice onto dinner plates, ladle chicken mixture over rice, then top with mushrooms and remaining chopped parsley.

Country Captain

4 SERVINGS

•

An old recipe, sometimes called East Indian Chicken Curry, brought home by a sea captain along with spices from the Orient. It's a Southern favorite.

½ stick (¼ cup) unsalted butter or
    vegetable oil
4 chicken breast halves, or 2½ to
    3½ pounds chicken parts,
    skin removed
½ cup chopped onion
½ cup chopped green bell pepper
2 cloves garlic, minced
1½ teaspoons curry powder
½ teaspoon salt

½ teaspoon freshly ground black
    pepper
½ teaspoon dried thyme
2 teaspoons sugar
1 (16-ounce) can stewed tomatoes,
    undrained
Cooked rice (page 289)
¼ cup currants or raisins
¼ cup slivered blanched almonds,
    toasted (page 441)

In a 2-quart casserole, microwave butter on HIGH 1 minute to melt. Place chicken in casserole, bony sides up and thicker parts toward outside of dish. Cover and microwave on HIGH 5 minutes.

Combine onion, bell pepper, garlic, curry powder, salt, black pepper, thyme, sugar, and tomatoes. Pour mixture over chicken, cover, and microwave on HIGH 5 minutes. Stir and rearrange chicken. Cover and cook on 70% power 7 to 10 minutes. Serve on a bed of rice, garnished with currants and almonds.

Herbed Baked Chicken

4 SERVINGS

•

This is a good dish to partially prepare ahead of time and marinate in the refrigerator overnight.

1 stick (½ cup) unsalted butter
½ cup Durkee's Famous Sauce
2 or 3 cloves garlic, minced
3 tablespoons mixed chopped
    fresh basil and thyme, or 1
    teaspoon dried basil or thyme

4 chicken breast halves, or 2½ to
    3½ pounds chicken parts,
    skin removed
Cooked noodles or rice (page 289)
¼ cup snipped chives or chopped
    scallions
Chopped fresh herbs
Cherry tomatoes

Place butter, sauce, garlic, and herbs in 2-quart shallow casserole and microwave on HIGH 1 to 2 minutes, or until butter is melted.

Place chicken in casserole, turning pieces to coat. Arrange chicken with thicker parts toward outside of dish. Cover, and microwave on HIGH 10 to 14 minutes, or until juices run clear. Arrange chicken on a bed of noodles or rice. Pour remaining sauce over chicken and sprinkle with chives. Garnish with fresh herbs and cherry tomatoes.

SESAME CHICKEN

1/3 cup soy sauce
1/4 cup, packed, brown sugar
1/4 cup wine vinegar
1 to 2 tablespoons Oriental sesame oil
3 to 5 cloves garlic, minced
2 teaspoons grated fresh ginger
1/2 teaspoon freshly ground black pepper
1 tablespoon cornstarch
1 pound boneless, skinless chicken breasts, cut into 1/2-inch strips

1 medium onion, thinly sliced
1 red bell pepper, cut into julienne strips
3 to 4 cups shredded cabbage
2 tablespoons water
1 (8-ounce) package egg noodles, cooked conventionally
3 tablespoons sesame seeds, toasted (page 441)
1/2 cup walnuts

4 TO 6 SERVINGS

▪

This meal can be prepared in 20 minutes, and it's simply scrumptious!

In 1-quart bowl, combine soy sauce, sugar, vinegar, oil, garlic, ginger, black pepper, and cornstarch and stir to blend. Add chicken and toss to coat with marinade. Cover and marinate chicken for at least 30 minutes or overnight in refrigerator.

Microwave chicken, covered, on HIGH 5 to 8 minutes, or until cooked. Allow chicken to stand, covered, while vegetables cook.

Place onion, bell pepper, cabbage, and water in 2-quart bowl and toss to mix well. Cover and microwave on HIGH 6 to 8 minutes, or until tender-crisp. Add chicken mixture and combine well with vegetables.

Place hot cooked noodles on large platter and arrange chicken-vegetable mixture over them. Sprinkle with sesame seeds and nuts and serve at once.

FLORENTINE CHICKEN ROLLS

4 SERVINGS

A wonderful entrée that can be prepared hours before guests arrive. Garnish with fresh herbs for a colorful presentation.

4 boneless, skinless chicken breast halves
1/2 cup cottage cheese
1 large egg, beaten
1/2 cup grated Gruyère or Monterey Jack cheese
1/3 cup freshly grated Parmesan cheese

1 teaspoon minced garlic
1 (10-ounce) package frozen chopped spinach, defrosted and drained
1 cup thinly sliced mushrooms
Freshly ground black pepper

Place chicken breasts between two sheets of wax paper and pound with mallet or roll with rolling pin until ¼ inch thick. Remove and discard top sheet of wax paper.

In small bowl, combine cottage cheese, egg, Gruyère, Parmesan, garlic, spinach, mushrooms, and pepper to taste and mix well. Divide mixture among chicken breasts, spreading out to edges. Roll up chicken loosely, from narrow end.

Place rolls seam sides down in a circle in shallow 2-quart dish and cover loosely with plastic wrap. Microwave on 70% power 15 to 18 minutes, or until chicken is cooked. Let stand, covered, 5 minutes.

LEMON-TARRAGON CHICKEN

4 SERVINGS

The distinctive flavors of lemon, tarragon, and fruity olive oil make this dish taste sublime. No need for salt at all.

1/4 cup fresh lemon juice
3 to 4 tablespoons fresh tarragon, or 1 teaspoon dried
2 or 3 cloves garlic, minced
1/4 cup extra-virgin olive oil

4 chicken breast halves, or 2½ pounds chicken pieces, skin removed
2 cups dry bread crumbs

Combine lemon juice, tarragon, garlic, oil, and chicken breasts in plastic bag. Marinate 2 to 3 hours or overnight, turning chicken several times.

Put crumbs in large bowl. Remove chicken from marinade and toss in crumbs, coating well. Place chicken in a circle in shallow 2-quart casserole, thicker parts toward outside of dish. Microwave, uncovered, on 70% power 12 to 16 minutes. Serve over buttered rice or noodles.

CHICKEN BREAST TARRAGON

4 chicken breast halves, skin
   removed
1 medium onion, thinly sliced
1 tablespoon fresh tarragon, or
   1/2 teaspoon dried
1/3 cup dry white wine

1 tablespoon cornstarch
1/2 cup heavy cream or plain
   low-fat yogurt
Salt
Freshly ground white pepper
1 cup sliced mushrooms

4 SERVINGS

•

Tarragon and chicken again, here combined with a distinctive wine and cream sauce. Especially good served over Perfect Rice (page 289) and decorated with sautéed cherry tomatoes.

Place chicken breasts, bony sides down, in a circle in 2-quart casserole. Spread the onion on top and sprinkle with tarragon. Microwave on HIGH 10 to 12 minutes.

Mix wine, cornstarch, cream, and salt and pepper to taste in 2-cup measure. Microwave on HIGH 2 to 3 minutes and pour over chicken. Top with mushroom slices and microwave on HIGH 2 to 3 minutes, just to heat mushrooms.

MEXICAN CHICKEN

4 chicken breast halves, skin
   removed
1 cup chopped onion
1/2 stick (1/4 cup) unsalted butter
1 (16-ounce) can tomatoes,
   undrained

1 (4-ounce) can green chilies,
   drained
8 ounces tortilla chips, crushed
1 to 2 cups grated Cheddar cheese
1 cup sliced black olives

4 TO 6 SERVINGS

•

A tasty, colorful dish with a wonderful texture contrast.

Place chicken breasts in 2-quart casserole, bony sides up and thicker parts toward outside of dish. Cover with plastic wrap and microwave on HIGH 12 to 14 minutes, or until chicken is cooked. Cool and remove bones. Chop meat into bite-size pieces and reserve.

Place onions and butter in same casserole and microwave on HIGH 3 to 4 minutes. Add tomatoes, chilies, and chicken. Microwave on 70% power 6 to 8 minutes.

Place tortilla chips in medium casserole and pour chicken-tomato mixture over them. Microwave on HIGH 1 to 2 minutes, or until very hot. Top with grated cheese and black olives and serve at once.

187

HOT CHICKEN AND PASTA SALAD

4 SERVINGS

Here's a different kind of hot chicken salad. Fettucine, cut from egg pasta, is a tender complement to the chicken. If you are planning to serve the salad cold, try using shells or penne, a ribbed, tubular pasta with a chewy texture that will hold up well in the refrigerator.

4 boneless, skinless chicken breast
    halves, cooked (page 169), and
    cut into strips
2 tomatoes, cut into $1/2$-inch dice
1 onion, thinly sliced
3 cloves garlic, minced
$2/3$ cup extra-virgin olive oil
$1/3$ cup cider vinegar
$1/2$ teaspoon salt
1 tablespoon capers, crushed

2 tablespoons chopped fresh basil
$1/2$ teaspoon dried oregano
$1/2$ teaspoon dried thyme
$1/4$ cup chopped arugula
8 ounces fettucine, shells, or
    penne, cooked according to
    package instructions
$1/2$ cup freshly grated Parmesan
    cheese

In 2-quart bowl, combine chicken, tomatoes, onion, garlic, oil, vinegar, salt, capers, basil, oregano, thyme, and arugula and microwave on HIGH 2 to 4 minutes, or until hot. Serve over fettucine and sprinkle with Parmesan cheese.

BAKED CHICKEN SALAD

4 TO 6 SERVINGS

A good way to use leftover chicken or turkey.

$1/2$ cup chopped onion
1 cup chopped celery
2 cups cooked chicken or turkey
    (page 167), cut into $1/2$-inch
    dice
1 cup croutons
$3/4$ cup mayonnaise (page 116) or
    salad dressing

2 tablespoons fresh lemon juice
$1/4$ teaspoon freshly ground white
    pepper
Salt
$3/4$ cup grated Cheddar cheese
    (optional)
$1/2$ cup slivered blanched almonds,
    toasted (page 441)

Place onion and celery in shallow 2-quart casserole and microwave, covered, on HIGH 2 to 3 minutes, or until tender-crisp. Stir in chicken, croutons, mayonnaise, lemon juice, pepper, and salt to taste. Cover, and microwave on 70% power 5 to 8 minutes, or until very hot and bubbly.

Sprinkle cheese, if desired, over chicken mixture and let stand 2 to 3 minutes to melt. Sprinkle with almonds and serve at once.

CHICKEN TACOS

2 cups cooked chicken or turkey (page 167), cut into ½-inch dice
½ cup chopped onion
1 (7-ounce) can jalapeño or taco sauce
8 taco shells

1 cup finely shredded iceberg lettuce
1 large tomato, chopped
4 ounces Monterey Jack cheese, grated
½ cup sour cream
Chopped fresh coriander (cilantro)
Chopped black olives (optional)

8 SERVINGS

Mix chicken, onion, and jalapeño sauce together in 1-quart measure. Microwave on HIGH 2 to 3 minutes until warm. Fill taco shells with mixture, and top with lettuce, tomato, and cheese. Garnish wih sour cream, coriander, and olives, if desired, and serve at once.

CREAMED CHICKEN

½ stick (¼ cup) unsalted butter
¼ cup all-purpose flour
1 teaspoon salt
½ teaspoon freshly ground white pepper
2 cups milk

3 cups cooked chicken or turkey (page 167), cut into ½-inch dice
½ cup chopped red bell pepper
1 cup diced (¼ inch) celery
1 (10-ounce) package frozen green peas

5 OR 6 SERVINGS

A comforting standby recipe for leftover chicken, turkey, or even ham. Serve it over rice, wide noodles, or hot biscuits.

Place butter in 2-quart casserole and microwave on HIGH 1 minute, or until melted. Stir in flour, salt, and white pepper and blend well. Pour in milk, stirring with wire whisk to combine smoothly. Microwave on HIGH 5 to 6 minutes, stirring several times. Stir in chicken and reserve.

Place bell pepper and celery in 1-quart casserole. Cover and microwave on HIGH 2 to 3 minutes, add peas and microwave on HIGH 2 to 3 minutes longer, or until peas are just cooked.

Add vegetables to chicken mixture, stirring to mix. Cover and microwave at 70% 2 to 3 minutes, or until hot.

CHICKEN SPAGHETTI SAUCE

6 SERVINGS

A savory dish that is low in calories and cholesterol. Substitute cooked turkey for the chicken, if that's what you have on hand.

1 medium onion, chopped
1 teaspoon minced garlic
2 tablespoons extra-virgin olive oil
1 teaspoon dried basil
1 teaspoon dried oregano
1 teaspoon dried thyme
1 teaspoon chopped parsley
1 teaspoon salt
1 teaspoon freshly ground black pepper

2 teaspoons sugar
1 (15-ounce) can tomato sauce
1 (16-ounce) can tomatoes, undrained, chopped
3 to 4 cups bite-size pieces cooked chicken (page 167)
16 ounces spaghetti or fettucine, cooked according to package instructions

In 3-quart casserole, combine onion, garlic, oil, basil, oregano, thyme, parsley, salt, pepper, and sugar. Cover and microwave on HIGH 4 to 5 minutes.

Add tomato sauce and tomatoes, cover, and microwave on HIGH 8 to 10 minutes, stirring once. Add chicken, cover again, and cook on 70% power 5 minutes. Serve over hot cooked pasta.

CRUNCHY ALMOND CHICKEN

4 TO 6 SERVINGS

1/2 cup finely chopped onion
1/2 cup chopped celery
2 cups cooked chicken or turkey (page 167), cut into 1/2-inch dice
1 cup cooked rice (page 289)
1 (10 3/4-ounce) can condensed cream of mushroom soup

1/2 cup mayonnaise (page 116)
1 tablespoon fresh lemon juice
2 or 3 hard-cooked eggs (page 122), sliced
Dry bread crumbs
1/2 cup sliced blanched almonds, toasted (page 441)

Place onion and celery in 2-cup measure, cover with plastic wrap, and microwave on HIGH 2 to 3 minutes, or until vegetables are tender-crisp.

In 2-quart casserole, layer chicken, rice, and onion mixture.

Combine soup, mayonnaise, and lemon juice and stir well. Spread soup mixture over onion mixture. Arrange sliced eggs over soup mixture and sprinkle with bread crumbs. Microwave on 70% power 5 to 7 minutes, or until hot and bubbly. Sprinkle almonds on top and serve.

CHICKEN CASSEROLE

16 ounces spaghetti, broken into 3-inch pieces, cooked according to package instructions
2 onions, chopped
2 green bell peppers, chopped
2 cups chopped celery
1 pound mushrooms, sliced, or 1 (8-ounce) can sliced mushrooms, drained

6 cups cooked chicken or turkey (page 167), cut into bite-size pieces
1 pound sharp Cheddar cheese, grated
4 cups Velouté Sauce (page 78)
1 tablespoon Worcestershire sauce
Juice of 2 lemons
1 teaspoon freshly ground white pepper
Salt

20 SERVINGS

■

A wonderful dish to prepare ahead of time for a crowd. It also freezes well.

While spaghetti is cooking, place onions, bell pepper, and celery in 2-quart measure, cover, and microwave on HIGH 5 to 7 minutes, or until tender-crisp. Transfer vegetables to large bowl. Add cooked, drained spaghetti. Put mushrooms into 2-quart measure, cover, and microwave on HIGH 4 to 6 minutes. Drain mushrooms and add to vegetables and spaghetti together with chicken, half the cheese, velouté sauce, Worcestershire, lemon juice, pepper, and salt to taste. Mix ingredients well, then divide between two 3-quart casseroles and sprinkle each with remaining cheese.

Recipe can be prepared ahead to this point. If dishes are still warm, allow to cool to room temperature, cover with plastic wrap, and refrigerate overnight.

To serve, microwave each casserole separately on 70% power 15 to 18 minutes, or until hot in center.

When serving both casseroles at once, reheat until hot and bubbly in conventional oven preheated to 350° F.

CHICKEN LIVERS AND ONIONS

4 SERVINGS

3 slices bacon
¼ cup all-purpose flour
1 teaspoon salt

½ teaspoon freshly ground black
  pepper
1 pound chicken livers
2 cups thinly sliced onions

Place bacon in a single layer in shallow 2-quart casserole and microwave on HIGH 2 to 4 minutes. Remove bacon and set aside, leaving drippings in casserole. Mix together flour, salt, and pepper and toss chicken livers in flour mixture.

Place chicken livers in bacon drippings and arrange onions over them. Cover and microwave on HIGH 4 to 5 minutes. Rearrange liver and onions and microwave on 50% power 4 to 7 minutes.

BARBECUED CORNISH HENS

4 SERVINGS

2 (1½- to 1¾-pound) Cornish
  hens, split
¼ cup fresh lemon juice
¼ cup chopped onion
2 or 3 cloves garlic, minced
3 tablespoons fresh thyme or
  chopped fresh basil, or 1
  teaspoon dried thyme or basil

½ teaspoon salt
¼ teaspoon freshly ground white
  pepper
1 teaspoon Worcestershire sauce
1 teaspoon sugar

Place hens in a heavy-duty plastic bag. Combine lemon juice, onion, garlic, thyme, salt, pepper, Worcestershire, and sugar in a small bowl and pour mixture over hens. Turn hens in marinade, seal bag tightly, pressing out all air, and place bag in a bowl. Refrigerate several hours or overnight, turning several times.

Prepare a barbecue grill.

Remove hens from marinade and place in 12 × 9-inch casserole with meatier portions toward outside of dish. Cover loosely with wax paper and microwave on HIGH 9 minutes. Turn pieces over, cover, and cook on HIGH 6 to 9 minutes, or until juices run clear. Let stand.

In 1-cup measure, heat marinade on HIGH 1 to 2 minutes.

Transfer hens to grill and cook over medium-hot coals 12 to 15 minutes, or until brown, turning birds and basting several times with heated marinade.

CORNISH HENS
WITH CURRIED APRICOTS

2 (1½- to 1¾-pound) Cornish hens

1 (7-ounce) package curry rice, cooked according to package directions

4 SERVINGS

SAUCE
2 tablespoons unsalted butter
1 medium onion, sliced
½ cup sliced celery
2 tablespoons all-purpose flour
½ teaspoon curry powder
2 teaspoons chicken bouillon granules, or 2 cubes

¼ teaspoon freshly ground white pepper
1 (16-ounce) can apricots, undrained
½ cup pitted black olives
Fresh herbs

Place hens, breast side down, in 12 × 9-inch baking dish. Tie legs together with string. Cover loosely with wax paper and microwave on HIGH 8 minutes. Turn hens breast side up and cook 8 to 10 minutes, or until juices run clear and leg moves freely in socket. Let stand, covered, while you make the sauce.

Combine butter, onion, and celery in a 1-quart measure. Cover tightly and microwave on HIGH 3 to 4 minutes, or until tender-crisp. Stir in flour, curry powder, bouillon, and pepper. Measure apricot syrup and add enough water to equal 1 cup. Stir into vegetable mixture. Cover and cook on HIGH 3 to 4 minutes, or until sauce boils 1 minute. Stir in apricot halves and microwave on HIGH for 1 minute.

Split hens, arrange on platter, and pour sauce over them. Garnish with olives and fresh herbs and serve with rice.

ORANGE-GLAZED CORNISH HENS

4 SERVINGS

■

Orange marmalade and soy sauce make a beautiful glaze.

¼ cup orange marmalade
¼ cup soy sauce
½ teaspoon minced garlic

½ teaspoon freshly ground black pepper
2 (1½- to 1¾-pound) Cornish hens

Combine marmalade, soy sauce, garlic, and black pepper in 2-quart plastic bag. Place hens in bag, turning to coat. Allow hens to marinate 4 hours, or overnight in the refrigerator, turning occasionally.

When ready to cook, place hens on baking rack, breast side down and legs toward center. Microwave on HIGH 10 minutes. Turn hens breast side up and microwave on HIGH 10 to 15 minutes, or until leg moves freely in socket and juices run clear. Let stand 5 minutes, then split and serve.

PEACH-GLAZED DUCK

4 TO 6 SERVINGS

■

Enjoy preparing for a festive affair.

½ cup peach preserves
⅓ cup soy sauce
1 teaspoon minced garlic
½ teaspoon freshly ground white pepper
1 (4½- to 5-pound) duckling, washed and drained, with giblets removed

1 apple, cored and quartered
1 medium onion, quartered
1 bunch parsley or watercress
4 to 6 prunes, plumped in hot water and drained
1 cup drained canned sliced peaches

Make glaze by combining peach preserves, soy sauce, garlic, and pepper in 2-cup measure. Microwave on HIGH 45 seconds. Set aside.

Fill duck cavity with apple and onion wedges. Use wooden toothpicks to secure neck skin to back. Place duck on baking rack, breast side down. Brush duck with half the glaze. Microwave on HIGH 10

minutes. Reduce power to 50% and cook 8 to 9 minutes per pound. Halfway through cooking, turn duck breast side up and drain fat. When duck is cooked, remove from oven and microwave remaining glaze 1 to 2 minutes to heat. Brush duck with glaze, place under a foil tent, and let stand 5 to 10 minutes before serving.

Arrange duck on platter and decorate with sprigs of parsley, prunes, and peach slices.

SAVORY TURKEY WITH SUMMER VEGETABLES

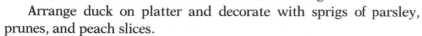

1 (2-pound) package frozen turkey thighs, defrosted (page 165)
1 clove garlic, minced
1 medium onion, sliced
2 medium yellow squash, sliced
2 medium tomatoes, peeled and quartered
1 teaspoon sugar
3 tablespoons chopped fresh basil, or 1 teaspoon dried
1/4 teaspoon freshly ground black pepper

4 SERVINGS

Place turkey thighs in 3-quart casserole. Cover tightly with plastic wrap and cook on HIGH 5 minutes. Reduce power level to 50% and cook 10 minutes longer. Turn pieces over, cover again, and cook on 50% power 10 minutes, or until meat near bone is no longer pink and juices are clear.

Combine garlic, onion, squash, tomatoes, sugar, basil, and pepper in 1½-quart casserole. Cover tightly with plastic wrap and cook on HIGH 4 to 5 minutes, or until vegetables are tender-crisp. Pour over turkey and let stand, covered, 5 minutes.

TURKEY CREOLE

4 TO 6 SERVINGS

▪

Turkey has remained popular in America since the Pilgrims feasted on it in 1621. Enjoy this Creole dish made with cooked turkey.

¼ cup (½ stick) butter, extra-virgin olive oil, or bacon drippings
1 medium onion, finely chopped
½ cup diced green bell pepper
½ cup sliced celery
½ teaspoon dried thyme
½ teaspoon freshly ground black pepper

1 teaspoon minced garlic
2 teaspoons Worcestershire sauce
1 bay leaf
1 teaspoon salt
2 teaspoons sugar
1 (16-ounce) can tomatoes, undrained, chopped
2 cups finely chopped cooked turkey (page 167)

Combine butter, onion, bell pepper, celery, thyme, black pepper, garlic, Worcestershire, bay leaf, salt, sugar, and tomatoes in 3-quart casserole. Cover and microwave on HIGH 6 to 8 minutes, or until boiling. Stir, add turkey, and microwave on 70% power 3 to 4 minutes, or until turkey is heated through. Serve with rice.

Meat

It will take you only a short while to master the skills necessary for selecting suitable cuts of meat for microwaving and matching those cuts with the appropriate cooking methods. As you become informed about microwaving meat and acquire experience in the kitchen, your skills will become honed and you will be free to experiment with your own meat recipes.

The major problem people encounter in microwave meat cookery is that the meat toughens, which results from using too high a power level. A very high power level cooks the meat at too high a temperature and simply extracts the juices from the meat without tenderizing the muscle fibers and connective tissues. In fact, you would have the same problems if you cooked most meats to 500° F. in the conventional oven.

One great advantage of microwaving meat is that no fat is needed to prevent the meat from sticking to the cooking vessel, nor is basting required to keep the meat moist.

Many meat dishes do very well in the microwave, among them chili, spaghetti sauces, meat loaves, meatballs, stir-fry recipes, precooked sausages and hot dogs, smoked and cured meats such as bacon and kielbasa, and frozen entrées.

For some other dishes, however, the microwave offers no real benefit. Meats that are best cooked conventionally are:

- large quantities of any kind
- foods with crisp coatings
- large, irregularly shaped cuts
- fried foods
- meats that can be very quickly sautéed in a conventional frying pan

SELECTION AND STORAGE

SELECTION

The grades of beef, lamb, and veal you will find at your butcher or in the supermarket are:

- *Prime*—the most superior quality, found primarily in restaurants and very fancy butcher shops.
- *Choice*—very high quality, usually found in supermarkets and most butchers.
- *Select*—(formerly known as "Good") has a higher ratio of lean to fat and is less tender. It may need moist heat to tenderize it.

For pork, retail cuts do not carry a grading, since much pork is cured or processed and carries the packer's brand name.

STORAGE

Microwaving allows the natural flavor of the meat to be enjoyed. Because no additional flavor is introduced during microwaving, such as the characteristic flavor of carbonized fat produced by conventional browning, it is even more important that microwaved meat be fresh. Off flavors from improperly stored meat will be even more obvious in microwave-cooked meat.

Refrigerate meat as soon as possible in the coldest part of the refrigerator for up to 2 days for ground meat, stew meat, and organ meats, and 2 to 4 days for other meats. Meats that are packaged for self-service can be refrigerated in the original packaging. Meat that is not prepackaged at the store should be rewrapped in a moistureproof, vaporproof material such as foil, freezer paper, or plastic.

To store meats longer than several days, freeze them wrapped in a moistureproof covering. Foil or wax-coated freezer paper are the best coverings to use in the freezer. Ground and smoked pork should be kept frozen for only 1 to 3 months. Ground and cubed beef or lamb and veal can be kept frozen for 3 to 4 months. Fresh pork and lamb roasts and chops will keep well for up to 6 months. Beef roasts and steaks will keep well frozen up to 8 or 9 months.

Basic Meat Cookery

EQUIPMENT

A few readily available pieces of equipment specifically designed for the microwave will help make cooking meat even easier.

- A bacon rack will hold bacon out of drippings and allow it to crisp.
- A browning dish is useful for cooking steaks, chops, and other small cuts of meat (see page 10).
- A roasting rack will prevent larger cuts of meat from sitting in their own juices as they cook.
- A microwavable plastic colander will allow ground meat and vegetables to partially cook and drain at the same time.
- A microwave thermometer will measure the temperature of roasts if your microwave is not equipped with a built-in temperature probe or food sensor.

COMBINATION COOKING

Combination cooking—that is, cooking partially in the microwave to reduce total cooking time and partially by a conventional method to brown the meat and develop flavor —is an excellent way to cook many meats.

Some cuts that benefit from combination cooking are:

- **Spareribs, short ribs, steaks, some roasts.** Cook first in the microwave, then grill or smoke for appearance and flavor.
- **Pot roasts and stews.** Brown conventionally on the rangetop, then finish in the microwave with other ingredients.
- **Chops** can be browned conventionally, then simmered in the microwave.
- **Tender roasts** that weigh 3 to 4 pounds, are uniform in shape, and have a thin, even coating of fat can cook in the microwave, then finish in the conventional oven to develop color and flavor.

DEFROSTING MEATS IN THE MICROWAVE

Meat that is wrapped in plastic or paper can be defrosted in its wrapping. Foil wrapping must be removed before defrosting. If the meat is packaged on Styrofoam trays, remove the tray as soon as it can be separated from the meat. Place the meat on a plate or dish to catch drippings.

Turn the meat over halfway through defrosting. For faster and more even defrosting, separate chops, steaks, stew meat, or other pieces of meat as soon as they can be pulled apart, spread them out in the dish, and continue defrosting.

Watch ground meat as it defrosts and remove the outer defrosted portions at several intervals. As soon as the meat is soft enough, break it up and spread it in the dish.

Roasts sometimes need to be shielded with foil in thin areas, areas with bone, or in other areas that become too hot during defrosting.

TIMETABLE FOR MEAT DEFROSTING

MEAT	30% POWER (MINUTES/POUND)	MEAT	30% POWER (MINUTES/POUND)
Bacon	6	Steaks or chops	5 to 7
Ground beef	5	Roasts	8 to 13
Bulk sausage	4 to 5	Organ meats	6 to 8
Link sausage	2 to 4	Spareribs	5 to 7

BROWNING

Meats that cook longer than 12 to 15 minutes, such as roasts, will brown acceptably while microwaving, although the color will not always be as dark as that produced in the conventional oven. Smaller cuts of meat—chops, for instance—cook so quickly that they don't have time to brown, and for these you might want to use a browning dish (page 10).

CHOPS

Four to 6 pork chops or lamb chops can be microwaved easily. We sometimes like to brown chops conventionally in a skillet and then simmer them in the microwave, although conventional browning isn't necessary. Chops will not cook long enough in the microwave to brown from microwave cooking alone. Cover them with a sauce, vegetables, or a crumb coating to help hold moisture in the meat and add eye appeal. Pork chops should be covered for even cooking. Rearrange chops during cooking so that all areas of the meat cook evenly. Chops may also be cooked on a browning dish.

GROUND MEAT

When a recipe calls for crumbled ground meat, the microwave oven is the easiest way to cook it. When browning ground meat, microwave on HIGH for about 5 minutes per pound. Either crumble and spread the meat evenly in a dish or crumble it in a microwavable plastic colander over a bowl to catch the drippings. Ground meat dishes microwave very well, especially when they can be stirred. When a dish cannot be stirred during cooking, such as lasagna, lower the power level and cover during cooking so that the food will cook in the center without overcooking the outer edges.

RIBS

Short ribs (beef) and spareribs (pork) are at their juiciest, tenderest, and most flavorful when cooked by a combination of microwaving and conventional grilling or broiling (see Combination Cooking, page 199). When time or other conditions don't permit either of these methods, microwaved ribs are good, too. Cook them, covered, with some liquid to steam, on HIGH for 5 to 10 minutes, then on 30 to 50% power until they are tender. A good bit of fat will cook out of the ribs; drain it off, then coat the ribs with a sauce and microwave, uncovered, on 50% power for 5 to 10 minutes.

ROASTS

DRY-ROASTING

Tender beef roasts and lamb can be microwaved, uncovered, with good results; however, we prefer to use a combination of the microwave to cook the roast with the conventional oven to brown and crisp its surface (see Combination Cooking, page 199).

Guidelines for roasting in the microwave:

- Well-marbled meat is more tender than very lean meat. An even layer of fat on the outside of the meat will help promote even cooking and browning. If the fat covering is not uniformly thick, trim the thick parts.
- Place the roast on a microwave roasting or baking rack in a dish. The rack should hold the roast up out of the drippings. (Meat that cooks in its drippings will overcook.)
- Begin cooking on HIGH 5 to 10 minutes to bring up the temperature of the roast quickly. Complete cooking at 30 to 50% power.
- Drain off the drippings several times during cooking. Microwaves are more attracted to fat than to water and, when they are attracted to the drippings, the roast will cook more slowly.
- Irregular shapes cook unevenly. To prevent overcooking thin areas of meat, or those that contain bone, shield those parts with foil (if your microwave oven permits the use of foil).
- Boneless roasts cook more evenly in general. Because bones conduct heat, a roast with a bone on one side will cook faster on that side. Roasts with a center bone surrounded by at least 1 inch of meat will cook fairly evenly.
- Begin roasting the meat with the fat side down, then turn the roast over halfway through cooking.
- If you prefer to determine the cooking time of certain cuts by internal temperature rather than by weight (see Cooking Chart for Meats, opposite), use the temperature probe of your microwave or a microwavable thermometer (page 11). Insert the sensing end of the thermometer into the center of a muscle so that it touches neither fat nor bone. (If the temperature climbs much more rapidly than it should, the thermometer is very likely in a fat pocket.) To check for doneness, simply remove the thermometer and reposition it. Continue microwaving and check the temperature again.
- Cook a roast until the thermometer registers 5 degrees below the desired doneness. Just as in conventional cooking, large cuts should stand 10 to 15 minutes to finish cooking and set the texture. In microwaving there is an even greater tendency for meats to continue cooking after they're taken from the oven than in conventional roasting: The internal temperature of a microwaved roast can rise by as much as 10 to 20 degrees during standing. Place a foil tent over the meat while it stands.

MOIST-ROASTING

Less tender roasts and lower grades of beef have less fat and more connective tissue; they need moist heat to tenderize them. Microwave them covered so that they cook in steam.

Although many cuts of pork are not tough, we recommend that all fresh pork be cooked by moist heat (see page 227).

- To tenderize meat, marinate it before cooking, use a meat tenderizer, or pound it with a mallet.

- Brown the roast conventionally or not, as you wish. Conventional browning helps to develop the flavor and adds color as well.
- Add liquid to the meat and cover while cooking so that the meat will steam.
- Cook on HIGH 5 to 10 minutes to heat the roast quickly, then cook at 30 to 50% power.

STEWS

Meat for stews should be cut into cubes of uniform size. The meat may or may not be conventionally browned before adding the remaining ingredients, but the flavor is best when this extra step is taken. Begin microwaving on HIGH 5 to 10 minutes, then, after adding seasonings and liquid, cook on 30 to 50% power. Vegetables are sometimes steamed separately from the meat and added to the meat at the end of cooking.

COOKING CHART FOR MEATS			
FOOD AND WEIGHT	**TIME**	**POWER LEVEL**	**TECHNIQUE**
BEEF			
Ground, crumbled	5 min	HIGH	Cook in bowl or in microwavable plastic colander placed in bowl to collect drippings. Stir and break up meat during cooking.
Ground, patties			
1, 4-ounce	1¼ min	HIGH	Form into patties. Place on
4, 4-ounce	3½ min	HIGH	roasting rack. Cover with wax paper. Turn over halfway through cooking time.
Ground, meat loaf			
1 lb	10 min	HIGH	Use a ring dish or form loaf into
1½ lb	14 to 15 min	HIGH	doughnut shape. Cover with wax paper. Let stand 10 minutes after cooking. Cover with a sauce.
Ground, meatballs			
12, 1-inch balls (1 lb)	7 to 9 min	HIGH	Place meatballs in a circle, leaving center of dish empty. Cover with wax paper. Turn meatballs over halfway through cooking. Drain. *(continued)*

COOKING CHART FOR MEATS (Continued)

FOOD AND WEIGHT	TIME	POWER LEVEL	TECHNIQUE
BEEF *(cont'd)*			
Roasts, pot roasts (2 to 3½ lb)			
arm, chuck	27 to 33 min/lb	HIGH for 5 minutes, 30% until cooked	Brown conventionally, then place in casserole. Add ¼ cup water, onion, garlic, and desired seasoning. Turn roast over halfway through cooking time. Let stand 10 to 15 minutes after cooking.
bone-in blade	23 to 29 min/lb		
boneless blade	32 to 39 min/lb		
boneless shoulder, eye of round, bottom round, sirloin tip	41 to 48 min/lb		
Roasts, tender cuts (3 to 4 lb)	11 to 13 min/lb (rare to med)	50%	Use roasting rack. Shield thin parts or areas with bone where needed. Turn over halfway through cooking time. Let stand 15 to 20 minutes after cooking.
rib eye, boneless top round, top loin, rump and cross rib, rib roast	18 to 22 min/lb (rare to med)	30%	
Roasts, corned beef (3 to 4 lb)	30 to 35 min/lb	HIGH for 15 minutes, 30% until cooked	Add ½ cup water (1 onion, sliced, if desired) and cover. Turn over halfway through cooking time. Let stand 10 minutes after cooking.
VEAL			
Roast (3 to 4 lb)	13 to 17 min/lb	HIGH for 5 minutes, 50% until cooked	Use roasting rack. Shield thin parts or areas with bone, if needed. Turn halfway through cooking. Let stand 10 minutes after cooking.
LAMB			
Roast, bone-in center leg (3 to 5 lb)	14 to 17 min/lb (rare)	30%	Use roasting rack. Shield thin parts or areas with bone if needed. Turn halfway through cooking. Let stand 10 minutes after cooking. *(continued)*
	18 to 21 min/lb (med)		
	22 to 26 min/lb (well)		

COOKING CHART FOR MEATS (Continued)

FOOD AND WEIGHT	TIME	POWER LEVEL	TECHNIQUE
PORK			
Bacon			
1 slice	1 min	HIGH	Arrange in single layer on roasting rack. Cover with paper towel to prevent splattering. For crisper bacon, let stand a few minutes after cooking.
4 slices	3 min	HIGH	
Canadian bacon			
whole, 1 lb	12 to 15 min	50%	Arrange slices in single layer, overlapping as needed. Add 2 tablespoons water. Cover with plastic wrap. Turn over halfway through cooking time. Let stand 10 minutes after cooking.
1 lb, ¼" slices	7 min	50%	
4, ¼" slices	1½ min	50%	
Crumbled, ground (1 lb)	6 min	HIGH	Place in bowl, or microwavable plastic colander in bowl to catch drippings. Cover with plastic wrap. Stir to break up pork halfway through cooking; stir again after cooking.
Cubes (boneless shoulder) cut in ½- to 1-inch cubes (1 lb)	18 to 25 min/lb	30%	Place in casserole with ¼ cup water. Rearrange halfway through cooking time.
Chops, fresh (5 to 7 oz; ¾" to 1" thick) boneless top loin, center cut rib, center cut loin			
1 chop	20 min/lb	30%	Place in single layer. Cover. Rearrange halfway through cooking time.
4 chops	18 min/lb		

(continued)

COOKING CHART FOR MEATS (Continued)

FOOD AND WEIGHT	TIME	POWER LEVEL	TECHNIQUE
PORK *(cont'd)*			
Ribs (3 to 3½ lb; 1″ thick portions) Backribs or spareribs (cut in serving-size portions, 3 to 3½ lb)	14 min/lb	50%	Place in large casserole or oven cooking bag with 1 cup water. Cover or close bag. Turn over, rearranging carefully, halfway through cooking time.
Roasts, boneless (3 to 3½ lb; 4-inch diameter)	22 min/lb	30%	Cook covered in large casserole or cooking bag. Turn over halfway through cooking time. Cook until internal temperature of roast reaches 165° F. Let stand, covered, 10 to 15 minutes after cooking. Temperature will rise above the recommended temperature of 170° F.
Roasts/bone-in (3 to 3½ lb)	20 min/lb	30%	Cook covered in large casserole. Turn over halfway through cooking. Cook until internal temperature of roast reaches 165° F. Let stand 10 to 15 minutes after cooking. Temperature of roast will rise above recommended temperature of 170° F.
Ham, "fully-cooked" whole, 3 lb	15 to 18 min/lb	30%	Use roasting rack. Turn over halfway through cooking time. Let stand 15 minutes after cooking.
slice, 2″ thick (3 lb)	20 to 35 min	50%	Cover. Turn over halfway through cooking. *(continued)*

COOKING CHART FOR MEATS (Continued)

FOOD AND WEIGHT	TIME	POWER LEVEL	TECHNIQUE
PORK *(cont'd)*			
slice, ¾ to 1" thick	14 min	50%	Cover. Turn the ham slice over halfway through cooking. Let stand several minutes.
slices, ¼" thick (1½ lb)	10 min	50%	Overlap slices. Add ¼ cup water. Cover.
Ham, "cook before eating" (3 lb)	22 min/lb	30%	Same as pork roasts.
Pork sausage links smoked (2)	1½ to 2 min	HIGH	Add ½ cup water. Cover. (For best flavor, cook conventionally.)
Pork sausage links, precooked (2 to 3)	2 min	HIGH	Cook on preheated browning skillet. (Or cook conventionally.)
Pork sausage, continuous link, fully-cooked, smoked (1 lb)	3 min	HIGH	Cook uncovered.
Hot dogs (2, in buns)	1½ min	HIGH	Wrap in paper napkin or paper towel to prevent excessive moisture loss.
Smoked rib or loin chops			
2, 1" thick	7 to 8 min	HIGH	Use roasting rack. Coat with
4, 1" thick	12 to 13 min	HIGH	glaze or sauce to hold in
2, ¾" thick	5½ to 6½ min	HIGH	moisture. Turn over halfway
4, ¾" thick	8½ to 10 min	HIGH	through cooking time.

Beef

Beef, the most popular meat in the American diet, offers a variety of cuts for many uses. Select beef that has firm white fat and avoid meat in which the fat is yellow, soft, or oily looking. The meat should have a firm, fine-grained texture; the color can vary from light to dark red.

HAMBURGERS

Hamburgers can be cooked conventionally or in the microwave. For reasons of color and flavor, we prefer to cook hamburgers conventionally, by grilling, broiling, or panbroiling, while a vegetable or other meal accompaniment is being microwaved.

However, sometimes the option of microwaving is the best choice as a timesaver, especially when preparing 1 or 2 hamburgers and when assertive seasonings or sauces are used and the burgers' flavor does not rest on the ground beef alone. Use the cooking chart on page 203.

MEATBALLS

Microwaving is an excellent way to cook meatballs. Follow the cooking chart on page 203. Be sure to drain the drippings, if a large amount has collected, when you turn the meatballs. If the drippings do not contain too much fat, they may be used later to add flavor to the sauce.

MEAT LOAF

Meat loaf from the microwave tastes delicious and can be quickly prepared. The most important guideline is to use extra-lean ground meat. Cook on HIGH, uncovered, so that moisture can evaporate. Drain any liquid that accumulates in the dish during cooking. A meat loaf microwaved in a ring-shaped dish or in a pie plate with a custard cup in the center cooks more evenly than it would in a traditional loaf or casserole shape. After cooking, let the meat loaf stand about 5 minutes to set. Invert the meat loaf onto a plate and fill the center with a complementary vegetable, such as mashed potatoes, broccoli flowerets, or green peas.

TENDER STEAKS

Ribeye, T-bone, club, Delmonico, rib, New York strip, Porterhouse, or sirloin—these steaks are best broiled or grilled conventionally because good flavor is dependent upon the carbonizing of the fat, which can happen only with radiant heat. Nevertheless, the microwave browning dish, used according to the manufacturer's instructions, can be a good alternative when cooking for 1 or 2 people, particularly in hot weather. Always turn steaks with tongs to avoid losing juices from piercing with a fork.

VEAL

Veal is usually tender, but unlike good beef, it has little or no marbling. For this reason it is often cooked in a sauce or coated with crumbs and covered during microwaving to hold in the moisture. Baby veal is pale pink, older veal a deep pink. Good veal should have firm exterior fat and porous bone.

CALF'S LIVER

When a recipe calls for simmering liver in a sauce, the microwave can be an efficient cooking choice. Otherwise, since liver can be sautéed on the rangetop as easily as it can be microwaved, we prefer the conventional cooking method.

STANDING RIB ROAST

1 (4-pound) standing rib beef roast

4 TO 6 SERVINGS

COOKING BY TIME

Place roast fat side down on roasting rack. Estimate total cooking time for doneness desired: rare, 9 to 12 minutes per pound; medium, 10 to 14 minutes per pound; well done, 11 to 15 minutes per pound. Microwave on HIGH 5 minutes, then on 50% power for remainder of cooking time. Halfway through cooking, turn roast over. Remove roast from oven and tent loosely with foil. Let stand 10 to 20 minutes before serving.

COOKING BY TEMPERATURE

Use a temperature probe, food sensor, or microwave thermometer. Insert sensing end of thermometer into center of meat. Do not let it rest against bone or in a fat pocket. Microwave on HIGH 5 minutes, then on 50% power until roast reaches desired temperature: rare, 120° F.; medium, 135° F.; well done, 150° F. Remove roast from oven and tent loosely with foil. Let stand 10 to 20 minutes before serving.

When reheating rare roast beef or steak, place a lettuce leaf over the meat so that the meat will become hot without cooking in the center.

GYPSY STEAK

5 OR 6 SERVINGS

■

½ cup all-purpose flour
¼ cup (½ stick) butter or olive oil
1½ pounds flank or sirloin steak
1 clove garlic, minced
1 cup sliced onions
1 cup Beef Stock (page 46) or
    canned beef broth
1 tablespoon vinegar

1 teaspoon mustard
½ cup tomato sauce
1 teaspoon prepared horseradish
¾ teaspoon salt
½ teaspoon freshly ground black
    pepper
½ cup cream or sour cream

In 2-quart dish, microwave flour and butter on HIGH 2 minutes. Stir and microwave on HIGH 3 to 5 minutes longer, or until roux is light brown.

Cut steak across grain into very thin slices. Stir steak and garlic into roux and microwave on HIGH 3 to 4 minutes.

Add onions and microwave on HIGH 3 minutes. Add to stock, vinegar, mustard, tomato sauce, horseradish, salt, and pepper and microwave on HIGH 3 to 5 minutes, or until very hot. Stir in sour cream. Serve over noodles or rice.

POT ROAST

8 TO 12 SERVINGS

■

½ cup all-purpose flour
1 teaspoon dried oregano
½ teaspoon dried dill
½ teaspoon garlic salt
½ teaspoon salt
1 teaspoon freshly ground black
    pepper
1 (3- to 4-pound) boneless beef
    chuck roast
¼ cup olive oil

3 tablespoons red wine vinegar
1 tablespoon Worcestershire sauce
4 potatoes, peeled and cut into
    1-inch chunks
2 carrots, cut into 1-inch chunks
2 onions, quartered
2 stalks celery, cut into large
    chunks
1½ cups Beef Stock (page 46) or
    canned beef broth

In large dish or paper bag, combine flour, oregano, dill, garlic salt, salt, and pepper. Dredge roast in flour, coating well on all sides.

Heat oil in heavy skillet over high heat on conventional rangetop.

When oil is hot but not smoking, add beef and brown on all sides.

Place roast in 4-quart casserole. Add vinegar, Worcestershire, potatoes, carrots, onions, celery, and stock. Cover and microwave on HIGH 10 minutes. Reduce power to 30% and microwave 1 hour longer, or until meat and vegetables are tender, turning roast and stirring vegetables halfway through cooking. Let stand, covered, 10 to 15 minutes before serving.

SAUERBRATEN

1 (3-pound) beef round steak, 2½
    inches thick
1 onion, sliced
1 stalk celery, sliced
1 carrot, sliced
1 teaspoon salt
1 teaspoon freshly ground black
    pepper
4 whole cloves

1 clove garlic, sliced
2 bay leaves
½ cup red wine vinegar
3 cups water
½ cup all-purpose flour
1½ tablespoons vegetable oil
1½ tablespoons butter
1 teaspoon grated fresh ginger
    (optional)

8 SERVINGS

Beef marinates for four
days in a flavorful mix-
ture of vegetables,
spices, and vinegar.

Place beef, onion, celery, carrot, salt, pepper, cloves, garlic, bay leaves, vinegar, and water in 1-gallon plastic bag. Press air from bag and secure top. (Meat will be completely immersed in marinade.) Place bag in bowl and refrigerate 4 days.

Remove meat from marinade, reserving marinade. Pat meat dry and dredge in flour, coating roast on all sides. Heat oil and butter in heavy skillet over high heat on conventional rangetop until butter melts and foam subsides. Add beef and brown on all sides.

Remove cloves from marinade and pour into 3-quart casserole. Place roast in casserole, cover, and microwave on HIGH 10 minutes, then cook on 50% power 20 minutes. Turn roast over, cover again, and cook on 50% power 25 to 40 minutes, or until tender. Let stand, covered, 10 to 15 minutes.

Place roast on cutting board. Remove bay leaves from cooking liquid and pour liquid and vegetables into food processor or blender and puree. Add grated ginger, if desired.

Cut meat into thin diagonal slices, arrange on platter and top with sauce.

BEEF ROULADES

6 TO 8 SERVINGS

Serve with steamed vegetables and a salad for a special occasion.

8 ounces mild pork sausage, crumbled

1 teaspoon dried sage

¼ teaspoon dried thyme

¼ teaspoon salt, plus salt to taste

¼ teaspoon freshly ground black pepper, plus pepper to taste

2 tablespoons chopped parsley, plus chopped parsley for garnish

3 cups cooked wild rice (page 295)

1 (10-ounce) can condensed cream of mushroom soup

2 (1-pound) flank steaks, pounded ⅜ inch thick

2 tablespoons unsalted butter

¼ cup canned beef broth

2 cups sliced mushrooms

1 cup half-and-half

1 tablespoon dry sherry

In 1-quart measure, microwave sausage, covered, on HIGH 3 to 4 minutes, or until cooked. Add sage, thyme, ¼ teaspoon each salt and pepper, 2 tablespoons parsley, wild rice, and half the mushroom soup, mixing well.

Sprinkle steaks with salt and pepper to taste. Spread rice mixture over steaks and roll up steaks from long side, jelly-roll fashion. Secure roulades with wooden toothpicks and tie with kitchen string.

Melt butter in heavy skillet over moderately high heat on conventional rangetop. Add roulades and brown on all sides. Transfer roulades to 3-quart casserole. Pour broth into skillet and deglaze, scraping up all browned bits. Pour broth over steak rolls, cover casserole, and microwave on 50% power 30 to 40 minutes, or until beef is tender.

Transfer roulades to serving platter, remove toothpicks and string, and slice beef.

To prepare sauce, add mushrooms to cooking liquid, cover and microwave on HIGH 2 to 3 minutes. Stir in half-and-half, sherry, and remaining mushroom soup. Microwave on HIGH 2 to 3 minutes longer, or until just boiling. Pour some sauce over beef, sprinkle roulades with remaining chopped parsley, and pass sauce separately.

Beef Goulash

¼ cup olive oil

1 pound boneless beef chuck, cut into 1-inch cubes

1 onion, chopped

1 green bell pepper, chopped

1 clove garlic, minced

2 tablespoons sweet Hungarian paprika

1½ teaspoons salt

¼ teaspoon freshly ground black pepper

1 teaspoon vinegar

2 cups Beef Stock (page 46) or canned beef broth

4 TO 6 SERVINGS

▪

This Hungarian specialty may be made with pork, lamb, or beef.

Heat oil in heavy skillet over high heat on conventional range-top. Add beef and brown on all sides.

Meanwhile, place onion, bell pepper, and garlic in 3-quart casserole. Cover and microwave on HIGH 5 minutes.

When beef is browned, stir in paprika, salt, pepper, vinegar, and stock and deglaze skillet, scraping up all browned bits. Stir beef mixture into casserole, cover, and microwave on HIGH 5 minutes. Reduce power to 50% and cook 30 minutes longer. Serve over buttered noodles.

TRANSYLVANIAN GOULASH

Prepare Beef Goulash as directed. After goulash has cooked, add 1 (1-pound) can sauerkraut, drained, and ½ cup sour cream. Reheat on 80% power 3 to 5 minutes, or to serving temperature.

Corned Beef

1 (3-pound) corned beef round or brisket, with seasonings

2 cups water

1 recipe Dijon Mustard Glaze (page 87)

8 TO 10 SERVINGS

▪

For a delicious accompaniment, add cabbage wedges to the cooking liquid after the corned beef is removed and cook until tender.

Place corned beef, seasonings, and water in 3-quart casserole. Cover and microwave on HIGH 10 minutes, then on 30% power 1½ to 2 hours, or until tender (30 to 40 minutes per pound). Halfway through cooking, turn beef over. Let stand, covered, 15 minutes. Remove beef from liquid, drain, and slice. Serve with sauce.

CORNED BEEF STEW

4 TO 6 SERVINGS

A quick and tasty one-dish meal.

4 potatoes, peeled and cut into
 large chunks
2 carrots, thickly sliced
1 large onion, sliced vertically
2 stalks celery, thickly sliced
2 cloves garlic, minced
½ teaspoon dry mustard
1 teaspoon salt

½ teaspoon freshly ground black
 pepper
1 tablespoon cornstarch
1 cup water
1 (12-ounce) can corned beef,
 drained and cut into large
 chunks

To help tenderize corned beef, slice it after first hour of cooking and return to cooking liquid.

Place potatoes and carrots in 2-quart casserole, pushing them to sides of dish. Place onion, celery, and garlic in center of dish, cover, and microwave on HIGH 6 to 9 minutes, or until potatoes are tender.

Combine mustard, salt, pepper, cornstarch, and water and pour over vegetables. Place corned beef evenly over vegetables, cover, and microwave on HIGH 5 to 6 minutes, or until sauce is thickened.

ENCHILADA CASSEROLE

8 TO 10 SERVINGS

2 pounds lean ground beef,
 crumbled
1 medium onion, chopped
½ teaspoon garlic powder
1 teaspoon chili powder, or to
 taste
¼ teaspoon ground cumin
Salt

1 (16-ounce) can refried beans
2 (15-ounce) cans red enchilada
 sauce
10 corn tortillas
8 ounces Cheddar cheese, grated
Sour cream
Chopped green chilies
Chopped black olives

In 2-quart measure, combine beef and onion and microwave on HIGH 7 to 10 minutes, or until beef is cooked, stirring several times during cooking. Drain off fat. Add garlic powder, chili powder, cumin, salt to taste, refried beans, and ½ can enchilada sauce. Microwave on HIGH 3 to 5 minutes, or until hot.

Wrap tortillas in plastic wrap and microwave on HIGH about 1 minute to warm them and make them pliable. Place 2 to 3 tablespoons meat filling on each tortilla. Roll up tortillas and place them, seam sides down, in 13 × 9-inch dish. Pour remaining enchilada sauce over tortillas and microwave on HIGH 3 to 6 minutes, or until thoroughly heated.

Sprinkle with cheese and microwave on 70% power 4 to 5 minutes, or until cheese is melted. Serve topped with sour cream, chilies, and olives to taste.

> To make extra-lean ground beef moister, add a grated raw potato to each pound of meat.

BEEF AND SPAGHETTI BAKE

1 onion, chopped
1 green bell pepper, chopped
2 stalks celery, chopped
1 pound lean ground beef
1 (29-ounce) can tomato sauce
1 cup burgundy wine
1 cup water
½ teaspoon dried oregano

½ teaspoon dried basil
½ teaspoon dried marjoram
1 clove garlic, minced
½ teaspoon salt
¼ teaspoon freshly ground black pepper
8 ounces spaghetti, broken in half
4 ounces Cheddar cheese, grated

8 TO 12 SERVINGS

The pasta cooks right in the sauce!

Place onion, bell pepper, and celery in large bowl, cover, and microwave on HIGH 4 minutes. Crumble beef over vegetables, cover, and microwave on HIGH 5 minutes. Add tomato sauce, wine, water, oregano, basil, marjoram, garlic, salt, and pepper and stir well.

Place spaghetti in 3-quart casserole and pour sauce over it, moving spaghetti around until well covered with liquid. Cover casserole and microwave on HIGH 10 minutes. Stir, cover again, and microwave on 50% power 30 minutes.

Spread grated cheese over spaghetti, cover, and let stand 15 minutes. Serve with a tossed salad and French bread. Casserole may be refrigerated for several days or frozen.

SPINACH MEAT LOAF PIE

4 TO 6 SERVINGS

·

This busy-day special is basically a spinach-and-beef meat loaf, cooked in a pie plate and served in wedges.

1 pound lean ground beef, crumbled
1 onion, chopped
1 clove garlic, minced
1/2 teaspoon dried basil
1/4 teaspoon dried marjoram
1/4 teaspoon dried oregano
1 teaspoon salt
1/4 teaspoon freshly ground black pepper
1 (10-ounce) package frozen chopped spinach, defrosted and drained
4 large eggs, beaten
1/4 cup shredded mozzarella cheese (optional)

Crumble beef into 2-quart measure, add onion, garlic, basil, marjoram, oregano, salt, and pepper and microwave on HIGH 5 minutes, or until beef is cooked.

Stir in drained spinach and eggs. Cover and microwave on HIGH 2 to 3 minutes, stirring several times. Press mixture into buttered 10-inch pie plate, cover with wax paper, and microwave on 70% power 4 to 6 minutes, or until set. Sprinkle with cheese, if desired, and let stand 3 to 4 minutes.

ITALIAN MEATBALLS

6 TO 8 SERVINGS

·

2 large onions, finely chopped
1 3/4 cups rolled oats
1 pound lean ground beef, crumbled
1/2 pound ground pork, crumbled
2 cloves garlic, minced
1/2 cup freshly grated Parmesan cheese
2 large eggs, beaten
1 teaspoon fennel seeds
1 teaspoon salt
1 teaspoon freshly ground black pepper
1/4 teaspoon dried oregano
1/4 teaspoon dried thyme

In large bowl, microwave onions on HIGH 2 minutes. Add rolled oats, beef, pork, garlic, Parmesan, eggs, fennel seeds, salt, pepper, oregano, and thyme and combine well.

Form mixture into balls 1 to 2 inches in diameter and arrange in a circle on 10-inch pie plate. Microwave on HIGH 5 minutes, then on 50% power 10 minutes. Serve plain or with Tomato-Basil Sauce (page 90) or Mushroom Sauce (page 89) over pasta.

CURRIED BEEF

3 to 4 cups sliced onions
1 stick (½ cup) unsalted butter
2 teaspoons ground coriander
1 tablespoon grated fresh ginger or
    1 teaspoon ground ginger
½ teaspoon turmeric
½ teaspoon freshly ground black
    pepper
½ teaspoon cayenne pepper

4 cloves garlic, minced
4 cardamom pods, crushed
½ teaspoon anise seeds, crushed
1 pound lean ground beef,
    crumbled, or 1 pound beef
    chuck, cut into ½-inch pieces
1 tablespoon fresh lemon juice
2 tablespoons water

4 OR 5 SERVINGS

▪

A good company dish that is very quick and easy to prepare.

In 3-quart casserole, place onions, butter, coriander, ginger, turmeric, black pepper, cayenne, garlic, cardamom, and anise seeds. Cover and microwave on HIGH 5 to 8 minutes, or until onions are tender.

Add beef, lemon juice, and water, cover, and microwave on 50% power 10 to 20 minutes, stirring every 5 minutes. Serve over rice.

CHILI CON CARNE

1½ pounds lean ground beef,
    crumbled
1 onion, chopped
3 cloves garlic, minced
2 (28-ounce) cans tomatoes,
    undrained, chopped
2 (16-ounce) cans red kidney
    beans, drained
1 bay leaf
2 teaspoons beef bouillon granules

3 tablespoons chili powder, or to
    taste
1 teaspoon ground cumin
½ teaspoon dried oregano
½ teaspoon paprika
½ teaspoon sugar
Salt
Freshly ground black pepper
Red pepper flakes or chopped
    jalapeño peppers (optional)

6 SERVINGS

▪

In 3-quart casserole, combine beef, onion, and garlic and microwave on HIGH 7 minutes. Stir in tomatoes, beans, bay leaf, bouillon granules, chili powder, cumin, oregano, paprika, sugar, salt and pepper to taste, and red pepper flakes to taste, if desired. Cover casserole and microwave on HIGH 10 minutes, then cook on 50% power 20 to 30 minutes.

JOHNNY MEZETTI

6 SERVINGS

A ground beef sauce to serve over fettucine or rice. This recipe can be completed in less than 30 minutes.

1 onion, chopped
1 green bell pepper, chopped
2 cloves garlic, minced
1 1/2 pounds lean ground beef, crumbled
1 (16-ounce) can tomatoes, undrained
1 (6-ounce) can tomato paste
2 cups fresh or frozen corn
2 teaspoons salt

1/2 teaspoon freshly ground black pepper
1 teaspoon dried oregano
1/2 teaspoon ground allspice
1 cup grated Cheddar cheese
16 ounces fettucine, cooked according to package instructions
1/2 cup sliced green olives

Place onion, bell pepper, and garlic in a 3-quart casserole, cover, and microwave on HIGH 5 minutes. Add beef, cover, and microwave on HIGH 5 to 8 minutes, stirring halfway through cooking.

Add tomatoes, tomato paste, corn, salt, pepper, oregano, and allspice. Cover and microwave on HIGH 10 minutes. Add cheese and stir until it melts. Serve over fettucine. Sprinkle with olives.

NOTE

To prepare ahead, layer fettucine and sauce in a casserole, cover, and refrigerate or freeze. To serve, defrost if frozen, and microwave, covered, on 70% power 10 minutes, or to serving temperature.

SAVORY MEAT LOAF

6 SERVINGS

1 1/2 pounds lean ground beef, crumbled
1 1/2 cups dry bread crumbs
1 (8-ounce) can tomato sauce
1 large egg, beaten
1 onion, chopped
2 tablespoons Worcestershire sauce

2 teaspoons dry mustard
1 clove garlic, minced
1/2 teaspoon dried oregano
1/2 teaspoon dried sage
1/2 teaspoon salt
1/4 teaspoon freshly ground black pepper
1 tablespoon brown sugar

In bowl, combine beef, bread crumbs, half the tomato sauce, egg, onion, 1 tablespoon Worcestershire, mustard, garlic, oregano, sage, salt, and pepper and mix well. Form into ring shape on 9-inch pie plate, and insert a custard cup in center.

Combine remaining tomato sauce, 1 tablespoon Worcestershire, and brown sugar. Spread over meat and microwave, uncovered, on HIGH 15 to 20 minutes. Let stand 5 minutes before serving.

Lotus Blossom Special

1½ pounds boneless sirloin or
    flank steak, partially frozen
1 carrot, thinly sliced
8 ounces snow peas, trimmed,
    strings removed
8 ounces mushrooms, sliced
1 stalk celery, diagonally sliced

1 small onion, sliced vertically
3 scallions, diagonally sliced
1 (5-ounce) can sliced bamboo
    shoots, drained
1 (3-ounce) can sliced water
    chestnuts, drained

6 SERVINGS

MARINADE

3 tablespoons peanut oil
2 to 3 tablespoons soy sauce
1½ teaspoons sugar
2 cloves garlic, minced

¼ teaspoon salt
¼ teaspoon freshly ground black
    pepper

Thinly slice meat across grain (this is easier to do when meat is partially frozen). Combine marinade ingredients in a bowl, add sliced beef, and stir to coat meat. Let stand 30 minutes. (Or cover bowl with foil and freeze for up to 1 month. To defrost, remove foil and microwave frozen meat mixture on 30% power 6 to 7 minutes and proceed with recipe.)

Place carrot slices against sides of shallow 2-quart casserole. Place pea pods, mushrooms, celery, onion, and scallions in dish and push them toward outer edge, next to carrots. Place meat and marinade in center of dish, cover, and microwave on HIGH 6 to 10 minutes, or until vegetables are tender-crisp. Add bamboo shoots and water chestnuts and stir well. Cover and microwave on HIGH 2 to 5 minutes. Serve with rice or Chinese noodles.

SPOONBURGERS

6 SERVINGS

1 pound lean ground beef
1 medium onion, finely chopped
1 carrot, finely shredded
1 stalk celery (strings removed),
    shredded
1/2 cup catsup

1/2 cup chili sauce
1 tablespoon Worcestershire sauce
1 teaspoon salt
1/4 teaspoon freshly ground black
    pepper
6 hamburger buns, split

Crumble beef into 2-quart measure and add onion, carrot, and celery. Cover and microwave on HIGH 7 to 10 minutes, or until meat is cooked and vegetables are tender.

Stir in catsup, chili sauce, Worcestershire, salt, and pepper. Microwave, uncovered, on HIGH 2 minutes, then on 50% power 5 minutes. Spoon mixture between split buns and serve.

NOTE

The carrot and celery may be omitted, but they do add flavor and vitamins. Children won't even know they're eating vegetables.

SPAGHETTI SAUCE

6 TO 8 SERVINGS

Tastes as though it had simmered for hours.

1 pound lean ground beef,
    crumbled
1/2 pound pork sausage, crumbled
1 1/2 cups chopped onions
1 to 2 teaspoons minced garlic
2 teaspoons dried oregano
2 teaspoons dried basil
2 whole star anise or 1 teaspoon
    fennel seeds

2 (28-ounce) cans tomatoes,
    undrained
1 (20-ounce) can tomato sauce
2 teaspoons beef bouillon granules
Salt
Freshly ground black pepper
Freshly grated Parmesan cheese

In 4-quart casserole, microwave beef, pork sausage, onions, and garlic, covered, on HIGH 8 to 10 minutes.

Add oregano, basil, star anise, tomatoes, tomato sauce, bouillon granules, and salt and pepper to taste. Cover and microwave on HIGH 15 minutes, then on 50% power 30 to 40 minutes. Serve over cooked spaghetti and sprinkle with grated Parmesan cheese.

Pepper Steak

1 pound flank steak or boneless
    sirloin, partially frozen
1/4 cup soy sauce
2 tablespoons cornstarch
1 tablespoon minced fresh ginger
    or 1 teaspoon ground ginger
1 teaspoon minced garlic
2 tablespoons vegetable oil

1 medium onion, sliced
1 large green bell pepper, sliced
1 (16-ounce) can tomatoes,
    undrained, chopped
1 tablespoon sugar
Salt
Freshly ground black pepper

**4 OR 5
SERVINGS**

Slice meat thinly across grain. In bowl, combine meat, soy sauce, cornstarch, ginger, garlic, and oil and let stand at least 30 minutes.

Cover bowl and microwave meat mixture on HIGH 4 to 6 minutes. Stir and add onion, bell pepper, tomatoes, sugar, and salt and pepper to taste. Cover again and microwave on HIGH 8 to 10 minutes, stirring halfway through cooking. Serve over rice.

Hot and Spicy Beef

1 pound sirloin or flank steak,
    partially frozen
2 tablespoons soy sauce
2 tablespoons dry sherry
1 teaspoon sugar
2 tablespoons peanut oil
1 tablespoon cornstarch

2 tablespoons water
1/2 teaspoon cayenne pepper
1 medium red bell pepper, cut into
    1-inch pieces
1 medium green bell pepper, cut
    into 1-inch pieces
2 cups sliced mushrooms

**4 TO 6
SERVINGS**

Slice meat thinly across the grain.

In bowl, combine steak, soy sauce, sherry, and sugar. Stir to blend and let marinate at least 20 minutes.

Place oil in 2-quart casserole, add beef mixture, and microwave on HIGH 3 to 5 minutes. Stir.

Dissolve cornstarch in water and add to beef mixture with cayenne, bell peppers, and mushrooms. Cover and microwave on HIGH 4 to 6 minutes. Serve with rice.

BEEF TACOS

10 TACOS

▪

Fun for teenagers to put together themselves. Other toppings such as chopped onion, chopped olives, sour cream, chopped avocado, salsa, or chopped cilantro may also be added.

1 ½ pounds lean ground beef
1 clove garlic, minced
½ teaspoon ground cumin
1 teaspoon chili powder
1 (8-ounce) can tomato sauce
Salt

Freshly ground black pepper
Hot pepper sauce
10 taco shells
Grated Monterey Jack or Cheddar
   cheese, shredded iceberg
   lettuce, and chopped tomatoes

Crumble beef into 2-quart measure, add garlic, and microwave on HIGH 7 to 8 minutes, or until beef is cooked. Stir several times to break up the meat. Drain. Stir in cumin, chili powder, tomato sauce, and salt, pepper, and hot pepper sauce to taste. Microwave, uncovered, on HIGH 2 to 3 minutes longer.

Fill taco shells with several tablespoons of meat mixture. Top with grated cheese, shredded lettuce, and chopped tomatoes.

BEEF TOSTADA CASSEROLE

6 SERVINGS

▪

1 pound lean ground beef,
   crumbled
1 large onion, chopped
⅔ cup chopped celery
1 (8-ounce) can tomato sauce
1 (16-ounce) can red kidney
   beans, drained
1 (12-ounce) can whole-kernel
   corn, drained
2 teaspoons chili powder
¼ teaspoon dried oregano

½ teaspoon salt
½ teaspoon freshly ground black
   pepper
½ cup grated Cheddar or
   Monterey Jack cheese
½ cup crushed corn chips
Sour cream, sliced avocado, sliced
   olives, hot peppers, chopped
   tomatoes, and/or shredded
   iceberg lettuce

Place ground beef, onion, and celery in 2- to 3-quart casserole, cover, and microwave on HIGH 5 to 6 minutes, or until meat is cooked and vegetables are tender-crisp. Drain.

Stir in tomato sauce, beans, corn, chili powder, oregano, salt, and pepper. Cover and microwave on HIGH 4 to 5 minutes, or until hot, stirring during cooking. Sprinkle with cheese and corn chips and microwave on HIGH 2 to 3 minutes, or until cheese melts.

Serve topped with sour cream, sliced avocado, sliced olives, hot peppers, chopped tomatoes, lettuce, or other toppings of your choice.

BEEF AND BROCCOLI

1 pound flank steak, partially
    frozen
1 tablespoon grated fresh ginger
1 teaspoon sugar
1 tablespoon cornstarch
3 tablespoons soy sauce
2 tablespoons dry sherry
1 onion, sliced

1 pound broccoli flowerets and
    peeled, diagonally sliced stems
4 to 6 scallions, thinly sliced
1 carrot, thinly sliced
1/3 cup peanut oil
1 chicken bouillon cube
1/3 cup hot water

4 SERVINGS

A simple and delicious stir-fry.

Thinly slice flank steak across grain (this is easier to do when meat is partially frozen). Place in bowl with ginger, sugar, cornstarch, soy sauce, and sherry and rub mixture into steak strips. Allow to marinate 30 minutes or longer. Stir well. (Recipe can be made ahead to this point. Transfer meat and marinade to a plastic storage bag and freeze for up to 1 month. To defrost, microwave on 30% power 6 to 7 minutes, then proceed with recipe.)

Place onion, broccoli, scallions, and carrot in 2-quart dish. Pour meat mixture into center of dish, pushing vegetables toward outer edge. Cover and microwave on HIGH 5 to 8 minutes, or until vegetables are cooked but still quite crisp. Add oil. Dissolve bouillon cube in water and add to beef mixture. Cook and stir on HIGH 2 to 3 minutes longer, if needed. Serve with Oriental noodles or rice.

PARMESAN MEAT LOAF

4 TO 6 SERVINGS

1 medium onion, chopped
1 medium green bell pepper,
    chopped
1 pound lean ground veal,
    crumbled
1 cup low-fat (1%) cottage cheese
1/2 cup rolled oats
2 large eggs, beaten

1 teaspoon minced garlic
1/2 teaspoon salt
1/4 teaspoon freshly ground black
    pepper
1/2 cup freshly grated Parmesan
    cheese
1/2 cup catsup

In 2-quart bowl, combine onions and bell pepper, cover, and microwave on HIGH 4 to 6 minutes. Add veal, cottage cheese, oats, eggs, garlic, salt, pepper, and Parmesan and toss gently. Lightly press mixture into a ring dish or round 2-quart casserole. (If using casserole, place custard cup in center and form meat loaf around it in a ring.)

Microwave on HIGH 5 minutes, then on 70% power 9 to 12 minutes. Spread catsup over meat and allow loaf to stand 5 minutes before serving.

STIR-FRIED LIVER AND ONIONS

4 SERVINGS

1 pound calf's liver, cut into
    1/4-inch strips
2 tablespoons soy sauce
1/4 teaspoon freshly ground black
    pepper
1/2 teaspoon dried oregano

1/4 teaspoon garlic salt
2 tablespoons cornstarch
2 tablespoons vegetable oil
1 large onion, cut into vertical
    strips
2 tablespoons catsup

In bowl, combine liver, soy sauce, pepper, oregano, garlic salt, and cornstarch. Let stand 10 to 15 minutes.

Pour oil into 2-quart measure and microwave on HIGH 1 to 2 minutes, or until hot. Add liver mixture and onions. Cover and microwave on HIGH 5 to 8 minutes, stirring several times, or until liver is cooked. Stir in catsup.

Veal Paupiettes

6 veal scallops or thin cutlets
    (1 pound)
4 ounces cooked ham
1 clove garlic
½ teaspoon dried marjoram
Pinch of freshly grated nutmeg
½ teaspoon fresh or dried
    rosemary leaves (optional)
2 tablespoons olive oil
2 tablespoons unsalted butter
1 onion, finely chopped

1 small carrot, finely chopped
1 small potato, peeled and finely
    chopped
2 tablespoons chopped parsley
½ cup dry white wine
¾ cup Beef Stock (page 46) or
    canned beef broth
½ teaspoon dried thyme
3 whole cloves
2 bay leaves

4 TO 6 SERVINGS

Serve these veal rolls with rice or potatoes for a special dinner.

Pound veal scallops until about ¼ inch thick. Trim into rectangles. In food processor fitted with steel blade, place veal trimmings, ham, garlic, marjoram, nutmeg, and, if desired, rosemary, and pulse to chop meat and combine ingredients. Spread mixture evenly over veal scallops and roll up. Secure with wooden toothpicks.

Place heavy skillet over moderately high heat on conventional rangetop, add olive oil and butter, and heat until butter melts. Add paupiettes and brown on all sides, 5 to 7 minutes. Transfer veal to 2-quart dish.

Add onion, carrot, and potato to veal drippings and cook over moderately high heat until golden, 4 to 5 minutes, stirring frequently. Add parsley, wine, stock, thyme, cloves, and bay leaves. Stir to loosen all browned bits at bottom of pan. Simmer 5 to 7 minutes, or until liquid is reduced by half, stirring frequently.

Pour sauce over paupiettes, cover, and microwave on 50% power 12 to 15 minutes, or until veal in center of dish is cooked.

Transfer veal to serving plate. Remove cloves and bay leaves from sauce and puree sauce in food processor or blender. Pour sauce over veal and serve at once.

LAMB

The term *spring lamb* is sometimes used to designate lamb under a year old, and sometimes simply means very young lamb. Spring lamb can be found year round, but it is most often available in the spring. Select lamb with firm, waxy fat and fine, smooth, lean meat. Young lamb has dark pink flesh and porous red bones. The lamb flavor becomes more pronounced as the animal matures. For this reason, spring lamb is preferred for its mild flavor. All lamb is tender.

SPICED LAMB CHOPS

4 SERVINGS

4 (1½-inch) loin lamb chops
½ cup mayonnaise
1 teaspoon mustard
½ teaspoon soy sauce
½ teaspoon crushed dried
    rosemary leaves

Place lamb chops in single layer in shallow baking dish, meaty portion toward outside of dish. Combine mayonnaise, mustard, and soy sauce and spread mixture over chops. Sprinkle with rosemary, cover with wax paper, and microwave on HIGH 5 minutes, then on 50% power for 10 to 15 minutes, depending on the degree of doneness desired.

LAMB CURRY

4 OR 5 SERVINGS

1½ pounds boneless lamb, cut
    into bite-size pieces
1 tablespoon ground coriander
1 teaspoon grated fresh ginger
½ teaspoon freshly ground black
    pepper
½ teaspoon cayenne pepper
2 cloves garlic, minced
⅛ teaspoon ground cinnamon
1 cup plain low-fat yogurt
4 medium onions, sliced
½ stick (¼ cup) butter
4 cardamom pods, crushed
1 cup slivered blanched almonds,
    toasted (page 441)
¼ cup golden raisins (optional)

In bowl combine lamb, coriander, ginger, black pepper, cayenne, garlic, cinnamon, and yogurt and mix well. Cover and let stand in refrigerator overnight.

In 3-quart casserole, combine onions, butter, and cardamom. Microwave on HIGH 4 to 5 minutes, or until onions are tender. Stir in lamb mixture, cover, and microwave on 70% power 6 to 8 minutes. Stir in almonds and, if desired, raisins. Let stand 3 to 4 minutes. Serve over rice.

PORK

Good fresh pork has a fine pink grain and firm white fat. It is often smoked or cured. Cured pork is pink; it becomes gray when exposed to light, but the color change does not affect the quality of the meat. Pork should always be cooked covered in the microwave. To prevent any possibility of trichinosis—an illness caused by trichinae, parasites sometimes present in uncooked pork—the meat should reach an internal temperature of 170° F. before it is served. If you cook a roast or large cut of meat to 165° F. and let it stand 10 to 15 minutes, the internal temperature will rise to 170° F. or above.

BACON

Microwaving is the best cooking method for bacon. Because of the high proportion of fat to lean in bacon, it microwaves beautifully brown and crisp. The bacon should be placed in a single layer on a bacon or baking rack. Bacon racks, designed especially for use in the microwave, will hold the bacon out of the fat drippings so that it will crisp. Cook on HIGH power for approximately 1 minute per slice. The cooking time will vary depending on the thickness of the bacon slices and the amount of fat and water in the bacon. Place a paper towel over the bacon to help prevent spattering in the oven.

HAM

Ham is from the hindquarter of the pig. Use the cooking chart beginning on page 203 for microwaving instructions.

SAUSAGES

When cooking fresh sausage, follow the guidelines for ground beef patties on page 203. Fresh sausages can be microwaved, but their flavor is enhanced by conventional browning.

Uncooked smoked sausage such as bauernwurst and Polish sausage (kielbasa) are cured and smoked, but must be thoroughly cooked. Use HIGH power to cook several servings, but for larger cuts or more servings, use a combination of HIGH power for 5 minutes and 50% power for the remainder of cooking time. Cook covered.

Cooked smoked sausages, such as bologna, frankfurters, hot dogs or wieners, bierwurst, Berliner bockwurst, Berliner blutwurst, smokies, and knockwurst, are usually made from fresh meats that have been smoked and fully cooked. These sausages are ready to eat but taste better when they are heated. They can be microwaved on HIGH power.

Cooked sausages made from fresh uncured or cured meats that have been thoroughly cooked—liver sausage, liverwurst, andouillette, scrapple, liver loaf, blood sausage, and braunschweiger are some examples—may also be heated in the microwave on HIGH to enhance their flavor.

Dry and semidry sausage—pepperoni, chorizos, salami, Lebanon bologna, mortadella, and summer sausage—are cured and ready to eat. When these are served as snacks they are not even heated. When they are used in food preparation, they can be heated in the microwave to extract some of the fat.

HONEY·BAKED PORK CHOPS

4 SERVINGS

■

A good recipe for combination cooking (page 199).

4 (1-inch-thick) pork chops

MARINADE

1/3 cup honey
1/4 cup cider vinegar
2 tablespoons soy sauce
2 tablespoons crystallized ginger, coarsely chopped

2 or 3 cloves garlic, sliced
1/2 teaspoon freshly ground black pepper

Arrange pork chops in single layer in 9-inch pie plate, meatier portions toward outside of plate. Combine honey, vinegar, soy sauce, ginger, garlic, and black pepper and pour marinade over chops. Cover with plastic wrap and refrigerate overnight.

Prepare charcoal or other outdoor grill, or preheat conventional broiler.

Microwave chops, still covered, on HIGH 3 minutes. Rearrange chops, cover again, and microwave on 50% power 5 minutes. Transfer chops to grill and continue cooking until done, about 15 minutes longer, turning several times and basting often with marinade.

If you prefer to cook chops entirely in the microwave, after first 3 minutes of cooking on HIGH, rearrange chops, cover again, and microwave on 50% power 15 to 18 minutes, or until cooked. Let stand, covered, 5 minutes.

BAKED PORK CHOPS WITH TOMATO SAUCE

4 pork chops or pork steaks (2 pounds)
1 large onion, cut into 4 thick slices
1 (15-ounce) can tomato sauce

1 tablespoon vinegar
2 teaspoons chili powder
¼ teaspoon ground allspice
1 clove garlic, minced
4 green bell pepper rings (optional)

4 SERVINGS

Trim fat from chops and place them in single layer in large pie plate. Arrange onion slices on top.

Combine tomato sauce, vinegar, chili powder, allspice, and garlic. Pour sauce over chops and onion, cover with plastic wrap, and microwave on HIGH 15 minutes.

Add green pepper rings, if desired, cover, and microwave on HIGH 3 to 5 minutes longer, or until the chops are cooked.

NOTE

This dish can be cooked successfully on HIGH because the sauce and onions "share" the microwaves with the meat.

STUFFED CABBAGE

1 onion, minced
1 clove garlic, minced
8 ounces ground pork or bulk pork
    sausage, crumbled
8 ounces cooked ham, finely
    chopped
1 cup cooked rice (page 289)
2 egg whites

1 tablespoon Dijon mustard
1/4 teaspoon ground sage
1/4 teaspoon dried thyme
1/2 teaspoon salt
1/4 teaspoon freshly ground black
    pepper
1 large head cabbage

SAUCE
2 egg yolks
1/4 cup fresh lemon juice
1 tablespoon cornstarch

1/4 teaspoon paprika
Water

Prepare stuffing: In 2-quart measure, microwave onions, garlic, and pork, covered, on HIGH 4 to 5 minutes, or until meat is cooked. Stir in ham, rice, egg whites, mustard, sage, thyme, salt, and pepper and combine well.

Prepare cabbage leaves: Wrap whole cabbage in plastic wrap and microwave on HIGH 3 to 4 minutes, or until 12 to 14 large outer leaves can be separated from head. Refrigerate remaining cabbage for another use.

Place cabbage leaves in 2-quart bowl or plastic bag and microwave on HIGH 2 to 3 minutes, or until soft and pliable. Cut away most of bottom of vein from each leaf. Place about 1/4 cup stuffing on each leaf, fold in sides, and roll up, beginning at stem end and rolling toward tip.

Place cabbage rolls in shallow 3-quart casserole, seam sides down. (Recipe can be made ahead to this point. Cover casserole with plastic wrap and freeze for up to 6 weeks. To defrost, microwave on 30% power 8 to 15 minutes, or until defrosted in center of dish. Proceed with recipe.) Microwave on HIGH 6 to 10 minutes, or until cabbage is tender and filling is hot.

Prepare sauce: In small bowl, beat egg yolks. Stir in lemon juice, cornstarch, and paprika. Drain cooking liquid from cabbage rolls and stir in sauce. Microwave on HIGH 1 to 2 minutes, or until slightly thickened. If sauce is too thick, thin with a little water. Spoon sauce over cabbage rolls and serve.

PORK BURRITOS

3 pounds boneless lean pork, cut
    into ½-inch cubes
3 large onions, chopped
2 green bell peppers, chopped
¾ cup chopped fresh coriander
    (cilantro)
2 tomatoes, chopped
2 cloves garlic, minced
1 tablespoon salt
½ teaspoon freshly ground black
    pepper
½ teaspoon ground cumin

Dash of ground cloves
½ teaspoon dried oregano
2 bay leaves
8 ounces fresh tomatillos, husked
    or 1 (10-ounce) can, drained
    (optional)
½ cup cornstarch
¼ cup water
12 flour tortillas
2 cups grated Monterey Jack or
    Cheddar cheese
2 cups Salsa (page 90)

12 SERVINGS

▪

The burritos can be prepared ahead and frozen for quick defrosting and reheating.

Place pork in 3- to 4-quart casserole and cover with onions, bell peppers, cilantro, tomatoes, garlic, salt, pepper, cumin, cloves, oregano, bay leaves, and tomatillos. Microwave, covered, on HIGH 10 minutes, then on 50% power 20 to 30 minutes, or until pork is very tender and tomatillos are soft.

With a slotted spoon, transfer pork and vegetables to food processor fitted with steel blade and pulse 5 or 6 times to shred meat. Return mixture to sauce. Combine cornstarch and water and stir into meat mixture. Microwave on HIGH 3 to 4 minutes, or until slightly thickened.

Wrap tortillas in wax paper and microwave on HIGH 45 to 60 seconds, or until warm.

To make burritos, place a heaping ½ cup pork filling a little below center of each tortilla. Fold sides of tortillas over filling, then roll up. Place burritos seam side down in 2 13 × 9-inch dishes. Recipe can be prepared ahead to this point. Cover with plastic wrap and refrigerate if desired. Or place burritos on baking sheet and freeze. Store frozen burritos in plastic freezer bags and defrost and reheat individually.

Remove covering, if any, from dish and sprinkle burritos with cheese. Microwave on HIGH until cheese melts, 3 to 4 minutes if burritos were at room temperature, or longer if refrigerated. Serve with Salsa.

PORK CANTONESE

4 SERVINGS

■

A delicious stir-fry.

1 pound boneless lean pork, cut
  into ½-inch cubes
2 tablespoons peanut or corn oil
1 (14-ounce) can pineapple
  chunks, drained
2 cups sliced mushrooms
2 to 3 tablespoons molasses

2 tablespoons white or rice wine
  vinegar
1 green bell pepper, cut into strips
2 medium onions, sliced
2 tablespoons cornstarch
2 tablespoons water

Place pork in 2-quart casserole, cover, and microwave on HIGH 3 to 5 minutes, stirring once. Add oil, pineapple, mushrooms, molasses, vinegar, bell pepper, and onions. Cover and microwave on HIGH 4 to 7 minutes. Combine cornstarch and water and stir into meat mixture. Microwave on HIGH 1 to 2 minutes. Serve over rice or Chinese noodles.

BARBECUED RIBS

4 SERVINGS

■

Cook ribs in the micro-
wave first and then
complete cooking on
the grill.

3½ pounds ribs (pork baby back,
  pork country-style, pork
  spareribs, or beef short ribs)

½ cup water
1 recipe Barbecue Sauce (page 86)
  or bottled barbecue sauce

Preheat charcoal or other outdoor grill or preheat conventional broiler.

Place ribs in 12 × 8-inch casserole, arranging thicker portions toward outside and overlapping thinner parts. Add water, cover with plastic wrap, and microwave on HIGH 5 minutes. Reduce power to 50% and cook 7 minutes. Turn meat over and rearrange. Microwave on 50% power 8 minutes.

Drain ribs and place on grill over hot coals. Grill 18 to 25 minutes, or until ribs are brown and fork-tender. Baste during grilling with barbecue sauce.

BRAISED PORK TENDERLOINS WITH CREAM SAUCE

2 pork tenderloins, 1 1/2 pounds
  each
3 or 4 cloves garlic, thinly sliced
1 tablespoon unsalted butter
2 tablespoons vegetable oil
1/2 cup dry white wine
2 to 3 tablespoons dry mustard

1 teaspoon freshly ground black
  pepper
1 teaspoon crushed dried
  rosemary
1 large onion, thinly sliced
1 cup heavy cream
1 tablespoon all-purpose flour
1 teaspoon salt

6 TO 8 SERVINGS

■

The blend of flavors in this dish is outstanding. Serve it with Lo-Cal Risotto (page 296).

With sharp knife, make slits in tenderloins and insert garlic slices.

Place butter and oil in heavy skillet and melt butter over moderately high heat on conventional rangetop. Add tenderloins and brown on all sides. Remove pork and place in 12 × 9-inch casserole. Deglaze skillet with white wine, scraping up all browned bits. Reserve wine mixture.

Combine mustard, pepper, and rosemary and rub mixture into pork. Pour reserved wine mixture over pork and top with onion slices. Cover and microwave on 50% power 12 to 15 minutes per pound. Turn meat over halfway through cooking. Transfer pork to cutting board.

Blend cream, flour, and salt and stir into cooking liquid. Microwave on 70% power 3 to 4 minutes, or until sauce is thickened, stirring several times.

Slice pork thin, arrange on heated platter, and pour sauce over it. Serve at once.

BAKED HAM AND WILD RICE WITH CELERY SAUCE

6 TO 8 SERVINGS

Great for a crowd! This dish can be made ahead and refrigerated or frozen. It's a good way to use leftover ham.

1 (6-ounce) package mixed long-grain and wild rice

1 (20-ounce) package frozen chopped broccoli, defrosted and blanched (page 245)

CELERY SAUCE

1½ cups sliced celery

1 cup finely chopped onion

1 cup sliced mushrooms

3 tablespoons unsalted butter

3 tablespoons all-purpose flour

1½ cups milk

½ teaspoon dried thyme

12 ounces cooked ham, cut into strips

1 cup grated sharp Cheddar cheese

1 cup mayonnaise (page 116)

1 teaspoon dry mustard

Salt

Freshly ground white pepper

½ cup freshly grated Parmesan cheese

Chopped parsley or paprika

Microwave rice according to package instructions. Spread rice evenly in 13 × 9-inch baking dish.

Drain broccoli and spread over rice. Sprinkle ham and Cheddar cheese over broccoli.

Make celery sauce: Place celery, onion, mushrooms, and butter in 1-quart measure, cover, and microwave on HIGH 4 to 5 minutes, or until vegetables are tender. Stir in flour, then slowly stir in milk. Microwave on HIGH 3 to 6 minutes, or until thickened, stirring several times. Stir in thyme, mayonnaise, mustard, and salt and pepper to taste. Pour sauce over broccoli mixture and sprinkle with Parmesan.

Microwave on 70% power 10 to 15 minutes, or until thoroughly heated. Garnish with parsley or other fresh herbs or a light sprinkling of paprika.

SCRUMPTIOUS HAM

1 (10- to 12-pound) smoked ham
6 bay leaves, crushed
1 tablespoon dried thyme
2 (2-inch long) cinnamon sticks
2 onions, sliced

2 cloves garlic, sliced
Whole cloves
½ cup, packed, dark brown sugar
⅓ cup honey
3 tablespoons Dijon mustard

20 TO 25 SERVINGS

In this unusual recipe, ham is boiled with seasonings, then baked in the microwave with a honey and mustard glaze. Prepare at least one day before serving or even several days ahead.

At least 1 day in advance, place ham in large stockpot, add water to cover, bay leaves, thyme, cinnamon sticks, onions, garlic, and 5 whole cloves. Cover and bring to a boil on conventional rangetop. Reduce heat and simmer until ham is tender, 3 to 3½ hours. Internal temperature of ham should be 170° F. Let ham stand in cooking liquid until room temperature.

Remove ham from liquid. (Strain liquid and use as stock for an interesting soup.) Cut skin from ham and trim fat, leaving a ¼-inch layer. Score fat and stud with cloves.

An hour before serving place ham, fat side down, on roasting rack in large dish and microwave on HIGH 10 minutes. Turn ham fat side up. Combine brown sugar, honey, and mustard and spread over ham. Microwave on 30% power 40 to 50 minutes, or until ham is thoroughly heated.

SAUSAGE AND RICE

1 pound smoked Polish sausage
    (kielbasa), sliced
1 cup rice
4 to 6 scallions, chopped
1 clove garlic, minced
1 (28-ounce) can tomatoes,
    undrained, chopped

1 cup water
1 chicken bouillon cube
1 bay leaf
1 teaspoon salt
½ teaspoon freshly ground black
    pepper
½ teaspoon dried thyme

6 SERVINGS

A lovely one-dish meal that can be assembled and cooked in less than one hour.

In 3-quart casserole, combine sausage, rice, scallions, garlic, tomatoes, water, bouillon cube, bay leaf, salt, pepper, and thyme. Cover and microwave on HIGH 10 minutes, then stir. Microwave on 50% power 30 minutes, or until rice is cooked.

RED BEANS AND SAUSAGE

6 SERVINGS

■

A Louisiana specialty! Delicious for informal entertaining

2 slices bacon, chopped
1 onion, chopped
1 stalk celery, chopped
1 clove garlic, minced
1 cup chopped cooked ham
1 bay leaf
1½ teaspoons salt
½ teaspoon freshly ground black pepper

½ teaspoon ground allspice
3 cups water
1 pound smoked or Polish sausage (kielbasa), cut into 2-inch pieces
1 (15½-ounce) can kidney beans, drained
3 to 4 cups hot cooked rice (page 289)

Place bacon, onion, celery, and garlic in 2-quart casserole, cover, and microwave on HIGH 3 to 5 minutes, or until vegetables are tender.

Add ham, bay leaf, salt, pepper, allspice, water, and sausage, cover, and microwave on HIGH 5 minutes, then on 50% power 15 minutes.

Stir in kidney beans, cover, and microwave on 50% power 10 to 15 minutes longer. Serve over rice.

SAUSAGE PITAS

6 SERVINGS

■

A tasty sandwich for a quick, easy meal.

8 ounces Italian sausage (sweet or hot), sliced
1 onion, chopped
1 clove garlic, minced
½ teaspoon dried oregano
½ cup chopped green bell pepper
½ cup diced celery
1 cup sliced mushrooms

Salt
Freshly ground black pepper
6 pita breads, slit open
2 cups grated Monterey Jack cheese
Chopped tomatoes
Shredded iceberg lettuce
Olives (optional)

Combine sausage, onion, garlic, oregano, bell pepper, and celery in 2-quart measure. Cover and microwave on HIGH 5 to 6 minutes, or until sausage is cooked and vegetables are tender-crisp. Drain.

In separate bowl, microwave mushrooms 2 minutes, or just until tender. Drain and add to sausage mixture. Season to taste with salt and pepper.

Stuff pita pockets with sausage mixture. Sprinkle filling with grated cheese.

Stand stuffed pitas upright against sides of 8- to 10-inch round casserole and microwave on HIGH 3 to 4 minutes, or until cheese is melted. Sprinkle tomatoes, lettuce, and, if desired, olives over cheese.

SAUSAGE AND RICE DRESSING

8 ounces bulk pork sausage
1 cup sliced celery
1 cup chopped onion
1 cup sliced mushrooms or
   1 (8-ounce) can sliced
   mushrooms, drained
2 cups cooked brown rice (page
   289)
1 teaspoon salt

1/4 teaspoon freshly ground black
   pepper
1 teaspoon crumbled dried sage
1 teaspoon poultry seasoning
1 chicken bouillon cube dissolved
   in 1/2 cup hot water
1/4 cup slivered blanched almonds,
   toasted (page 441)

8 SERVINGS

▪

Use as delicious stuffing for an already cooked turkey or as a casserole that stands alone!

Crumble sausage into 2-quart casserole and microwave on HIGH 2 to 3 minutes. Drain. Add celery, onion, and mushrooms, cover, and microwave on HIGH 4 to 6 minutes, or until vegetables are tender-crisp.

Add rice, salt, pepper, sage, poultry seasoning, and bouillon mixture. Cover and microwave on 70% power 5 to 8 minutes, or until thoroughly heated. Stir in almonds.

QUICK CASSOULET

**4 TO 6
SERVINGS**

•

This is a specialty of the Toulouse region in the south of France. Leftover bits of pork, lamb, or duck are very good in this dish, but it's equally delicious made with sausage. Cassoulet tastes even better when the flavors have a chance to blend. If you have time, make it a day or two ahead and let it sit, tightly covered, in the refrigerator, then reheat in the microwave just before serving.

4 slices bacon
1 large onion, chopped
2 cloves garlic, minced
1 chicken bouillon cube dissolved
   in ½ cup boiling water
3 (16-ounce) cans great northern
   beans, drained
1 pound sausage (smoked, Italian,
   or French *saucisson*), cut into
   ½-inch slices

1 to 2 cups chopped cooked lamb,
   duck, or pork (optional)
1 teaspoon dried thyme
1 bay leaf
3 tablespoons chopped parsley
½ teaspoon salt
¼ teaspoon freshly ground black
   pepper
1 tablespoon tomato paste
   (optional)

Place bacon in 2-quart casserole and microwave on HIGH 4 minutes or until cooked. Remove bacon and reserve. To drippings, add onion and garlic, cover, and microwave on HIGH 3 minutes. Add bouillon, beans, sausage, lamb, thyme, bay leaf, parsley, salt, pepper, and, if desired, tomato paste. Stir well, cover, and microwave on HIGH 10 to 15 minutes. Crumble bacon and stir in. Delicious with crusty French bread and a simple tossed salad.

GAME

Game, as a rule, is leaner and less tender than a commercially raised animal of similar size. When cooking game in the microwave, follow conventional guidelines for preparing each type of game and for selecting a suitable cooking method. Then microwave either by a dry or a moist method, just as you would conventionally, following the techniques and cooking times described in this chapter.

VENISON ROAST

1 (2- to 3-pound) venison roast
1/2 cup all-purpose flour
1 1/2 tablespoons vegetable oil
1 1/2 tablespoons butter
1/4 cup soy sauce
1/2 cup water
1 onion, sliced

1 lemon, sliced
2 cloves garlic, minced
1 tablespoon finely chopped
    parsley
1 teaspoon salt
1/2 teaspoon freshly ground black
    pepper

**4 TO 6
SERVINGS**

Dredge venison in flour, shaking off excess. In heavy skillet, heat oil and butter over high heat on conventional rangetop. Add venison and brown on all sides. Transfer venison to 3-quart casserole.

Add soy sauce and water to skillet and deglaze over high heat on rangetop, scraping up all brown bits. Add deglazing liquid to venison with onion, lemon, garlic, parsley, salt, and pepper. Cover and microwave on HIGH 5 minutes, then on 30% power 40 to 50 minutes, or until meat is tender. Turn roast over halfway through cooking. Let meat stand, covered, 10 minutes before slicing.

VENISON STEW

6 TO 8 SERVINGS

2 pounds venison, cut into
    uniform 1-inch cubes
1 cup buttermilk
1 cup all-purpose flour
1 teaspoon salt
1/2 teaspoon freshly ground black
    pepper
3/4 cup vegetable oil
8 ounces raw mushrooms,
    cleaned and stemmed, or
    1 (8-ounce) can whole
    mushrooms, undrained

1 onion, cut in wedges
1 tablespoon Worcestershire sauce
1/4 teaspoon hot pepper sauce
2 bay leaves
2 cloves garlic, minced
1 (16-ounce) can tomatoes,
    undrained

In bowl, combine venison cubes and buttermilk, stirring to coat meat. Cover and refrigerate overnight.

Combine flour, salt, and pepper. Drain venison, pat dry with paper towels, and dredge in flour mixture. Pour vegetable oil in heavy skillet and place over high heat on conventional rangetop. Add venison and brown meat on all sides.

Place browned meat in 3-quart casserole. Add mushrooms, onion, Worcestershire, hot pepper sauce, bay leaves, garlic, and tomatoes, breaking up tomatoes with fork. Cover and microwave on HIGH 10 minutes. Stir, cover again, and microwave on 50% power 50 to 60 minutes, or until meat is tender. Let stand, covered, 10 minutes.

Vegetables

Some people think that fresh vegetables cooked in the microwave are the best they've ever eaten! For a fresh-from-the-garden taste, there is no better way to cook corn on the cob, or cream-style corn, or almost any other vegetable.

Steamed vegetables—asparagus, broccoli, cabbage, carrots (and the list goes on)—retain their bright natural colors and, because flavor is at its peak, require little seasoning. Except for special occasions, rich sauces, butter, and salt won't be necessary.

Researchers have found that cooking vegetables in a microwave can be more nutritious than using a conventional rangetop or oven. The reason is that microwave cooking requires little water, is much faster, and requires no fat to prevent sticking. This means that the water-soluble vitamins B and C complex are not as easily lost in cooking water or totally destroyed by long periods of cooking, as in conventional methods.

GUIDELINES FOR COOKING VEGETABLES

- Wash vegetables just before cooking. In many cases no extra water is needed unless cooking dense vegetables, such as carrots or potatoes. If a softer texture is desired, add about an extra ¼ cup water per pound of vegetables.
- Don't salt vegetables until after cooking, when less will be required. If you prefer to salt before cooking, dissolve salt in water before adding it to the vegetables. Undissolved salt will cause spots to appear on the vegetable and dehydration to occur.
- Smaller, uniform pieces will cook more evenly and faster than larger pieces.
- Arrange whole vegetables, such as potatoes, acorn squash, or corn on the cob, in a circle on a platter before microwaving.
- Always place vegetables such as broccoli and asparagus with the stem ends pointing toward the outside of the dish, where they will cook faster and more evenly.
- Pierce the skin of whole, unpeeled vegetables to allow steam to escape and to prevent some vegetables, such as spaghetti squash, potatoes, or pumpkin, from bursting.
- Cook fresh and frozen vegetables on HIGH to best capture their flavor and nutrients.
- Stir or rearrange vegetables midway through cooking so they will cook evenly.

- Standing time varies with the vegetable. Larger, denser vegetables should stand longer to give the center time to become soft and tender. Take standing time into consideration as part of the cooking process when cooking vegetables, because they overcook easily.
- When heating canned vegetables, cook at 70% power to prevent overcooking and to maintain texture.
- Make every drop of flavor count; when using olive oil to season vegetables, use the finest you can afford.
- Frozen vegetables may be cooked in the package. Always pierce the carton first to allow steam to escape. As a general rule, cook 1 pound of frozen vegetables on HIGH 4 to 6 minutes. Cook 2 pounds for 9 to 12 minutes, or follow the microwaving directions on the package.

PREPARING
VEGETABLES FOR FREEZING

Vegetables must be blanched (scalded) before they are frozen. The heating process destroys the enzymes that cause foods to ripen and produce off-flavors.

The microwave oven is a convenient tool for blanching up to 2 to 3 pounds (or 2 to 3 pints) of vegetables at a time. In conventional blanching, vegetables are scalded in a large pot of boiling water. In microwave blanching, only a small amount of water is used, and the vegetables retain more of their water-soluble vitamins and minerals, texture, and flavors.

Wash the vegetable and peel it, if necessary. Cut it into cubes, slices, or other shapes in the amounts called for in the chart that follows. Place the vegetables and the water in a casserole and cover. Do not add salt. Microwave for the recommended time, stirring midway through cooking. Remove the vegetable from the microwave at once and transfer to a bowl of ice water to stop the cooking. When the vegetables are cool, drain them completely, then package, label, and quick-freeze them in freezer bags or freezer cartons.

Prepare cream-style corn for the freezer by blanching or precooking in the microwave —much easier than conventional cooking because you won't have to stir continuously to prevent scorching.

TIMETABLE FOR BLANCHING VEGETABLES

VEGETABLES	AMOUNT	TABLESPOONS OF WATER	MINUTES OF COOKING TIME ON HIGH
Artichoke hearts	1 pound	2	6 to 7
Asparagus (2" pieces)	2 cups	2	2½
Beans, snap,	2 cups	2	3
green, or wax	4 cups	3	6
Broccoli (2" pieces)	4 cups	4	3
Carrots (¼" slices)	2 cups	3	3
Corn on the cob	4 ears	None	3½ to 4½
Corn kernels	2 cups	3	4½
Lima beans	2 cups	2	3½ to 5
Peas, green	2 cups	None	3
Spinach	1 pound	None	2 to 3½
Squash, summer, yellow crookneck, or zucchini	1 pound	None	4

For vegetables not listed, blanch 3 to 4 minutes per pound.

BASIC VEGETABLE COOKERY

Certain leafy greens, such as mustard, collard, beet greens, and kale, have been omitted from this list and from the vegetable recipes that follow it. So much time and so much stirring go into cooking these vegetables that we believe they are best prepared by conventional methods.

Season vegetables to taste after they are cooked with herbs, salt and pepper, extra-virgin olive oil, butter, bacon drippings, vegetable oil, chicken or beef granules, or other seasonings. When using dried herbs and spices, follow these guidelines:

Strong-flavored herbs and spices, such as bay leaves, cardamom, curry, ginger, hot pepper, mustard, black pepper, rosemary, and sage, should be added with a light hand since they can overpower other foods; use about 1 teaspoon for every 6 servings, depending on other seasonings and flavors in dish.

Medium-flavored seasonings, such as basil, celery seed, cumin, dill, oregano, tarragon, fennel, marjoram, mint, savory, thyme, and turmeric, can be added a little more generously: 2 to 3 teaspoons for 6 servings.

Delicate-flavored seasonings, such as burnett, chives, parsley, and chervil, combine well with other herbs and spices and can be added to taste.

ARTICHOKES

Fresh (2 globe artichokes): Rinse and cut leaf tips from artichokes, trim stem bottoms, and peel stems. Rub all over with cut lemon. Place in small dish, add 2 tablespoons water, and cover tightly with plastic wrap. Microwave on HIGH 6 to 10 minutes, or until leaves can be pulled off easily. For 4 artichokes, microwave on HIGH 12 to 16 minutes.

    Frozen artichoke hearts (10-ounce package): Cook, covered, on HIGH 7 to 9 minutes.

ASPARAGUS

Fresh spears (1 pound): Rinse, snap off tough bottoms, and place in a circle in casserole or pie plate with stems pointing outward. Cover with plastic wrap and microwave on HIGH 6 to 8 minutes, or until tender-crisp, rearranging spears halfway through cooking. Drain.

    Frozen (10-ounce package): Cook, covered, on HIGH 7 to 9 minutes.

BEANS (SNAP, GREEN, AND WAX)

Fresh (1 pound): Wash and remove ends and strings; break or cut into 2-inch pieces. Place in 1½-quart casserole with ⅔ cup water, cover tightly, and cook on HIGH 5 to 7 minutes, or until tender. Drain.

    Frozen (10-ounce package): Cook, covered, on HIGH 5 to 7 minutes.

BEAN SPROUTS

Fresh (1 pound): Rinse and place in 1-quart dish. Cover tightly and cook on HIGH 4 to 6 minutes, stirring halfway through cooking.

BEETS

Fresh (1 pound): Wash and trim, leaving 1-inch tops to prevent color loss. Place in 2-quart casserole, cover tightly, and microwave on HIGH 10 to 15 minutes, or until fork-tender. Drain.

BOK CHOY

Fresh (1 pound): Rinse and cut stalks into ¼-inch slices and leaves into 1-inch pieces. Place in 1½-quart casserole, cover tightly, and cook on HIGH 3 to 5 minutes, or until tender-crisp. Drain.

BROCCOLI

Fresh (1 pound): Rinse, trim off tough stalk ends, and peel remaining stems. Divide spears. Place, with stems facing outward, in 12 × 8-inch casserole, cover tightly, and microwave on HIGH 6 to 8 minutes, or until tender.

    Frozen (10-ounce package): Cook, covered, on HIGH 7 to 9 minutes.

BRUSSELS SPROUTS

Fresh (1 pound): Rinse, trim off stem bottoms, cutting a small cross in each one, and remove any loose leaves. Place in a 1½-quart casserole, cover tightly, and microwave on HIGH 5 to 8 minutes, or until tender.

    Frozen (10-ounce package): Cook, covered, on HIGH 4 to 7 minutes.

CABBAGE (GREEN OR RED)

Fresh (1 pound): Shred, place in 2-quart casserole, and add 2 tablespoons water. Cover tightly with plastic wrap and microwave on HIGH 8 to 10 minutes, stirring once. Drain.

CARROTS (BABY WHOLE OR SLICED)

Fresh (1 pound): Trim and place in 1-quart casserole with 2 tablespoons water. Cover tightly and microwave on HIGH until tender, 7 to 10 minutes for baby whole carrots and 5 to 8 minutes for sliced, stirring and rearranging once.

CAULIFLOWER

Fresh (whole, large): Wash, trim off stem end and leaves, and place in pie plate. Cover tightly with plastic wrap and microwave on HIGH 12 to 15 minutes, turning over once. Let stand, covered, 5 minutes before serving.

    Flowerets (1 pound): Arrange in 10-inch round casserole. Add 2 tablespoons water, cover tightly, and microwave on HIGH 7 to 10 minutes, or until tender.

CELERY

Fresh sliced (2 cups): Place in 1-quart casserole with 1 tablespoon water, cover, and cook on HIGH 4 to 5 minutes.

CHINESE CABBAGE

Fresh (1 pound): Rinse, drain, shred, and place in 2-quart casserole with 2 tablespoons water. Cover tightly and cook on HIGH 6 to 9 minutes, stirring once. Drain.

CORN

Fresh kernels (3 cups): Place in 1-quart casserole and add 2 to 3 tablespoons water or milk. Cover tightly and microwave on HIGH 7 to 8 minutes, stirring once.

    Frozen kernels (2 cups): Cook, covered, on HIGH 5 to 8 minutes.

EGGPLANT

Fresh (1 pound): Peel and cut into 1-inch cubes. Place in 1-quart casserole, cover tightly, and cook on HIGH 4 to 7 minutes, stirring once. Drain.

JERUSALEM ARTICHOKES

Fresh (1 pound): Scrub well, peel if desired, and cut into ¼-inch slices. Place in 1 quart of salted water until ready to cook (to prevent darkening). Drain and place in 2-quart casserole with ⅓ cup water and 1 teaspoon fresh lemon juice. Cover and cook on HIGH 7 to 10 minutes, or until tender. Let stand, covered, 5 minutes, then drain.

JICAMA

Fresh (1 pound): Wash, peel, and cut into ½-inch cubes or ¼-inch slices. Place in 2-quart casserole with ¼ cup water, cover tightly, and microwave on HIGH 3 to 6 minutes, or until tender-crisp.

KOHLRABI

Fresh (1 pound): Trim ends and stems, peel and slice. Place in 2-quart casserole with 2 tablespoons water, cover, and cook on HIGH 10 to 15 minutes, or until tender. Drain.

LEEKS

Fresh (2 pounds): Trim root ends and split leeks lengthwise. Wash thoroughly and place in 9-inch square dish with 2 tablespoons water. Cover tightly and cook on HIGH 4 to 7 minutes, or until tender.

LIMA BEANS

Fresh (1 pound, shelled): Place in casserole and add 1 cup water. Cover tightly and microwave on HIGH 5 minutes, then on 50% power 25 to 35 minutes, or until tender.

    Frozen (10-ounce package): Cook, covered, on HIGH 8 to 9 minutes.

MUSHROOMS

Fresh (1 pound): Wipe with damp cloth or wash just before cooking. Place in a 2-quart casserole, cover, and microwave on HIGH 4 to 7 minutes. Drain.

OKRA

Fresh whole or sliced (1 pound): Rinse and place in 1-quart casserole with ¼ cup water. Cover tightly with plastic wrap and microwave on HIGH 7 to 10 minutes, stirring once. Drain.

    Frozen (10-ounce package): Cook, covered, on HIGH 5 to 7 minutes.

ONIONS

Fresh whole (4 large or 2½ to 3 pounds): Peel, slice off tops to expose all layers, and trim off root ends. Place in 9-inch pie plate, cover tightly with plastic wrap, and microwave on HIGH 8 to 10 minutes, turning over halfway through cooking.

Fresh chopped (2 cups): Place in 1-quart casserole, cover, and cook on HIGH 4 to 5 minutes.

PARSNIPS

Fresh (1 pound): Scrape and cut into ¼-inch slices. Place in 1-quart casserole with ¼ cup water, cover tightly, and microwave on HIGH 6 to 8 minutes, or until tender. Drain.

PEAS

Fresh shelled (2 cups, about 2 pounds in shell): Place in 1-quart casserole with ¼ cup water, cover tightly, and cook on HIGH 6 to 8 minutes, or until tender. Drain.

Frozen (10-ounce package): Cook, covered, on HIGH 5 to 7 minutes.

TIMETABLE FOR COOKING POTATOES			
POTATO TYPE & PREPARATION	NUMBER & SIZE OF POTATOES	MINUTES OF COOKING TIME ON HIGH	DIRECTIONS
Baking (unpeeled)	1 (7-ounce)	4 to 5	Scrub potatoes, pierce skin, and place on paper towel. Turn over halfway through cooking. Remove from oven, wrap in kitchen towel, and let stand 5 to 10 minutes.
	2 medium	7 to 10	Place at least 1 inch apart.
	3	11 to 13	Place in a triangle at least 1 inch apart.
	4	13 to 16	Place in a circle at least 1 inch apart.
New, whole (peeled)	8 medium	6 to 8	Place in casserole, add 2 to 3 tablespoons water. Cover.
All-purpose (peeled and cut into 1-inch cubes)	5 or 6 medium	8 to 11	Place in a casserole and add 2 to 3 tablespoons water. Cover.
All-purpose (peeled and cut into ¼-inch slices)	5 or 6 medium	9 to 12	Place in a casserole and add 2 to 3 tablespoons water. Cover.

PEPPERS (GREEN, RED, AND YELLOW BELL)

Fresh (2 large, or about 1 pound): Cut into strips and place in 1-quart casserole. Cover and cook on HIGH 3 to 6 minutes, or until tender-crisp.

POTATOES

Fresh: Cook according to timetable opposite.

PUMPKIN

Fresh (2 to 3 pounds): Cut into quarters, peel, and scrape out seeds and membranes. Cut into 1-inch cubes and place in 2-quart casserole. Cover tightly with plastic wrap and cook on HIGH 12 to 15 minutes, or until tender. Drain.

RUTABAGA

Fresh (1½ pounds): Peel and cut into 1-inch cubes. Place in 2-quart casserole with ¼ cup water. Cover tightly and microwave on HIGH 15 to 18 minutes, or until tender. Drain.

SNOW PEAS

Fresh (1 pound): Trim ends and remove strings. Place in 1-quart casserole with 2 tablespoons water, cover, and microwave on HIGH 3 to 5 minutes, stirring once. Drain.

    Frozen (6-ounce package): Cook, covered, on HIGH 2½ to 3 minutes.

SPINACH

Fresh (1 pound): Wash well and tear into bite-size pieces. Place in 2-quart casserole, cover tightly, and microwave on HIGH 2 to 4 minutes, or until cooked to taste. Drain.

    Frozen (10-ounce package): Cook, covered, on HIGH 6 to 8 minutes.

SQUASH (HUBBARD OR BANANA)

Fresh (1 pound): Wash and cut in half. Place in 12 × 8-inch casserole, cover tightly with plastic wrap, and microwave on HIGH 6 to 9 minutes per pound, or until tender. Serve in shell.

SQUASH (PATTY PAN)

Fresh (1 pound): Rinse, cut into cubes, and place in casserole with 1 to 2 tablespoons water. Cover tightly and microwave on HIGH 9 to 12 minutes, or until tender.

SQUASH (SPAGHETTI)

Fresh (2½ to 3 pounds): Wash and pierce rind deeply with knife in several places. Place in microwave and cook on HIGH 14 to 18 minutes, or until squash yields to pressure. Let stand 5 minutes. Cut in half and scrape out seeds and fibers. Pull out long strands of flesh by twisting with a fork.

SQUASH (SUMMER—YELLOW OR ZUCCHINI)

Fresh (1 pound): Cut into ¼-inch slices and place in 1½-quart casserole. Cover tightly with plastic wrap and cook on HIGH 6 to 8 minutes, or until tender. Drain.

SQUASH (WINTER—ACORN OR BUTTERNUT)

Fresh (1 to 1½ pounds): Pierce skin with fork and place in microwave. Cook on HIGH 6 to 8 minutes. Let stand 5 minutes. Cut in half and scrape out seeds and membranes.

SWEET POTATOES OR YAMS

Fresh whole (7 to 8 ounces each): Scrub potatoes and pierce with fork. Place in a circle on a microwavable dish, cook according to timetable below, and let stand 5 minutes.

TIMETABLE FOR COOKING SWEET POTATOES			
NUMBER OF POTATOES	MINUTES OF COOKING TIME ON HIGH	NUMBER OF POTATOES	MINUTES OF COOKING TIME ON HIGH
1	4 to 6	3	9 to 12
2	6 to 8	4	12 to 15

SWISS CHARD

Fresh (1 pound): Remove stems and cut leaves into 1-inch strips. Place in 1½-quart casserole, cover tightly, and microwave on HIGH 3 to 6 minutes, or until tender. Drain.

TOMATOES

Fresh (1 pound): Peel and chop. Place in 1½-quart dish, cover, and cook on HIGH 4 to 6 minutes. Puree, if desired.

TURNIPS

Fresh (1 pound): Peel, cut into cubes, and place in 1-quart casserole with ¼ cup water. Cover tightly with plastic wrap and cook on HIGH 9 to 12 minutes, or until tender. Drain.

STEAMED ARTICHOKES WITH GARLIC AND OLIVE OIL

2 medium artichokes
1/2 lemon plus 2 to 3 slices lemon
2 cloves garlic

2 teaspoons extra-virgin olive oil
2 tablespoons water

2 SERVINGS

■

Pull off small tough bottom leaves of artichokes, then, with a sharp knife, cut off about 1 inch from tops, rubbing cut edges with lemon half to prevent discoloration. Cut off bottom of stem and peel stem, starting at base of artichoke. Rub stem with lemon half.

Place artichokes upside down in 8-inch square casserole, add lemon slices, garlic, olive oil, and water. Cover tightly with plastic wrap and microwave on HIGH 6 to 10 minutes, or until bottom of artichokes can be pierced by a fork and leaves at base can be pulled out easily. Let artichokes stand, covered, in liquid 3 to 4 minutes. Drain and serve hot with melted butter, lemon butter, or Hollandaise sauce (page 84), or serve cold with vinaigrette or mayonnaise (pages 114 and 116).

ARTICHOKE HEARTS AND SCALLOPED TOMATOES

1 medium onion, finely chopped
3 tablespoons extra-virgin olive oil
    or unsalted butter
1 tablespoon chopped fresh basil,
    or 1/2 teaspoon dried
1 tablespoon sugar

1 (28-ounce) can whole tomatoes,
    undrained
1 (14-ounce) can artichoke hearts,
    drained and quartered
1 teaspoon minced garlic
Salt
Freshly ground black pepper

6 TO 8 SERVINGS

■

Easy to make. This is a good side dish with chicken, pork, or beef.

Place onion and olive oil in 2-quart casserole, cover, and microwave on HIGH 2 to 4 minutes.

Add basil, sugar, tomatoes, artichoke hearts, garlic, and salt and pepper to taste. Stir gently, cover, and microwave on HIGH 8 to 12 minutes.

ASPARAGUS IN ORANGE-WALNUT SAUCE

4 SERVINGS

In ancient Rome, asparagus, a rare and treasured food, was sometimes frozen in the snow of the Italian Alps and retrieved months later for special dinners. It undoubtedly tastes even better today prepared in the microwave.

Juice and pulp of 1 orange
1 tablespoon white wine vinegar
1 stick (¹/₂ cup) unsalted butter
2 tablespoons chopped walnuts, toasted (page 441)

1 pound asparagus, trimmed, cooked (page 245), and drained
Salt
Freshly ground white pepper

In small bowl, combine orange juice and pulp, vinegar, butter, and walnuts. Microwave on HIGH 1 minute, or until butter is melted. Cook on 70% power 1 to 2 minutes and pour over hot asparagus. Add salt and pepper to taste.

ASPARAGUS ORIENTAL

4 TO 6 SERVINGS

3 cups diagonally sliced fresh asparagus (1¹/₂-inch pieces)
2 tablespoons water
1 tablespoon Oriental sesame oil

¹/₂ teaspoon salt
¹/₂ teaspoon freshly ground white pepper

Combine asparagus, water, and oil in 1-quart casserole. Cover tightly with plastic wrap and microwave on HIGH 2 minutes. Stir, cover, and microwave on HIGH 2 to 3 minutes, then stir in salt and pepper.

An alternate cooking method: Place trimmed spears in 2-cup measure, stem side up. Cover tightly with plastic wrap and microwave on HIGH 4 to 7 minutes.

SAVORY GREEN BEANS

1 pound green beans
1/4 cup water
1 tablespoon extra-virgin olive oil
1 tablespoon finely chopped onion

1 teaspoon finely chopped fresh
    basil
1 clove garlic, minced

4 SERVINGS

■

Wonderful texture and flavor.

Trim beans, cut into 2- to 3-inch lengths, and place in a 1½-quart casserole with water. Cover tightly with plastic wrap and microwave on HIGH 3 to 4 minutes, or until cooked but still crunchy.

Drain cooked beans and return to casserole. Add olive oil, onion, basil, and garlic, cover again, and let stand 3 to 4 minutes.

TARRAGON GREEN BEANS

1 pound green beans, cut into
    3-inch pieces and cooked
    (page 245)
1 cup sliced mushrooms
1/2 cup sliced onions

1 tablespoon unsalted butter or
    margarine
1 tablespoon fresh tarragon, or
    1 teaspoon dried

**4 OR 5
SERVINGS**

■

Let cooked beans stand in cooking dish, covered, 3 to 4 minutes. Drain beans, add mushrooms, onions, butter, and tarragon. Cover and microwave on HIGH 2 to 4 minutes.

STEAMED BELGIAN ENDIVES

4 SERVINGS

4 medium Belgian endives,
washed and cut into ¼-inch
slices
¼ cup Chicken Stock (page 47) or
canned chicken broth

2 tablespoons unsalted butter
¼ teaspoon freshly ground white
pepper
Salt

Place endives in 2-quart casserole with broth, butter, pepper and salt to taste. Cover tightly with plastic wrap and microwave on HIGH 2 minutes. Stir, cover again, and cook on HIGH 1½ to 2½ minutes, or until tender-crisp.

BOK CHOY

4 SERVINGS

3 or 4 large stalks bok choy
1 tablespoon unsalted butter or
margarine
1 tablespoon Oriental sesame oil

1 or 2 cloves garlic, minced
1 tablespoon soy sauce
1 teaspoon Worcestershire sauce
1 teaspoon sugar

Cut bok choy stalks into ⅛-inch slices, cut leaves into 1-inch strips, and place in 2-quart casserole. Add butter, oil, garlic, soy sauce, Worcestershire, and sugar, cover tightly with plastic wrap, and microwave on HIGH 2 to 3 minutes. Stir, cover again, and cook on HIGH 2 to 3 minutes.

LEMON BROCCOLI

1½ pounds broccoli spears,
   trimmed
2 tablespoons water
2 or 3 cloves garlic, minced
2 tablespoons extra-virgin olive oil

½ teaspoon salt
¼ teaspoon freshly ground black
   pepper
½ lemon, sliced
2 teaspoons grated lemon zest

**4 TO 6
SERVINGS**

•

Enjoy this versatile veg-
etable fresh all year
long. It combines well
with almost any meat.

Place broccoli in 12 × 8-inch casserole with tender heads facing
center. Add water, cover tightly with plastic wrap, and microwave on HIGH 8 to 10 minutes. Let stand 5 minutes.

Combine garlic, oil, salt, pepper, and lemon slices in 1-cup measure. Microwave for 1 to 1½ minutes. Pour over broccoli. Sprinkle
with lemon zest.

BRAISED CABBAGE

4 cups coarsely shredded cabbage
1 medium onion, choppped
2 tablespoons water

¼ cup fresh lemon juice
Freshly ground black pepper

4 SERVINGS

•

Try this low-cal, salt-
free dish when
counting calories.

Combine cabbage, onion, and water in 1-quart casserole. Cover
tightly with plastic wrap and microwave on HIGH 6 to 8 minutes. Add lemon juice and pepper to taste.

CHOW MEIN CABBAGE

4 OR 5 SERVINGS

■

Simple and so fresh-tasting.

5 cups shredded cabbage
1 cup sliced celery
1 cup sliced green bell pepper
1 cup sliced onions

3 tablespoons bacon drippings, butter, or chicken broth
Salt
Freshly ground black pepper

Combine cabbage, celery, bell pepper, onions, and bacon drippings in 2-quart casserole. Cover tightly and microwave on HIGH 7 to 10 minutes. Stir and add salt and pepper to taste.

GERMAN-STYLE SWEET-AND-SOUR CABBAGE

4 TO 6 SERVINGS

■

An interesting blend of flavors and textures.

3 slices bacon
6 cups shredded red cabbage
1 cup sliced onions
3 medium tart apples, peeled, cored, and sliced
1 cup Chicken Stock (page 47) or canned broth
1/3 cup cider vinegar

3 tablespoons sugar
Salt
Freshly ground black pepper
1 tablespoon cornstarch
2 tablespoons water
1 apple, with peel, cored and sliced

Place bacon in single layer in 3-quart casserole and microwave on HIGH 3 to 5 minutes, or until cooked. Remove bacon from dish and reserve for garnish.

Combine cabbage, onions, peeled and sliced apples, stock, vinegar, and sugar in the bacon drippings. Cover and microwave on HIGH 7 to 10 minutes. Stir and microwave on HIGH 4 to 6 minutes longer.

Add salt and pepper to taste. Blend cornstarch with water and add to cabbage. Cover and cook on HIGH 1 to 2 minutes, or until liquid is thickened. Sprinkle with crumbled bacon and garnish with unpeeled apple slices.

MARINATED CARROTS

4 cups (about 1¼ pounds) sliced
    carrots (¼-inch slices)
2 tablespoons water
1 green bell pepper, sliced
1 onion, sliced
1 teaspoon minced garlic
1 (10½-ounce) can condensed
    tomato soup

½ cup vegetable oil
¾ cup sugar
¾ cup cider vinegar
2 teaspoons mustard
2 teaspoons Worcestershire sauce
Salt
Freshly ground black pepper

6 TO 8 SERVINGS

▪

A good do-ahead dish.

In 2-quart casserole, microwave carrots and water, covered, on HIGH 8 to 12 minutes, or until carrots are tender-crisp.

Add bell pepper, onion, garlic, soup, oil, sugar, vinegar, mustard, Worcestershire, and salt and pepper to taste. Cover and refrigerate. Serve within a week.

LEMON-BASIL CARROTS

1 pound carrots, thinly sliced or
    cut into strips
3 tablespoons water
3 tablespoons unsalted butter or
    extra-virgin olive oil

½ teaspoon salt or garlic salt
2 tablespoons chopped fresh basil,
    or 1 teaspoon dried
1 tablespoon fresh lemon juice

4 TO 6 SERVINGS

▪

Good served with butter or olive oil.

Combine carrots and water in 1-quart casserole. Cover and cook on HIGH 9 to 12 minutes. Drain and add butter, salt, basil, and lemon juice and microwave on HIGH 1 minute. Stir and serve at once.

CARROT PUREE

6 SERVINGS

This luxurious puree is delicious served simply as a casserole. Or, for a beautiful presentation, spoon the puree into a pastry bag fitted with a large star tip and pipe it as a border of rosettes around a roast or other vegetables.

1 1/2 pounds carrots, sliced and cooked (page 246)
1/2 stick (1/4 cup) unsalted butter, softened
2/3 cup heavy cream
1/2 teaspoon dry mustard

Pinch of sugar
Pinch of freshly grated nutmeg
Salt
Freshly ground white pepper

Drain cooked carrots and transfer to food processor. Add butter, cream, mustard, sugar, nutmeg, and salt and pepper to taste. Process until smooth. Transfer to 2-quart baking dish, cover, and microwave at 70% power 5 to 6 minutes.

BABY CARROTS WITH ORANGE MANDARIN GLAZE

6 TO 8 SERVINGS

2 pounds whole baby carrots, trimmed and cooked (page 246)
1/3 cup unsalted butter, melted

1/4 cup, packed, light brown sugar
1/3 cup frozen orange juice concentrate
1/2 teaspoon salt

While carrots cook, combine butter, sugar, orange juice concentrate, and salt in 2-cup measure. Remove cooked carrots from microwave and cook orange juice concentrate mixture on HIGH 4 to 5 minutes. Pour mixture over carrots and serve.

CAULIFLOWER DELUXE

1 large head cauliflower, cooked whole (page 246)
2 or 3 cloves garlic, minced
¼ cup extra-virgin olive oil or unsalted butter, melted

¼ teaspoon freshly ground white pepper
½ cup freshly grated Parmesan cheese

6 SERVINGS

▪

Pretty served on a platter surrounded with colorful vegetables.

Drain cauliflower and let stand covered. Combine garlic, oil, pepper, and cheese, pour over cauliflower and serve at once.

CORN ON THE COB

The wonderful fresh taste can't be beat by any other cooking method.

1. Place butter on a piece of wax paper and microwave at 20% power 20 to 30 seconds to soften. Roll husked corn in butter.
2. Wrap ears of corn individually in wax paper or plastic wrap (or place in a casserole and cover with plastic wrap). Cooking time will vary with the size of ears of corn.

TIMETABLE FOR COOKING CORN ON THE COB		
NUMBER OF EARS (HUSKED)	TABLESPOONS BUTTER (SALTED OR UNSALTED)	MINUTES OF COOKING TIME ON HIGH
1	1	3 to 5
2	2	4 to 8
4	3	8 to 13

CONFETTI CORN

4 OR 5 SERVINGS

■

A colorful side dish.

1 pound frozen corn
1 large red or green bell pepper, chopped
$1/2$ cup chopped celery
$1/2$ cup chopped onion

$1/3$ cup unsalted butter or margarine
1 ($3^1/2$-ounce) can pimiento, drained and chopped
Salt
Freshly ground white pepper

Place the corn, bell pepper, celery, onion, and butter in 2-quart casserole. Cover and microwave on HIGH 6 to 8 minutes. Stir, cover again, and cook on HIGH 2 to 4 minutes.

Stir in pimiento and salt and pepper to taste. Serve at once.

CREAM-STYLE FRESH CORN

6 TO 8 SERVINGS

■

6 to 8 ears tender young corn or 5 to 6 cups frozen corn, defrosted
$1/2$ cup unsalted butter, bacon drippings, or margarine
1 cup milk

1 to 2 tablespoons cornstarch or 2 tablespoons self-rising cornmeal
Salt
Freshly ground black pepper

Remove corn from cob by cutting halfway through kernels from top to bottom of cob. Scrape remaining corn from each cob. Place corn in 2-quart casserole, add butter and ½ cup milk. Cover and microwave on HIGH 5 to 7 minutes. Stir.

Combine remaining milk with cornstarch and stir into corn mixture. Cover and microwave on 70% power 4 to 5 minutes. Season to taste with salt and pepper and add more milk, if needed.

ITALIAN EGGPLANT

1 medium eggplant (1 pound)
3 tablespoons extra-virgin olive oil
1 clove garlic, minced
1/4 teaspoon dried oregano leaves

1/4 teaspoon salt
1 medium tomato, sliced
2 to 3 tablespoons freshly grated
    Parmesan cheese

2 SERVINGS

∎

Cut eggplant in half lengthwise and place cut sides up on 9-inch pie plate. Combine oil, garlic, oregano, and salt and brush mixture over cut surfaces of eggplant. Arrange tomato slices on top. Cover and microwave on HIGH 4 to 5 minutes. Allow to stand several minutes. Sprinkle cheese over tomatoes and serve.

MUSHROOM DELIGHT

1 pound mushrooms, sliced
3 tablespoons unsalted butter
1 cup chopped onions
3 tablespoons all-purpose flour
1 cup sour cream

1/4 cup chopped parsley
1 teaspoon minced garlic
Salt
Freshly ground white pepper

**4 TO 6
SERVINGS**

∎

A delicious side dish with grilled steak or chops!

In 2-quart casserole, microwave mushrooms on HIGH 4 to 5 minutes. Drain and reserve.

Melt butter in another 2-quart casserole. Stir in onions and flour and microwave on HIGH 2 to 3 minutes. Stir in sour cream and microwave on 70% power 2 to 3 minutes. Add mushrooms, parsley, garlic, and salt and pepper to taste and toss to mix. Microwave on 70% power 5 to 7 minutes.

BRAISED MUSHROOMS

4 TO 6 SERVINGS

▪

Wonderful served with a thick, juicy steak from the grill.

1 pound mushrooms, sliced
½ stick (¼ cup) unsalted butter or margarine
1 tablespoon fresh lemon juice

1 teaspoon salt
½ teaspoon freshly ground white pepper

Place mushrooms in 1½-quart casserole and microwave, uncovered, on HIGH 4 to 6 minutes. Drain. Add butter, lemon juice, salt, and pepper and microwave on HIGH 1 minute.

HAM-MUSHROOM DUXELLES

MAKES ABOUT 1½ CUPS

▪

Use duxelles as a stuffing for vegetables such as other mushrooms and zucchini, or for rolled flank steak or chicken breasts. Freeze the duxelles in an ice cube tray and add a cube to sauces or soups to season them.

1 pound mushrooms, finely chopped
¼ cup chopped scallions
½ stick (¼ cup) unsalted butter
½ teaspoon dried marjoram
1 tablespoon all-purpose flour

½ teaspoon salt
Pinch of freshly ground black pepper
2 tablespoons finely chopped parsley
½ cup finely chopped cooked ham

In 1½-quart measure, combine mushrooms and scallions, cover, and microwave on HIGH 5 minutes. Stir in butter, marjoram, flour, salt, and pepper and microwave on HIGH 3 to 4 minutes. Stir in parsley and ham.

TOMATOES STUFFED WITH OKRA EVANGELINE

1 pound fresh or frozen okra,
  sliced
1 cup chopped onions
1/4 cup bacon drippings or
  unsalted butter
1 cup chopped cooked ham

2 or 3 cloves garlic, minced
Salt
Freshly ground black pepper
1 1/2 cups cooked rice (page 289)
4 large tomatoes

4 OR 5
SERVINGS

■

A tasty dish from the
bayou. Make it when
okra and tomatoes are
plentiful. Okra that
cooks too long turns
gummy, so be careful
not to overcook it.

Combine okra, onions, and bacon drippings in 1 1/2-quart casserole, cover, and microwave on HIGH 6 to 9 minutes. Add ham, garlic, salt, pepper, and rice and stir to mix.

Cut off stem ends from tomatoes and carefully scoop out pulp. Set tomato shells aside. Stir pulp into okra mixture.

Stuff tomatoes with okra mixture, place in shallow casserole, and microwave on HIGH 3 to 6 minutes.

OKRA PILAF

3 slices bacon
2 cups sliced fresh or frozen okra
1 medium onion, chopped
1 cup rice
2 cups Chicken Stock (page 47) or
  canned chicken broth

1 teaspoon salt (do not use with
  canned chicken broth)
1/2 teaspoon freshly ground black
  pepper
2 cups tomatoes, peeled and diced,
  or 1 (16-ounce) can, drained

6 SERVINGS

■

A good side dish to
serve with pork.

Place bacon in 2-quart casserole. Cover with paper towel and microwave on HIGH 4 to 5 minutes. Remove bacon and set aside. Add okra and onion to casserole, cover, and cook on HIGH 5 to 8 minutes.

Add rice, stock, salt, pepper, and tomatoes. Cover and cook on HIGH 8 minutes. Stir and microwave, covered, on 50% power 12 to 14 minutes.

TWICE-BAKED POTATOES

6 TO 8 SERVINGS

■

Prepare the potatoes hours ahead, then heat for a few minutes at serving time.

4 medium baking potatoes, cooked (page 248)
½ stick (¼ cup) unsalted butter, melted
½ cup buttermilk

1 teaspoon salt
½ teaspoon freshly ground black pepper
Grated Cheddar cheese

Wrap cooked potatoes in a kitchen towel and allow to stand 5 to 10 minutes to soften.

Cut potatoes in half lengthwise, scoop out flesh, reserving shells, and place flesh in mixing bowl. Add butter, buttermilk, salt, and pepper, and mash with potato masher or fork. Spoon mixture into potato shells and place in shallow 2-quart casserole.

When ready to serve, reheat on HIGH 4 to 6 minutes and sprinkle with Cheddar.

PARMESAN POTATOES

5 OR 6 SERVINGS

■

Use a ricer or an old-fashioned potato masher to mash potatoes. Electric mixers and food processors tend to release too much starch from the potatoes, resulting in a gummy mass.

4 medium baking potatoes, cooked (page 248)
½ cup skim milk
¾ cup plain low-fat yogurt

¼ cup freshly grated Parmesan cheese
½ teaspoon salt
¼ teaspoon freshly ground white pepper

While potatoes are still hot, peel and mash them or press through a ricer into a mixing bowl. Stir in milk, yogurt, cheese, salt, and pepper and serve at once.

POTATO PUREE

2 medium baking potatoes,
    cooked (page 248)
½ stick (¼ cup) unsalted butter
½ cup heavy cream or sour cream

2 tablespoons milk (omit if
    making rosettes)
½ teaspoon salt
½ teaspoon freshly ground white
    pepper

4 SERVINGS

▪

If you aren't counting calories or cholesterol, this dish is the ultimate in indulgence. For a special dinner, use a pastry tube to make potato rosettes. Pipe directly on a platter of meat and vegetables.

While potatoes are still hot, peel them and put through ricer into 1-quart casserole.

Add butter, cream, milk, salt, and pepper and mix well. Microwave on HIGH 1½ minutes to heat well. Stir and serve at once.

MASHED POTATOES

3 medium baking potatoes,
    cooked (page 248)
⅔ cup milk or half-and-half
3 tablespoons unsalted butter

½ teaspoon salt
½ teaspoon freshly ground white
    pepper

4 SERVINGS

▪

Comfort food—plain, simple, and delicious.

While potatoes are still hot, peel them and put through ricer into 1½-quart casserole.

Stir in milk, butter, salt, and pepper. Serve hot.

COLCANNON

4 OR 5 SERVINGS

▪

This dish originated in Ireland, where potatoes and cabbage are always plentiful.

4 to 5 cups shredded green
    cabbage
2 to 3 tablespoons water
4 medium baking potatoes,
    cooked (page 248)

1 stick (½ cup) unsalted butter
1 cup milk
1 teaspoon salt
½ teaspoon freshly ground white
    pepper

Place cabbage and water in 2-quart casserole, cover, and microwave on HIGH 6 to 8 minutes, or until tender.

Peel potatoes while still hot and press through the ricer or mash directly in a serving bowl. In 2-cup bowl, microwave butter, milk, salt, and pepper on HIGH 3 to 3½ minutes. Add to mashed potatoes, along with cabbage, and stir to blend. Reheat if necessary.

CREAMED POTATOES

4 TO 6 SERVINGS

▪

1 cup chopped onions
½ stick (¼ cup) unsalted butter
3 tablespoons all-purpose flour
1½ cups milk
½ cup freshly grated Parmesan
    cheese

1 teaspoon salt
½ teaspoon freshly ground white
    pepper
4 cups cubed cooked all-purpose
    potatoes (page 248)

Place onions, butter, and flour in 1-quart measure and microwave on HIGH 4 to 5 minutes. Stir in milk, cheese, salt, and pepper and microwave on HIGH 5 to 6 minutes.

Place potatoes in 2-quart casserole, pour sauce over them, and microwave on HIGH 5 to 7 minutes.

BAKED POTATO SKINS

4 medium baking potatoes,
   cooked (page 248)
1/2 stick (1/4 cup) unsalted butter,
   melted
Freshly ground black pepper

3 or 4 slices bacon, cooked (page
   227) and crumbled (optional)
1 cup grated sharp Cheddar
   cheese (optional)

8 SERVINGS

■

Use combination cook-
ing to save lots of time
and energy.

Cut potatoes in half, scoop out flesh and reserve it for another
use. Cut skins in half lengthwise again, then into 2 or 3 pieces.
Brush skins all over with melted butter and sprinkle with pepper.

Preheat a conventional broiler.

Place potato skins on a baking sheet and broil on top rack 5 to 7
minutes, or until lightly browned. Sprinkle with bacon and cheese, if
desired, and broil 2 to 3 minutes longer.

BASQUE POTATOES

6 medium red or all-purpose
   potatoes, thinly sliced
1 teaspoon minced garlic
1 cup chopped onions
3 tablespoons extra-virgin olive oil

1/2 cup chopped parsley
1 (4-ounce) jar chopped
   pimientos, drained
Salt
Freshly ground black pepper

**6 TO 8
SERVINGS**

■

In 2-quart casserole, combine potatoes, garlic, onions, olive oil,
parsley, pimientos, and salt and pepper to taste. Cover and microwave on HIGH 10 minutes. Stir, cover again, and cook 3 to 5 minutes
longer, or until potatoes are tender.

PUMPKIN SOUFFLÉ

6 TO 8 SERVINGS

▪

Easy and delicious!

1 (16-ounce) can unsweetened
    pumpkin puree
¾ cup, packed, light brown sugar
1 cup milk or half-and-half
4 large eggs, beaten

½ teaspoon salt
½ teaspoon ground cinnamon
½ teaspoon ground cloves
½ teaspoon ground ginger

Place pumpkin, sugar, milk, eggs, salt, cinnamon, cloves, and ginger in food processor or electric mixer and blend. Pour into 1-quart casserole and microwave on HIGH 5 to 7 minutes. Gently stir, rotating the mixture at outside of dish to center. Cover and microwave on 70% power for 12 to 14 minutes.

GARLIC-SAUTÉED SPINACH

4 SERVINGS

▪

¼ cup (½ stick) unsalted butter,
    margarine, or extra-virgin
    olive oil
2 cloves garlic, minced
1½ to 2 pounds spinach, well
    washed and trimmed

Salt
Freshly ground black pepper

In 2-quart bowl, microwave butter and garlic on HIGH 1 to 2 minutes to melt butter and sauté garlic. Stir in spinach, cover, and microwave on HIGH 4 to 6 minutes, or until cooked. Serve at once.

SQUASH AU GRATIN

1 pound yellow squash, sliced
1 medium onion, finely chopped
½ stick (¼ cup) unsalted butter
2 large eggs, beaten
1 cup grated Cheddar cheese

Salt
Freshly ground white pepper
1 cup toasted bread or cracker
  crumbs

5 OR 6 SERVINGS

In 2-quart casserole, microwave squash and onion, covered, on HIGH 5 to 7 minutes. Drain and add butter and eggs, stirring to blend.

Stir in half the cheese and salt and pepper to taste. Cover with plastic wrap and microwave on 70% power 4 to 7 minutes. Uncover and top with crumbs and remaining cheese. Microwave on 70% power 2 to 3 minutes.

SQUASH CASSEROLE

1 pound yellow squash, sliced
1 medium onion, chopped
2 carrots, coarsely grated
1 stick (½ cup) unsalted butter
1 cup sour cream

1 (10¾-ounce) can condensed
  cream of chicken soup
2 cups packaged cornbread
  stuffing mix

8 SERVINGS

In 2-quart measure, microwave squash, onion, carrots, and butter, covered, on HIGH 8 to 10 minutes, or until carrots are tender. Stir in sour cream and soup.

Spread half the stuffing mix on bottom of 2-quart casserole. Spread squash mixture evenly over stuffing. Cover and microwave on HIGH 6 to 8 minutes, or until thoroughly heated. Sprinkle with remaining stuffing mix.

SPAGHETTI SQUASH WITH CHEESE

6 SERVINGS

1 (3- to 4-pound) spaghetti squash
2 tablespoons unsalted butter or
    olive oil
1/4 cup chopped onion
1/4 cup chopped green bell pepper
1/4 cup chopped red bell pepper
1/2 teaspoon dried basil

1/2 teaspoon dried oregano
1/4 teaspoon dried marjoram
2 or 3 garlic cloves, minced
1 teaspoon salt
1 to 2 cups grated Monterey Jack
    cheese
1/4 cup sliced black olives

Wash squash and pierce rind with knife 2 to 3 inches deep in several places. Place in pie plate and cook on HIGH 5 to 6 minutes per pound, or until squash yields to slight pressure and feels soft. Let stand 5 to 10 minutes. Cut in half crosswise and scrape out seeds and fibers. With a fork, twist out long strands of flesh and remove to 3-quart casserole.

In separate dish, combine butter, onion, bell pepper, basil, oregano, marjoram, garlic, and salt. Cover and microwave on HIGH 3 to 5 minutes. Combine with squash strands and add cheese. Let stand several minutes to melt cheese. Top with black olives.

SUMMER SQUASH AND TOMATOES

6 SERVINGS

3 tablespoons unsalted butter
1 cup sliced onion
4 cups sliced yellow squash or
    zucchini
1/2 teaspoon salt
1/2 teaspoon freshly ground black
    pepper

2 tablespoons chopped fresh basil,
    or 1 teaspoon dried
2 medium tomatoes, cut into
    1/2-inch dice
1 cup grated Cheddar cheese
    (optional)

Place butter, onion, squash, salt, pepper, and basil in 2-quart casserole. Cover and microwave on HIGH 3 to 5 minutes.

Stir in tomatoes and microwave on HIGH 2 to 6 minutes. Top with cheese and allow casserole to stand several minutes until cheese is melted.

SWEET POTATOES
WITH PRALINE-NUT TOPPING

3 medium sweet potatoes (about 1 1/2 pounds), cooked (page 250)
3/4 cup half-and-half or evaporated milk
1/3 cup unsalted butter or margarine

PRALINE NUT TOPPING
1/2 stick (1/4 cup) unsalted butter
1/2 cup, packed, brown sugar
1/4 cup all-purpose flour

2 large eggs
1/2 cup, packed, light brown sugar
1/2 teaspoon salt
1 1/2 teaspoons butter and nut flavoring or lemon extract

1/2 cup chopped pecans or walnuts, toasted (page 441)

8 SERVINGS

▪

Perfect for a special holiday meal. This dish can be prepared several days in advance and refrigerated.

Peel potatoes and place in food processor with half-and-half, butter, eggs, brown sugar, salt, and flavoring and blend until smooth.

Pour into 1 1/2-quart casserole, cover, and cook on HIGH 9 to 10 minutes, stirring once.

Make topping: Combine butter, sugar, and flour in 2-cup measure and microwave on HIGH for 1 minute. Stir and pour over potatoes. Cook on HIGH 6 to 8 minutes. Top with toasted nuts.

LACED SWEET POTATOES

8 SERVINGS

•

A wonderful blend of flavors.

3 pounds sweet potatoes, cooked (page 250)
½ cup bourbon
1 stick (½ cup) unsalted butter
½ cup fresh orange juice

¾ cup sugar
3 large eggs, beaten
½ teaspoon freshly grated nutmeg
½ cup chopped pecans or walnuts, toasted (page 441)

Peel and cube sweet potatoes. In food processor, combine sweet potatoes, bourbon, butter, orange juice, sugar, eggs, and nutmeg and process until smooth. Transfer to 2-quart casserole, cover, and microwave on HIGH 15 to 18 minutes. Stir. Cook on HIGH 2 to 3 minutes longer, sprinkle with nuts, and serve.

SWEET POTATO SURPRISE

6 TO 8 SERVINGS

•

Cook the sweet potato immediately after it is grated to prevent it from discoloring. This is a good do-ahead dish for busy holiday times.

1 large (1 pound) sweet potato, peeled and grated
¾ cup sugar
1 cup milk
1 stick (½ cup) unsalted butter, melted

2 large eggs, beaten
1 teaspoon cinnamon
½ teaspoon ground cloves
½ teaspoon freshly grated nutmeg
½ cup golden raisins

Place grated potato in 2-quart measure, cover, and microwave on HIGH 5 to 6 minutes, stirring once. Add sugar, milk, butter, eggs, cinnamon, cloves, nutmeg, and raisins, stir, and cook on HIGH 5 minutes, stirring once.

Pour into 1-quart casserole, cover with plastic wrap, and microwave on 50% power 5 to 8 minutes.

BAKED BEANS

3 or 4 slices of bacon
1 medium onion, chopped
1 green bell pepper, chopped
1 (16-ounce) can navy beans,
    drained
1 (16-ounce) can kidney beans,
    drained

1 (16-ounce) can butter beans,
    drained
1/2 cup, packed, brown sugar
1/2 cup catsup
1 teaspoon dry mustard
1 teaspoon liquid smoke
1 teaspoon Worcestershire sauce

8 TO 10 SERVINGS

▪

A good dish to take on a picnic or to a covered dish supper.

Place bacon in 2-quart casserole, cover, and cook on HIGH 3 to 5 minutes. Remove bacon and drain on paper towels. Add onion and bell pepper to bacon drippings, cover, and microwave on HIGH 3 to 5 minutes.

Stir in beans, sugar, catsup, mustard, liquid smoke, and Worcestershire and microwave on HIGH 15 minutes, stirring once. Cover and microwave on 70% power for 8 to 12 minutes. Crumble bacon over beans and serve at once.

TOMATO-POTATO BAKE

3 slices bacon
2 cups sliced peeled all-purpose
    potatoes
1 (16-ounce) can tomatoes,
    undrained
1 green bell pepper, chopped

1 medium onion, sliced
1/2 teaspoon dried basil
1 teaspoon salt
1/2 teaspoon freshly ground black
    pepper

6 SERVINGS

▪

It is only since the nineteenth century that tomatoes have become widely accepted as a food "fit for humans." Serve this fittest of dishes with ham or beef.

Place bacon in 2-quart casserole and microwave on HIGH 3 to 4 minutes. Remove bacon and drain on paper towels. Add potatoes, tomatoes, bell pepper, onion, and basil, breaking up tomatoes with fork. Cover and cook on HIGH 12 to 18 minutes, stirring several times. Stir in salt and pepper. Crumble bacon over top and serve.

GRATED ZUCCHINI

6 SERVINGS

3 tablespoons unsalted butter or
   margarine
1 clove garlic, minced
3 medium zucchini, coarsely
   grated

Pinch of freshly grated nutmeg
Salt
Freshly ground black pepper

In 2-quart casserole, microwave butter and garlic on HIGH 1 minute to melt butter. Stir in zucchini, cover, and microwave on HIGH 3 to 5 minutes, or to desired doneness. Stir in nutmeg, salt, and pepper.

TO MAKE ZUCCHINI FANS

Slice zucchini ¼ inch thick lengthwise to within 1 inch of stem end. Fan out. Place stem end facing inside of baking dish. Cover with plastic wrap and microwave on HIGH 1 to 1½ minutes for each medium zucchini. Brush with olive oil and sprinkle with salt and pepper to taste.

STUFFED ZUCCHINI

6 SERVINGS

This delicious side dish can be prepared hours before serving and refrigerated. Microwave at the last minute to heat.

6 medium zucchini
1 onion, chopped
½ stick (¼ cup) unsalted butter or
   margarine, melted
3 cups soft bread crumbs
½ cup freshly grated Parmesan
   cheese

3 tablespoons chopped parsley
1 teaspoon salt
¼ teaspoon freshly ground black
   pepper
2 large eggs, beaten
Paprika or cherry tomatoes

Place whole zucchini in a circle in microwave and cook on HIGH 6 minutes, turning halfway through cooking. Remove.

Place onion and 2 tablespoons butter in small bowl, cover, and microwave on HIGH 3 to 4 minutes, or until onions are tender-crisp.

Cut zucchini in half lengthwise and scoop out flesh with spoon, leaving a shell about ¼ inch thick. Add pulp to onion mixture with remaining butter, bread crumbs, cheese, parsley, salt, pepper, and eggs.

Stuff zucchini shells and arrange on plate like spokes of a wheel. Microwave on HIGH 8 to 10 minutes, or until shells and stuffing are cooked. Sprinkle with paprika or garnish with cherry tomatoes to serve.

MICROWAVING MIXED VEGETABLES

There are an almost infinite number of vegetable combinations that taste extraordinarily good when cooked in the microwave. The recipes that follow differ from each other enough in ingredients and technique to give you a basis for making combinations of your own. Anything goes, as long as you use the freshest vegetables you can find and follow the guidelines on pages 242 and 243. Use the cooking instructions that begin on page 244 for preparation techniques and cooking times.

VEGETABLE GARDEN BOUQUET

8 ounces carrots, cut into
    1/4-inch slices
1 pound fresh broccoli spears
1 pound cauliflowerets

8 ounces mushrooms
2 tablespoons water
1 large tomato, cut into wedges
1 recipe Cheese Sauce (page 76)

6 TO 8 SERVINGS

■

Cook the vegetables on a platter with the denser ones forming the outside of a circle. This makes a colorful presentation.

Arrange carrots along the perimeter of a 12- to 14-inch microwavable platter, with inner circles of broccoli, cauliflower, and mushrooms. Sprinkle water on carrots. Cover tightly with plastic wrap and microwave on HIGH 7 to 10 minutes, or until tender-crisp. Arrange tomato wedges in center. Cover and allow to stand 5 minutes. Serve with cheese sauce.

QUICK AND EASY MIXED VEGETABLES

4 TO 6 SERVINGS

■

1 (10-ounce) package frozen green beans
2 or 3 cloves garlic, minced
1 cup thinly sliced mushrooms
1 cup thinly sliced green bell pepper
1 cup thinly sliced celery
1 cup thinly sliced carrots
1/2 cup Chicken Stock (page 47) or 1 bouillon cube, dissolved in 1/2 cup water
1 tablespoon soy sauce
1 teaspoon Oriental sesame oil

In 2-quart casserole, combine frozen green beans, garlic, mushrooms, bell pepper, celery, carrots, chicken stock, soy sauce, and sesame oil. Cover tightly with plastic wrap and microwave on HIGH 6 to 8 minutes, or until vegetables are cooked but still crunchy, stirring once during cooking.

STIR-FRY VEGETABLES

6 TO 8 SERVINGS

■

You don't need a wok to make a delicious stir-fry. Use the microwave for excellent results.

2 tablespoons vegetable oil
1 large clove garlic, minced
1 (1/2-inch) piece fresh peeled ginger, minced
2 cups cauliflowerets
2 cups small broccoli flowerets
1 cup diagonally sliced celery
1/2 cup chopped scallions
1 teaspoon salt
1 teaspoon freshly ground black pepper
1/2 teaspoon Oriental sesame oil
2 tablespoons soy sauce

In 2-quart casserole, microwave oil on HIGH 45 to 60 seconds. Add garlic and ginger and microwave on HIGH 1 minute.

Add cauliflower, broccoli, celery, and scallions, cover, and microwave on HIGH 3 minutes. Stir, cover, and cook on HIGH 3 to 5 minutes. Add salt, pepper, sesame oil, and soy sauce and toss. Serve at once.

FRESH VEGETABLE DELIGHT

4 cups shredded green cabbage
1 medium onion, sliced
2 or 3 carrots, cut into 1/4-inch
  slices
1 medium potato, cut into
  1/4-inch slices

3 tablespoons water
1/2 teaspoon freshly ground white
  pepper
Salt (optional)
2 to 3 tablespoons unsalted butter
  or bacon drippings (optional)

4 TO 6 SERVINGS

∙

If you're on a low-fat, low-sodium diet, try this combination of vegetables with freshly ground pepper as the only seasoning. The flavor is wonderful, and the salt and fat won't be missed.

Combine cabbage, onion, carrots, and potato in 1½-quart casserole. Add water, cover tightly with plastic wrap, and microwave on HIGH 8 to 10 minutes.

Stir in pepper, and, if desired, salt and butter. Let stand 5 minutes before serving.

FESTIVE VEGETABLE RING

1 cup cherry tomatoes, or 1 large
  tomato cut into 6 wedges
5 cups broccoli flowerets
4 cups cauliflowerets

1/2 cup chopped onion
2 to 3 tablespoons water
1 recipe Cheese Sauce (optional;
  page 76)

6 TO 8 SERVINGS

∙

This dish tastes good served simply with melted butter and lemon juice to taste.

Place tomatoes in bottom of 6-cup glass ring mold. Arrange broccoli and cauliflower over tomatoes. (Vegetables will rise 1 to 1½ inches above top of dish, but will settle into dish as they cook.) Sprinkle chopped onion and water over cauliflower.

Cover tightly with plastic wrap and microwave on HIGH 9 to 12 minutes. Drain. Gently press vegetables into mold. Invert onto serving platter. Serve with cheese sauce, if desired.

HOT VEGETABLES IN MUSTARD MAYONNAISE

6 SERVINGS

3 carrots, cut into chunks
8 small red new potatoes,
    quartered
1 pint fresh Brussels sprouts, or
    1 (10-ounce) package frozen

2 stalks celery, thickly sliced
1 to 2 tablespoons water
5 or 6 scallions, chopped

MUSTARD MAYONNAISE

1 large egg
1 tablespoon Dijon mustard
3 tablespoons cider vinegar
1 teaspoon celery seeds

$2/3$ cup extra-virgin olive oil
1 tablespoon walnut oil (optional)
Salt
Freshly ground black pepper

Arrange vegetables on large plate, with carrots around perimeter, potatoes next, and Brussels sprouts and celery in center. Sprinkle water over the vegetables, cover tightly with plastic wrap, and microwave on HIGH 9 to 12 minutes, or until vegetables are tender. Uncover and let stand to cool slightly.

In blender or food processor or with wire whisk, combine egg, mustard, vinegar, and celery seeds. Slowly beat in olive oil and, if desired, walnut oil. Season to taste with salt and pepper. Toss dressing with vegetables and scallions. Serve warm.

Pasta, Grains, and Breads

Pasta and grain dishes made in the microwave taste delicious, but since the time required to cook them is about the same as for conventional methods, we find it more practical to use the conventional range for cooking these foods.

A significant exception is rice. Perfectly cooked rice can be achieved every time, with no stirring and no possibility of burning or sticking. And once the rice is removed from the oven, it can stand, covered, and will remain hot while you cook other foods in the microwave.

For the same reasons, we also prefer to cook grains such as bulgur, couscous, grits, wild rice, and individual servings of cereal in the microwave.

COOKING CEREALS						
CEREAL	AMOUNT	CASSEROLE OR CUP SIZE	WATER	SALT	MINUTES OF COOKING TIME ON HIGH	GENERAL DIRECTIONS
Cream of rice	⅔ cup	2 quarts	2⅔ cups	½ teaspoon	3½ to 4½	Stir after 2 minutes.
Enriched Cream of Wheat (regular and quick)	⅔ cup	3 quarts	3½ cups	½ teaspoon	7 to 8	Stir after 4 minutes.
Grits, quick	⅔ cup	2 quarts	2⅔ cups	¾ teaspoon	8 to 9	Stir after 5 minutes.
Oat bran cereal	⅓ cup	2-cup cereal bowl	1 cup		2 to 2½	Stir after 1½ minutes.
Oatmeal, old-fashioned	1⅓ cups	3 quarts	3 cups	¾ teaspoon	8 to 9	Stir after 5 minutes.
Oatmeal, quick	1⅓ cups	2 quarts	3 cups	¾ teaspoon	6 to 7	Stir after 3 minutes.

FETTUCINE ALFREDO

1 stick (¹/₂ cup) unsalted butter
1 cup heavy cream
1 cup (4 ounces) freshly grated
    Parmesan cheese
¹/₃ cup chopped red bell pepper
1 (10-ounce) package frozen
    artichoke hearts, thawed and
    halved

16 ounces fettucine, cooked
    according to package
    instructions
Salt
¹/₂ teaspoon freshly ground white
    pepper

**6 TO 8
SERVINGS**

Serve this version of
Fettucine Alfredo when
unexpected company
arrives. It's so easy to
prepare at the last
minute.

Combine butter, cream, cheese, bell pepper, and artichoke hearts in 2-quart casserole. Microwave on 70% power 4 to 6 minutes, or until cheese is melted.

While sauce is in microwave, cook fettucine on rangetop. Drain pasta and add to sauce, tossing until pasta is coated. Add salt and pepper to taste and serve at once.

FETTUCINE ALLA ROMANA

8 ounces fettucine, cooked
    according to package
    instructions
¹/₂ stick (¹/₄ cup) unsalted butter
3 or 4 cloves garlic, minced
¹/₄ cup minced prosciutto

¹/₂ cup green peas
¹/₂ cup heavy cream
1 large egg, beaten
¹/₂ cup freshly grated Parmesan
    cheese
Freshly ground white pepper

**2 OR 3
SERVINGS**

Enjoy with a crisp
green salad and crusty
bread.

While pasta cooks, place butter, garlic, prosciutto, and green peas in 2-quart casserole. Cover and cook on HIGH 3 to 4 minutes, or until mixture is boiling. Add cream, egg, and cheese and toss to combine. Microwave on 70% power 1 to 2 minutes, or until cheese is melted. Drain pasta, add to sauce, and toss lightly to coat noodles. Add pepper to taste and serve at once.

MANICOTTI

16 TO 18
SERVINGS

■

This recipe makes enough to serve 16 to 18 people. Freeze one casserole to enjoy when you don't have time to cook. The meat sauce and cheese filling may also be made in advance, with the casserole being assembled at the last minute.

16 ounces manicotti, cooked according to package instructions

MEAT SAUCE

1½ pounds lean ground beef
1 pound sweet or hot Italian sausage, removed from casings
2 medium onions, finely chopped
4 or 5 cloves garlic, minced
1 (32-ounce) jar chunky-style spaghetti sauce
1 (15-ounce) can tomato sauce

2 teaspoons dried basil
2 teaspoons dried oregano
1 teaspoon dried marjoram
1 teaspoon dried thyme
2 teaspoons sugar
1 teaspoon salt
1 teaspoon freshly ground black pepper

CHEESE FILLING

1½ pounds ricotta or cottage cheese
1 pound mozzarella cheese, shredded
⅔ cup freshly grated Parmesan cheese

2 large eggs
1 (10-ounce) package frozen chopped spinach, defrosted and well drained

Drain cooked manicotti, place in a bowl of cold water, and set aside.

Place ground beef, sausage, onions, and garlic in 2-quart casserole. Cover and cook on HIGH 5 minutes. Stir, cover, and cook on HIGH 5 to 7 minutes, or until meat is almost cooked. Stir and drain all fat.

Add spaghetti sauce, tomato sauce, basil, oregano, marjoram, thyme, sugar, salt, and pepper. Microwave on HIGH 10 to 15 minutes, or until boiling.

Combine ricotta, mozzarella, Parmesan, eggs, and spinach in a bowl, and stir until well mixed. Stuff manicotti shells with cheese filling. Put 1 cup meat sauce in each 13 × 9-inch casserole. Arrange manicotti in single layer over sauce and cover with remaining sauce.

Cover and microwave each casserole separately on 70% power 15 to 20 minutes, or until hot in center. (When serving this entire recipe at one time, it is more efficient to heat both dishes at once in a conventional oven. Bake 20 to 30 minutes at 350° F.)

LASAGNA

Substitute 16 ounces lasagna noodles, cooked, for manicotti. Layer noodles, cheese mixture, and meat sauce. Sprinkle additional grated mozzarella and Parmesan over top during last 5 minutes of final heating.

LASAGNA PESTO SWIRLS

8 lasagna noodles, cooked according to package instructions
1 (10-ounce) package frozen chopped spinach
1 cup cottage cheese

PESTO

1 teaspoon minced garlic
2½ cups, tightly packed, fresh basil leaves
⅓ cup freshly grated Parmesan cheese

1 cup freshly grated Parmesan cheese
¼ teaspoon freshly grated nutmeg
½ teaspoon salt
½ teaspoon freshly ground white pepper
Cherry tomatoes or tomato slices

½ cup extra-virgin olive oil
2 tablespoons parsley
3 tablespoons pine nuts (optional)

4 TO 6 SERVINGS

■

Another delicious pasta dish can be made simply by tossing 16 ounces hot, cooked fettucine with pesto. Sprinkle with additional Parmesan cheese.

Drain cooked lasagna noodles, place in a bowl of cold water, and set aside.

Remove wrapper, puncture spinach carton, and microwave on HIGH 3 to 4 minutes to defrost. Drain spinach in sieve, pressing out all liquid. Transfer to mixing bowl, add cottage cheese, Parmesan, nutmeg, salt, and pepper and mix well.

Drain lasagna noodles and spread out on a flat surface. Divide spinach filling among noodles, spreading evenly along entire length. Roll up noodles and stand on end in shallow 3-quart round casserole.

To make sauce, in food processor or blender, combine garlic, basil, Parmesan, oil, and parsley, and, if desired, pine nuts, and process until smooth.

Spoon pesto over each lasagna roll, cover, and microwave on HIGH 6 to 9 minutes, or until heated through. Serve with cherry tomatoes.

NOODLE RING

6 SERVINGS

▪

Serve plain egg noodles in a festive ring. You can fill the center with vegetables and surround the noodles with sliced meat, if you like.

8 ounces egg noodles, cooked according to package directions
½ stick (¼ cup) unsalted butter, melted
2 large eggs, beaten
1 teaspoon salt
¼ to ½ teaspoon freshly ground white pepper
1 tablespoon chopped parsley

Combine drained noodles, butter, eggs, salt, pepper, and parsley in a bowl and mix well. Pour into 5-cup glass ring mold, cover with plastic wrap and microwave on HIGH 4 to 7 minutes. Unmold on large round platter.

CHEESE NOODLE RING
Add 1 cup grated sharp Cheddar cheese and ⅓ cup half-and-half.

NOODLES SUPREME

6 TO 8 SERVINGS

▪

2 or 3 cloves garlic, minced
1 medium onion, chopped
½ stick (¼ cup) unsalted butter
1 cup sour cream
1 cup cottage cheese
½ teaspoon hot pepper sauce
½ teaspoon salt
¼ teaspoon freshly ground white pepper
½ cup freshly grated Parmesan cheese
5 ounces thin egg noodles, cooked according to package instructions

Combine garlic, onion, and butter in 1½-quart casserole. Cover and microwave on HIGH 3 to 4 minutes, or until onions are translucent. Add sour cream, cottage cheese, hot pepper sauce, salt, pepper, and cheese. Stir in drained egg noodles, cover, and cook on 70% power 5 to 6 minutes or until hot, stirring once.

POPPY SEED NOODLES

8 ounces egg noodles, cooked
    according to package
    instructions
1/2 stick (1/4 cup) unsalted butter
2 tablespoons poppy seeds

2 or 3 cloves garlic, minced
1 teaspoon salt
1/2 teaspoon freshly ground black
    pepper

4 TO 6 SERVINGS

·

While noodles cook, place butter in 1½-quart casserole and microwave on HIGH 1 minute to melt. Add poppy seeds, garlic, salt, and pepper and cook on 50% power 1 to 2 minutes. Drain noodles and combine with butter mixture. Serve at once.

SPICED NOODLE PUDDING

8 ounces egg noodles, cooked
    according to package
    instructions
2 large eggs, beaten
1/2 cup evaporated milk or
    half-and-half

2 teaspoons cinnamon
1 apple, peeled and grated
1 cup raisins
1/2 stick (1/4 cup) unsalted butter,
    melted
1/2 teaspoon salt

8 SERVINGS

·

A different and delicious dish to serve with turkey and chicken. Garnish with unpeeled apple slices.

TOPPING

1/2 teaspoon cinnamon

1/4 cup sugar

In 2-quart casserole, combine drained hot noodles, eggs, milk, cinnamon, grated apple, raisins, butter, and salt. Cover tightly with plastic wrap and microwave on HIGH 5 minutes. Stir.

To make topping, mix cinnamon and sugar and sprinkle over noodle mixture. Cover and microwave on 50% power 5 to 6 minutes. Let stand 5 minutes before serving.

BARLEY CASSEROLE

6 TO 8 SERVINGS

▪

This is a wonderful dish to serve with a pork roast. Cook the dish the day before and refrigerate. Leftovers also freeze well.

$^{1}/_{3}$ cup unsalted butter
1 cup pearl barley
1 medium onion, chopped
1 (2-ounce) envelope dehydrated
　onion soup
2 cups Chicken Stock (page 47) or
　canned chicken broth

1 to 2 cups sliced mushrooms or 1
　(5$^{1}/_{2}$-ounce) jar sliced
　mushrooms, drained
1 (5-ounce) can water chestnuts,
　drained and sliced
$^{2}/_{3}$ cup slivered blanched almonds,
　toasted (page 441)

Place butter, barley, onion, and onion soup mix in 2-quart casserole. Cover tightly with plastic wrap and cook on HIGH 3 to 4 minutes. Add stock, mushrooms, and water chestnuts. Cover again and microwave on HIGH 5 minutes, then cook on 50% power 25 to 30 minutes, or until barley is tender. Sprinkle top with toasted almonds and let stand 5 minutes.

BASIC BULGUR

4 TO 6 SERVINGS

▪

This crunchy grain with a nutty flavor is a staple in Middle Eastern countries and one of the oldest forms of wheat. Bulgur is very high in the B vitamins, niacin, protein, riboflavin, and thiamine. It's delicious served with duck, chicken, pork, roast, and lamb.

1 cup bulgur (cracked wheat),
　rinsed and drained
2 cups Chicken Stock (page 47) or
　canned chicken broth

Salt
$^{1}/_{2}$ teaspoon freshly ground pepper
1 teaspoon vegetable or olive oil

In 1-quart dish, combine bulgur, stock, salt to taste, pepper, and oil. Cover and microwave on HIGH 4 to 5 minutes. Reduce power to 50% and cook 14 to 17 minutes. Let stand about 5 minutes until all liquid is absorbed.

BULGUR PILAF

1 large onion, chopped
2 tablespoons unsalted butter
1 teaspoon salt
1/2 teaspoon freshly ground black
    pepper

1 cup bulgur (cracked wheat),
    rinsed and drained
2 cups Chicken Stock (page 47),
    Beef Stock (page 46), or
    canned chicken or beef broth

**4 TO 6
SERVINGS**

■

Place onion and butter in 1-quart casserole, cover, and micro-wave on HIGH 2 to 3 minutes. Stir in salt, pepper, bulgur, and stock, cover again, and cook on HIGH 4 to 5 minutes. Reduce power to 50% and cook 14 to 17 minutes. Allow to stand about 5 minutes, until all liquid is absorbed.

COUSCOUS

1 onion, chopped
1 stick (1/2 cup) unsalted butter
3 cloves garlic, minced
1 teaspoon curry powder
2/3 teaspoon paprika

2 cups couscous
1 quart Chicken Stock (page 47)
    or canned chicken broth
Salt
Freshly ground black pepper

**8 TO 10
SERVINGS**

■

A North African spe-
cialty. Serve as a side
dish or with lamb stew
ladled over it.

In 2-quart casserole, combine onion, butter, garlic, curry powder, and paprika, cover, and microwave on HIGH 3 to 5 minutes, or until onion is tender. Add couscous, stock, and salt and pepper to taste. Microwave, uncovered, on HIGH 10 minutes. Let stand 5 min-utes until liquid is absorbed.

GOLDEN GRANOLA

6 TO 7 CUPS

·

Granola and yogurt make a delicious quick breakfast. The mixture is perfect to take on a camping trip as a snack or breakfast.

1/4 cup honey
1/3 cup vegetable oil
1 teaspoon vanilla extract
1 1/2 teaspoons cinnamon
1/2 teaspoon salt (optional)
3 cups old-fashioned rolled oats
1/4 cup whole wheat flour

1/2 cup sunflower seeds, wheat germ, or sesame seeds
1 cup unsweetened shredded coconut
1 cup coarsely chopped nuts
1/4 cup, packed, brown sugar
3/4 cup raisins

In small bowl, combine honey, oil, vanilla, cinnamon, and, if desired, salt.

In shallow 3-quart dish, stir together oats, flour, sunflower seeds, coconut, nuts, and brown sugar. Drizzle honey mixture over oat mixture and stir to coat dry ingredients. Spread evenly in dish and microwave, uncovered, on HIGH 8 to 10 minutes, or until golden brown, stirring several times during cooking. Stir in raisins and let stand until cool. Store tightly covered.

CHEESE GRITS SOUFFLÉ

6 TO 8 SERVINGS

·

Grits, made from coarsely ground corn, have been a Southern staple from the time of America's pioneer days. Serve this wonderful side dish at brunch or dinner.

1 cup quick-cooking (not instant) grits
1 teaspoon salt
3 cups water
1 stick (1/2 cup) unsalted butter
4 large eggs, beaten
1/2 cup milk

2 cups grated sharp Cheddar cheese plus grated Cheddar for garnish
1/2 teaspoon freshly ground white pepper
1/2 teaspoon garlic powder

Cook grits, salt, water, and butter in 2-quart measure 10 to 12 minutes, stirring several times. Add eggs, milk, 2 cups of cheese, pepper, and garlic. Stir until well mixed and pour into 1 1/2-quart casserole. (Recipe may be prepared ahead to this point. Cover casserole and refrigerate until 15 minutes before serving.)

Place covered casserole in microwave and cook on HIGH 5 minutes. Stir and microwave, covered, on 70% power 5 to 8 minutes. Sprinkle with additional grated cheese and serve at once.

PERFECT RICE

Convenience is the best reason for making rice in the microwave. Although the cooking time is about the same as for conventional rangetop methods, in the microwave there is no concern about sticking or scorching, and you can turn your attention to other elements of the meal.

We suggest that you cook more rice than is required in the recipes. Leftover rice can be frozen in ½- to 1-cup portions and used in recipes calling for cooked rice.

MOLDED RICE

Cooked rice that has been molded into various shapes looks attractive on a dinner plate or serving platter.

Rice Timbales: Press hot cooked rice into buttered or oiled plastic or paper cups (easier to unmold because they are somewhat flexible) or into custard cups, or even coffee cups or teacups. To unmold, run a thin-bladed knife around the side of mold and invert on plate.

Rice Ring: Lightly press hot rice into a heavily buttered or oiled microwavable ring mold. The rice should fill the mold slightly above the rim. Cover with plastic wrap. The ring can be refrigerated at this point. When almost ready to serve, microwave ring on HIGH 2 to 4 minutes (3 to 5 minutes, if mold was refrigerated), or until hot. Press down lightly on the rice and let stand, covered, 1 to 2 minutes. To unmold, run a knife around sides of mold and invert on a serving platter. Fill the center with vegetables or stews, if desired.

TIMETABLE FOR COOKING RICE

Place rice and liquid in 1-quart dish, cover tightly with plastic wrap, and microwave as directed below.

1 CUP RAW RICE	LIQUID	COOKING TIME
Brown	2 to 2½ cups	5 minutes on HIGH, then 40 to 55 minutes on 50% power
White, long-grain	2 cups	5 minutes on HIGH, then 12 to 15 minutes on 50% power
White, short-grain	1½ cups	5 minutes on HIGH, then 12 to 15 minutes on 50% power

CALIFORNIA RICE

4 TO 6 SERVINGS

Terrific served with almost any meat dish.

Rice is a nonallergenic food—a versatile choice when dietary restrictions prohibit wheat, rye, oats, or barley.

1 cup long-grain rice
2 cups water
2 bay leaves
2 tablespoons unsalted butter
1 cup chopped onion
2 cups sour cream or plain low-fat yogurt

½ teaspoon freshly ground white pepper
1 (4-ounce) can green chilies, drained and chopped
2 cups grated Monterey Jack or sharp Cheddar cheese

Place rice, water, and bay leaves in 1-quart casserole. Cover with plastic wrap and microwave on HIGH 4 to 5 minutes. Reduce power to 50% and cook 14 to 15 minutes.

In 2-cup measure, microwave butter and onion on HIGH 3 to 4 minutes. Combine with cooked rice and stir in sour cream, pepper, and chilies.

Layer rice mixture and cheese in 2-quart casserole. Microwave on 70% power 10 to 12 minutes. Let stand 5 minutes.

BASMATI RICE

4 OR 5 SERVINGS

Basmati is a variety of long-grain rice often used in India and the Middle East. It is especially good in pilafs. If imported *basmati* rice is not available, Texmati, a Texas-grown hybrid, is an excellent substitute.

1 cup basmati *rice*
1¾ cups water

¾ teaspoon salt

Wash rice in several changes of cold water, removing any small stones or seeds, then drain (not necessary if using Texmati rice). Combine rice, water, and salt in 2-quart casserole. Cover tightly with plastic wrap and cook on HIGH 5 to 6 minutes, or until boiling. Reduce power to 50% and cook 8 to 10 minutes.

Let stand covered for 5 minutes until all liquid is absorbed.

CAROLINA RED RICE

3 slices bacon
1 medium onion, finely chopped
1 (16-ounce) can tomatoes,
    undrained, chopped
1 tablespoon brown sugar

1 teaspoon salt
1/2 teaspoon freshly ground black
    pepper
1/8 teaspoon cayenne pepper
1 cup long-grain rice

**4 to 6
SERVINGS**

▪

South Carolina was the first colony to grow rice successfully. Rice was called "Carolina gold" and was an important cash crop for over 200 years. This is a good dish to serve with chicken, pork, or fried fish.

Microwave bacon in 2-quart casserole on HIGH 3 to 5 minutes. Remove bacon and drain on paper towels. Add onions to bacon drippings, cover, and cook on HIGH 3 to 4 minutes.

Stir in tomatoes, sugar, salt, black pepper, cayenne, and rice. Cover and cook on HIGH 5 to 6 minutes. Reduce power to 50% and cook 12 to 14 minutes. Crumble bacon on top and let stand 5 minutes.

CUMIN RICE

1 cup long-grain rice
2 tablespoons bacon drippings
1/2 cup chopped onion
1/4 cup chopped green or red bell
    pepper
1/2 to 3/4 teaspoon cumin seeds or
    1/4 teaspoon ground cumin

2 1/2 cups water
3 teaspoons beef bouillon granules
1 tablespoon Worcestershire sauce
1/2 teaspoon salt
1/4 teaspoon freshly ground black
    pepper

4 SERVINGS

▪

In 2-quart bowl, toss rice and bacon drippings together to coat rice. Microwave on HIGH 3 to 5 minutes, or until the rice is lightly browned, stirring every minute. Add onion and bell pepper, cover, and microwave on HIGH 3 minutes longer, or until vegetables are tender.

Add cumin, water, bouillon granules, Worcestershire, salt and pepper. Cover and microwave on HIGH 10 minutes, then on 50% power 15 minutes, or until cooked. Let stand 5 minutes.

CHEESE RICE

4 SERVINGS

1 cup long-grain rice
2 cups water or canned chicken or
 beef broth
1 cup grated Cheddar cheese
1/4 teaspoon salt

1/2 teaspoon freshly ground white
 pepper
1/2 cup evaporated milk or plain
 low-fat yogurt
2 slices bacon, cooked (page 227;
 optional)

Combine rice and water in 2-quart casserole, cover, and microwave on HIGH 10 minutes, then on 50% power 15 minutes, or until cooked. Stir in cheese, salt, pepper, and evaporated milk. Top with crumbled bacon, if desired, and let stand 5 minutes.

GREEN RICE

**4 TO 6
SERVINGS**

This combination of spinach and rice is delightful!

1 (10-ounce) package frozen
 chopped spinach, defrosted
1 cup chopped onion
3 tablespoons unsalted butter
1 cup cooked long-grain rice
 (page 289)

1 cup freshly grated Parmesan
 cheese
Salt
Freshly ground black pepper

Drain spinach well and set aside.
 Place onion and butter in 1-quart casserole and microwave on HIGH 2 to 3 minutes. Add spinach, rice, and ¾ cup Parmesan cheese. Season to taste with salt and pepper. Cover and microwave on 70% power 6 to 9 minutes. Sprinkle with remaining Parmesan.

HOPPIN' JOHN

1 cup chopped onion
2 tablespoons bacon drippings or
    vegetable oil
1/2 to 1 teaspoon hot pepper sauce
1 to 2 cups chopped cooked ham

2 (15-ounce) cans blackeyed peas,
    drained
3 cups cooked long-grain rice
    (page 289)
Salt
Freshly ground black pepper

6 TO 8
SERVINGS

■

In the South, eating Hoppin' John on New Year's Day is a tradition said to bring good fortune in the coming year. It's also a good way to use leftover ham or rice. Enjoy with cornbread and a salad.

Place onion and bacon drippings in 2-quart casserole and microwave on HIGH 3 minutes. Add hot pepper sauce, ham, and peas. Cover and cook on HIGH 5 to 7 minutes.

Stir in rice, cover, and microwave on HIGH 2 to 3 minutes, or until very hot, then add salt and pepper to taste.

PALAU

1 1/2 cups long-grain rice
3 cups water
1 teaspoon salt
1 cinnamon stick (about 3 inches)
8 cardamom pods, broken
1 teaspoon whole black
    peppercorns

4 whole cloves
2 cups sliced onions
1/2 stick (1/4 cup) unsalted butter
1/4 teaspoon cumin seeds

4 TO 6
SERVINGS

■

An aromatic dish with origins in India.

■ ■ ■ ■ ■ ■ ■ ■ ■ ■ ■

Cardamom, a member of the ginger family and one of the world's most precious spices, is native to India. Use scissors to snip open the pod and remove the black seeds before cooking.

■ ■ ■ ■ ■ ■ ■ ■ ■ ■ ■

Combine rice, water, and salt in deep 2-quart casserole and set aside.

Tie cinnamon stick, cardamom, peppercorns, and cloves in cheesecloth bag and place in 1-quart measure with onions, butter and cumin. Cover and microwave on HIGH 5 to 6 minutes, stirring once. Add onion mixture to rice, cover, and microwave on HIGH 10 minutes. Reduce power to 50% and cook 10 minutes longer, or until rice is cooked. Let stand 5 minutes. Remove spice bag before serving.

PECAN PILAF

4 TO 6 SERVINGS

▪

An excellent side dish to serve with any meat.

½ stick (¼ cup) unsalted butter
½ cup chopped scallions
1 cup long-grain rice
2 cups Chicken Stock (page 47) or
* canned chicken broth*

¼ teaspoon dried thyme
Salt
Freshly ground white pepper
1 tablespoon chopped parsley
1 cup chopped pecans

Combine butter and scallions in 2-quart casserole. Cover and microwave on HIGH 2 minutes. Add rice, stock, thyme, salt and pepper to taste, and parsley. Cover tightly with plastic wrap and microwave on HIGH, 6 minutes, or until boiling. Cook on 50% power 12 to 14 minutes. Let stand 5 minutes.

Spread nuts on a plate and toast on HIGH 2 to 3 minutes, stirring after each minute. Stir into rice just before serving.

PERSIAN RICE

4 TO 6 SERVINGS

▪

The orange flavor combines well with pork.

1 cup long-grain rice
½ cup frozen orange juice
* concentrate, thawed*
1½ cups water
2 tablespoons unsalted butter
1 teaspoon salt

½ teaspoon freshly ground white
* pepper*
½ cup golden raisins
½ teaspoon grated orange zest
½ cup blanched almonds, toasted
* (page 441)*

In 1½-quart bowl or casserole, combine rice, orange juice concentrate, water, butter, salt, and pepper. Cover and cook on HIGH 5 to 6 minutes, or until boiling. Reduce power to 50% and cook, covered, 12 to 14 minutes, or until water has almost been absorbed.

Add raisins and orange zest and let stand 5 minutes. Stir in almonds.

WILD RICE

1 cup wild rice, rinsed
2 cups water

½ stick (¼ cup) unsalted butter
1 teaspoon salt

4 SERVINGS

■

Wild rice was once an important food for the American Indians who introduced it to French explorers.

Place wild rice in a bowl, barely cover with hot water, and allow to stand 1 hour, or until all water is absorbed. Drain.

Place wild rice, 2 cups water, butter, and salt in 1-quart measure. Cover and cook on HIGH 10 minutes, then on 50% power 30 to 35 minutes. Let stand 5 minutes.

WILD RICE WITH SAUTÉED SHRIMP AND CHICKEN

1 (6-ounce) package Uncle Ben's
    Long Grain and Wild Rice
½ cup golden raisins
4 slices bacon, cooked (page 227)
    and crumbled, drippings
    reserved
1 cup chopped celery
¼ cup chopped scallions
¼ to ½ teaspoon freshly ground
    white pepper

1 pound boneless skinless chicken
    breasts, cooked (page 169)
    and cut into strips
1 pound shrimp, steamed (page
    155) and peeled
½ cup chopped pecans, toasted
    (page 441)
Parsley sprigs

5 OR 6 SERVINGS

■

Just right for a special occasion or small dinner party. To serve as a side dish, omit the shrimp and chicken.

Cook rice in 2-quart casserole according to microwave directions on package. Add raisins while rice is hot. Cover again to allow raisins to plump.

In 2-cup measure, combine 2 tablespoons bacon drippings with celery, scallions, and pepper. Cover and cook on HIGH 2 to 3 minutes, until tender-crisp. Add to rice and stir.

Mound rice on a serving platter or dish. Surround with chicken and shrimp and sprinkle with toasted pecans and bacon. Place parsley around outside edge for an eye-appealing main dish.

LOW-CAL RISOTTO

**4 OR 5
SERVINGS**

·

½ cup long-grain rice
½ cup wild rice
1 medium onion, finely chopped
2 teaspoons chicken bouillon
    granules

½ teaspoon freshly ground black
    pepper
2 cups water

Combine long-grain and wild rice, onion, bouillon granules, pepper, and water in 1½-quart casserole. Microwave on HIGH 5 to 6 minutes, or until boiling. Stir, cover, and cook on 50% power 20 to 25 minutes. Let stand 5 minutes, until water is absorbed.

YEAST BREADS

We like our bread brown and crusty, and we prefer to bake most yeast breads in a conventional oven. Even so, the microwave is very convenient to use when proofing yeast dough.

In 1-quart measure, microwave 3 cups water on HIGH 4 to 5 minutes, or until boiling. Place yeast dough in a bowl, cover with plastic wrap, and place next to boiling water in the microwave. Microwave on 10% power 10 minutes. Turn off microwave and let dough rest in oven 10 minutes with water. Test for rising and repeat if further proofing is necessary.

An alternative method is to microwave the dough and boiling water at 30% power for 1 to 2 minutes, then allow bread to stand in the oven 15 minutes.

For the second rise, shape the bread into a loaf and place in a glass bread pan. Cover loosely with wax paper and follow the same instructions, but leave bread in for a shorter time and watch carefully to see that it does not rise too high.

DEFROSTING COMMERCIAL FROZEN YEAST BREAD DOUGH

1. Pour 2 cups water in a 12 × 8-inch casserole and microwave on HIGH until boiling, about 3 to 4 minutes.
2. Heavily butter the frozen dough on all sides and place in a greased 8-inch loaf dish. Set the dish in the casserole of boiling water, cover loosely with wax paper, and cook on 50% power 2 minutes. Turn dough over and cook on 50% power 2 minutes longer. Allow to stand 5 minutes, or until dough is defrosted. Proceed with proofing instructions (opposite).

REHEATING BREADS

Wrap the bread in a napkin or paper towel and heat. When warming several rolls or a whole loaf of bread (weighing 1 pound), place in a bread basket or a cloth or paper napkin and cover with a second cloth or napkin to absorb moisture.

TIMETABLE FOR REHEATING BREADS

BREAD	MICROWAVE TIME ON HIGH	BREAD	MICROWAVE TIME ON HIGH
1 roll	8 to 10 seconds	6 rolls	25 to 30 seconds
2 rolls	12 to 16 seconds	1 loaf bread	1 to 1½ minutes
4 rolls	20 to 25 seconds	1 refrigerated pancake or waffle	45 to 60 seconds

Oat Bran Muffins I

**MAKES
36
MUFFINS**

■

An easy way to get extra oat bran into your diet. Enjoy a hot muffin for breakfast.

3 cups oat bran cereal
1/2 cup oat bran
1 cup water
1/2 cup corn oil
1 cup, packed, light or dark brown sugar

3 large eggs, beaten
2 cups all-purpose flour
2 1/2 teaspoons baking soda
1/2 teaspoon salt
2 cups buttermilk
1 cup raisins

Place cereal and oat bran in mixing bowl. In 1-cup measure, microwave water on HIGH 1 to 2 minutes, or until boiling. Pour boiling water over bran, stir to mix, and set aside.

In 4-quart bowl, combine oil, sugar, eggs, flour, baking soda, salt, and buttermilk and stir to mix. Add oat bran mixture and raisins to batter, stirring to blend.

Transfer mixture to 2-quart container, cover tightly, and refrigerate for up to 5 weeks.

To cook 6 muffins, place paper liners in microwave muffin pan. Remove batter from refrigerator; do not stir. Spoon batter into muffin cups, filling half full. Cook on HIGH 3 to 4 minutes, or until top looks damp but not wet. Let stand 2 to 3 minutes.

To cook 1 muffin, place paper liner in 1-cup custard cup and half-fill with batter. Microwave on HIGH 30 to 40 seconds. Let stand 1 minute.

To bake conventionally, preheat oven to 400° F. Grease 12 muffin cups and fill two-thirds full with batter. Bake 12 to 15 minutes.

OAT BRAN MUFFINS II

2¼ cups oat bran
1 tablespoon baking powder
¼ cup sugar
1 cup skim milk
2 egg whites

2 tablespoons dark or light corn
  syrup
1 teaspoon salt (optional)
½ cup raisins (optional)

**MAKES
12 MUFFINS**

■

A good low-cholesterol muffin. Store the batter in the refrigerator and cook one muffin at a time—in one minute!

Combine oat bran, baking powder, sugar, milk, egg whites, syrup, and, if desired, salt and raisins in 2-quart bowl and stir to mix. Cover tightly with plastic wrap and store in refrigerator for up to 3 days.

To cook 1 muffin, grease 1-cup custard cup (or line it with a paper baking cup), fill two-thirds full with batter, and microwave on HIGH 50 to 60 seconds, or until surface looks damp but not wet. To cook 6 muffins, microwave on HIGH 3 to 4 minutes. To reheat 1 muffin, microwave on HIGH 30 to 40 seconds.

To bake conventionally, preheat oven to 425° F. Grease 12 muffin cups and divide batter among them. Bake 10 to 15 minutes.

Desserts

Dessert can be a glorious finale or a subtle finishing touch for a meal. Desserts figure prominently in culinary history, and there are special sweets associated with almost every international festive event and with other celebrations and holidays.

People love sweets. Even the most rigorous weight-loss diets include some form of dessert. The key to satisfying a sweet tooth within the framework of a healthy diet is to limit the number of desserts you eat and to control the portion size.

The microwave oven can be used to simplify the preparation of some desserts and to produce a superior flavor in others. Those most successfully made in the microwave are

JUST DESSERTS

Drive away those midwinter blues with an afternoon dessert party. Ask friends to bring some of these sweets—they're so easy to make in the microwave that you'll find willing helpers.

Serve one or two dessert wines, an assortment of teas, regular and decaffeinated coffee, and some milk and soft drinks for the kids.

Carolina Trifle (page 366)
Fresh Berry Shortcake (page 312)
Bread Pudding (page 361)
Lemon Curd (page 317) in Pastry Shells
Queen of Sheba (page 342)
Amaretto Cheese Pie (page 307)
Peach Truffles (page 397)
Irish Cream Truffles (page 396)
Scrumptious Nut Brittle (page 412)
Yogurt-Coated Nuts (page 416)

fruit desserts, puddings and pie fillings, custards, buttercreams and other icings and cake fillings, crumb pie crusts, some cakes, and bar cookies.

Desserts that cannot be microwaved with the best results are pastries, puff pastry, crisp meringues, crepes, pancakes, fritters, pies in which the filling is baked in the pastry, soufflés, and most cakes. These, as well as other desserts that are fried or have crisp textures, should be cooked conventionally.

However, even for these, the microwave can save or simplify tedious preparation steps—toasting and blanching nuts, plumping fruit, melting chocolate and butter, bringing ingredients to room temperature or defrosting them, softening butter without melting, and many more.

We have included here a wide variety of desserts, some of them rich and elegant, others very simple but no less delicious.

PIES

Pies are perhaps America's best-loved dessert after ice cream. As a rule, the recipes that follow consist of a microwaved crumb crust that is then assembled with a cooked filling and garnished spectacularly or modestly, but always appropriately.

CHOCOLATE COOKIE CRUST

24 cream-filled chocolate wafer cookies (such as Oreos)

½ stick (¼ cup) unsalted butter

MAKES
1 (9-INCH)
CRUST

•

Crush cookies with a rolling pin or in a food processor. In 2-quart measure, microwave butter on HIGH 30 to 60 seconds, or until melted. Add crushed cookies and combine well. Using back of spoon, press mixture against bottom and side of oiled 9-inch pie plate. Microwave on HIGH 2 minutes. Let stand until cool.

COCONUT ALMOND CRUST

**MAKES
1 (9-INCH)
CRUST**

1 cup sliced blanched almonds
1 cup shredded coconut
2/3 cup all-purpose flour

1/4 cup sugar
1/2 stick (1/4 cup) unsalted butter,
  softened

Process almonds, coconut, flour, sugar, and butter in a food processor until mixture resembles crumbs. Using back of spoon, press mixture against bottom and side of oiled 9-inch pie plate. Microwave on HIGH 2 to 3 minutes, or until surface looks dull. Let stand until cool.

GRAHAM CRACKER CRUST

**MAKES
1 (9-INCH)
CRUST**

1/3 cup unsalted butter
1 1/2 cups graham cracker crumbs

1/3 cup sugar

In 1-quart measure, microwave butter on HIGH 30 to 60 seconds, or until melted. Stir in crumbs and sugar. Using back of spoon, press mixture against bottom and side of oiled 9-inch pie plate. Microwave on HIGH 2 minutes. Let stand until cool.

CHOCOLATE GRAHAM CRUST
Add 3 tablespoons Dutch-process cocoa powder to crumb mixture.

COCONUT GRAHAM CRUST

**MAKES
1 (9-INCH)
CRUST**

1 cup graham cracker crumbs
1 cup shredded coconut

1/3 cup sugar
1/3 cup unsalted butter, melted

Combine crumbs, coconut, sugar, and butter and mix well. Press mixture against bottom and side of oiled 9-inch pie plate using back of spoon. Microwave on HIGH 2 minutes. Let stand until cool.

GRANOLA CRUST I

1 stick (1/2 cup) unsalted butter
1 1/2 cups quick-cooking oats
1/3 cup, packed, light brown sugar
1/3 cup all-purpose flour

1/2 cup finely chopped nuts
1/4 cup wheat germ, sesame seeds,
    or oat bran (optional)

**MAKES
1 (9-INCH)
CRUST**

•

In 2-quart measure, microwave butter on HIGH 1 minute, or until melted. Stir in oats, sugar, flour, nuts, and, if desired, wheat germ. Stir to combine.

Transfer mixture to oiled 9-inch pie plate and, using back of spoon, press it against bottom and side of plate. Microwave on HIGH 2 to 3 minutes, then let stand until cool. If mixture slides down in plate during cooking, simply press it back in place immediately after removing from oven. Crust will become crisp while cooling.

For added nutrients and an even nuttier flavor use the wheat germ or sesame seeds.

GRANOLA CRUST II

1/2 cup vegetable oil
3 tablespoons water
1 1/2 cups quick-cooking oats

1/3 cup, packed, light brown sugar
1/3 cup all-purpose flour
1/4 cup oat bran

**MAKES
1 (9-INCH)
CRUST**

•

In bowl, combine oil, water, oats, sugar, flour, and oat bran and mix well. Using back of spoon, press mixture against bottom and side of oiled 9-inch pie plate. Microwave on HIGH 2 to 3 minutes. If mixture slides down in plate during cooking, simply press it back in place immediately after removing from oven. Crust will become crisp while cooling.

A delicious low-cholesterol dessert crust. With a fruit pie filling, this makes a dessert that is hard to surpass for good nutrition and flavor.

VANILLA WAFER CRUST

**MAKES
1 (9-INCH)
CRUST**

¹/₃ cup unsalted butter
1¹/₃ cups vanilla wafer crumbs

¹/₄ cup sugar

In 2-quart measure, microwave butter on HIGH 30 to 60 seconds to melt. Stir in crumbs and sugar. Using back of spoon, press mixture against bottom and side of oiled 9-inch pie plate. Microwave on HIGH 2 minutes. Let stand until cool.

WHOLE WHEAT PIE CRUST

**MAKES
1 (9-INCH)
CRUST**

1 cup whole wheat flour
1 tablespoon sugar (optional)
¹/₂ teaspoon salt
*3 tablespoons solid vegetable
    shortening*

*3 tablespoons unsalted butter,
    softened*
3 tablespoons ice water

In bowl, combine flour, sugar, if desired, and salt. Using a pastry blender or 2 forks, cut in shortening and butter until mixture forms coarse crumbs. Sprinkle with ice water, stirring with fork. When mixture holds together, knead dough 2 to 3 times.

Place dough on floured surface and roll into 13-inch circle. Transfer dough to 9-inch pie plate and let rest 5 to 10 minutes. Trim and crimp edges and prick crust in several places with fork. Microwave on HIGH 5 to 7 minutes, or until cooked. Surface will appear dry and opaque. Use for fruit and cream pie fillings.

ZWIEBACK PIE CRUST

**MAKES
1 (9-INCH)
CRUST**

1¹/₂ cups zwieback crumbs
¹/₃ cup sifted confectioners' sugar

¹/₃ cup unsalted butter, melted

In bowl, combine crumbs, sugar, and butter. Using back of spoon, press mixture against bottom and side of oiled 9-inch pie plate. Microwave on HIGH 2 minutes. Let stand until cool.

AMARETTO CHEESE PIE

CRUST

1 stick (¹/₂ cup) unsalted butter
1¹/₂ cups almond-flavored cookie
   crumbs or graham cracker
   crumbs

2 tablespoons sugar
1 tablespoon Dutch-process cocoa
   powder
¹/₄ teaspoon cinnamon

FILLING

2 (8-ounce) packages cream
   cheese (or 16 ounces
   Neufchâtel or ricotta)
²/₃ cup sugar

3 large eggs, beaten
¹/₄ cup Amaretto or other almond-
   flavored liqueur

TOPPING

1 cup sour cream
2 tablespoons sugar
1 tablespoon Amaretto or other
   almond-flavored liqueur
Blanched almonds, toasted (page
   441)

Shaved chocolate or Chocolate
   Curls (page 394)
Melted bittersweet or semisweet
   chocolate (page 392) or
   chocolate syrup (optional)

Prepare crust: In bowl, microwave butter on HIGH 1 to 2 minutes to melt. Add crumbs, sugar, cocoa, and cinnamon and stir to mix well. Press mixture against bottom and side of buttered 9-inch pie plate and microwave on HIGH 1¹/₂ minutes. Let cool.

Make filling: In 2- to 3-quart bowl, microwave cream cheese on HIGH 1 minute to soften. Beat in sugar, eggs, and Amaretto. Microwave on HIGH 5 minutes. Pour into crust and microwave on 50% power 5 to 7 minutes.

Make topping: In bowl, combine sour cream, sugar, and Amaretto and spoon over the hot pie filling. Microwave on 50% power 3 minutes. Chill and garnish with toasted almonds and shaved chocolate. Drizzle melted chocolate or chocolate syrup over the top, if desired.

RUM CHEESE PIE

Use graham cracker crumbs in crust and substitute dark rum for Amaretto in filling and topping.

APPLE PIE

6 TO 8 SERVINGS

6 cups peeled, cored, and sliced
    cooking apples, preferably
    Granny Smith (about 2 1/2
    pounds)
2/3 to 3/4 cup sugar
1/3 cup all-purpose flour
1/2 stick (1/4 cup) unsalted butter

1/2 teaspoon cinnamon (optional)
1/2 teaspoon freshly grated nutmeg
    (optional)
Granola Crust I or II (page 305)
Whipped cream, ice cream, or
    sliced Cheddar cheese

Place apples in 2-quart measure or casserole. Combine sugar and flour and toss with apple slices. Add butter, cover, and microwave on HIGH 7 minutes. Stir, cover, and cook on HIGH 6 to 9 minutes longer, or until apples are tender. Add cinnamon and nutmeg, if desired.

Cool mixture slightly and pour into pie crust. Serve warm topped with whipped cream, ice cream, or cheese slices.

BROWNIE PIE

8 SERVINGS

1 stick (1/2 cup) unsalted butter
3 ounces semisweet chocolate
1 cup sugar
1/2 cup all-purpose flour
3 large eggs, beaten

1 teaspoon vanilla extract
Pinch of salt
1/2 cup chopped nuts (optional)
Ice cream or whipped cream

Place butter and chocolate in 2-quart measure and microwave on 70% power 2 to 3 minutes, or until melted. Stir.

Add sugar, flour, eggs, vanilla, salt, and, if desired, nuts. Stir until smooth. Pour into oiled 9-inch pie plate and microwave on HIGH 4 to 5 minutes. Let stand 5 minutes. Cut into wedges and serve warm topped with ice cream or whipped cream.

BAKED ALASKA

Mound ice cream over cooled Brownie Pie. Spread Meringue (recipe opposite) over surface to edges of cake, sealing in ice cream. Microwave on HIGH 3 minutes, or broil conventionally until meringue is browned.

BUTTERMILK LEMON MERINGUE PIE

1 cup sugar
¼ cup cornstarch
1¼ cups buttermilk
3 eggs yolks, beaten
⅓ cup fresh lemon juice
1 teaspoon grated lemon zest

2 tablespoons unsalted butter
1 (9-inch) conventionally baked
    pie crust or Graham Cracker
    Crust (page 304)
Meringue (recipe follows)

8 SERVINGS

Sweetened whipped cream is a good alternative to the meringue topping.

In 2-quart measure, combine sugar and cornstarch. Stir in buttermilk and microwave on HIGH 3 to 5 minutes, or until boiling.

Add about ½ cup hot buttermilk mixture to egg yolks, stirring constantly. Stir egg mixture into remaining buttermilk mixture. Microwave on HIGH 3 to 5 minutes, or until thickened, stirring several times during cooking.

Stir in lemon juice, zest, and butter. Cool and pour into crust. Top with sweetened whipped cream or meringue.

MERINGUE

3 egg whites

5 tablespoons sugar

MAKES ENOUGH FOR ONE 9- OR 10- INCH PIE

In large bowl, microwave egg whites and sugar on 10% power 4 to 5 minutes. Beat with electric mixer until stiff peaks form.

To use on pies, pile meringue lightly on pie filling, spreading to edges of crust and enclosing filling completely. Microwave on HIGH 2 to 3 minutes, or until tender and firm, but not browned. If you prefer a browned meringue, instead of microwaving preheat a conventional oven to 350° F. and bake pie 10 to 15 minutes.

YOGURT CREAM PIE

8 SERVINGS

∎

Very quick and easy to prepare for the family or company— delicious, too.

1 (8-ounce) package cream cheese
2 cups plain low-fat yogurt
1 (3-ounce) package instant vanilla pudding
1 cup sifted confectioners' sugar
1 (9-ounce) carton frozen whipped topping, thawed

Graham Cracker Crust (page 304)
1 to 2 cups fresh fruit (sliced peaches, blueberries, or strawberries) or 1 (20-ounce) can blueberry or cherry pie filling
1/3 cup red currant or apricot jelly

In 1-quart measure, microwave cream cheese on HIGH 45 to 60 seconds, or until softened. Blend in yogurt, pudding mix, sugar, and whipped topping. Spread mixture in pie crust and top with single layer of fruit.

If pie is topped with fresh fruit, make a jelly glaze. In cup, microwave jelly on HIGH 30 to 45 seconds to melt, then brush over fruit. Chill pie before serving.

CHOCOLATE CHEESE PIE

8 TO 10 SERVINGS

∎

2 (8-ounce) packages cream cheese
1 cup sugar
3 large eggs, separated
1 teaspoon vanilla extract
1 teaspoon instant coffee powder
1 ounce unsweetened chocolate

8 ounces semisweet chocolate
Chocolate Cookie Crust (page 303), Coconut Almond Crust (page 304), or Zwieback Pie Crust (page 306)
Whipped cream
Shaved chocolate

In 2-quart measure, microwave cream cheese on HIGH 1 minute to soften. Beat in sugar, egg yolks, vanilla, and coffee powder.

In 2-cup measure microwave unsweetened and semisweet chocolate on 70% power 2 to 3 minutes to melt, then beat into cheese mixture. Beat egg whites until stiff peaks form and fold into cheese mixture. Microwave filling on HIGH 2 minutes, stirring several times.

Pour filling into crust and microwave on 50% power 5 to 8 minutes, or until set. Cool and refrigerate several hours or overnight. Serve garnished with whipped cream and shaved chocolate.

GRASSHOPPER PIE

1 (10-ounce) package
    marshmallows
⅔ cup half-and-half
¼ cup green crème de menthe
¼ cup white crème de cacao

2 cups heavy cream, whipped
Chocolate Cookie Crust (page 303)
Chocolate Curls (page 394) or
    chocolate cookie crumbs

**6 TO 8
SERVINGS**

Prepare filling: In 2-quart measure, microwave marshmallows and half-and-half on HIGH 2 to 2½ minutes, or until marshmallows puff up and begin melting. Stir well to completely melt them. Let stand 2 to 3 minutes, then stir in crème de menthe and crème de cacao. Refrigerate about 15 to 20 minutes, until mixture thickens.

Fold in half the whipped cream and pour into crust. Refrigerate until firm. Garnish with remaining 2 cups whipped cream and chocolate curls or chocolate cookie crumbs. You may freeze pie for longer storage and firmer texture.

BRANDY ALEXANDER PIE

Substitute ¼ cup brandy and ¼ cup dark crème de cacao for crème de menthe and white crème de cacao.

CHOCOLATE PEPPERMINT PIE

Omit crème de menthe and add ½ teaspoon peppermint extract or ¼ cup peppermint liqueur and, if desired, several drops red food coloring. Garnish with chocolate curls or crushed soft peppermint sticks.

CREAMY AMARETTO PIE

Substitute ½ cup Amaretto for crème de menthe and crème de cacao.

KAHLÚA CREAM PIE

Substitute ¼ cup Kahlúa for crème de menthe and add 2 tablespoons Dutch-process cocoa powder and 2 teaspoons instant coffee powder.

Fresh Berry Pie

6 TO 8
SERVINGS

■

The exceptionally vivid flavor of fresh berries is captured in this recipe. The amount of sugar added to the berry puree will depend on the ripeness of the fruit and your own sweet tooth. This pie tastes best if it's assembled close to serving time so the pastry won't become soggy.

5 to 6 cups fresh blueberries, blackberries, or strawberries, picked over
1 cup sugar, or to taste
3 tablespoons cornstarch

2 to 3 drops food coloring (optional)
1 (9-inch) conventionally baked pie crust
Whipped cream

Place 2 to 3 cups berries in a food processor and puree. Transfer to 2-quart bowl, add sugar to taste and cornstarch, stir, and microwave on HIGH 2 to 3 minutes, or until mixture reaches a boil. Stir and microwave on 70% power 5 to 7 minutes, or until thickened, stirring several times. Stir in food coloring, if desired. Cool fruit glaze to room temperature.

If using strawberries, halve or quarter remaining ones, if large. Spread about 1 cup glaze on bottom of pie crust and arrange remaining berries in shell. Spread remaining glaze over berries. Garnish generously with whipped cream.

FRESH BERRY SHORTCAKE
Cut a sponge cake (page 339) into 2 or 3 layers. Spread each layer with fresh berry glaze and whole berries and stack layers. Garnish with mounds of whipped cream.

Georgia Peach Pie

6 TO 8
SERVINGS

■

6 cups peeled, sliced fresh peaches (about 3 pounds)
2 tablespoons fresh lemon juice
1¼ cups sugar
3 tablespoons cornstarch

1 tablespoon peach schnapps or brandy (optional)
1 (9-inch) conventionally baked pie crust
Whipped cream
Sprigs of mint

Place 3½ cups peaches in bowl and sprinkle with lemon juice. Stir to coat peaches to prevent their darkening.

To make glaze, puree remaining 2½ cups peaches in a food pro-

cessor. Transfer puree to a bowl, combine with sugar and cornstarch, and microwave on HIGH 3 to 4 minutes, or until mixture begins to boil. Cook on 70% power 4 to 5 minutes, or until thickened. Stir in the schnapps, if desired. Cool to room temperature. (Flavor is best if glaze is used on same day it is made and is not refrigerated.)

Spread about ½ cup glaze on bottom of pie crust. Arrange peach slices over glaze, reserving 5 or 6 slices. Pour remaining glaze over fruit. Top with whipped cream. Garnish with reserved peach slices and fresh mint. Enjoy!

COLONIAL STEWED PEACH MERINGUE PIE

7 ounces dried peaches (about
    1½ cups)
1 cup water
2 large eggs, separated
1¼ cups sugar
3 tablespoons cornstarch
2 cups evaporated milk

½ cup cold water
1 teaspoon vanilla extract
1 tablespoon fresh lemon juice
1 tablespoon unsalted butter
Pinch of salt
Graham Cracker Crust (page 304)

6 TO 8 SERVINGS

In bowl, combine dried peaches and water, cover, and microwave on HIGH 2 to 3 minutes, or until hot. Let stand until cool, then cut peaches into 1-inch pieces.

In another bowl, combine egg yolks, 1 cup sugar, cornstarch, evaporated milk, and cold water and beat well with wire whisk. Microwave on HIGH 2 minutes. Stir and microwave on 70% power 2 to 4 minutes, or until thickened. Add vanilla, lemon juice, butter, and salt, stir and let cool.

Spread stewed peaches over pie crust, then spread custard over fruit.

Preheat conventional oven to 350° F.

Prepare meringue: Beat egg whites until fluffy. Slowly add remaining ¼ cup sugar while continuing to beat until stiff peaks form. Mound meringue over filling and brown in conventional oven 10 to 15 minutes. Chill and serve.

MILE-HIGH LEMONADE PIE

8 TO 10 SERVINGS

■

1 cup evaporated milk, well chilled
1 envelope unflavored gelatin
¾ cup water
⅔ cup sugar
1 (8-ounce) can frozen lemonade
   concentrate, thawed

1 teaspoon lemon extract
½ teaspoon grated lemon zest
Graham Cracker Crust (page 304)

Place chilled evaporated milk in the freezer.

Stir gelatin into ¼ cup water and let stand for 3 to 4 minutes. In 2-quart measure, microwave remaining ½ cup water on HIGH 1 to 1½ minutes until boiling. Add gelatin mixture and stir until dissolved. Stir in sugar, lemonade, lemon extract, and lemon zest. Chill until thickened.

Beat evaporated milk with electric mixer until light and fluffy. Fold into chilled lemon mixture. Refrigerate about 5 minutes to thicken more. Pile high in crust and refrigerate several hours.

SWEET POTATO PIE

6 TO 8 SERVINGS

■

A traditional favorite.

2 medium sweet potatoes
1 stick (½ cup) unsalted butter
1½ cups sugar
2 large eggs
2 tablespoons bourbon or
   1 tablespoon vanilla extract

Granola Crust I or II (page 305)
Whipped cream
Toasted nuts (page 441) or
   shredded coconut

Pierce potatoes with fork and microwave on HIGH 8 to 12 minutes, or until soft. Peel potatoes and place pulp in a mixer or food processor. Add butter, sugar, eggs, and bourbon and beat until smooth.

Transfer mixture to 2-quart measure and microwave on HIGH 7 to 8 minutes, stirring several times. Let stand until warm. Spread in pie crust. Garnish with whipped cream and toasted nuts or coconut.

Pie Crust
and Filling Combinations

Here are some of the wonderful combinations of pie crusts and fillings that we put together as we developed the recipes for this book. You'll enjoy inventing your own combinations.

PIE	CRUST	FILLING	GARNISH
Chocolate Cream Pie	Granola I or II (page 305)	Chocolate Pastry Cream (page 319)	whipped cream
Vanilla Cream Pie	Graham Cracker, Vanilla Wafer, or Chocolate Cookie (pages 303, 304, and 306)	Vanilla Cream (page 319)	whipped cream
Butter Rum Pie	Chocolate Cookie (page 303)	Butter Rum (page 319)	Chocolate Curls (page 394)
Coconut Cream Pie	Graham Cracker or Granola I or II (pages 304 and 305)	Coconut Cream (page 319)	whipped cream
Banana Cream Pie	Graham Cracker or Granola I or II (pages 304 and 305)	sliced bananas brushed with lemon juice; spread with Vanilla Cream or Butter Rum Filling (page 319)	whipped cream
Grand Marnier Pie	Chocolate Graham (page 304)	Frozen Grand Marnier Soufflé (page 368); pour soufflé mixture into crust and freeze	

DESSERT FILLINGS AND FROSTINGS

The microwave oven is the first cooking method to consider for pie and cake fillings and frostings because it makes the job so much easier. The recipes that follow give perfect results, but you can also use your favorite conventional recipes, following microwave technique.

Use a container that is two to three times the volume of the ingredients so that even milk mixtures can cook without boiling over. Our recipe instructions call for stirring with a wire whisk several times during cooking to keep the mixture smooth. But even if you neglect to stir at all during cooking, and the mixture becomes lumpy, in most cases it can be made silky smooth by pureeing it for several seconds in a blender or food processor.

Most of these recipes are cooked on HIGH power, uncovered to allow some of the moisture to evaporate, which will aid the thickening process.

GANACHE

**MAKES
2½ CUPS**

Ganache is an extremely rich chocolate filling and glaze. Use it to fill sponge cake layers and cream puffs.

1 cup heavy cream
10 ounces semisweet chocolate, coarsely chopped

2 tablespoons cognac, rum, or orange-flavored liqueur

In 2-quart measure, microwave cream on HIGH 2 to 3 minutes, or just until it simmers. Add chocolate and stir with wire whisk until chocolate has melted and mixture is smooth. Let ganache cool, but do not refrigerate. Stir in cognac. Ganache will be liquid. At this point it can be poured over cake as a glaze.

To transform ganache into a filling, beat cooled mixture with an electric mixer 5 to 10 minutes, or until it doubles in volume, becomes lighter in color, and holds its shape.

VARIATION
Omit cognac and use 2 tablespoons additional cream.

LEMON CURD

4 eggs yolks, beaten
1 cup sugar
⅓ cup fresh lemon juice

1 stick (½ cup) unsalted butter,
    cut into 8 pieces
1 tablespoon grated lemon zest

**MAKES
2 CUPS**

▪

An old English teatime favorite, sweet yet tart. Spread it on muffins, toast, and nut breads or use it as a cake or tart filling. Lemon curd, tightly covered, keeps for several weeks in the refrigerator.

Combine egg yolks, sugar, and lemon juice in 4-cup measure. Cover with plastic wrap and microwave on HIGH 4 to 7 minutes, stirring several times, or until mixture thickens and coats the back of a spoon.

    Stir butter into lemon mixture, one piece at a time. Stir in grated zest. Process in food processor or blender until velvety smooth. Transfer to tightly covered container and chill.

LEMON MOUSSE FILLING
Fold ½ to 1 cup sweetened whipped cream into the lemon curd and use as a filling for pies and tart shells.

LIME CURD
Substitute lime juice and zest for lemon.

ORANGE CURD
Substitute ⅓ cup frozen orange juice concentrate, thawed, for lemon juice and 1 to 2 tablespoons finely grated orange zest for lemon zest.

CITRUS CURD
Use 2 tablespoons each: lemon juice, lime juice, orange juice, and grapefruit juice instead of lemon juice.

LEMON VELVET FILLING

4 egg yolks
1 cup sugar
⅓ cup fresh lemon juice

1 tablespoon grated lemon zest
Pinch of salt
1 cup heavy cream, whipped

**MAKES
2½ CUPS**

▪

In bowl, beat egg yolks, then stir in sugar, lemon juice, zest, and salt. Microwave on HIGH 4 to 6 minutes, or until thick. Cool.
    Fold in whipped cream and chill. Use as pie, tart, or cake filling.

CHOCOLATE ANGEL FILLING

**MAKES
ABOUT
1 QUART, OR
ENOUGH TO
FILL 3 OR 4
CAKE LAYERS**

·

A delicious filling that
further enhances a
sponge or angel food
cake.

⅓ cup all-purpose flour
⅓ cup granulated sugar
2 cups half-and-half
2 sticks (1 cup) unsalted butter, at
    room temperature

1 cup sifted confectioners' sugar
¼ cup Dutch-process cocoa
    powder
2 teaspoons vanilla extract

In 2-quart measure, combine flour and granulated sugar, then whisk in milk. Microwave on HIGH 5 to 8 minutes, or until very thick, stirring several times. Cover surface with plastic wrap to prevent a skin from forming, and cool.

With electric mixer, cream butter, confectioners' sugar, cocoa, and vanilla until light and fluffy. Gradually add cooled milk mixture, beating constantly. Continue beating until smooth. Store in tightly covered container in refrigerator up to 1 week.

CAPPUCCINO ANGEL FILLING

Dissolve 2 tablespoons instant coffee powder in milk and add 2 to 3 tablespoons brandy to cooled milk mixture.

PRALINE ANGEL FILLING

Substitute light brown sugar for granulated sugar. Stir ½ to 1 cup Praline Powder (page 382) into finished filling.

PASTRY CREAM (CRÈME PATISSIÈRE)

**MAKES
3 CUPS**

·

Pastry cream is a custard filling for sponge
cake layers, cream
puffs, pastry shells, or
crepes.

⅔ cup sugar
½ cup all-purpose flour
6 egg yolks
2 cups half-and-half or milk

½ stick (¼ cup) unsalted butter,
    cut into 4 pieces
1 teaspoon vanilla extract
Pinch of salt

In bowl, stir together sugar and flour. Stir in egg yolks.
In 2-quart measure, microwave half-and-half on HIGH 2½ minutes. Add 2 to 3 tablespoons half-and-half to egg yolk mixture, beating constantly. Add 4 to 5 tablespoons more half-and-half, still beating. Pour egg mixture into remainder of half-and-half and beat well.

Microwave custard on HIGH 4 to 7 minutes, or until mixture is thickened. Add butter, vanilla, and salt and beat for about 1 minute, or until mixture is shiny. Cool to room temperature.

CHOCOLATE PASTRY CREAM
Add ¼ cup Dutch-process cocoa powder with sugar and flour.

CUSTARD SAUCE
Prepare pastry cream, omitting flour.

VANILLA CREAM FILLING

¾ cup sugar
2 tablespoons cornstarch
3 large eggs, beaten
1 teaspoon vanilla extract

1 stick (½ cup) unsalted butter,
   cut into 8 pieces and softened
2 cups heavy cream

**MAKES
ENOUGH FOR
1 (9-INCH)
PIE**

•

This deliciously rich filling is excellent for pies and pastries. It may be stored for several days in the refrigerator or frozen for future use.

In bowl, combine sugar, cornstarch, and eggs. Microwave, uncovered, on 10% power 5 minutes, stirring once during cooking. Beat with electric mixer until very thick. Cover with plastic wrap and microwave on 50% power 2 to 3 minutes, stirring every minute.

Place bowl in larger bowl of ice water and stir to cool to room temperature. Beat again, adding vanilla and butter, 1 tablespoon at a time.

In another bowl, whip heavy cream and fold into egg mixture. Cover tightly and refrigerate.

BUTTER RUM FILLING
Add 2 tablespoons dark rum to cooked filling. Good with Chocolate Cookie Crust (page 303).

CHOCOLATE CREAM FILLING
Add ⅓ cup Dutch-process cocoa powder with sugar.

COCONUT CREAM FILLING
Stir ½ to 1 cup fresh or frozen grated coconut into cooked filling. Use to fill conventionally baked pie crust, Graham Cracker Crust (page 304), or Granola Crust I or II (page 305).

MOCHA CREAM FILLING
Add ⅓ cup Dutch-process cocoa powder and 1 tablespoon instant coffee powder with sugar.

BUTTERCREAM FROSTING

MAKES 1½ CUPS, OR ENOUGH TO FROST TOP AND SIDES OF A 9-INCH LAYER; DOUBLE RECIPE TO FROST A 2- OR 3-LAYER CAKE

•

Rich, light, and delicious. Chill the buttercream until it holds its shape before frosting the cake.

¾ cup granulated sugar
¼ cup all-purpose flour
1 cup milk

1½ sticks (¾ cup) unsalted butter, softened
3 tablespoons confectioners' sugar
1 teaspoon vanilla extract

In 1-quart measure, combine sugar and flour, then beat in milk. Microwave on HIGH 3 to 5 minutes, or until mixture is very thick and pastelike. Cover surface with plastic wrap to prevent a skin from forming, and cool.

In mixing bowl, cream butter, confectioners' sugar, and vanilla with electric mixer until light and fluffy. Slowly add cooked mixture, beating constantly. Continue beating until buttercream is light and fluffy. Store frosting or frosted cake in refrigerator during hot weather.

CARAMEL BUTTERCREAM

Substitute light brown sugar for granulated sugar. Add 1 or 2 tablespoons of caramel syrup (see Caramel Dome, page 383), praline powder (page 382), hazelnut liqueur, or macadamia liqueur with vanilla extract.

CHOCOLATE BUTTERCREAM

Add ¼ cup Dutch-process cocoa powder with flour.

ORANGE BUTTERCREAM

Add 1 or 2 drops of yellow and red food coloring (if desired) and 2 tablespoons orange liqueur instead of vanilla.

PEPPERMINT BUTTERCREAM

Substitute peppermint extract for vanilla.

CUSTARD FROSTING

Beat 1 large egg into sugar mixture before beating in milk. Proceed with recipe. Especially good with moist, fruit-filled cakes.

• • • • • • • • • • • •

Microwave refrigerated icings at 10 to 40% power to make them spreadable. The length of time will depend on the amount of frosting.

• • • • • • • • • • •

CARAMEL FROSTING

3 cups, packed, light brown sugar
1 cup heavy cream or evaporated
   milk
Pinch of salt

1 stick (¹/₂ cup) unsalted butter,
   cut into 8 pieces and softened
1 teaspoon vanilla extract

MAKES ENOUGH FROSTING FOR TWO 9-INCH LAYERS

•

Use as soon as it is made.

In 2-quart measure, microwave sugar, cream, and salt on 70% power 5 to 6 minutes, or until sugar is dissolved. Stir and microwave on 70% power 15 to 20 minutes longer or until mixture registers 234° F. (very soft-ball stage) on candy thermometer. Add butter and let frosting stand, without stirring, until it cools to lukewarm.

Add vanilla and beat with an electric mixer until frosting is creamy and begins to hold its shape. Quickly spread on cake.

BLACK WALNUT FROSTING
Add ½ cup coarsely chopped black walnuts with vanilla.

COCONUT PECAN FROSTING

1 (12-ounce) can evaporated milk
1¹/₂ cups sugar
3 large egg yolks
1¹/₂ sticks (³/₄ cup) unsalted butter,
   softened

1 tablespoon vanilla extract
2 cups shredded coconut
1¹/₂ cups chopped pecans, toasted
   (page 441)

MAKES ABOUT 6 CUPS, OR ENOUGH TO FROST A 9-INCH CAKE

•

In 2-quart measure beat together milk, sugar, egg yolks, butter, and vanilla. Microwave on HIGH 5 to 8 minutes, or until thickened. Add coconut and pecans. Let cool, beat, and spread on chocolate or spice cake.

CHOCOLATE GLAZE

MAKES
ABOUT
½ CUP

■

Shiny and luscious!

2 tablespoons unsalted butter
1 ounce semisweet chocolate
2 tablespoons heavy cream

½ cup sifted confectioners' sugar
1 teaspoon vanilla extract

In 2-cup measure, microwave butter and chocolate on 50% power 1 to 2 minutes, or until melted. Add cream, sugar, and vanilla and beat until smooth. Pour over cake.

CHOCOLATE SOUR CREAM FROSTING

MAKES
2½ CUPS

■

Very rich. Good for cupcakes.

12 ounces semisweet chocolate
    chips

1 cup sour cream
1 teaspoon vanilla extract

In 2-quart measure, microwave chocolate on 70% power 3 to 5 minutes, or until melted. Stir until smooth. Blend in sour cream and vanilla with a wire whisk. If frosting is too liquid, refrigerate several minutes and beat. Store frosted cake in refrigerator.

PENUCHE FROSTING

MAKES
ABOUT 3
CUPS, OR
ENOUGH TO
FROST AN
8-INCH CAKE

■

1 cup, packed, light brown sugar
½ cup milk
1 stick (½ cup) unsalted butter
2 cups sifted confectioners' sugar

1 teaspoon vanilla extract
½ cup chopped pecans, toasted
    (page 441; optional)

In 2-quart measure microwave brown sugar, milk, and butter on HIGH 3 to 5 minutes, or until sugar is completely dissolved and mixture boils. Cool.

Beat syrup, gradually adding confectioners' sugar. Add vanilla and beat to spreading consistency. Stir in nuts, if desired.

MOCHA FROSTING

1 cup sugar
⅓ cup water
¼ teaspoon cream of tartar
3 large egg yolks
2 sticks (1 cup) unsalted butter,
    cut into 8 pieces and softened

1½ ounces unsweetened chocolate
1 tablespoon instant coffee
    powder
1½ tablespoons dark rum

MAKES ABOUT 2 CUPS, OR ENOUGH TO FROST TWO 8-INCH LAYERS

▪

A rich, smooth, creamy texture—a classic buttercream. Be sure that the egg yolk mixture and butter are the same temperature when you begin beating in the butter.

In 2-quart measure, microwave sugar, water, and cream of tartar on HIGH 5 to 10 minutes, or until syrup registers 240° F. (soft-ball stage) on a candy thermometer.

While syrup cooks, in mixing bowl beat egg yolks with electric mixer until light and fluffy. Gradually add hot syrup, beating constantly. Continue beating until mixture is room temperature.

Beat in butter, 2 tablespoons at a time, and continue beating until mixture is smooth and creamy.

In cup, microwave chocolate on 70% power 1 to 2 minutes to melt. Combine coffee powder and rum. Beat chocolate and coffee mixture into buttercream. If making ahead, store, covered, in refrigerator for up to 1 week. Microwave on 10% power 2 to 3 minutes to bring back to spreading consistency.

ROCKY ROAD FROSTING

3 tablespoons unsalted butter
3 ounces unsweetened chocolate
3 cups sifted confectioners' sugar
7 tablespoons milk

⅛ teaspoon salt
1 teaspoon vanilla extract
12 large marshmallows
½ cup chopped nuts (optional)

MAKES 3 CUPS, OR ENOUGH TO FROST A 9-INCH CAKE

▪

In small bowl, microwave butter and chocolate on 70% power 2 to 3 minutes to melt. In another bowl, blend sugar, milk, salt, and vanilla. Stir in melted chocolate mixture, then fold in marshmallows and, if desired, nuts. Let frosting stand 3 to 4 minutes, or until marshmallows are almost melted and frosting is of spreading consistency.

FLUFFY FROSTING

This light-as-air frosting is best eaten the same day it is made.

Mint Patty Frosting is a very quick topping for a snack cake, brownies, or cupcakes. Place cream-filled chocolate mint patties or buttermints on the hot cake immediately after cooking. Cover with plastic wrap to hold in the heat and melt the mints. If there isn't enough heat to melt them, microwave on HIGH 30 to 60 seconds. When the mints are melted, spread to cover the cake.

1 cup sugar
¼ cup water
2 tablespoons corn syrup

Pinch of salt
3 egg whites
1 teaspoon vanilla extract

In 2-quart measure, stir together sugar, water, corn syrup, and salt. Microwave on HIGH 4 to 6 minutes, or until the mixture registers 260° F. (hard-ball stage) on a candy thermometer.

Meanwhile, in an electric mixer beat egg whites until soft peaks form. Continuing to beat at medium speed, pour hot syrup in a thin, steady stream, into egg whites. Add vanilla and beat at high speed about 5 minutes, or until stiff peaks form.

FLUFFY CHOCOLATE FROSTING

In cup, microwave 2 ounces unsweetened chocolate on 70% power 1 to 3 minutes, or until melted. Gently fold chocolate into frosting.

FLUFFY COCONUT FROSTING

Frost cake with Fluffy Frosting and sprinkle with shredded coconut.

FLUFFY ORANGE FROSTING

Substitute fresh orange juice for water. Add 1 teaspoon grated orange zest and several drops orange food coloring with vanilla.

SEAFOAM FROSTING

Substitute light brown sugar for granulated sugar.

QUICK BUTTER FROSTING

½ stick (¼ cup) unsalted butter
1 pound confectioners' sugar,
*   sifted*

4 to 5 tablespoons heavy cream
1 teaspoon vanilla extract
Pinch of salt

MAKES
2 TO 3 CUPS,
OR ENOUGH TO
FROST A
9-INCH CAKE

∎

In 2-quart measure, microwave butter at 10% power 45 seconds to soften. Place butter and 1 cup sugar in mixing bowl and cream until light and fluffy. Add remaining sugar alternately with cream, beating constantly. Add enough cream to make good spreading consistency. Stir in vanilla and salt.

QUICK PEPPERMINT BUTTERCREAM

Crush 4 or 5 soft peppermint sticks in heavy cream, microwave on 50% power 2 to 3 minutes, if needed, to help dissolve candy. Prepare frosting as directed, using peppermint cream.

QUICK CHOCOLATE FUDGE FROSTING

Add ⅓ cup Dutch-process cocoa powder with sugar.

PEANUT BUTTER FROSTING

Blend ½ cup creamy peanut butter into finished frosting.

CREAM CHEESE FROSTING

1 stick (½ cup) unsalted butter
1 (8-ounce) package cream cheese
1 pound confectioners' sugar,
*   sifted*

2 teaspoons vanilla extract
Milk or heavy cream (optional)

MAKES
ABOUT 3 CUPS,
OR ENOUGH TO
FROST A
9-INCH CAKE

∎

In 2-quart measure, microwave butter and cream cheese at 70% power 1 to 2 minutes, or until softened. Add sugar and vanilla and beat until smooth and fluffy. Add a little milk or cream to thin, if desired.

PINEAPPLE FROSTING

Stir ½ cup crushed, well-drained canned pineapple into finished frosting.

CREAM CHEESE NUT FROSTING

Stir ½ cup chopped pecans or walnuts into finished frosting.

ROYAL ICING

**MAKES
2 CUPS**

*1 pound confectioners' sugar,
   sifted*

*½ teaspoon cream of tartar
3 egg whites*

This is the icing used by cake decorators. Because it hardens when it dries, it is used to make flowers and other elaborate decorations.

In microwavable mixing bowl, stir sugar, cream of tartar, and egg whites together and microwave on 10% power 5 minutes. Beat with an electric mixer until light and fluffy. Keep a damp towel over bowl, even while using icing, to prevent a crust from forming. Use a pastry tube to make flowers, or trace designs on wax paper that can be lifted when dry and placed on a cake.

WHIPPED CREAM FROSTING

**MAKES
3 ½ TO 4 CUPS,
OR ENOUGH
TO FROST A
9-INCH CAKE**

*2 cups heavy cream (35%
   butterfat content)*
*⅓ to ½ cup sifted confectioners'
   sugar*

*1 teaspoon vanilla extract
Pinch of salt*

A perfect frosting for sponge cake. The cream used in this frosting must have a high butterfat content (at least 35%) to hold up for several days. The bowl, beaters, and cream should be very cold when whipping cream to make it light and fluffy.

Beat cream with an electric mixer until it begins thickening. Add sugar, vanilla, and salt. Beat until stiff peaks form. Use to frost or fill a cake. Keep cake refrigerated.

CHOCOLATE WHIPPED CREAM FROSTING
Fold in ⅓ to ½ cup Dutch-process cocoa powder. One teaspoon instant coffee powder and 1 tablespoon rum may also be added.

PEPPERMINT WHIPPED CREAM FROSTING
Fold in ⅓ cup crushed soft peppermint sticks and add sugar to taste.

CAKES

Our most successful microwave cakes are those that are kept moist with fruits or vegetables—Chocolate Date Ring and Carrot Cake are good examples—or those, like sponge cake, that are sliced into layers and used as a base for fillings, which help return moisture if the cake has dried out a little in the microwave.

We have included several microwave cake recipes for occasions when nothing but a cake will do and preparation time is short. Most cakes, however, are best baked conventionally, with the filling and frosting or glaze made in the microwave.

CAKE MIXES
Cakes from mixes bake well in the microwave. As a general rule, follow the instructions given on the box of cake mix, combining all ingredients and mixing at a medium speed for 2 minutes.

SLICING A CAKE INTO LAYERS
It's easier to slice a firm cake, so if there is time, chill or partially freeze it. Measure the cake vertically with a ruler and mark each layer with 6 to 8 toothpicks placed around the circumference. Use a sharp serrated knife to cut the cake. Brush away any crumbs before decorating the cake.

BAKING THE CAKE

- Fill the dish no more than half full, because microwave cakes rise more than conventional ones. Extra batter may be used to make cupcakes (page 330).
- To promote even cooking, particularly in the center of the cake, we have found that it is helpful to microwave the cake batter on HIGH 1 to 2 minutes to heat it throughout before baking begins. Heat the batter in either the mixing bowl or the baking dish, then stir to equalize the heat. If the batter is heated after it is poured into the baking dish, stir very carefully and rotate the outside portions of batter to the center, without disturbing the coating on the dish. Then proceed with the baking instructions.
- Cakes are usually cooked uncovered so that moisture from the batter can evaporate. Sometimes covering the dish loosely with wax paper helps equalize the heat in the dish and aid even cooking.
- Usually, after the batter is heated, cakes are baked at 50 to 70% power to allow the cake to rise, then on HIGH to complete the cooking.
- Even cooking is more critical in baked products than in other types of cooking. In microwave ovens that do not cook evenly, turn the dish several times during cooking

and elevate the cake dish to the center of the oven by placing it on an inverted pie plate or soufflé dish.

TESTING FOR DONENESS

Microwaved cakes are very tender. Because moisture is being pulled from the batter very quickly—almost more quickly than the moisture can evaporate—the cake is actually done before it appears dry. Overcooking produces tough cakes. Keep this in mind when determining doneness.

- The first test for doneness is to turn the cake dish gently from side to side. If the cake moves like liquid, it probably is not yet done. If, when you jiggle or turn the dish, the cake seems solid, it may be done. Then use one of the following tests to further check doneness.

- The cake should appear damp on top. If the surface of the cake is completely dry, the cake is probably overcooked. Touch a damp area with your finger or the back of a spoon; the surface of the cake will stick to the spoon or finger when you lift it. If the batter that is revealed beneath looks liquid or raw, the cake is not done. If baked cake is revealed beneath the moist surface, the cake is done, and the moisture on top is only surface moisture that has not yet had time to evaporate. If this is the case, the surface moisture will evaporate when the cake stands a few minutes.

- Microwaved cakes, just as conventional ones, are done when a toothpick or straw inserted near the center comes out clean, or with no batter on it. Microwaved cakes also come away from the sides of the dish and spring back when lightly pressed with a finger, just as conventional cakes do.

- When you are uncertain about whether the cake is done, stop cooking and allow the cake to stand for 5 to 10 minutes, then check doneness again. If, at this point, you decide that the cake was not done, simply put it back in the microwave and cook it a little longer.

STANDING TIME

The cake must be cooled to firm up and achieve a desirable texture. Standing time should be considered part of the cooking process, especially in microwaving. Let the cake stand directly on the countertop rather than on a cake rack for 5 to 10 minutes before attempting to invert it from the dish. Lightly cover with a piece of wax paper to help prevent excessive moisture loss. If, when the cake is inverted from the dish, it is not done, place the dish over the cake, invert the cake back into the dish, and microwave longer. Many cakes have been salvaged this way.

GUIDELINES FOR MICROWAVING CAKES

BAKING DISHES

Microwaved foods cook more evenly in round dishes than in square ones, so when there is an option, use a round dish. If you do use a square dish, place a triangular piece of foil over each corner to shield it and to prevent the cake from overcooking in the corners. Check the manufacturer's operator manual before using foil to be sure that the metal will not damage your oven.

Loaf pans and oblong baking dishes produce uneven results, which can be improved somewhat by placing a strip of foil over each end of the dish. Bundt and ring shapes are excellent choices.

Clear glass or plastic dishes allow you to look at the bottom of the cake to check for doneness.

DISH PREPARATION

No preparation is required if the cake will be served from the dish—cake squares or bar cookies, for instance. If the cake will be inverted from the dish, place a layer of brown or parchment paper in the bottom of the dish.

Fluted or other shaped cake dishes should be greased to help unmold the cake. Coat the dish thoroughly with solid shortening, butter, oil, or nonstick vegetable spray, then shake granulated sugar or dry crumbs over the dish to coat it completely. The crumbs will color the outside of the cake. For a chocolate cake, use granulated sugar; for other batters, a mixture of 3 tablespoons granulated sugar and 2 teaspoons of cocoa looks attractive. Or use dry crumbs that are toast-colored, such as graham cracker, vanilla wafer, and fine toasted bread crumbs. **Never coat the dish with flour as you would in conventional baking; the flour only becomes gummy during baking, which defeats its original purpose.**

CUPCAKES

Microwaved cupcakes will not brown, and only 6 cupcakes should be put into the microwave oven at one time. For these reasons, we find the conventional oven preferable for baking cupcakes. However, because microwave cupcakes cook so fast they're fun for children to make. Chocolate or yellow cake mixes give the best results. Just follow package instructions for making the batter and bake as instructed below.

DIRECTIONS FOR BAKING CUPCAKES IN THE MICROWAVE

1. Put paper cupcake liners in the muffin or custard cups to help absorb excess moisture.

2. Fill the cups one-third to one-half full.

3. Arrange custard cups in a circle on a microwavable plate or tray. If the cupcakes must be rotated during cooking, turn the plate instead of repositioning each cup.

4. After cooking, remove the cupcakes from the dish or custard cups and place on a rack to cool. Excess moisture will evaporate as they cool. (If not cooled on a rack or towel, the cupcakes will tend to be soggy.)

5. Since the cupcakes won't brown, cover them with crumb, nut, or spice toppings, or frosting for eye appeal.

TIMETABLE FOR MICROWAVING CUPCAKES	
NUMBER OF CUPCAKES	**COOKING TIME ON HIGH**
1	25 to 30 seconds
2	45 seconds to 1¼ minutes
3	1 to 1½ minutes
4	1½ to 2 minutes
5	2 to 2½ minutes
6	2 to 3 minutes

APPLESAUCE CAKE

3 tablespoons granulated sugar
3 teaspoons Dutch-process cocoa
    powder
2¼ cups all-purpose flour
2 teaspoons baking soda
1 teaspoon salt
2½ teaspoons cinnamon
1¾ cups, packed, brown sugar

¾ cup salad oil
3 large eggs
2 cups applesauce
1 cup chopped walnuts
½ cup raisins
1 recipe Cream Cheese Frosting
    (page 325) or confectioners'
    sugar

12 SERVINGS

■

A moist, delicious cake.

Prepare cake dish: Combine granulated sugar and cocoa. Thoroughly grease a 6- to 8-cup fluted tube dish. Sprinkle cocoa mixture into dish, turning to coat it evenly and completely. Shake out excess cocoa mixture.

In small bowl, combine flour, baking soda, salt, and cinnamon. In electric mixer or food processor, beat brown sugar, oil, and eggs until light and fluffy. Add applesauce and then flour mixture, beating just until blended. Stir in walnuts and raisins.

Pour batter into prepared dish and cover with wax paper. Microwave on HIGH 2 minutes, gently stir, then microwave on 50% power 8 minutes, and again on HIGH 3 to 6 minutes, or until done.

Let cake stand directly on countertop or towel, uncovered, 10 minutes. Invert cake onto serving plate. Spread Cream Cheese Frosting or sift confectioners' sugar over cake.

Opening the microwave oven door while baking a cake will not cause the cake to fall, as can happen in conventional baking, since there is no heat in the microwave oven.

BUTTERNUT CAKE

Substitute 1 tablespoon vanilla, butter and nut flavoring, for cinnamon. Omit raisins. Substitute granulated sugar for brown sugar, if desired. Frost with Cream Cheese Frosting.

LE GATEAU AU VIN (WINE CAKE)

Substitute 2 teaspoons cocoa for cinnamon and 1 cup semisweet red wine, such as marsala, and 1 cup applesauce for 2 cups applesauce.

CARROT CAKE

3 tablespoons granulated sugar
3 teaspoons Dutch-process cocoa
   powder
2 cups all-purpose flour
1½ teaspoons baking powder
1 teaspoon baking soda
1 teaspoon cinnamon
1 teaspoon salt
1½ cups, packed, light brown
   sugar

¾ cup salad oil
3 large eggs
1 (8-ounce) can crushed
   pineapple, undrained
1½ cups shredded carrots
   (3 carrots)
1 cup chopped pecans or walnuts
1 recipe Cream Cheese Frosting
   (page 325; optional)

Prepare cake dish: Combine granulated sugar and cocoa thoroughly. Grease a 6- to 8-cup fluted tube cake dish. Sprinkle cocoa mixture into dish, turning to coat it evenly and completely. Shake out excess cocoa mixture.

In small bowl, combine flour, baking powder, baking soda, cinnamon, and salt. In large bowl, beat brown sugar, oil, and eggs until light and fluffy. Add flour mixture and mix. Stir in pineapple, carrots, and nuts.

Pour batter into prepared dish and cover with wax paper. Microwave on HIGH 2 minutes, gently stir, then microwave on 50% power 10 minutes, and again on HIGH 2 to 5 minutes, or until done.

Let cake stand directly on countertop or towel, uncovered, 10 minutes. Invert cake onto serving plate. Serve as a nut bread or frost with Cream Cheese Frosting.

To soften brown sugar, add a few drops of water or a slice of apple, cover tightly, and microwave on HIGH 15 seconds or longer, if needed.

CARROT CAKE SQUARES

Prepare half the recipe for Carrot Cake (use 2 eggs). Pour into 9-inch square dish and cover lightly with wax paper. Microwave on HIGH 2 minutes, then gently stir and microwave on 50% power 5 minutes, or until done.

SWEET POTATO CAKE

Substitute grated raw sweet potato for carrot.

CHEESECAKE

CRUST
½ stick (¼ cup) unsalted butter
1 cup graham cracker crumbs

2 tablespoons light brown sugar
¼ teaspoon grated lemon zest

FILLING
3 large eggs, separated
*2 (8-ounce) packages cream
    cheese*

½ cup granulated sugar
1 tablespoon fresh lemon juice

TOPPING
¾ cup sour cream

3 tablespoons granulated sugar

**6 TO 8
SERVINGS**

▪

This is classic cheese-
cake at its best. Serve
the cake right out of the
baking dish.

Prepare crust: Butter 9-inch, 6-cup cake dish. In 2-cup measure, microwave butter on HIGH 30 to 45 seconds to melt. Stir in crumbs, brown sugar, and lemon zest and mix well. Press into prepared dish.

Make filling: Beat egg whites until stiff peaks form and set aside. In large microwavable mixing bowl, microwave cream cheese on HIGH 1 to 1½ minutes to soften. Add egg yolks, sugar, and lemon juice and beat with an electric mixer until light and smooth. Fold in egg whites. Microwave on HIGH 3 to 4 minutes, or until custard is thoroughly hot, stirring several times. Mixture will not be smooth. Pour hot custard into crust and microwave on 50% power 4 to 6 minutes, or until almost set in center.

Make topping: In 2-cup measure, combine sour cream and sugar and microwave on HIGH 1½ minutes. Spread evenly over cheesecake. Chill before serving. Delicious as is or with fresh fruit.

PRALINE CHEESECAKE

Use ½ cup each light brown and granulated sugar in filling and 3 tablespoons light brown sugar in topping. Serve with Praline Sauce (page 384).

**BEATING EGG
WHITES:**
Egg whites will whip
to a higher volume
when they are at room
temperature. Micro-
wave them at 10%
power for one minute
or longer to warm
them before beating.
The bowl, beater, and
egg whites should be
totally free of fat. Even
a speck of egg yolk
will keep the whites
from beating properly.
Adding a pinch of salt
or cream of tartar, or
a dash of lemon juice
or vinegar after the
egg whites have been
beaten to the foamy
stage will help stabi-
lize them further and
enable them to be
beaten longer and into
stiffer peaks.

ANGEL CUSTARD CAKE

8 SERVINGS

•

Light!

1 envelope unflavored gelatin
¼ cup milk
4 egg yolks
1 cup sifted confectioners' sugar

1 teaspoon vanilla extract
2 cups heavy cream, whipped
1 (1-pound) angel food cake

In a cup combine gelatin and milk and let stand.

Beat egg yolks until light and lemon colored. Add sugar and continue beating until thick. Transfer to a 2-quart measure, cover, and microwave on 50% power 2 to 3 minutes, stirring several times. Mixture should remain smooth.

Add gelatin mixture to egg mixture and stir to dissolve gelatin and combine thoroughly. Cool, add vanilla and fold in whipped cream. Refrigerate 5 to 10 minutes, or until mixture is thickened, but not set.

Slice cake into 3 layers. Spread custard between layers and on side and top of cake. Refrigerate overnight.

EGGNOG CAKE

Reduce milk to 2 tablespoons and add ½ cup bourbon or rum to egg yolk mixture. Toasted almond macaroons may be crumbled over custard after it is spread over cake layers.

> If you ever overcook a cake, lace it with your favorite liqueur while it is still hot. It will be moist and delicious!

DEVIL'S FOOD CAKE

6 SERVINGS

•

1 ounce unsweetened chocolate
⅔ cup sugar
⅓ cup vegetable oil
⅓ cup milk

2 large eggs
½ teaspoon vanilla extract
¾ cup all-purpose flour
¼ teaspoon salt

Place a circle of brown paper or wax paper in the bottom of 8-inch round dish, 3 to 4 inches deep.

Combine chocolate, sugar, oil, milk, eggs, vanilla, flour, and salt in mixing bowl and beat with electric mixer 2 minutes. Spread batter in prepared dish and microwave on 50% power 5 minutes, then on HIGH 1 to 3 minutes. Cover with plastic wrap and let stand directly on countertop 5 to 10 minutes.

FUDGE UPSIDE-DOWN CAKE

CAKE
1 cup all-purpose flour
2 teaspoons baking powder
¼ cup Dutch-process cocoa
    powder
¼ teaspoon salt
1 cup, packed, light brown sugar

½ cup milk
2 tablespoons unsalted butter,
    melted
1 teaspoon vanilla extract
¾ cup chopped pecans, toasted
    (page 441)

**6 TO 8
SERVINGS**

FUDGE SAUCE
¾ cup, packed, light brown sugar
¼ cup Dutch-process cocoa
    powder

1¼ cups evaporated milk, heated

Prepare cake: In mixing bowl combine flour, baking powder, cocoa, salt, brown sugar, milk, butter, and vanilla. Mix well. Stir in toasted nuts and spread batter in ungreased 9-inch square dish.

Prepare fudge sauce: In 1-quart measure, combine brown sugar and cocoa. Stir in evaporated milk. Microwave on HIGH 3 to 4 minutes, or until mixture boils.

Pour sauce over cake batter and microwave on HIGH 5 to 7 minutes, or until the top becomes cakelike and bottom is sauce. Let stand 3 to 4 minutes. Spoon cake and sauce into dessert dishes.

BLACK FOREST UPSIDE-DOWN CAKE
Spread 1 (21-ounce) can pitted tart cherries, drained, on bottom of baking dish, pour batter over cherries, and proceed with recipe.

CHOCOLATE DATE RING

10 TO 12 SERVINGS

1½ cups chopped dates
1 cup water
3 tablespoons plus 1¼ cups sugar
3 tablespoons Dutch-process cocoa powder
1 stick (½ cup) unsalted butter, softened
2 large eggs, beaten
1 teaspoon vanilla extract
1½ cups all-purpose flour
1 teaspoon salt
1½ teaspoons baking powder
1 teaspoon cinnamon (optional)
¾ cup semisweet chocolate chips
½ cup chopped walnuts or pecans

Place dates and water in 1-quart measure, cover, and microwave on HIGH 2½ to 3 minutes, or until boiling. Let stand, covered, at least 30 minutes.

Prepare cake dish: Combine 3 tablespoons sugar and cocoa. Thoroughly grease 12-cup glass ring mold. Sprinkle cocoa mixture into dish, turning to coat on all sides. Shake out excess cocoa mixture.

In large bowl, microwave butter on 10% power 1 to 2 minutes to soften. Add 1¼ cups sugar and cream mixture until light and fluffy. Add eggs and vanilla. Sift together flour, salt, baking powder and, if desired, cinnamon. Add flour and date mixtures to creamed mixture and beat until well combined. Stir in chocolate chips and nuts.

Pour batter into prepared dish. Place a piece of plastic wrap over dish, but do not seal tightly. Microwave on 70% power 15 to 18 minutes, or until cake tests done.

Let cake stand in dish 10 minutes, then invert onto serving dish.

CHOCOLATE MOUSSE CAKE

8 TO 12 SERVINGS

This cake is a good quick dessert for chocolate lovers.

6 ounces semisweet chocolate chips
1 ounce unsweetened chocolate
8 large eggs, separated
¾ cup sugar
Pinch of salt
1 teaspoon vanilla extract
1 tablespoon instant coffee powder
2 tablespoons hot water
Whipped cream

In cup, microwave semisweet and unsweetened chocolate on 70% power for 3 minutes, or until melted.

Beat egg whites until stiff peaks form, then gradually beat in ½ cup sugar and pinch of salt. Set aside.

Beat egg yolks until thick and pale yellow. Slowly beat in remaining ¼ cup sugar. Dissolve coffee powder in hot water and add to egg yolks with vanilla. Stir in melted chocolate, then fold in egg whites.

Place a circle of brown or wax paper in bottom of 9-inch glass pie plate.

Reserve 4 cups mousse in a bowl, cover, and refrigerate until later. Pour remaining mousse into pie plate. Microwave on HIGH 2 minutes, then stir mousse to rotate the outer portions to center of dish. Cover with plastic wrap and microwave on 50% power 5 to 7 minutes, or until firm.

Cool. (As cake cools it will shrink.) After cake has cooled, remove from pie plate and place on cake plate. Spread reserved mousse over cake and garnish with whipped cream. Chill and serve. A raspberry sauce may be drizzled over the individual slices, if desired, but cake is delicious without sauce.

LANE CAKE

LANE FILLING

1 stick (½ cup) unsalted butter
1 cup sugar
4 large eggs, beaten
1½ cups chopped pecans

1½ cups chopped seedless raisins
1½ cups shredded coconut
1 teaspoon vanilla extract
⅓ cup bourbon

Sponge Cake (page 339), cut into
    4 layers

1 recipe Fluffy Frosting (page 324)

10 TO 12 SERVINGS

■

A traditional Southern treat that tastes best if the cake and filling are assembled and refrigerated several days before serving so that the flavors can mellow. This is an adaptation of a recipe created by Emma Rylander Lane of Clayton, Alabama, in her cookbook *Some Good Things to Eat*, published in 1898.

Prepare filling: In microwavable bowl, cream butter and sugar, then beat in eggs. Microwave on HIGH for 5 to 8 minutes, or until thickened. Add pecans, raisins, coconut, vanilla, and bourbon and mix well.

Spread filling evenly over all 4 cake layers, then stack layers. Cover cake with foil and refrigerate 2 to 3 days.

Just before serving, frost sides with Fluffy Frosting.

DOBOSTORTE

An Austrian specialty of sponge cake layered with chocolate butter-cream and raspberry jam, then finished with a caramel glaze.

½ cup raspberry jam
1 tablespoon framboise (raspberry brandy)
1 tablespoon fresh lemon juice
Chocolate Buttercream (page 320)
Sponge Cake (page 339), cut into 6 layers

10 to 12 whole hazelnuts, toasted (page 441)
½ cup finely chopped toasted hazelnuts

CARAMEL GLAZE
½ cup sugar

¼ cup water

In small bowl, combine raspberry jam, framboise, and lemon juice. Assemble cake: Spread 3 to 4 tablespoons Chocolate Buttercream over first cake layer. Spread 2 tablespoons of raspberry mixture on a second layer. Stack second layer on first, jam side down. Repeat with remaining layers. Spread remaining buttercream on top and sides of cake.

Line 8-inch cake pan with foil and grease foil or spray with vegetable spray.

Prepare glaze: In 1-cup measure, combine sugar and water. Cover tightly with plastic wrap and microwave on HIGH 5 to 8 minutes, or until caramel colored. Watch carefully after first 4 minutes; once color starts to change, syrup caramelizes quickly and can easily burn. Pour about two-thirds of the caramel into foil-lined pan. Lightly score caramel into wedges. Quickly stir whole nuts into remaining caramel, then lift out nuts one at a time using a spoon and place in center of each wedge. Place several nuts in the center of caramel disk. If caramel hardens before nuts are coated, microwave 2 to 3 seconds to soften.

Carefully lift foil with hardened caramel disk out of pan and remove disk. Place caramel disk on top of cake. Smooth buttercream around caramel. Press chopped hazelnuts around sides of cake.

Except for caramel disk and nut garnish, this cake may be made and assembled several days in advance. Disk and nuts should be put in place just before serving.

SPONGE CAKE

5 large eggs, separated
¾ teaspoon cream of tartar
1½ cups sugar
½ teaspoon salt
½ cup ice water

1 teaspoon vanilla or almond
   extract
1 cup all-purpose flour
⅓ cup cornstarch
½ teaspoon baking powder

**MAKES
ONE 8-INCH
CAKE**

▪

This all-purpose cake can be sliced into 3 or 4 layers and used as a base for a wide variety of fillings to create many elegant, light desserts. (See Sponge Cake Combinations, pages 342 and 343.) The cake is also a good accompaniment for tea, served plain or sprinkled with a little confectioners' sugar.

Prepare baking dish: Place a circle of brown or wax paper in bottom of 8-inch, 12-cup round baking dish. Make a 6-inch collar of doubled wax paper and attach with tape so that collar extends 3 inches above top of dish.

In large bowl, beat egg whites and cream of tartar with an electric mixer until stiff peaks form. Set aside.

In another bowl, beat egg yolks until thick, gradually adding sugar and salt. Add ice water and vanilla, beating constantly until mixture is very thick and cream colored.

Sift together flour, cornstarch, and baking powder and add mixture slowly to egg yolk mixture, beating constantly at lowest speed. Gently fold in egg whites.

Pour batter into prepared dish and microwave on HIGH 4 to 6 minutes, or until cake tests done. Let sponge cake stand directly on countertop 10 minutes and invert from dish. Cool before cutting into layers.

CHOCOLATE SPONGE CAKE

Sift ⅓ cup Dutch-process cocoa powder with flour, cornstarch, and baking powder.

SPICE SPONGE CAKE

Substitute light brown sugar for granulated sugar. Add ½ teaspoon cinnamon with flour.

ITALIAN RUM CAKE

8 TO 10 SERVINGS

•

Must be made at least one day ahead.

RUM SYRUP
1/3 cup water
1/3 cup sugar

1/3 cup dark rum

Sponge Cake (page 339), cut into 4 layers
Pastry Cream (page 318)
Whipped Cream Frosting (page 326) flavored with 1 tablespoon dark rum

Toasted nuts (page 441), Chocolate Curls (page 394), candied or glazed fruit, or sugared flowers

Prepare rum syrup: In 2-cup measure, microwave water and sugar on HIGH 45 seconds or until boiling. Add rum and stir until sugar dissolves.

Assemble cake: Place 1 layer on cake plate, brush with one-quarter of syrup and spread with one-third of pastry cream. Repeat with 2 more cake layers and finish with last layer brushed with rum syrup. Cover and refrigerate at least overnight.

When ready to serve, frost with Whipped Cream Frosting and garnish with toasted nuts, Chocolate Curls, candied fruit, or sugared flowers.

PINEAPPLE PUDDING CAKE

6 TO 8 SERVINGS

•

The cake rises to the top of the baking dish and floats on the sauce at the bottom.

1/2 stick (1/4 cup) unsalted butter, softened
1 1/2 cups, packed, light brown sugar
1 large egg, beaten
1 cup all-purpose flour
2 teaspoons baking powder

1/2 teaspoon salt
1 1/4 cups milk
1 (8-ounce) can crushed pineapple, drained and juices reserved
1 teaspoon vanilla extract
Whipped cream (optional)

In mixing bowl, cream butter and 3/4 cup brown sugar with electric mixer. Beat in egg. Combine flour, baking powder, and salt. Add flour mixture, ½ cup milk, drained pineapple, and vanilla to creamed mixture. Spread evenly in 8-inch round dish.

In 1-quart measure, combine pineapple juice, remaining ¾ cup each milk and sugar, and microwave on HIGH 3 to 4 minutes, or until mixture boils. Gently pour over batter and microwave cake on HIGH 6 to 10 minutes, or until cake tests done. Serve from baking dish, either warm or cold, garnished with whipped cream, if desired.

To make cold butter spreadable, microwave 1 stick on 10% power 1 minute.

GINGERBREAD

1 ¼ cups all-purpose flour
½ cup, packed, light brown sugar
½ teaspoon baking soda
½ teaspoon salt
½ teaspoon ground cloves
1 teaspoon cinnamon

1 teaspoon ground ginger
⅓ cup vegetable oil
2 large eggs
1 cup dark molasses
¼ cup water

9 SERVINGS

Place flour, sugar, baking soda, salt, cloves, cinnamon, ginger, oil, eggs, molasses, and water in 2-quart measure and beat with wire whisk until well blended.

Microwave batter on HIGH 2 minutes. Stir and pour into buttered 8-inch square dish. Shield corners of dish with foil (if your oven permits) and microwave on HIGH 3 to 5 minutes, or until cake tests done. Let stand directly on countertop 10 minutes. Serve cake from baking dish.

To heat an individual serving of cake, cover it with wax paper and microwave on HIGH 10 to 15 seconds.

341

SPONGE CAKE COMBINATIONS

The combinations suggested below will serve as a guide to using some of the fillings and frostings found in this chapter. All recipes call for one 8-inch Sponge Cake (page 339), either plain (P) or chocolate (C). Unless otherwise indicated, use one recipe of all fillings and frostings.

These cakes serve from 8 to 12 people, depending on how much else is being served at the meal.

CAKE	LAYERS	FILLINGS	FROSTING	GARNISH
Queen of Sheba	3 (C)	Ganache (page 316)	Ganache (same recipe)	Chocolate Curls (page 394)

ASSEMBLY: Reserve ⅓ ganache in liquid stage for frosting. Beat remaining ⅔ ganache until stiff. Spread equally over 2 layers. Stack all 3 layers; chill 30 minutes. Pour liquid ganache over cake, then quickly spread over top and sides with spatula. Refrigerate until 30 to 45 minutes before serving.

CAKE	LAYERS	FILLINGS	FROSTING	GARNISH
Lemon Cake	4 (P)	Lemon Curd (page 317)	Whipped Cream Frosting (page 326)	

ASSEMBLY: Spread each layer with ¼ lemon curd; stack layers. Frost sides with frosting. Refrigerate until 30 minutes before serving.

CAKE	LAYERS	FILLINGS	FROSTING	GARNISH
Black Forest Cake	3 (C)	Crème de cacao or cherry liqueur (optional); 1 (29-ounce) can cherry pie filling	Whipped Cream Frosting (page 326)	

ASSEMBLY: Sprinkle 3 layers with liqueur, if desired. Spread 2 layers with pie filling, then stack all 3 layers. Frost top and sides. Refrigerate until serving.

CAKE	LAYERS	FILLINGS	FROSTING	GARNISH
Boston Cream Pie	2 (P)	1 tablespoon rum or cognac; Pastry Cream	Chocolate Glaze (page 322)	

ASSEMBLY: Sprinkle layers with rum, if desired. Spread pastry cream over 1 layer; stack second layer on top. Carefully pour glaze over cake, letting it drip down sides. Refrigerate until 30 minutes before serving.

CAKE	LAYERS	FILLINGS	FROSTING	GARNISH
Banana Cream Cake	3 (P)	Banana liqueur (optional); 2 or 3 ripe bananas, sliced and brushed with lemon juice; Praline Angel Filling (page 318)	Whipped Cream Frosting (page 326)	Reserved banana slices

ASSEMBLY: Sprinkle 3 layers with banana liqueur, if desired. Set 1 layer aside. Reserving ⅓ slices for garnish, arrange banana slices on 2 layers, then spread both layers with praline filling. Stack 3 layers. Frost top and sides with frosting. Garnish with remaining bananas.

CAKE	LAYERS	FILLINGS	FROSTING	GARNISH
Cappuccino Torte	4 (C)	½ cup coffee, orange, chocolate, or hazelnut liqueur (optional); Cappuccino Angel Filling (page 318)	Whipped Cream Frosting (page 326)	Cocoa powder

ASSEMBLY: Sprinkle each layer with 1 tablespoon liqueur, if desired. Spread filling equally over all layers. Stack layers. (Cake may be frozen at this point.) Place a lacy paper doily over top of cake and sprinkle with cocoa. Carefully lift away doily, leaving cocoa design. Frost sides with frosting and refrigerate until serving.

CAKE	LAYERS	FILLINGS	FROSTING	GARNISH
Chocolate Walnut Brandy Cake	3 (C)	¼ cup brandy; ½ to 1 cup chopped walnuts; Chocolate Buttercream (page 320)	Whipped Cream Frosting (page 326)	Chopped walnuts; Chocolate Curls (page 394)

ASSEMBLY: Beat 1 tablespoon brandy into chocolate buttercream. Sprinkle each layer with 1 tablespoon brandy and ⅓ of nuts. Spread each layer with ⅓ chocolate buttercream. Stack layers. (Cake may be frozen at this point for later use.) Frost sides of cake with whipped cream frosting. Garnish with additional nuts and Chocolate Curls.

CAKE	LAYERS	FILLINGS	FROSTING	GARNISH
Crème de Menthe Cake	3 or 4 (C)	2 to 3 tablespoons crème de menthe; Buttercream Frosting (page 320), with 2 to 3 drops green food coloring added (optional)	Whipped Cream Frosting (page 326)	Chocolate Curls (page 394)

ASSEMBLY: Sprinkle each layer with liqueur, if desired. Spread each layer with buttercream and stack layers. Frost sides with whipped cream frosting. Garnish with Chocolate Curls. Refrigerate until serving.

COOKIES

Bar cookies baked in a square dish or cookie wedges baked in a round one are the best selections for the microwave. Most recipes can be prepared and cooked in less than 10 minutes (about the same time it takes to preheat a conventional oven). Bar cookies baked in oblong dishes do not cook as uniformly as they do in square or round ones.

Individual cookies, such as drop, rolled, molded, and cut-out cookies, must be microwaved 6 to 12 at a time, and it is almost always more efficient to cook them conventionally. For this reason we have included only bar cookie recipes in this chapter. If you would like to microwave individual cookies, place them on a wax-paper-lined dish, 2 inches apart, in a circle. Remember that for microwaving cookies, you will need a much stiffer dough, one that is almost crumbly, to prevent excessive spreading during cooking. Most individual cookies are microwaved at 50% power.

GUIDELINES FOR SUCCESSFUL BAR COOKIES

- To help prevent overcooking in the corners of the dish, place a triangle of foil over each corner. (Check your oven manufacturer's owner manual to be sure that the use of metal is permitted in your particular oven.) Do not allow the foil to touch the sides of the oven.
- When making layered bars, the bottom layer should be cooked before the next layer is added. When a filling is used, it is sometimes best to partially cook the filling before spreading it on the crust.
- For added eye appeal, sprinkle cookies with confectioners' sugar, cover them with frosting or glaze, or place them under a conventional broiler to brown and crisp. Many cookies need none of these enhancements.
- To prevent undercooking in the center of the dish, microwave the batter on HIGH 1 to 2 minutes and stir so the batter will be uniformly hot before beginning baking.
- Cool completely before cutting into bar cookies and serving. Bar cookies are very tender and do not hold together well until they are cold. To hurry them along, they can be placed in the refrigerator or freezer.
- Suggestions for converting conventional recipes: Microwaved baked foods are more tender than those conventionally baked. Reduce the amount of leavening called for in the conventional recipe by about one-half. Add an extra egg if the cookies are too crumbly. Decrease the amount of liquid by about one-fourth, especially if using a mix.

PEPPERMINT BROWNIES

1 stick (¹/₂ cup) unsalted butter
1 cup granulated sugar
2 large eggs
¹/₂ cup Dutch-process cocoa
　　powder

¹/₂ cup all-purpose flour
¹/₂ teaspoon baking powder
1 teaspoon vanilla extract

**MAKES 16
BAR COOKIES**

■

FROSTING

5 tablespoons unsalted butter
2 cups sifted confectioners' sugar

1 tablespoon milk
¹/₂ teaspoon peppermint extract

GLAZE

1 tablespoon unsalted butter

1 ounce unsweetened chocolate

In mixing bowl, microwave butter on HIGH 30 to 60 seconds to melt. Add granulated sugar and cream mixture. Add eggs, 1 at a time, beating constantly. Add cocoa, flour, baking powder, and vanilla and beat to mix well. Spread in 8-inch square glass dish and shield corners with foil (if permitted in your oven). Microwave on HIGH 5 to 6 minutes.

Prepare frosting: In bowl, microwave butter on HIGH 30 to 60 seconds to melt. Blend in confectioners' sugar, milk, and peppermint and beat until smooth. Spread frosting over brownies while they are still warm.

Prepare glaze: In cup, microwave butter and chocolate on 70% power 2 to 3 minutes, or until chocolate is melted. Blend well and drizzle over frosting.

Chill brownies and cut into squares.

■ ■ ■ ■ ■ ■ ■ ■ ■ ■
Make a quick birthday
cake to delight a child
by preparing a bar
cookie recipe in a
round dish and deco-
rating the top. Cut in
thin wedges to serve.
■ ■ ■ ■ ■ ■ ■ ■ ■ ■

BANANA NUT BARS

MAKES
16 TO 24
BAR COOKIES

1/2 stick (1/4 cup) unsalted butter
3/4 cup granulated sugar
1 large egg
1/2 cup sour cream or evaporated
milk
3/4 cup mashed bananas (1 large
banana)

1 cup all-purpose flour
1/2 teaspoon baking powder
1/4 teaspoon salt
1 teaspoon vanilla extract
1/2 cup chopped walnuts or pecans

GLAZE

2 tablespoons unsalted butter
1 cup sifted confectioners' sugar

1 1/2 tablespoons milk or plain low-
fat yogurt

In 2-quart measure, microwave butter on HIGH 30 to 60 seconds, or until melted. Add granulated sugar, egg, sour cream, bananas, flour, baking powder, salt, and vanilla and beat until well mixed. Stir in nuts.

Microwave on HIGH 1 to 2 minutes, or until very hot. Gently stir. Spread in 8-inch square glass dish. Shield corners with foil (if permitted in your oven). Microwave on 70% power 5 to 7 minutes or until done. Let stand until warm.

Prepare glaze: In 2-cup measure, combine butter, confectioners' sugar, and milk. Microwave on HIGH 30 to 60 seconds, or until butter is melted. Stir until smooth and spread over baked surface. Cool and cut into bars.

PEANUT BUTTER BROWNIES

MAKES 24
BAR COOKIES

A treat kids love!

6 tablespoons unsalted butter
1/2 cup, packed, light brown sugar
1/2 cup granulated sugar
2 large eggs, beaten
1/2 cup smooth or crunchy peanut
butter
1 cup all-purpose flour
1 1/2 teaspoons baking powder

1/2 teaspoon salt
1 teaspoon vanilla extract
1 cup semisweet chocolate chips
Confectioners' sugar or 2
tablespoons confectioners'
sugar mixed with 2
tablespoons Dutch-process
cocoa powder

In 2-quart measure, microwave butter on HIGH 30 to 60 seconds, or until melted. Stir in brown sugar, granulated sugar, eggs, peanut butter, flour, baking powder, salt, and vanilla. Beat until well mixed and microwave on HIGH 1 to 2 minutes, or until hot.

Stir batter and spread in 8-inch square glass dish. Sprinkle chocolate chips evenly over batter. Shield corners with foil (if permitted in your oven). Microwave on 70% power 5 to 7 minutes, or until done.

Let stand several minutes, then sprinkle with confectioners' sugar. Cool completely and cut into squares.

ROCKY ROAD BROWNIES

1/3 cup unsalted butter
2 ounces unsweetened chocolate
1 cup granulated sugar
2 large eggs, beaten
1 cup all-purpose flour

1/2 teaspoon baking powder
1/4 teaspoon salt
1 teaspoon vanilla extract
1/2 cup chopped nuts
1 cup miniature marshmallows

GLAZE

1 cup sifted confectioners' sugar
1 tablespoon unsalted butter
2 tablespoons milk

2 tablespoons Dutch-process
*   cocoa powder*

**MAKES 12
BAR COOKIES**

■

They're yummy.

• • • • • • • • • • •
Freshen and soften stale marshmallows (2 cups) by placing them in a bowl with 1 tablespoon water. Cover and microwave on 50% power 30 to 40 seconds, or longer if needed.
• • • • • • • • • • •

Combine butter, chocolate, and granulated sugar in 2-quart measure. Microwave on HIGH 2 to 2½ minutes, stirring once, or until chocolate is melted. Add eggs, flour, baking powder, salt, vanilla, and nuts, stirring only until batter is smooth. Cook on HIGH 2 minutes.

Pour batter into 8-inch square glass dish. Shield corners (if permitted in your oven) and cook on 70% power 4 to 5 minutes, or until top is damp but no longer wet. Sprinkle with miniature marshmallows. Cover with plastic wrap and let set until the marshmallows are soft enough to spread.

Prepare glaze: Combine confectioners' sugar, butter, milk, and cocoa in 2-cup measure. Microwave on HIGH 1 to 1½ minutes, or until butter melts. Stir and spread over marshmallows. Cool and cut into squares.

CHINESE CHEWS

**MAKES
36 TO 48
COOKIES**

2 tablespoons unsalted butter
¾ cup granulated sugar
2 large eggs, beaten
⅔ cup all-purpose flour
1 teaspoon baking powder

½ teaspoon salt
1 teaspoon vanilla extract
1 cup chopped dates
1 cup chopped pecans or walnuts
¼ cup confectioners' sugar

In a bowl, microwave butter on HIGH 30 to 60 seconds, or until melted. Blend in granulated sugar and eggs. Add flour, baking powder, salt, vanilla, dates, and nuts and stir well. Microwave on HIGH 1 to 2 minutes, or until hot. Stir.

Spread batter evenly in 8-inch square glass dish. Shield corners with foil (if permitted in your oven). Microwave on HIGH 4 to 7 minutes, or until done.

Cool and cut into 1-inch squares. Roll squares in your hands to form balls. Put confectioners' sugar in a plastic bag. Drop balls into bag and shake to coat with sugar.

CONGO SQUARES

**MAKES 24
BAR COOKIES**

1 stick (½ cup) unsalted butter
1¼ cups, packed, dark or light
    brown sugar
2 large eggs
1¼ cups all-purpose flour
1½ teaspoons baking powder

¼ teaspoon salt
½ cup chopped nuts
6 ounces semisweet chocolate
    chips
Confectioners' sugar (optional)

In bowl, microwave butter on HIGH 1 minute, or until melted. Add brown sugar and cream mixture. Beat in eggs.

Combine flour, baking powder, and salt and stir into egg mixture. Stir in half the nuts and the chocolate chips.

Spread mixture in 8-inch square glass dish. Shield corners with aluminum foil (if permitted in your oven). Microwave on HIGH 1 to 2 minutes, or until hot. Stir, rotating batter on outside to center. Sprinkle remaining nuts and chips over batter. Microwave on 70% power 5 to 8 minutes. Cool and cut into squares. Sprinkle with confectioners' sugar, if desired.

CHOCOLATE TOFFEE BARS

BASE
1 stick (¹/₂ cup) unsalted butter
¹/₂ cup, packed, light brown sugar

1 cup all-purpose flour

MAKES 24 BAR COOKIES

■

Very rich.

FILLING
1 stick (¹/₂ cup) unsalted butter
2 tablespoons light corn syrup
1 cup, packed, light brown sugar
¹/₄ cup heavy cream or evaporated milk

1 cup chopped walnuts or pecans
1 ounce semisweet chocolate
1 teaspoon vanilla extract

Prepare base: In cup, microwave butter on 50% power 30 to 60 seconds to soften. In bowl, combine sugar and flour, then cut in softened butter until mixture resembles coarse crumbs. Press evenly in greased 8-inch square glass dish. Microwave on HIGH 3 to 4 minutes, or until surface looks dull.

Prepare filling: In 2-quart measure, microwave butter on HIGH 1 minute to melt. Stir in corn syrup and brown sugar. Microwave on HIGH 3 to 4 minutes, or until mixture registers 260° F. (hard-ball stage) on candy thermometer. Stir in cream and nuts. Microwave on HIGH 1 to 3 minutes, or to 240° F. (soft-ball stage). Stir in chocolate and vanilla and stir until chocolate is melted. Pour filling over base and spread evenly. Chill for several hours, then cut into bars.

OATMEAL RAISIN BARS

**MAKES
24 BAR
COOKIES**

•

1 stick (¹/₂ cup) unsalted butter
¹/₂ cup, packed, light brown sugar
¹/₂ cup all-purpose flour
1¹/₂ cups quick-cooking oats

¹/₂ teaspoon baking powder
1 teaspoon cinnamon
1 large egg, beaten
¹/₂ cup raisins

ICING

1 (3-ounce) package cream cheese
2 tablespoons unsalted butter
2 cups sifted confectioners' sugar

1 teaspoon applejack or vanilla
    extract

In 2-quart bowl, microwave butter on HIGH 30 seconds, or until melted. Stir in brown sugar and flour and microwave on HIGH 2 minutes. Stir and add oats, baking powder, cinnamon, egg, and raisins. Mix well and pour into greased 8-inch square glass dish. Shield corners with foil (if permitted in your oven). Microwave on HIGH 1 to 2 minutes, or until surface looks dull.

　　Make icing: In bowl, microwave cream cheese and butter on HIGH 30 to 45 seconds to soften. Add sugar and applejack and beat until smooth. Spread icing over oatmeal base while surface is still warm. Cool and cut into bars.

LEMON SQUARES

**MAKES
24 BAR
COOKIES**

•

BASE

1 stick (¹/₂ cup) unsalted butter
1 cup all-purpose flour

¹/₄ cup sifted confectioners' sugar
¹/₂ teaspoon grated lemon zest

FILLING

2 large eggs
1 cup granulated sugar
3 tablespoons fresh lemon juice

2 tablespoons all-purpose flour
¹/₂ teaspoon baking powder
Confectioners' sugar

Prepare base: In bowl, microwave butter on HIGH 1 to 2 minutes to melt. Blend in flour, confectioners' sugar, and lemon zest.

Press evenly in 8-inch square glass dish. Shield corners with foil (if permitted in your oven) and microwave on HIGH 3 to 4 minutes.

Prepare filling: In microwavable mixing bowl, beat eggs and granulated sugar with an electric mixer. Add lemon juice and beat until mixture is pale yellow, about 5 minutes. Combine flour and baking powder and fold into egg mixture. Microwave on HIGH 1 minute. Stir filling and pour over base. Cover baking dish with plastic wrap and microwave on 50% power 5 minutes. Uncover and microwave on HIGH 1 to 2 minutes, or just until set in center. Completely cool, sprinkle with confectioners' sugar, and cut into squares.

GINGER CAKES

¹/₂ stick (¹/₄ cup) unsalted butter
¹/₃ cup granulated sugar
¹/₄ cup light molasses
²/₃ cup all-purpose flour
¹/₂ teaspoon baking soda
¹/₂ teaspoon ground ginger

¹/₄ teaspoon freshly grated nutmeg
¹/₄ teaspoon cinnamon
Pinch of ground cloves
2 large eggs, beaten
2 tablespoons hot water

MAKES

16 TO 24 BAR

COOKIES

■

An old-fashioned treat.

ICING

¹/₂ cup confectioners' sugar
2 tablespoons fresh orange juice
    or milk
2 tablespoons unsalted butter

¹/₂ teaspoon vanilla extract
1 to 2 drops red food coloring
    (optional)

In bowl, microwave butter on HIGH 30 to 60 seconds, or until melted. Add granulated sugar, molasses, flour, soda, ginger, nutmeg, cinnamon, cloves, eggs, and hot water and beat until well mixed. Microwave on HIGH 1 minute, then stir.

Spread batter in buttered 8-inch square glass dish. Shield corners with foil (if permitted in your oven). Microwave on 70% power 6 to 8 minutes, or until done.

Prepare icing: In 2-cup measure, combine confectioners' sugar, orange juice, butter, vanilla, and food coloring, if desired. Microwave on HIGH 30 to 60 seconds, or until butter is melted. Beat until blended and spread over baked surface. Cool and cut into bars.

GRANOLA BARS

MAKES 24 BAR COOKIES

▪

Low in cholesterol and high in fiber.

1½ cups rolled oats
½ cup wheat germ or unsweetened shredded coconut
2 tablespoons brown sugar
2 tablespoons honey

2 tablespoons margarine, melted
2 egg whites
½ teaspoon vanilla
Pinch of salt

Place oats and wheat germ in 2-quart measure and microwave on HIGH 3 minutes. Stir in brown sugar, honey, margarine, egg whites, vanilla, and salt and combine well.

Spread batter in 8-inch square glass dish. Shield corners of dish with foil (if permitted in your oven). Microwave on HIGH 5 minutes, or until done. Cool and cut into bars.

DATE-NUT BARS

MAKES 16 BAR COOKIES

▪

½ stick (¼ cup) unsalted butter, melted
½ cup, packed, light brown sugar
2 large eggs, beaten
¾ cup all-purpose flour
1 teaspoon baking powder
¼ teaspoon salt

1 tablespoon Dutch-process cocoa powder
1 teaspoon vanilla extract
1 cup chopped dates
½ cup chopped walnuts or pecans
Confectioners' sugar

In bowl, combine butter, brown sugar, eggs, flour, baking powder, salt, cocoa, vanilla, dates, and walnuts. Mix well. Microwave on HIGH 1 minute and stir.

Spread in greased 8-inch square glass dish. Shield corners of dish with foil (if permitted in your oven). Microwave on 70% power 5 to 7 minutes, or until done. Let stand about 10 minutes, then sprinkle with confectioners' sugar. Cool and cut into bars.

PEANUT BUTTER BARS

1 cup sugar
1 cup light corn syrup
1 (12-ounce) jar crunchy peanut
    butter
1/2 cup raisins

4 cups toasted rice cereal
1 cup chopped nuts, toasted (page
    441; optional)
1/2 cup semisweet chocolate chips
    (optional)

MAKES ABOUT 36 BAR COOKIES

In 2-quart measure, combine sugar, corn syrup, and peanut butter. Microwave on HIGH 3 to 6 minutes, or until boiling, stirring twice during cooking. Stir in raisins, cereal, and, if desired, nuts. Press evenly into well-greased 13 × 9-inch dish. Let cool.

Place chocolate, if desired, in small bowl and microwave on 70% 1 to 2 minutes, or until melted. Stir until smooth and drizzle over peanut butter base. Chill and cut into bars.

MARSHMALLOW CEREAL SQUARES

1/2 stick (1/4 cup) unsalted butter
5 cups miniature or 40 large
    marshmallows (10 ounces)

5 cups crisp cereal (crispy rice,
    cereal checks, or cereal O's)

MAKES 24 TO 36 BAR COOKIES

In 2-quart bowl, microwave butter and marshmallows on HIGH 2 to 3 minutes, or until marshmallows have puffed up and butter is melted. Stir until smooth. Stir in cereal. Press mixture evenly in buttered 13 × 9-inch dish. Cool and cut into squares.

VARIATIONS

- Add 1/2 cup peanut butter to butter and marshmallows before microwaving.
- Add chopped nuts, raisins, or chopped dried fruit along with cereal.
- Drizzle melted chocolate over cereal squares.

HELLO DOLLIES

**MAKES 24
BAR COOKIES**

2½ cups graham cracker crumbs
2 teaspoons baking powder
1 (14-ounce) can condensed milk

6 ounces semisweet chocolate
  chips
1 cup coarsely chopped walnuts
  or pecans

In bowl, combine crumbs and baking powder. Stir in condensed milk, chocolate chips (reserving about ¼ cup chips), and nuts.

Spread batter evenly in greased 8- or 9-inch square glass dish. Sprinkle reserved chocolate chips over mixture. Shield corners and microwave on HIGH 5 to 9 minutes, or until done. Cool and cut into squares.

CREAMY RAISIN BARS

**MAKES
24 BAR
COOKIES**

A delicious cheese-cake-type bar cookie.

⅓ cup unsalted butter
⅓ cup, packed, brown sugar
1 cup all-purpose flour
½ cup raisins
½ cup chopped walnuts

1 (8-ounce) package cream cheese
¼ cup granulated sugar
1 large egg
1 tablespoon fresh lemon juice
½ teaspoon vanilla extract

In 2-quart measure, microwave butter on HIGH 1 minute, or until melted. Add brown sugar and blend in flour. Stir in raisins and walnuts.

Reserve ½ cup raisin mixture and press remainder evenly in 8-inch square glass dish. Shield corners and microwave on HIGH 4 to 5 minutes, or until surface looks dull.

In 1-quart measure, microwave cream cheese on HIGH 45 to 60 seconds to soften. Add granulated sugar, egg, lemon juice, and vanilla and beat until smooth. Microwave on HIGH 30 to 45 seconds, or just until hot. Spread evenly over crust. Sprinkle reserved raisin mixture on top. Cover with plastic wrap and microwave on 50% power 5 minutes. Uncover and cook on HIGH 1 to 2 minutes, or until set in center. Cool completely and cut into bars. Store in refrigerator.

SHORTBREAD

*1 1/4 cups all-purpose or whole
    wheat flour*
1/4 cup cornstarch, sifted
1/3 cup, packed, light brown sugar
1/2 teaspoon dry yeast (optional)*

*1 stick (1/2 cup) unsalted butter,
    cut into 1-inch pieces*
1 teaspoon vanilla extract
2 tablespoons cold water
Granulated sugar

**MAKES
16 WEDGES**

∎

A simple and elegant
cookie that is good with
tea or served with
fresh fruit or other light
desserts.

In food processor, process flour, cornstarch, brown sugar, and, if desired, yeast, to mix. Add butter and pulse processor several times until mixture resembles crumbs. Add vanilla and water and pulse several times, just until dough holds together. (If you do not have a food processor, mix by hand using a pastry blender.)

Shape dough into two balls and flatten into disks about 8 to 9 inches in diameter. Place disks on a piece of brown or wax paper and place on pie plate.

Microwave one disk at a time, uncovered, on HIGH 3 to 5 minutes, or until surface is slightly puffy and dry. Lift brown paper with shortbread to a towel spread out on countertop.

Cut shortbread into 16 wedges and sprinkle with granulated sugar. Lift paper with shortbread to wire rack and let cool. If bubbles form, gently pierce with tip of sharp knife or a fork.

LEMON SHORTBREAD

Omit vanilla and water and use 3 tablespoons fresh lemon juice. Before cooking, sprinkle 1 teaspoon grated lemon zest evenly over dough and lightly press it in.

ALMOND SHORTBREAD

Substitute almond extract for vanilla. Before cooking, sprinkle 1 cup toasted sliced blanched almonds evenly over disks and lightly press nuts into dough.

* The yeast is not used as leavening; instead, it complements and enhances the flavor of the vanilla.

Prune Squares

MAKES
16 BAR
COOKIES

■

Delicious and nutritious!

1 cup diced prunes
1 cup, packed, light brown sugar
¾ cup all-purpose flour
1½ teaspoons baking powder
¼ teaspoon salt

Pinch of cinnamon
2 large eggs, beaten
½ cup chopped walnuts or pecans
Confectioners' sugar

In bowl, combine prunes, brown sugar, flour, baking powder, salt, and cinnamon. Add eggs and beat well. Spread batter evenly in 8-inch square dish.

Microwave on HIGH 1 minute, then stir. Spread batter evenly again and sprinkle nuts over batter. Shield the corners with foil (if permitted in your oven). Cover with wax paper and microwave on HIGH 4 to 6 minutes, or until done. Let stand several minutes. Sprinkle with confectioners' sugar. Cool and cut into squares.

Toffee Bars

MAKES 18
BAR COOKIES

■

1 tablespoon plus one stick (½ cup) unsalted butter
9 graham crackers
½ cup, packed, light brown sugar

½ cup nuts (sliced almonds, or chopped pecans or walnuts)
½ cup milk chocolate or semisweet chocolate chips

Microwave 1 tablespoon of the butter in 8-inch square dish on HIGH 30 to 60 seconds, or until melted. Tilt dish to spread butter evenly over bottom. Cover bottom of dish with a single layer of graham crackers.

In 1-quart measure, combine 1 stick of butter and sugar. Microwave on HIGH 1 minute. Blend mixture well with a wire whisk, then microwave on HIGH 2 minutes longer. Spread evenly over crackers. Sprinkle top with nuts.

Microwave on HIGH 1½ to 3 minutes, or until mixture bubbles in center for 1 minute. Let stand several minutes, then sprinkle with chocolate chips. Let stand several minutes until melted, then spread chocolate over base. Cut into bars. Store in tightly covered container.

TURTLE BARS

1½ cups quick-cooking oats
½ cup, packed, light brown sugar
½ cup all-purpose flour
1 stick (½ cup) unsalted butter

20 caramel candies
1 tablespoon milk
½ cup milk chocolate chips
½ cup broken pecans

**MAKES 24
BAR COOKIES**

▪

Place oats, brown sugar, flour, and butter in 2-quart bowl and microwave on HIGH 2 to 4 minutes. Stir and press into buttered 8-inch square glass dish. Cook on HIGH 1 minute. Cool.

In bowl, microwave caramels and milk on HIGH 1 minute or longer to melt caramels. Stir until smooth and pour over crust. Sprinkle chocolate chips over hot caramel and let stand 1 to 2 minutes, or until melted; spread chocolate over caramel. Sprinkle pecans over chocolate. Cool and cut into bars.

CUSTARDS, PUDDINGS, AND MOUSSES

Excellent custards and steamed puddings can be cooked in the microwave in about one-quarter of the time it takes conventionally—and without resorting to special pans or using a *bain-marie* (water bath). Steamed pudding batter should be tightly covered (we use plastic wrap held tightly in place with a rubber band).

This section contains some of our most luxurious desserts, all of them based on custards—Bavarian Cream, Chocolate Decadence, and a series of ravishing cold soufflés and mousses, which alone are worth the price of the microwave.

BAKED CUSTARD

6 SERVINGS

2½ cups milk
½ cup sugar
2 teaspoons cornstarch
4 large eggs

1 teaspoon vanilla extract
¼ teaspoon freshly grated nutmeg
Pinch of salt

Microwave milk in 1-quart measure on HIGH 3 to 5 minutes, or until very hot. Meanwhile, combine sugar, cornstarch, eggs, vanilla, nutmeg, and salt in food processor or blender and blend well. With motor running, add hot milk in a stream.

Pour mixture into six 1-cup custard cups or an 8-inch round glass dish. If using custard cups, place in oven in a circle with at least 1 inch of space between them. Microwave on 50% power 12 to 18 minutes, or until custard is almost set; center should be slightly liquid and edges will begin to shrink from sides of cups. For cups, begin to watch carefully after 12 minutes of cooking; for large custard, begin watching after 15 minutes.

Cover with large piece of plastic wrap and let stand until cooled. Custard will become firm while standing. Serve warm or chilled. To unmold, loosen sides with thin-bladed knife and invert on serving plate(s).

CHOCOLATE CREAM CUSTARDS
Omit nutmeg. Add 3 ounces finely chopped semisweet chocolate to hot milk and process until smooth.

CRÈME CARAMEL
Combine 6 tablespoons sugar and 2 tablespoons water in 8-inch round glass dish. Microwave on HIGH 3 to 5 minutes, or until syrup is caramel colored. Rotate dish so that caramel covers bottom. Prepare all ingredients for Baked Custard, omitting nutmeg, and pour custard into caramel-glazed dish to cook.

PRALINE CREAM CUSTARDS
Omit nutmeg. Stir ⅓ to ½ cup Praline Powder (page 382) into hot milk.

CARAMEL RICE PUDDING

1 cup milk or half-and-half
2 large eggs
⅔ cup raisins
⅓ cup, firmly packed, light brown
   sugar

1½ cups cooked rice (page 289)
3 tablespoons unsalted butter,
   melted
1 teaspoon vanilla extract
Pinch of salt

4 SERVINGS

In 2-quart measure, beat together milk and eggs. Add raisins, brown sugar, rice, butter, vanilla, and salt and stir until well blended. Microwave on HIGH 5 minutes. Stir, cover, and microwave on 70% power 4 to 6 minutes. Let stand, covered, 5 minutes.

BANANA PUDDING

2½ cups milk or half-and-half
1 cup sugar
3 tablespoons cornstarch
2 large eggs, beaten
¼ teaspoon salt
1 teaspoon vanilla extract

½ stick (¼ cup) unsalted butter,
   cut into 4 to 6 pieces
1 (12-ounce) box vanilla wafers
4 to 6 bananas
Whipped cream

10 TO 12 SERVINGS

In 2-quart measure, microwave milk on HIGH 4 to 6 minutes, or until boiling. In small bowl, combine sugar and cornstarch. Blend in eggs and salt and beat well. Add ½ cup hot milk to egg mixture, stirring constantly. Stir egg mixture into remaining milk and cook on 70% power 5 to 8 minutes, or until thickened. Stir in vanilla and butter. Let cool.

To assemble pudding, line bottom and side of 2-quart bowl with vanilla wafers. Slice 2 to 3 bananas to make a single layer and place in bowl. Add one-third of filling. Repeat layering, ending with pudding. Chill. Before serving, garnish with whipped cream.

STEAMED CHOCOLATE DATE-NUT PUDDING

8 SERVINGS

8 ounces chopped pitted dates
   (about 2 cups)
¾ cup milk
3 tablespoons rum or brandy or 1
   teaspoon vanilla extract
4 ounces unsweetened chocolate
1 stick (½ cup) unsalted butter
1⅓ cups, packed, light brown
   sugar

3 large eggs
1½ cups all-purpose flour
1 teaspoon baking powder
½ teaspoon salt
1 cup chopped walnuts or pecans
Hard Sauce (recipe follows) or
   whipped cream

Place dates and milk in 1-quart measure and microwave on HIGH 1½ to 2 minutes, or until hot but not boiling. Stir in the rum, and set aside.

Place chocolate in small bowl and microwave on 70% power 3 to 4 minutes, or until melted. Set aside.

In 2-quart measure, cream the butter and sugar. Beat in eggs. Combine flour, baking powder, and salt and beat into creamed mixture. Beat in date mixture and melted chocolate. Stir in nuts.

Pour into buttered 2-quart measure or mold. Microwave on HIGH 2 minutes. Gently stir and microwave on HIGH 1 minute longer. Some parts of batter will begin to cook (but don't worry). Gently stir, pushing any lumps to center, but don't try to smooth them out. Cover tightly with plastic wrap (secure with a rubber band, if necessary) and microwave on 50% power 9 to 12 minutes, or until set. Let stand, covered, 5 to 10 minutes. Invert on serving plate and serve with Hard Sauce or whipped cream.

HARD SAUCE

1 stick (¹/₂ cup) unsalted butter
2 cups sifted confectioners' sugar
Pinch of salt

2 or more tablespoons brandy, or
   1 teaspoon vanilla extract

MAKES

1 CUP

■

In 1-quart measure, microwave butter on 50% power 1 to 2 minutes to soften. Add sugar, salt, and brandy and cream all ingredients until light and fluffy. Chill. Serve with steamed puddings.

BREAD PUDDING

8 ounces French bread, cut into
   2-inch cubes (5 to 6 cups)
2 cups half-and-half
2 tablespoons unsalted butter
2 large eggs, beaten

³/₄ cup granulated sugar
1 teaspoon almond extract
¹/₂ cup slivered blanched almonds,
   toasted (page 441)
¹/₂ cup golden raisins

SAUCE

¹/₂ stick (¹/₄ cup) unsalted butter
¹/₂ cup sifted confectioners' sugar

1 large egg
2 tablespoons bourbon

6 TO 8
SERVINGS

■

A standard of excellence. This delicious wintertime favorite is the best bread pudding we have ever tasted.

Place bread in large bowl, pour half-and-half over bread, and let stand in refrigerator 1 hour.

Place butter in 2-cup measure and microwave on HIGH 20 to 30 seconds, or until melted. Add the eggs, granulated sugar, and almond extract and whisk together. Gently fold egg mixture, almonds, and raisins into milk-soaked bread. Microwave on HIGH 2 minutes, then on 50% power 6 to 7 minutes, or until set.

Prepare sauce: In 2-cup measure, microwave butter on HIGH 45 seconds, or until melted. Stir in confectioners' sugar, egg, and bourbon and microwave on 50% power 1 to 2 minutes, stirring several times. If sauce is not smooth, process in blender or food processor for a few seconds. Serve sauce over warm pudding.

Heat brandy (2 to 4 tablespoons) for flaming desserts on HIGH for 15 seconds.

STEAMED CRANBERRY PUDDING

6 SERVINGS

Serve this holiday favorite with Hard Sauce (page 361) or Custard Sauce (page 319).

2 cups fresh or frozen cranberries
¾ cup, packed, light brown sugar
½ cup golden raisins
¼ cup dark rum
½ stick (¼ cup) unsalted butter

2 large eggs
¾ cup all-purpose flour
1½ teaspoons baking powder
½ teaspoon salt
⅔ cup chopped walnuts

Chop cranberries in blender or food processor and transfer to bowl. Stir in 2 tablespoons brown sugar. Combine raisins and rum in small dish. Cover and microwave on HIGH 1 to 2 minutes, or until boiling. Let stand, covered, 5 to 10 minutes to soften.

Cream butter and remaining brown sugar with electric mixer. Beat in eggs. Add flour, baking powder, and salt and combine well. Stir in cranberries, raisins and rum, and nuts.

Pour mixture into buttered 2-quart measure or other mold. Microwave on HIGH 2 minutes. Gently stir. Cover tightly with plastic wrap and microwave on 50% power 6 to 10 minutes, or until set. Let stand, covered, 5 minutes.

TAPIOCA PUDDING

4 OR 5 SERVINGS

1 large egg, separated
2 cups milk
3 tablespoons quick-cooking tapioca

½ cup sugar
Pinch of salt
½ teaspoon vanilla extract

In 2-quart measure, combine egg yolk, milk, tapioca, 2 tablespoons sugar, and salt. Beat well, then let mixture stand 5 minutes.

In another bowl, beat egg white until foamy. Gradually beat in remaining sugar and vanilla and continue beating until soft peaks form. Set aside.

Stir tapioca mixture well and microwave, covered, on HIGH 5 to 7 minutes, stirring after first 3 minutes. Fold in egg white mixture. Chill before serving.

CHOCOLATE DECADENCE

¹/₄ cup raisins
¹/₄ cup brandy
5 tablespoons unsalted butter
¹/₃ cup all-purpose flour
¹/₂ cup heavy cream
³/₄ cup sugar

4 large eggs, separated
6 ounces semisweet chocolate
¹/₂ teaspoon baking powder
1 teaspoon almond extract
Whipped cream

GLAZE

4 ounces semisweet chocolate   *¹/₂ cup heavy cream*

6 TO 8
SERVINGS

•

This is a five-star dessert and one of our favorites for special occasions. Some say it's a soufflé; others that it's a mousse cake; everyone says it's delicious! For an extra glamorous touch, serve it in a pool of raspberry sauce.

In cup, soak raisins in brandy overnight. Or if time doesn't permit, cover raisins and brandy and microwave on HIGH 1 minute; let stand 15 minutes.

In 1-quart measure, microwave butter on HIGH 1 minute to melt. Stir in flour and cream and microwave on HIGH 1 to 1½ minutes. Stir in sugar, egg yolks, raisins, and brandy and blend well.

In small bowl, microwave chocolate on 70% power 3 to 4 minutes, or until melted. Stir into egg mixture. With electric mixer, beat egg whites until peaks form. Fold in baking powder and almond extract. Fold egg whites into egg yolk mixture. Spread evenly in oiled 6-cup mold. Cover tightly with plastic wrap and do not vent. Microwave on 30% power 15 to 20 minutes. Let stand 10 minutes, then unmold and chill.

Prepare glaze: In 2-cup measure, microwave chocolate on 70% power 2 to 3 minutes to melt. Add cream and whisk until smooth. Spread over dessert. Serve with whipped cream. This dessert will keep in refrigerator for 1 week.

BAVARIAN CREAM

6 SERVINGS

■

Light, creamy, and rich Bavarian cream is a flavored custard containing gelatin for firmness and whipped cream and beaten egg whites for lightness. The custard may be frozen and defrosted without diminishing its smooth, luxurious texture.

1 1/2 cups milk
1 envelope unflavored gelatin
3 large eggs, separated
1/2 cup sugar

1 teaspoon vanilla extract
1/8 teaspoon freshly grated nutmeg
1/8 teaspoon cream of tartar
1 cup heavy cream (35% butterfat)

Pour 1/2 cup milk in small bowl and stir in gelatin. Let stand to soften.

In 2-quart measure, beat remaining 1 cup milk, egg yolks, and 1/4 cup sugar. Microwave on HIGH 2 minutes, stir, and microwave on 70% power 2 to 3 minutes, stirring every minute. Custard should be thick enough to coat a spoon. (If mixture has separated a little, don't worry.) Add vanilla and nutmeg. Stir in softened gelatin mixture and stir until blended and dissolved. Chill until mixture starts to set, about 45 to 60 minutes.

Oil and chill 6 1-cup molds or butter 6-cup mold and chill.*

With electric mixer, beat egg whites with cream of tartar until almost stiff. Gradually add remaining sugar, beating constantly. Whip cream until it holds soft peaks.

Gently fold egg whites and whipped cream into gelatin mixture. Pour mixture into prepared molds and chill until gelatin is set, about 1 hour.

Use Bavarian Cream as a filling for Sponge Cake (page 339) or Graham Cracker Crust (page 304).

ALMOND BAVARIAN CREAM

Omit nutmeg. Substitute 1 teaspoon almond extract for vanilla. Before adding gelatin mixture, combine half the hot custard mixture with 8 ounces almond paste, then whisk almond paste mixture into remaining custard. Proceed with recipe. Serve in Chocolate Cookie Crust (page 303), in a mold lined with ladyfingers, or as filling for Chocolate Sponge Cake (page 339).

BANANA BAVARIAN CREAM PIE

Omit nutmeg from Bavarian Cream. Line conventionally baked pie crust or Graham Cracker Crust with sliced bananas that have been

The quickest way to cool a hot food is to place the bowl of food in ice water. Since water is a better heat conductor than air, it will cool the food faster than ice alone.

* Molds may be lined with ladyfingers.

coated with lemon or lime juice. Spoon Bavarian over bananas and chill.

BRANDIED COFFEE BAVARIAN CREAM

Omit nutmeg. Add 2 to 4 tablespoons instant coffee powder, and additional ½ cup sugar, and 1 tablespoon cornstarch to egg yolk mixture before cooking. After mixture has cooked and cooled, stir in 2 tablespoons brandy.

CHESTNUT BAVARIAN CREAM

Omit nutmeg. Combine chilled custard with 1 (17-ounce) can sweetened chestnut puree, 2 tablespoons brandy, and 2 tablespoons Dutch-process cocoa powder.

CHOCOLATE BAVARIAN CREAM

Omit nutmeg. In cup, microwave 2 ounces semisweet chocolate on 70% power 2 to 3 minutes to melt. Blend into hot custard before adding gelatin mixture.

COCONUT BAVARIAN CREAM

Omit nutmeg. Fold ½ cup fresh or frozen grated coconut into finished Bavarian mixture.

EGGNOG BAVARIAN CREAM

Omit nutmeg. Add 1 to 2 tablespoons bourbon, brandy, or rum or a combination of these spirits to cooled custard.

■ ■ ■ ■ ■ ■ ■ ■ ■ ■ ■

Stabilized whipped cream will hold its shape when piped through a pastry tube or when it has to stand for several hours or longer. To stabilize 1 cup of cream, soften ½ teaspoon unflavored gelatin in 2 tablespoons cold water and let stand for 2 to 3 minutes. Microwave ¼ cup of the cream on HIGH 30 seconds, or just until boiling. Add the hot cream to the gelatin mixture and stir until the gelatin is dissolved. Refrigerate until chilled but not set, about 20 minutes. Whip the remaining ¾ cup cream until stiff, add the chilled gelatin mixture, and finish whipping.

■ ■ ■ ■ ■ ■ ■ ■ ■ ■ ■

CAROLINA TRIFLE

10 SERVINGS

3 cups milk or half-and-half
2 tablespoons cornstarch
1/4 teaspoon salt
3/4 cup sugar
2 large eggs
3 tablespoons unsalted butter

1 1/2 teaspoons vanilla extract
1 (1-pound) pound cake
3/4 cup dry sherry
3 cups sweetened whipped cream
1 (16-ounce) can cherry, blueberry
 or strawberry pie filling

In 2-quart measure, microwave milk on HIGH 4 to 5 minutes, or until very hot. In another bowl, combine cornstarch, salt, and sugar. Add eggs and stir until blended. Add about 1/2 cup hot milk to egg mixture and whisk until well blended. Add egg mixture to remaining hot milk and whisk. Cook on 70% power 6 to 8 minutes, or until thickened. Stir in butter and vanilla.

Cut pound cake into 1/2-inch slices and sprinkle with 1/2 cup sherry. Gently stir remaining sherry into whipped cream. Layer custard and cake in trifle dish or clear glass bowl. Make layers as follows: half the cake slices, half the custard, one-third of whipped cream, half the fruit filling. Top with whipped cream. Repeat layers and refrigerate several hours or overnight.

WHITE CHOCOLATE MOUSSE

8 SERVINGS

4 large eggs, separated
1 cup sugar
1 tablespoon unflavored gelatin
1/4 cup cold water
3 sticks (1 1/2 cups) unsalted butter

1 tablespoon vanilla extract
8 ounces white chocolate
Chocolate Sauce (page 385)
Fresh raspberries

In large microwavable bowl, whisk egg whites and sugar together, then microwave on 10% power 5 minutes, or until sugar is dissolved. Beat with electric mixer to a stiff meringue. Set aside.

In cup, combine gelatin with water and let stand 5 minutes. In another bowl, cream butter until light and fluffy. Add vanilla.

In bowl, microwave white chocolate on 50% power 3 minutes, or until melted, being careful not to overheat it. Beat egg yolks into chocolate. Add chocolate mixture to butter, beating until smooth.

Microwave gelatin and water mixture on 50% power 1 minute, or until gelatin is dissolved, then beat into butter mixture. Fold butter mixture into egg white mixture.

Pour mousse into a buttered 9-inch springform pan and chill. To serve, remove mousse from pan and slice into wedges. Serve with chocolate sauce and fresh raspberries.

CHOCOLATE PRALINE MOUSSE

¼ cup, packed, brown sugar
3 tablespoons heavy cream
¼ cup rum
6 ounces semisweet chocolate
    chips

2 egg whites, stiffly beaten
1 cup heavy cream (35%
    butterfat), whipped
Sweetened whipped cream and
    Chocolate Curls (page 394)

8 SERVINGS

•

Smooth and rich!

In 2-cup measure, combine sugar and cream and microwave on HIGH 1 to 2 minutes, or until sugar dissolves. Stir in rum and set aside.

In another bowl, microwave chocolate on 70% power 2 to 3 minutes, or until melted. Stir in sugar mixture, blending well. Cool.

Fold chocolate mixture into egg whites, then fold in whipped cream. Turn mousse into a serving bowl and chill. Garnish with sweetened whipped cream and Chocolate Curls and serve.

FROZEN GRAND MARNIER SOUFFLÉ

8 TO 10 SERVINGS

▪

Sublime!

¾ cup sugar
7 egg yolks
¼ cup frozen orange juice
    concentrate
3 tablespoons Grand Marnier
2 tablespoons cognac

2 cups heavy cream
    (35% butterfat)
Whipped cream
Orange sections, cut away from
    membrane
Chocolate Curls (page 394)

Cut a strip of brown or wax paper 5 inches wide and long enough to wrap around 1-quart soufflé dish with 1½ inches of overlap. Lightly oil one side of strip and tape it, oiled side facing inward, around soufflé dish with at least 2 inches of strip extending over top of dish.

In 2-quart bowl, beat sugar and egg yolks until thick and lemon colored. Beat in orange juice. Microwave on HIGH 3 minutes, stirring every minute. Mixture should be smooth.

Stir in Grand Marnier and cognac. Whip cream until soft peaks form and fold into egg yolk mixture. Pour into prepared soufflé dish and smooth top. Freeze soufflé overnight. Garnish with whipped cream, orange slices, and Chocolate Curls.

FROZEN LEMON BISQUE

8 TO 10 SERVINGS

▪

2 large eggs
¾ cup sugar
⅔ cup fresh lemon juice
1 tablespoon grated lemon zest

2 cups heavy cream
    (35% butterfat)
1 cup graham cracker crumbs
1 (10-ounce) package frozen
    raspberries

Combine eggs and sugar in 1-quart measure. Add lemon juice and beat until smooth. Microwave on HIGH 3 to 4 minutes, stirring halfway through cooking. Stir in lemon zest and chill.

Beat heavy cream and fold into lemon mixture. Sprinkle crumbs over bottom of 8-inch square dish. Pour lemon bisque mixture over crumbs, cover with plastic wrap, and freeze 4 to 5 hours, or until firm.

To serve, microwave raspberries on HIGH 2 minutes. Cut bisque into squares and top with raspberries.

COLD LEMON SOUFFLÉ

1 envelope unflavored gelatin
¼ cup cold water
6 large eggs, separated
1¼ cups sugar
⅔ cup fresh lemon juice

Grated zest of 2 lemons
1½ cups heavy cream
(35% butterfat)
Whipped cream
Thin lemon slices

8 SERVINGS

Cut a strip of brown or wax paper 6 inches wide and long enough to wrap around 1-quart soufflé dish with 1½ inches of overlap. Lightly oil one side of strip and tape it, oiled side facing inward, around soufflé dish with at least 3 inches of strip extending over top of dish.

In cup, combine gelatin and water and let stand 5 minutes. With electric mixer, in microwavable bowl, beat egg yolks and sugar until thick and light. Stir in lemon juice and microwave on 70% power 4 to 5 minutes, or until thickened but not boiling, stirring several times.

Add gelatin mixture to egg mixture and stir until dissolved. Beat in zest and refrigerate until mixture is cool, but do not let it set. Transfer to a large bowl.

In another bowl, with electric mixer, beat egg whites until stiff peaks form and fold into lemon mixture. Whip cream and fold it in. Pour into prepared soufflé dish and freeze. To serve, remove paper collar and garnish with whipped cream and thin lemon slices.

Orange Mousse

2 envelopes unflavored gelatin
1 cup water
1 cup sugar
1 cup fresh orange juice

1 cup orange sections, cut away
   from membranes
1 tablespoon grated lemon zest
1 cup heavy cream (35% butterfat)
Orange Cups (recipe follows)

In cup, stir gelatin into ½ cup cold water and let stand several minutes. In 2-quart measure, microwave remaining ½ cup water on HIGH 1 to 1½ minutes, or until boiling. Stir gelatin mixture into boiling water. Add sugar and stir until dissolved or microwave on HIGH 1 minute longer to dissolve sugar, if necessary.

Stir in orange juice, orange sections, and lemon zest. Chill until partially set. Whip cream and fold into orange mixture. Refrigerate until set. Serve in Orange Cups or sherbet dishes.

Orange Cups

6 large thick-skinned oranges

Slice off top quarter of each orange and discard tops. With spoon, scoop out pulp, leaving hollow shells. Reserve pulp for another use. With small sharp knife, cut edge of each orange into decorative scallop or zigzag shape, if desired. Chill before filling with mousse.

RASPBERRY SOUFFLÉ WITH CHOCOLATE SAUCE

1 envelope unflavored gelatin
2 tablespoons cold water
1 (10½-ounce) package frozen
   raspberries, defrosted
5 egg whites
¾ cup sugar
1 cup heavy cream (35% butterfat)

Whipped cream (optional)
Chocolate Curls (page 394;
   optional)
Fresh mint leaves (optional)
Fresh or defrosted frozen
   raspberries (optional)
Chocolate Sauce (page 385)

8 SERVINGS

Pretty for a dessert
buffet.

Cut a strip of brown or wax paper 6 inches wide and long enough to wrap around a 6-cup soufflé dish with 1½ inches of overlap. Lightly oil one side of strip and tape it, oiled side facing inward, around soufflé dish with at least 3 inches of strip extending over top of dish.

In cup, combine gelatin and water and let stand 5 minutes.

Place berries in food processor fitted with steel blade or blender and puree. Add gelatin mixture and process until well combined.

Transfer puree to microwavable bowl, and microwave on HIGH 2 to 3 minutes, stirring several times, to dissolve gelatin. Chill until mixture begins to thicken, about 30 minutes.

With electric mixer, beat egg whites until they hold soft peaks. Gradually add sugar, beating constantly, until whites are very stiff. In another bowl, whip cream. Gently fold berry mixture, meringue, and whipped cream together.

Spoon soufflé into prepared dish. Cover with plastic wrap and refrigerate or freeze.

To serve, remove paper collar. Garnish soufflé with additional whipped cream, Chocolate Curls, mint leaves, and berries, if desired. Serve with Chocolate Sauce.

ITALIAN CREAM

**MAKES
1 QUART**

■

Served with ginger
snaps or fresh fruit,
this light dessert is
good for parties or as
an addition to an after-
dinner fruit and cheese
assortment.

1 envelope unflavored gelatin
1/4 cup water
2 (8-ounce) packages cream
    cheese
1 stick (1/2 cup) unsalted butter,
    softened

1/2 cup sour cream
2/3 cup sifted confectioners' sugar
1 cup chopped walnuts
1 cup golden raisins
Grated zest of 2 lemons

In cup, combine gelatin and water and let stand several minutes.
Microwave on HIGH 20 to 30 seconds to dissolve gelatin.

Microwave cream cheese and butter in bowl on 70% power 1 to
2 minutes, or until softened. Transfer to food processor fitted with
steel blade.

Add gelatin mixture, sour cream, and confectioners' sugar and
process until smooth and well blended. Stir in walnuts, raisins, and
lemon zest. Pour into oiled 1-quart mold and chill. Unmold (see page
95) on a serving plate.

FRENCH VANILLA ICE CREAM

**MAKES
6 CUPS**

■

3/4 cup sugar
2 tablespoons all-purpose flour
1/8 teaspoon salt
1 (8-inch-long) vanilla bean, cut
    into 1/2-inch pieces, or 2
    teaspoons vanilla extract

2 cups half-and-half or milk
2 large eggs
2 cups heavy cream

In food processor or blender, combine sugar, flour, salt, and vanilla
bean pieces. Process until vanilla bean is finely chopped. (If using
vanilla extract, add later with heavy cream.)

Transfer mixture to 2-quart measure and beat in half-and-half.
Microwave on HIGH 5 to 6 minutes, or until slightly thickened, stirring several times.

Beat eggs in microwavable 2-quart bowl. Gradually add hot half-
and-half mixture, whisking constantly. Cook on 70% power 2 to 3
minutes, or until custard is just at a simmer. Cover tightly with
plastic wrap and chill, or place bowl in a larger bowl of ice water

and stir custard until it is cold. Stir in cream and vanilla extract, if using, and freeze in an ice cream maker, following manufacturer's instructions.

BANANA ICE CREAM

Omit vanilla bean and use 1 teaspoon vanilla extract. Add 2 cups mashed ripe bananas.

CHOCOLATE ICE CREAM

Add ½ to ¾ cup Dutch-process cocoa powder with sugar and flour. Omit vanilla bean and use 1 teaspoon vanilla extract instead.

FRENCH SILK

In 1- or 2-cup measure, microwave 6 ounces semisweet chocolate and 2 ounces unsweetened chocolate on 70% power 3 to 4 minutes, or until melted. Stir into hot custard. Add 1 cup toasted sliced almonds (page 441) to cream before freezing.

FRESH BERRY OR PEACH ICE CREAM

Add 2 to 3 cups cold berry or peach puree to chilled custard.

SPICE ICE CREAM

Omit vanilla bean and use 1 teaspoon vanilla extract. Add 1 (3-inch) cinnamon stick to half-and-half before microwaving. Add ½ teaspoon each ground cloves and freshly grated nutmeg to hot custard. Remove cinnamon stick before freezing ice cream.

> ■ ■ ■ ■ ■ ■ ■ ■ ■ ■ ■
> Ice cream terrines are made like a bombe but in a loaf pan that has been lined with plastic wrap. Strips of cake, fruit, or nuts may be layered in the terrine with the ice cream.
> ■ ■ ■ ■ ■ ■ ■ ■ ■ ■ ■

ICE CREAM BOMBE

An ice cream bombe is a combination of two or more flavors of ice cream or sherbet layered in a bowl or mold.

To soften the ice cream or sherbet to a workable consistency, microwave it at 10 to 40% power. Microwave 1 pint of ice cream on 40% power 15 to 30 seconds, or 1 quart of ice cream on 40% power 45 to 60 seconds. If the ice cream begins to melt before it softens, reduce the power level.

Spread the ice cream in a mold or bowl that has been oiled and then lined with plastic wrap. Freeze until hard, then make another layer. Freeze and repeat the process until the bombe is complete. Unmold and garnish with whipped cream or fresh fruit.

FRUIT

Fresh fruit is nutritious and never more delicious than when it is cooked in the microwave oven—except perhaps when it is fresh-picked. Unlike conventionally cooked fruit, which takes on a "cooked" flavor, fruit prepared in the microwave retains its fresh taste.

Fruits are usually microwaved covered so that they steam. Unless you are poaching in a flavored liquid, such as wine, there is no need to add liquid since the fruit can cook in its own juices.

CHUNKY APPLE SAUCE

MAKES ABOUT 2½ CUPS

•

6 cooking apples (Granny Smith, Golden Delicious, or Rome)

⅓ cup sugar
¼ teaspoon cinnamon (optional)

Peel and core apples. Cut into small chunks and place in 2-quart casserole. Cover and microwave on HIGH 7 to 9 minutes, stirring several times. Stir in sugar and microwave on HIGH 2 minutes more. Serve sprinkled with cinnamon, if desired.

CRANBERRY-STUFFED BAKED APPLES

4 SERVINGS

•

This festive-looking side dish, especially tasty served with pork or turkey, is also a comforting dessert.

4 Granny Smith apples
¼ cup whole cranberry sauce

2 tablespoons dark brown sugar
½ teaspoon cinnamon

Core each apple to within 1 inch of base. Combine cranberry sauce, brown sugar, and cinnamon and stuff each apple. Arrange apples evenly in a circle in 9-inch casserole, leaving space between apples. Cover tightly and microwave on HIGH 7 to 10 minutes, or until fork-tender.

SCRUMPTIOUS BAKED APPLES

½ cup sugar
½ teaspoon cinnamon
¼ teaspoon freshly grated nutmeg
1½ cups apple juice or 1 cup
  applejack and ½ cup water
6 cups apple slices (about 2½
  pounds; Rome preferred)

½ cup cake, cookie, or vanilla
  wafer crumbs
½ cup chopped dates or raisins
⅔ cup heavy cream
½ cup coarsely chopped walnuts

6 TO 8 SERVINGS

•

Cream makes this dish extra special. Serve as a dessert or a side dish.

• • • • • • • • • • •

When cooking apple slices, add sugar before cooking so that slices retain their shape.

• • • • • • • • • • •

Combine sugar, cinnamon, nutmeg, and apple juice in 2-cup measure. Microwave on HIGH 2 minutes, or until hot. Place apple slices in 2-quart casserole and pour apple juice mixture over them. Sprinkle with cake crumbs and dates.

Cover and microwave on HIGH 15 to 20 minutes, or until apples are tender, stirring midway through cooking. Stir in cream and top with walnuts. Serve warm.

BAKED MINCEMEAT APPLES

4 medium baking apples
1 cup mincemeat

2 tablespoons brandy
4 teaspoons butter

4 SERVINGS

•

Delicious and different as a light dessert.

Core unpeeled apples, taking care not to cut through to bottom. Combine and mix mincemeat and brandy and fill apple cavities. Top filling with a pat of butter.

Place apples in a circle on pie plate or in casserole and microwave on HIGH 8 to 12 minutes, or until apples are tender.

FRESH APPLESAUCE

MAKES
3 CUPS

∎

The flavor is wonderful!

2½ pounds cooking apples, peeled,
cored, and roughly chopped
(about 8 medium apples)

¼ cup water
¼ to ⅓ cup sugar

Combine apples, water, and sugar in casserole. Cover and microwave on HIGH 10 to 13 minutes, or until tender, stirring several times.

If you prefer a smooth sauce, puree apples in food processor or blender for a few seconds.

APRICOT RING MOLD

8 TO 10
SERVINGS

∎

∎∎∎∎∎∎∎∎∎∎∎

Remember to use the microwave when preparing your favorite gelatin salad or dessert. Simply microwave water or juice on HIGH until boiling (see timetable, page 422) and stir in flavored gelatin. If gelatin is slow to dissolve smoothly, microwave the liquid and gelatin on HIGH for 1 to 2 minutes, or until boiling.

∎∎∎∎∎∎∎∎∎∎∎

2 (3-ounce) packages apricot,
peach, or orange gelatin
1 (16-ounce) can apricot halves,
drained and pureed
¾ cup water
1 cup dry or sweet white wine

1 cup sour cream
Fresh fruit of choice: pineapple
chunks, sliced apples or pears,
strawberries, honeydew,
cantaloupe, and others

Combine gelatin, apricot puree, and water in 2-quart measure and microwave on HIGH 5 to 7 minutes, or until gelatin is dissolved.

Stir in wine and sour cream and beat until smooth. Pour mixture into oiled 6-cup ring mold and chill until set. Unmold and fill the center with fresh fruit.

BANANAS FOSTER

¹/₂ stick (¹/₄ cup) unsalted butter
¹/₂ cup, packed, light brown sugar
3 ripe bananas
1 tablespoon banana liqueur
    (optional)

2 to 4 tablespoons rum or brandy
French Vanilla Ice Cream or
    Banana Ice Cream (page 372)
¹/₂ cup chopped hazelnuts, toasted
    (page 441; optional)

4 TO 6
SERVINGS

▪

A showy but very easy dessert.

In 2-quart casserole microwave butter and sugar on HIGH 2 minutes. Stir, then cook on 50% power 4 minutes, or until caramelized.

Halve bananas lengthwise, then cut into thirds. Stir bananas into caramelized mixture, cover, and cook on HIGH 2 to 3 minutes. Stir in liqueur, if desired. Pour rum or brandy over the bananas, but do not stir. Bring casserole to dining table along with bowls of ice cream. Flame banana mixture and, with long-handled ladle, spoon flaming bananas and sauce over ice cream. Sprinkle with nuts, if desired.

GLAZED ORANGES

³/₄ cup fresh orange juice
1 teaspoon grated orange zest
3 tablespoons sugar
1 tablespoon cornstarch

¹/₄ cup orange liqueur or brandy
4 large navel oranges, peeled and
    sliced

4 TO 6
SERVINGS

▪

Serve as a dessert or a side dish. Especially good with pork or chicken.

Combine juice, zest, sugar, cornstarch, and liqueur in 1-quart measure. Microwave on HIGH 3 to 4 minutes, stirring several times.

Place sliced oranges in serving dish and pour orange mixture over them. Chill.

PEACH MELBA

6 TO 8 SERVINGS

▪

This is an adaptation of *Pêches Melba*, which was created by Georges Auguste Escoffier to honor Dame Nellie Melba for her outstanding operatic performances.

1 cup water
1/2 cup sugar
1/2 teaspoon vanilla extract
4 peaches, peeled, halved, and
    pitted

French Vanilla Ice Cream (page
    372)
Fresh Berry Sauce (page 384)

Combine water, sugar, and vanilla in a shallow 2-quart casserole. Microwave on HIGH 2 minutes to dissolve sugar. Place peach halves, cut side down, in syrup. Cover tightly with plastic wrap and microwave on HIGH 5 to 7 minutes, or until the peaches are just hot and tender, rearranging fruit halfway through cooking. Let peaches cool, covered, in syrup.

To serve, spoon ice cream into chilled shallow dessert dishes. Place a peach half, cut side down, in center of each dish and drizzle with Fresh Berry Sauce.

POACHED PEACHES
Serve poached peaches splashed with raspberry or blueberry liqueur, amaretto, or champagne.

POACHED FRUIT

Although fresh fruits are delicious raw, poaching offers a way to serve a nutritious warm dessert during the winter, or when fresh fruit is hard, underripe, or not very flavorful. Fruits can be poached in a wine, sugar, or fruit juice syrup. The sugar in the syrup renders the fruit soft, but not mushy, and, at the same time the flavor of the syrup is infused into the fruit.

Serve the fruit standing in a pool of custard sauce, pureed raspberries, or chocolate sauce, or garnish with whipped cream, *crème fraîche*, or ice cream.

POACHED PEARS OR APPLES

4 firm ripe pears or apples
Fresh lemon juice
2 cups water
1¼ cups sugar

¼ teaspoon anise seeds (optional)
1 teaspoon vanilla extract or 1
    (3-inch) cinnamon stick
Zest of 1 lemon

4 SERVINGS

■

Peel fruit, leaving stems intact and cutting thin slices from bases so that fruit will stand upright. Coat fruit with lemon juice to prevent discoloration.

Combine water, sugar, anise seeds, if desired, vanilla, and lemon zest in 1-quart measure and microwave on HIGH 5 minutes. Stir to be sure sugar is dissolved.

Place fruit in a plastic cooking bag. Pour hot syrup over fruit and secure top of bag, pressing out air so that fruit is immersed in syrup. (If a plastic cooking bag is not available, use a pie plate covered with plastic wrap. Place fruit in a circle with large ends toward perimeter of dish.) Microwave on HIGH 8 to 10 minutes, or until fruit is fork-tender.

Serve fruit with the syrup at room temperature or chilled. Poached fruit and syrup can be stored in refrigerator for several days and reheated in the microwave, if desired.

FRUIT FOOL
Puree leftover poached fruit and swirl with sweetened whipped cream. Chill and serve.

PEARS À LA RELIGIEUSE
Prepare Poached Pears and let cool in syrup. Remove pears from syrup and blot with paper towel to dry. Pour Chocolate Glaze (page 322) over pears to completely coat them. Chill. Serve garnished with whipped cream or standing in a pool of Fresh Berry Sauce (page 384) made with raspberries.

PEARS ALMA
Serve pears sprinkled with Praline Powder (page 382) and garnished with whipped cream. Stand pears in a small pool of Chocolate Sauce (page 385).

RUBY-RED POACHED PEARS OR APPLES
Substitute red wine or cranberry juice for the water.

Make a spur-of-the-moment dessert sauce: At serving time, microwave ice cream on 30% power until softened but not melted. Blend in liqueur to taste. Some flavor combinations you might want to try: Chocolate ice cream and Kahlúa; vanilla ice cream and Amaretto served over peaches.

PEAR CRISP

4 SERVINGS

•

Serve with pork or chicken.

4 cups peeled, cored, and sliced
    pears (about 1 ½ pounds
    Anjou or Bosc)
¾ cup, packed, brown sugar
⅔ cup all-purpose flour

¾ cup quick-cooking oats
1 teaspoon cinnamon
¼ teaspoon ground cloves
1 stick (½ cup) unsalted butter

Place pears in bottom of 9-inch pie plate or 1½-quart casserole. In bowl, combine sugar, flour, oats, cinnamon, cloves, and butter. Mix with your fingers until mixture is crumbly. Sprinkle over fruit. Microwave on HIGH 8 to 10 minutes, or until topping is bubbly.

SHERRIED FRUIT

**6 TO 8
SERVINGS**

•

A savory dish to accompany meat and oh, so quick!

¼ cup sherry
½ cup sugar
1 (16-ounce) can black cherries,
    drained

1 (20-ounce) can pineapple
    chunks, drained
1 (16-ounce) can sliced peaches,
    undrained
1 cup pitted prunes

Combine sherry, sugar, cherries, pineapple, peaches, and prunes in a 2-quart casserole and microwave on 70% power 8 to 10 minutes, stirring once.

VARIATION
Add 1 teaspoon curry powder to fruit and omit sherry.

PORT WINE SHERBET

1 quart water
1 cup sugar
1 tablespoon grated lemon zest

1 teaspoon vanilla extract
2 cups port wine

10 SERVINGS

.

Serve with fresh fruit: melons, berries, and grapes are good choices.

In 2-quart measure, microwave water and sugar on HIGH 5 to 8 minutes, or until boiling. Add lemon zest and vanilla and microwave on HIGH 3 minutes longer. Cool. Stir in port and chill.

Freeze mixture in an ice cream freezer, following manufacturer's instructions. If an ice cream freezer is not available, pour mixture into shallow dish and freeze several hours, or until ice crystals form. Beat with electric mixer or in food processor and return to freezer until firm.

FROZEN DUTCH APPLE CUSTARD

$1/3$ cup, packed, light brown sugar
$1/4$ teaspoon cinnamon
3 apples, peeled, cored, and
    chopped
$1/4$ cup golden raisins (optional)

3 tablespoons dark rum
1 quart French Vanilla Ice Cream
    (page 372)
$2/3$ cup chopped walnuts, toasted
    (page 441)

4 TO 6
SERVINGS

.

An apple, rum, and raisin frozen dessert that can be formed in a terrine or bombe or scooped into dessert dishes.

In 2-quart bowl, combine sugar, cinnamon, apples, and raisins. Cover and microwave on HIGH 3 to 5 minutes, or until apples are tender. Add rum and cool.

If ice cream is hard, soften by microwaving on 40% power 30 to 45 seconds. Add ice cream and nuts to apple mixture and combine well. Freeze until firm.

ICE CREAM PIE
Pour Frozen Dutch Apple Custard into a Graham Cracker Crust (page 304) and freeze.

CRÈME DE MENTHE ICE CREAM

**MAKES
2 QUARTS**

▪

A refreshing light dessert.

¹/₄ to ¹/₂ cup crème de menthe
1 quart vanilla or chocolate chip
*   ice cream*
1 pint pineapple sherbet

1 pint lime sherbet
2 to 3 drops green food coloring
*   (optional)*

In 1-cup measure, microwave crème de menthe on HIGH 1 minute to evaporate alcohol. Cool.

In bowl, microwave ice cream and sherbet on 40% power 45 to 60 seconds to soften. Blend in crème de menthe and, if desired, food coloring. Transfer to storage container, cover, and freeze.

PRALINE POWDER

**MAKES
ABOUT
1 CUP**

▪

One of the most useful dessert condiments, Praline Powder is used as a garnish or to flavor whipped cream, buttercream, ice cream, or fillings.

1 cup sugar
¹/₂ cup water

1 cup blanched almonds,
*   hazelnuts, or pecans, toasted*
*   (page 441)*

Combine sugar and water in 1-quart measure. Cover tightly with plastic wrap and microwave on HIGH 8 to 12 minutes, or until syrup is golden. Watch closely after first 8 minutes to prevent burning.

Spread toasted nuts on oiled baking sheet and pour syrup over them. Let cool. When hard, break praline into small pieces and place in food processor. Process to a fine powder. Store in airtight container until ready to use.

CARAMEL DOME

1 cup sugar   *½ cup water*

Combine sugar and water in 2-cup measure. Cover tightly with plastic wrap and microwave on HIGH 8 to 12 minutes, or until syrup is caramel colored. Watch very carefully after first 5 minutes to prevent burning; once syrup begins to change color, it caramelizes very quickly and burns easily.

To form individual domes, hold an inverted ladle (dome side up) over cup of caramel or over a dish (or, using tongs, invert a metal measuring cup over caramel). Dip a fork into hot caramel and drizzle caramel over back of ladle or metal cup. Working quickly, continue to drizzle the syrup over ladle in a lacy pattern until the nest looks substantial enough to hold its shape.

Gently pop the caramel from the ladle. Repeat until you have made 6 caramel cages. If caramel in measure becomes too hard before you finish, microwave it 15 to 20 seconds to liquefy it again. Store cages in tightly covered container until ready to use.

To form a large dome, use back of a metal mixing bowl.

CARAMEL DISK OR WEDGES
Pour hot caramel syrup into an oiled pie pan or foil form and let stand 15 to 20 seconds. Score surface into wedges where dessert will be sliced. Use entire disk as finishing garnish for a cake, or break wedges apart and stick them into icing of a cake.

ENOUGH FOR 1 LARGE DOME OR 6 INDIVIDUAL DOMES

•

The caramel dome makes an especially impressive presentation. A webbed cage of hardened caramel, it can be made large enough to crown an entire dessert or more manageable, smaller "nests" can be shaped to encase individual servings of custard or ice cream.

TANGY LEMON SAUCE

1 stick (½ cup) unsalted butter   *2 tablespoons water*
1 cup sugar   *1 tablespoon grated lemon zest*
3 tablespoons fresh lemon juice   *2 large eggs, beaten*

Place butter, sugar, lemon juice, and water in 1-quart bowl and microwave on HIGH 2 to 3 minutes, or until butter is melted and sugar is dissolved. Stir in lemon zest and eggs. Cook on 50% power 3 to 5 minutes, or until thickened.

MAKES 1½ CUPS

•

Delightful served warm over gingerbread.

FRESH BERRY SAUCE

**MAKES
1½ CUPS**

•

Use blueberries, strawberries, blackberries, or raspberries, whatever is in season. Serve over fresh fruit, cake, or ice cream for a quick dessert.

2 cups fresh berries
½ to ⅔ cup sugar

4 teaspoons cornstarch

Place berries, sugar, and cornstarch in food processor or blender and process into smooth puree. Transfer mixture to 1-quart measure and microwave on HIGH 4 to 6 minutes, or until slightly thickened. Cool to room temperature before serving.

BUTTERSCOTCH SAUCE

**MAKES
2 CUPS**

•

½ cup, packed, light brown sugar
½ cup, packed, dark brown sugar
*1 cup maple syrup or maple-
   flavored pancake syrup*

½ teaspoon salt
⅓ cup unsalted butter
2 teaspoons vanilla
⅔ cup heavy cream

Combine sugars, syrup, and salt in 2-quart measure. Cover tightly with plastic wrap and microwave on 70% power 3 to 4 minutes, or until sugar is dissolved, stirring halfway through cooking. Stir again and microwave, uncovered, on HIGH 2 to 3 minutes, or until syrup starts to thicken. Add butter, vanilla, and cream and stir until well blended. Microwave on HIGH 1 to 2 minutes, or until creamy. Serve warm over cake or ice cream.

PRALINE SAUCE
Add 2 to 4 tablespoons bourbon and ½ to ¾ cup chopped pecans with butter, vanilla, and cream.

CHOCOLATE SAUCE

6 ounces semisweet chocolate
　chips
1 ounce unsweetened chocolate
½ teaspoon instant coffee powder
¾ cup heavy cream

2 tablespoons light rum (optional)
2 tablespoons unsalted butter
Milk (optional)

**MAKES
1⅓ CUPS**

■

Delicious over ice
cream, sundaes, or
soufflés.

Place semisweet and unsweetened chocolate in 2-quart bowl and microwave on 70% power 2 to 3 minutse or until melted. Slowly stir in the instant coffee and cream, then add rum, if desired, and butter. Serve warm.

For thinner sauce, blend in a little milk. This sauce may be made ahead and refrigerated. To reheat, microwave on 50% power 1 to 3 minutes.

HOT FUDGE SAUCE

1 stick (½ cup) unsalted butter
1½ cups sugar
½ cup Dutch-process cocoa
　powder

2 ounces unsweetened chocolate
1 cup heavy cream
2 teaspoons vanilla extract

**MAKES
3 CUPS**

■

A good sauce for choc-
olate lovers!

In 1½- or 2-quart bowl, combine butter, sugar, cocoa, and unsweetened chocolate. Microwave on HIGH 2 to 3 minutes to melt chocolate. Stir. Add cream and vanilla, stirring to blend, and microwave on HIGH 3 to 4 minutes longer. To reheat, microwave on 50% power 1 to 3 minutes.

■ ■ ■ ■ ■ ■ ■ ■ ■ ■ ■

Melted milk chocolate
makes a quick dessert
topping. Microwave 6
ounces milk chocolate
on 50% power 2 to 3
minutes. Stir until
smooth.

■ ■ ■ ■ ■ ■ ■ ■ ■ ■ ■

MOCHA FUDGE TOPPING

**MAKES
2¾ CUPS**

■

4 ounces semisweet chocolate
⅔ cup sugar
1 cup heavy cream

¼ cup coffee liqueur
1 stick (½ cup) unsalted butter,
    cut into chunks

Place chocolate, sugar, cream, liqueur, and butter in 2-quart measure and microwave on HIGH 4 to 5 minutes, or until chocolate and butter are melted and sauce is very hot. Stir halfway through cooking. Microwave on 50% power 2 to 3 minutes, then beat with whisk 2 to 3 minutes. Serve warm or at room temperature over ice cream or cake.

DATE-NUT SAUCE

**MAKES
1½ CUPS**

■

Serve with vanilla, chocolate, or coffee ice cream.

1 cup, packed, light brown sugar
½ cup water
4 ounces pitted dates, chopped
    (about 1 cup)

2 to 3 tablespoons brandy
½ cup chopped walnuts or pecans
Pinch of freshly grated nutmeg

Place sugar and water in 1-quart measure and stir. Cover tightly and microwave on HIGH 1 to 2 minutes to dissolve sugar. Stir and cook on 70% power 3 to 4 minutes, or until slightly thickened. Stir in dates, brandy, nuts, and nutmeg.

Candy

Homemade candies are almost always tastier and less costly than those made commercially. Using the microwave oven, you can give new life to old family recipes, even if you're a novice candy-maker.

The winter holiday season is our favorite time for making candy for family and friends. It is true that a few basic skills are necessary. The most important one—knowing how to judge when a syrup has reached a particular stage of doneness—can be acquired only with practical experience. But because the microwave oven eliminates the most troublesome pitfalls in candy-making—burning and scorching—we have come to expect success with every attempt.

Candy supplies—items such as coating chocolate, flavoring oils, candy-dipping tools, molds, and other equipment and ingredients—are sold through mail order sources, some discount department stores, specialty food stores, and some supermarkets.

Convenience ingredients, such as sweetened condensed milk, marshmallows, and caramel candies, have made some candies simply a matter of melting ingredients together. We have included recipes for a wide variety of these candies that give foolproof results in a minimum of time.

Also included are such old-fashioned favorites as divinity, penuche, taffy, lollipops, and brittles. These must be cooked to precisely the correct temperature, whether conventional or microwave cooking is used. Good results are hindered by either undercooking or overcooking. Although the microwave makes the job much easier, the ability to estimate doneness (see box, opposite) is the secret for both conventional and microwave success.

About Candy-Making

SUGAR CRYSTALS

In conventional rangetop candy-making, sugar crystals, which can cause syrup to turn granular, sometimes form on the sides of the saucepan. To prevent the formation of crystals, the sides of the saucepan must be swabbed often with a brush that has been dipped in cold water.

This tedious procedure is unnecessary in microwaving. Since there is no heat source, and the cooking container gets hot only by conduction of heat from the candy itself, crystallization is rarely a problem.

SUGAR SYRUPS

There are two methods for testing sugar syrup doneness. To assure success, use both methods.

TEMPERATURE TEST

A microwave candy thermometer, made especially for use in the microwave oven, can be left in the dish during cooking.

A regular candy thermometer, while it cannot be used in the microwave oven when the oven is in operation, can be placed in the candy syrup after microwaving is stopped. Make sure the thermometer doesn't touch the side or bottom of the dish. Check the temperature after the minimum suggested cooking time. It will take 1 to 2 minutes to get an accurate reading. Remove the thermometer and microwave longer if needed.

COLD-WATER TEST

Fill a custard cup with ice water, drop several drops (up to ½ teaspoon) of the boiling candy syrup into the water. Lift the ball of candy from the water with your fingers and determine its consistency and stage of doneness following the chart below.

TESTING SUGAR SYRUP FOR DONENESS		
TYPE OF CANDY	**STAGE OF COOKING TESTED IN COLD WATER**	**DEGREES ON CANDY THERMOMETER AT SEA LEVEL**
Fudge, fondant, penuche, pralines	Soft-ball (can be picked up but flattens)	234 to 240° F.
Caramels	Firm-ball (holds shape unless pressed)	242 to 248° F.
Divinity, taffy, caramel corn, marshmallows, nougats	Hard-ball (holds shape though pliable)	250 to 268° F.
Butterscotch, English toffee	Soft-crack (separates into hard but not brittle threads)	270 to 290° F.
Brittles, hard candies	Hard-crack (separates into hard, brittle threads)	300 to 310° F.

Corn syrup, which acts as an "interfering agent" in the prevention of sugar crystals, is called for in many candy recipes.

WEATHER

The weather affects both conventional and microwave candy-making. A dry, cool day offers the best conditions. Candy-making on a rainy day is risky. However, if you must make candy on a rainy day, you may want to cook it a little longer than you normally would to compensate for the extra moisture in the atmosphere.

COOKING CONTAINER

Choose a microwave cooking container that can withstand high temperatures and is two to three times the volume of the candy. A 2-quart measure is ideal. Candy syrups boil higher in the microwave than on the conventional rangetop, and there should be sufficient space in the dish so that the syrup doesn't boil over. Although microwaves do not heat the container, candy syrups are so much hotter than boiling temperature that a lot of heat is conducted from the hot syrup to the container. Use thick pot holders when handling the container and be *very* careful when lifting the plastic wrap used as covering.

STORAGE

Candies should be stored in airtight containers. Fudge, fondants, penuche, and pralines will dry out if left uncovered, while hard candies such as brittle and lollipops will absorb moisture and become soft and sticky. Store these two types of candies separately.

CHOCOLATE

From mild, creamy milk chocolate, to intense bittersweet truffles, there is a chocolate to suit every taste. Fortunately, it is now possible to buy many kinds of chocolate in supermarkets across the country.

Other substances, such as white chocolate, chocolate coating (also known as confectioners' candy coating, summer coating, or compound coating), and other commercial products, are not real chocolate. These substitutes are available in retail and discount department stores and through mail order sources as well.

True chocolates differ widely in flavor, texture, and other culinary properties depending on how much pure chocolate (chocolate solids), cocoa butterfat, milkfat, and sugar, among other ingredients, they contain. Some differences are attributable to national origin:

- **Belgian chocolate,** which is typically a very fine chocolate, usually has a high cocoa butter content and is darker and less sweet than chocolates from other countries. It melts into a very smooth liquid and is an excellent choice for dipping.

390

- **French chocolate** is a little grainier and sweeter than Belgian.
- **Swiss chocolate** is rich and smooth. It is a little sweeter and milder than Belgian.
- **Mexican chocolate** is lower in cocoa butter and is sweeter than all of the European chocolates.
- **American chocolate** is generally sweet and mild, but varies greatly from one manufacturer to another.

TYPES OF CHOCOLATE

- **Unsweetened chocolate,** also known as baking chocolate, is composed of chocolate and cocoa butter. It gives the purest chocolate flavor and is used primarily for baking. Because it is very fluid when melted, it can be piped easily into very thin scrolls and other designs.
- **Bittersweet and semisweet chocolate** must contain at least 35% pure chocolate. Bittersweet is mildly sweetened and semisweet a little more heavily sweetened. The manufacturer may add additional cocoa butter, sugar, and flavorings. These chocolates are ideal for decorative use, baking, and eating.
- **Sweet baking chocolate,** also known as German chocolate, must contain at least 35% pure chocolate. It is more heavily sweetened than semisweet.
- **Milk chocolate** is similar in taste and texture to sweet baking chocolate but contains only 1% pure chocolate, at least 12% milk solids and over 3.5% milkfat. Milk chocolate does not work well for dipping.
- **White cocoa butter coating (white chocolate)** is actually not a chocolate because it contains no chocolate solids although it does contain cocoa butter. It is sweeter and more heat-sensitive than chocolate.
- **Summer coating,** confectioners' candy coating, or compound coating is not chocolate at all, but is made from artificially flavored vegetable fat. These are more manageable than real chocolate for the novice to use at home to produce molded chocolates and confections.

STORING CHOCOLATE

Wrap chocolate in a moisture- and vaporproof covering because it can absorb odors as well as moisture; white chocolate is especially vulnerable. Exposure to prolonged light can also deteriorate white chocolate.

Store chocolate in a cool, dry place in a tightly closed container. Never freeze or refrigerate chocolate because it could easily absorb moisture, which would prevent it from melting properly. Chocolate that is stored for a long period of time can become dry;

although it does not melt as well, it may still be used, especially with the addition of a little vegetable oil to soften the texture. Storage at too high a temperature can cause some of the cocoa butter crystals to melt and rise to the surface, producing a gray so-called bloom. Bloom does not affect the quality of the chocolate, only its appearance.

Chocolate is a cool-weather ingredient. The room temperature should be no higher than 65° F., and 60° F. is preferred when dipping or molding chocolates. There should be no steam in the room.

MELTING CHOCOLATE

The microwave is unquestionably the best way to melt chocolate for cooking and candy-making.

1. Chips or chopped chocolate melt faster and more evenly than a solid block. Quantities larger than 2 ounces should be chopped, either with a large, heavy knife or in the food processor. One-ounce pieces of unsweetened chocolate can be placed on a plate or in a cup and melted in their paper wrapping.

2. Place chocolate in a glass measure or on a plate. Never cover chocolate when melting it because steam condensation on the bottom of the covering can fall into the chocolate and cause it to become stiff and grainy. Even a drop of moisture can have this effect.

3. For best results, melt imported chocolate, milk chocolate, white chocolate, and flavored chips, such as butterscotch chips, on 50% power. Semisweet and bittersweet chocolate can usually be melted successfully on 70% power, but if your microwave cooks unevenly, use 50% power for these chocolates as well.

4. Fully melted chocolate continues to hold its shape but will become soft and shiny. Stir the chocolate to pourable consistency.

TIMETABLE FOR MELTING CHOCOLATE		
CHOCOLATE	AMOUNT	MICROWAVING TIME
Unsweetened, bittersweet, or semisweet	1 to 4 ounces	2 to 3 minutes on 70% power
	4 to 8 ounces	3 to 4 minutes on 70% power
Milk chocolate or white chocolate	1 to 4 ounces	2 to 3 minutes on 50% power
	4 to 8 ounces	3 to 5 minutes on 50% power

DIPPING CHOCOLATE

Many candies and confections are finished with a chocolate coating. For the home cook, there are two alternatives:

- **Chocolate coating** (see page 391), available in white, pastel, and dark wafers, is easier to use than real chocolate for dipping candies. Place 10 ounces of the coating in a 1-quart bowl or glass measure and microwave on 50% power 3 to 4 minutes. This will yield enough chocolate to dip 25 to 30 candy centers.
- **Real chocolate,** which requires more care and handling than coating chocolate, must be tempered before it can be used for dipping, but it certainly tastes far better. Tempering—the heating, cooling, and reheating of chocolate —helps the chocolate "set up" when it is used as a coating. The microwave oven and a microwave food sensor or thermometer make tempering chocolate easy.

Bittersweet and unsweetened chocolate are good for dipping, as is a combination of 12 ounces of semisweet and 1 ounce of unsweetened chocolate, which makes a rich but not too sweet coating, best used with a nonchocolate center.

TO TEMPER CHOCOLATE

Place 12 to 16 ounces dark chocolate chips or grated chocolate in a 1-quart glass measure and microwave on 70% power (use 50% power for white chocolate) for 3 or 4 minutes, or until the chocolate registers 115 to 120° F. (If your oven cooks unevenly, use 50% power and cook for 4 to 6 minutes.) Watch carefully after the temperature rises above 100° F. and do not allow chocolate to burn.

Remove chocolate from oven and allow to cool to: 85° F. for white chocolate; 80° F. for dark chocolate; and 78° F. for milk chocolate. Microwave it again to 115° F., or until it is the consistency of thick icing. Tempered chocolate sets quickly and has a shiny finish. Allow 1 pound of chocolate to dip 1 pound of candy centers, or 40 to 50 pieces, depending on the size of the centers and the temperature of the dipping chocolate.

Using a candy-dipping tool or a two-pronged fork, lower a piece of candy, or the candy center, into the chocolate, turning it to coat evenly. Lift candy, shaking excess chocolate back into measure, and place on wax paper to dry.

Before they dry, decorate dipped candies with finely chopped nuts, cookie crumbs, candied fruit, nut halves, or other garnishes. To "thread" dipped candies, drizzle them with fine lines in a contrasting color.

CHOCOLATE DESSERT CUPS

**MAKES
4 CHOCOLATE
CUPS**

▪

Since chocolate must be stored at room temperature, it's best to make these charming confections in cool weather.

6 ounces semisweet chocolate chips
Ice cream, White Chocolate Mousse (page 366), or Chocolate Praline Mousse (page 367)

Chocolate Curls (recipe below)

In 1-quart measure, microwave chocolate on 70% power 2 to 3 minutes, or until melted. Stir. While chocolate is still warm, brush onto bottom and sides of 2½-inch foil baking cups, building up a layer of about ⅛ inch in each cup. Place cups in muffin tins so they will retain their shape. Chill a few minutes, just until firm. Store at cool room temperature in tightly covered containers up to 3 months.

To serve, peel foil from chocolate, fill cups with ice cream, and garnish with Chocolate Curls.

MINIATURE CHOCOLATE CUPS

Brush inside of 8 to 12 foil bonbon cups with melted semisweet chocolate, making a layer ⅛ inch thick. Chill a few minutes until hardened and peel off foil. Store at cool room temperature in tightly covered containers up to 3 months.

To serve, fill with whipped cream and serve with after-dinner coffee. Delicious when cream-filled cup is dropped into a cup of hot coffee and stirred.

CHOCOLATE SHELLS

Coat inside of 4 scallop shells with ⅛-inch layer of melted semisweet chocolate. Chill or freeze for 5 minutes to harden chocolate. Press shell to release chocolate. Store at cool room temperature in tightly covered container up to 3 months.

To serve, fill one shell with buttercream, ice cream, or mousse, then top with a second shell, if desired.

CHOCOLATE CURLS

Place sheet of wax paper on baking sheet. Pour melted chocolate on paper and, with spatula, spread into rectangle ⅛ inch thick. Place in refrigerator until set but not hard, about 10 minutes. With sharp long-bladed knife, scrape chocolate off paper so that it rolls over onto itself into long, luxurious curls. Store at cool room temperature in tightly covered container up to 3 months.

To make short curls, microwave 1 square semisweet chocolate in wrapper on HIGH about 10 to 15 seconds to slightly soften surface. Scrape vegetable peeler across top of square scraping chocolate into short curls.

CHOCOLATE RASPBERRY TRUFFLES

8 ounces bittersweet or semisweet
    chocolate, chopped
1 large egg, beaten
1/3 cup strained red raspberry jam
1 tablespoon Chambord (black
    raspberry liqueur), or to taste

1 1/2 sticks (3/4 cup) unsalted butter
3/4 cup Dutch-process cocoa
    powder

**MAKES
24 CANDIES**

∎

The ultimate chocolate!

In 2-quart measure, microwave chocolate on 70% power 3 to 4 minutes, or until it is shiny and melted. Stir in egg and then jam and liqueur. Let mixture stand 1 minute to cool slightly.

If butter is hard, microwave on 20% power 1 minute to soften. Place chocolate in food processor and process, adding butter a chunk at a time. Beat until all butter is added and mixture is smooth. Chill 2 to 3 hours, or until firm.

Mixture may be made ahead to this point and frozen 1 to 2 months. Microwave frozen mixture on 20 to 30% power several minutes to soften slightly.

Form mixture into balls and roll in cocoa powder. Truffles will keep in airtight container in refrigerator up to 2 weeks.

CAPPUCCINO TRUFFLES
Substitute strained orange marmalade for raspberry jam and use 3 tablespoons coffee liqueur instead of Chambord.

IRISH CREAM TRUFFLES

**MAKES
36 TO 48
CANDIES**

•

A wee bit of heaven!

8 ounces white chocolate, grated
4 ounces milk chocolate chips
3 egg yolks
1/3 cup Irish cream liqueur
1 tablespoon Irish whiskey (or Scotch)

1 teaspoon coconut flavoring
1 1/2 sticks (3/4 cup) unsalted butter, softened
Dipping chocolate (page 393; a combination of half white and half dark)

Microwave white and milk chocolates in 2-quart measure on 50% power 3 to 4 minutes, or until shiny and melted. Stir until smooth. Stir in egg yolks, then liqueur and whiskey. Microwave on 50% power 1 minute to thicken.

Transfer mixture to food processor or mixer and beat. With motor running, add coconut flavoring and then butter, 1 tablespoon at a time. Process 2 to 3 minutes longer; mixture should be very thick. Drop by tablespoonfuls on a baking sheet and chill. (Truffle centers may be frozen for 4 to 6 weeks before dipping them.)

Form mixture into balls. Microwave the white and dark dipping chocolate together on 50% power until melted (3 to 4 minutes per pound). Dip balls into the melted chocolate coating and place on wax paper to dry. Truffles will keep in tightly covered container in refrigerator up to 2 weeks.

BRANDY ALEXANDER TRUFFLES
Substitute brandy for the Irish whiskey and omit coconut flavoring.

CRÈME DE MENTHE TRUFFLES
Substitute crème de menthe for the Irish cream liqueur and dip truffles in white dipping chocolate that has been tinted pale green.

PEACH TRUFFLES

10 ounces white chocolate
2 large eggs, beaten
1 (3-ounce) package peach-
 flavored gelatin
2 to 4 tablespoons peach liqueur
 or schnapps

2 sticks (1 cup) unsalted butter,
 softened
White dipping chocolate (page
 393)
Food coloring

**MAKES
36 TO 48
CANDIES**

•

White chocolate fruit-
flavored centers are
dipped into tinted white
chocolate! They're
often called summer
truffles because of
their cool, inviting pas-
tel colors. This fresh,
peach-flavored version
is reminiscent of Geor-
gia peaches in the
summer.

Microwave white chocolate in 2-quart measure on 50% power 3 to 4 minutes, or until melted. Stir in eggs, gelatin, and liqueur. Microwave on 70% power 2 minutes, stirring after 1 minute.

Transfer mixture to food processor or mixer and beat for 2 to 3 minutes, adding butter 1 tablespoon at a time.

Drop mixture by tablespoonfuls onto a baking sheet and chill. Form into balls, return to baking sheet, and chill in freezer 10 to 15 minutes. (The truffle centers may be stored in a plastic bag for 4 to 6 weeks before dipping.)

Dip truffles in melted white chocolate to which drops of red and yellow food coloring have been added to make a peach color. Place truffles on wax paper to harden.

VARIATIONS

Substitute other gelatin flavors and coordinating liqueurs. Tint white dipping chocolate with food coloring to suggest that flavor. Some suggestions are:

CHERRY TRUFFLES

Cherry-flavored gelatin, cherry liqueur; dip in dark tempered chocolate.

GRAND MARNIER TRUFFLES

Orange-flavored gelatin; Grand Marnier or Triple Sec; pale-orange white chocolate threaded with dark chocolate.

RASPBERRY TRUFFLES

Raspberry-flavored gelatin; Chambord or raspberry liqueur; dip in dark tempered chocolate

STRAWBERRY TRUFFLES

Strawberry-flavored gelatin; strawberry liqueur; dip in pink white chocolate

TRUFFLES AU PRALINE

**MAKES
36 CANDIES**

This is a candy of distinction. The centers may be frozen up to 2 months before dipping, or store them in an airtight container in the refrigerator up to 2 weeks.

12 ounces milk chocolate, chopped
2 large eggs, beaten
1/3 cup praline liqueur
1 stick (1/2 cup) unsalted butter (no substitute)

1 pound semisweet dipping chocolate
Praline Powder (page 382; optional)

In 1-quart measure, microwave chocolate on 50% power 3 to 4 minutes, or until shiny and melted. Stir until smooth. Stir in the eggs, then beat in liqueur. Transfer chocolate mixture to food processor or mixer.

If butter is hard, microwave on 10 to 30% power 1 to 3 minutes to soften, but not melt. With processor motor running, add butter to chocolate one chunk at a time until all butter is added.

Turn truffle mixture into a bowl and chill for several hours, or until firm. Form into balls, place on baking sheet, and chill.

In 1-quart measure, microwave chocolate coating on 70% power 3 to 4 minutes, or until melted. Dip truffles into chocolate coating, place on wax paper, and let dry until chocolate is almost firm. Roll in Praline Powder, if desired.

CHOCOLATE MOUNDS

**MAKES
60 TO 72
CANDIES**

2/3 cup evaporated milk
1 cup granulated sugar
1 teaspoon vanilla extract
2 (14-ounce) packages shredded coconut
1 (7-ounce) jar marshmallow cream

1 1/2 pounds confectioners' sugar, sifted
1 1/2 pounds semisweet chocolate coating

Combine milk, granulated sugar, and vanilla in a 2-quart measure and microwave on HIGH 5 to 6 minutes, or to hard-ball stage (250 to 260° F.), stirring halfway through cooking. Stir in coconut, marshmallow cream, and confectioners' sugar. When mixture is cool enough to handle, shape into patties, place on baking sheets, and freeze overnight.

Microwave chocolate in 2-quart measure on 70% power 3 to 5 minutes to melt. Using a fork or toothpick, dip frozen patties into the chocolate, let excess chocolate drip back into measure, and place candy on wax paper to dry.

VARIATION

Of course, a toasted almond pressed into the pattie before it is frozen is good, too.

CHOCOLATE-COVERED EASTER EGGS

3 cups granulated sugar
¾ cup light corn syrup
½ cup water
2 egg whites
1 teaspoon flavoring extract
(vanilla, raspberry,
strawberry, or others)

Confectioners' sugar
1 pound dipping chocolate (page
393)

MAKES
24 CANDIES

▪

Combine granulated sugar, corn syrup, and water in 2-quart measure. Cover with plastic wrap and microwave on 70% power 6 to 7 minutes, or until sugar is dissolved. Stir, rotating measure to mix into syrup any sugar or crystals on side of bowl. Microwave on 70% power 8 to 10 minutes, or to firm-ball stage (245° F.).

Meanwhile, with electric mixer beat egg whites until stiff peaks form. Gradually add hot syrup, beating constantly. Add flavoring and beat until mixture holds its shape and is very stiff, 5 to 10 minutes.

Let mixture stand until cool enough to handle, 20 to 30 minutes. Dust your hands with confectioners' sugar and form candy into egg shapes (or any other shape that pleases you) and place on baking sheet. Chill until firm.

Dip candies in dipping chocolate. Store in refrigerator in tightly covered container up to 5 days.

SPONGE CANDY

MAKES
1 POUND
CANDY

1 cup sugar
1 cup light or dark corn syrup
1 tablespoon cider vinegar

1 tablespoon baking soda
1 pound dipping chocolate (page
393; optional)

Line 8-inch square dish with foil and oil it.
Combine sugar, corn syrup, and vinegar in 2-quart measure and microwave on HIGH 3 minutes. Stir and microwave on HIGH 5 to 10 minutes, or to hard-crack stage (300° F.).

Stir in baking soda and, while mixture is still foaming, pour into prepared dish. Let mixture stand. When candy begins to harden, score it into squares with buttered knife. Let cool completely, then break apart along scored lines.

Candies may be dipped in chocolate, if desired.

BUCKEYES

MAKES
ABOUT
100 CANDIES

1 stick (¹/₂ cup) unsalted butter
1¹/₂ cups creamy peanut butter
2 cups sifted confectioners' sugar

1 teaspoon vanilla extract
16 ounces semisweet chocolate
chips

A delicious combination of peanut butter and chocolate.

In 2-quart measure, microwave butter on HIGH 1 to 2 minutes, or until melted. Add peanut butter, sugar, and vanilla and blend until smooth. Form into ³/₄-inch balls and place on a wax-paper-lined baking sheet. Freeze 1 hour.

In 1-quart measure, microwave chocolate on 70% power 3 to 4 minutes, or until melted. Stir until smooth. Remove peanut butter balls from freezer and, piercing balls with a toothpick or fork, dip into chocolate, coating three-quarters of each ball. Let excess chocolate drip off and place on wax paper to dry.

DIVINITY

2½ cups sugar
⅔ cup light corn syrup
½ cup water
3 egg whites

Pinch of salt
1 teaspoon vanilla extract
1 cup chopped pecans or walnuts
    (optional)

MAKES

36 CANDIES

■

Combine sugar, corn syrup, and water in 2-quart measure. Cover with plastic wrap and microwave on HIGH 12 to 18 minutes, or to hard-ball stage (260° F.). Meanwhile, with electric mixer, beat egg whites until stiff peaks form, adding salt while still beating.

Pour hot syrup in thin stream into egg whites, beating constantly. Add vanilla and continue beating until candy loses its gloss and holds its shape. Stir in nuts, if desired, and drop by tablespoonfuls onto wax paper. Let stand to dry. Store in airtight container.

CHOCOLATE RIPPLE DIVINITY

Omit nuts. After divinity has been beaten until it holds its shape, fold in 6 ounces semisweet chocolate chips. Stir to swirl the chocolate a little. Drop by teaspoonfuls onto wax paper to dry.

BLACK WALNUT DIVINITY

Substitute ¼ cup finely chopped black walnuts for pecans or walnuts.

STRAWBERRY DIVINITY

**MAKES
60 CANDIES**

■

You can make any color
or flavor you like by
varying the gelatin.
Raspberry, cherry,
lime, and orange are
good choices. This
divinity freezes beauti-
fully for several weeks.

2¾ cups sugar
¾ cup light corn syrup
⅔ cup hot tap water
3 egg whites
1 (3-ounce) package strawberry-
    flavored gelatin

1 cup chopped pecans (optional)
½ cup shredded coconut
    (optional)

Combine sugar, corn syrup, and water in 2-quart measure. Microwave, uncovered, on HIGH 12 to 18 minutes, or to hard-ball stage (260° F.). Meanwhile, with electric mixer beat egg whites until fluffy. Slowly add gelatin, beating constantly until stiff peaks form.

Pour hot syrup in thin stream into egg white mixture, beating constantly. Beat until candy holds its shape. Fold in nuts and coconut, if desired. Quickly drop by teaspoonfuls onto wax paper. Let stand until divinity is cooled and set. (This version takes longer to set than traditional divinity.) Store in airtight container.

CHERRY DIVINITY
Substitute cherry-flavored gelatin for strawberry; ½ cup chopped candied cherries may be folded in with, or instead of, coconut and nuts.

SEAFOAM

**MAKES
36 CANDIES**

■

2 cups, packed, light brown sugar
¼ cup dark corn syrup
⅓ cup water
3 egg whites

Pinch of salt
1 teaspoon vanilla extract
½ cup chopped walnuts or pecans

Combine brown sugar, corn syrup, and water in a 2-quart measure. Microwave, uncovered, on HIGH 8 to 15 minutes, or to hard-ball stage (267° F.). (This temperature is higher than that given for white divinity because brown sugar tends to make the candy stickier.) Meanwhile, with electric mixer, beat egg whites until stiff peaks form. Beat salt and vanilla into whites.

Pour hot syrup in thin stream into egg whites, beating constantly. Continue beating until candy loses its gloss and holds its shape. Fold in nuts.

Pour into lightly oiled 9-inch square dish or drop by tablespoonfuls onto wax paper. Let stand to dry. Store in airtight container.

MAPLE NUT DIVINITY

Substitute 1 teaspoon maple flavoring for vanilla. Maple syrup may be substituted for the dark corn syrup, if desired.

COCONUT RIBBON FUDGE

3 cups sugar
1 (13-ounce) can evaporated milk
3 tablespoons unsalted butter
2 envelopes unflavored gelatin
2 tablespoons water
1 (8-ounce) package shredded
    coconut

1 teaspoon vanilla extract
2 ounces unsweetened chocolate
1 (3-ounce) package strawberry-
    flavored gelatin

**MAKES
64 PIECES**

Place sugar, milk, and butter in 2-quart measure and microwave on HIGH 5 minutes. Stir and microwave on 70% power 10 to 15 minutes, or to soft-ball stage (234 to 240° F.).

In cup, sprinkle unflavored gelatin on water and let stand 2 to 3 minutes. Microwave on HIGH 20 to 25 seconds to dissolve gelatin, then add to syrup with coconut and vanilla.

Divide mixture into thirds. Pour one-third of mixture into buttered 8-inch square dish. Add chocolate to another third of mixture and microwave on 70% power 1 to 2 minutes to melt chocolate. Stir to blend and pour over coconut mixture in dish. Add strawberry gelatin to the remaining mixture and microwave on HIGH 1 to 2 minutes, stirring to blend. Pour over the chocolate layer. Cool and cut into pieces 2 inches long and ½ inch wide.

CARAMEL FUDGE

MAKES ABOUT 50 PIECES

■

1 stick (¹/₂ cup) unsalted butter
1 cup, packed, dark brown sugar
¹/₄ cup milk
1 teaspoon vanilla extract

1 pound confectioners' sugar,
  sifted
¹/₃ cup chopped pecans or walnuts

In 2-quart measure, microwave butter on HIGH 30 to 60 seconds, or until melted. Stir in brown sugar and microwave on HIGH 2 minutes, or until boiling. Let mixture stand 1 to 2 minutes and stir again. Slowly add milk and vanilla. Add confectioners' sugar and stir until well blended. (Or use a food processor.) Stir in nuts and press into lightly oiled 8-inch square dish. Chill until firm, then cut into small squares. Store in tightly covered container.

CHOCOLATE FUDGE

MAKES ABOUT 50 PIECES

■

This has been called the devil's fudge because it is so tempting!

2 cups sugar
³/₄ cup evaporated milk
2 tablespoons unsalted butter
6 ounces semisweet chocolate
    chips

1 cup nuts
1 teaspoon vanilla extract

In 2-quart measure, combine sugar and evaporated milk. Cover and microwave on HIGH 4 to 5 minutes, or until boiling, stirring once or twice during cooking to dissolve sugar crystals on sides of bowl. Cover again and microwave on 50% power 4 to 6 minutes, until mixture reaches soft-ball stage (234 to 240° F.).

Add butter, chocolate, nuts, and vanilla. Stir until blended. Pour into buttered 8-inch square dish. Let cool, then cut into small squares.

SCRUMPTIOUS FUDGE

2 tablespoons unsalted butter
2 (3-ounce) packages cream
   cheese
1 pound confectioners' sugar,
   sifted
$1/2$ cup Dutch-process cocoa
   powder

1 teaspoon vanilla extract
Pinch of salt
$1/2$ to 1 cup chopped walnuts or
   pecans

**MAKES
ABOUT 50
PIECES**

■

This rich, creamy fudge
is quick to make and
delicious.

Place butter and cream cheese in small bowl and microwave on
HIGH 1½ to 2 minutes, or until cream cheese is softened.

Transfer mixture to food processor or mixer and add sugar,
cocoa, vanilla, and salt. Process or mix until smooth. Stir in nuts and
press into 8-inch square dish. Chill until firm, then cut into small
squares.

ALMOND FUDGE
Substitute almond extract for vanilla and toasted almonds (page 441)
for walnuts.

PEANUT BUTTER FUDGE

2 (3-ounce) packages cream
   cheese
1 cup creamy peanut butter
1 pound confectioners' sugar,
   sifted

2 tablespoons evaporated milk
1 teaspoon vanilla extract
Pinch of salt
$1/2$ to 1 cup coarsely chopped
   unsalted roasted peanuts

**MAKES
ABOUT 50
PIECES**

■

Place cream cheese in 2-quart measure and microwave on HIGH
1 to 2 minutes, or until softened. Stir in peanut butter and
microwave on HIGH 1 minute longer. Stir until smooth.

Transfer cream cheese and peanut butter mixture to food processor or mixer and add sugar, milk, vanilla, and salt. Process or mix
until smooth. Stir in nuts. Spread in lightly oiled 8-inch square dish.
Chill until firm, then cut into small squares. Store candy in airtight
container.

HONEY BITS

MAKES

30 PIECES

A honey-flavored taffy.

. . . .

Honey keeps best stored in a cool, dry place, but not the refrigerator. With time, it will crystallize. To dissolve the crystals, cover the honey tightly with plastic wrap and microwave on HIGH for about 1 minute.

. . . .

1 cup sugar
1/2 cup honey

1/2 cup water
1 tablespoon unsalted butter

Combine sugar, honey, and water in 2-quart measure and microwave on HIGH for 10 to 15 minutes, or to soft-crack stage (280° F.). Let mixture stand 2 to 3 minutes, then add butter. When bubbling subsides, stir just until butter is mixed in. Pour mixture onto oiled marble slab or baking sheet and let stand about 5 minutes, or until cool enough to handle.

With oiled hands, pull and twist taffy about 15 minutes, or until it becomes firm and light in color. Twist into long rope and cut into bite-size pieces with oiled scissors. Individually wrap each piece with plastic wrap and store in a cool place.

SALTWATER TAFFY

MAKES

ABOUT 30

PIECES

Children still enjoy pulling and eating taffy. Make an assortment of pastel colors and flavors.

1 cup sugar
1/2 cup light corn syrup
1/2 cup water
3/4 teaspoon salt
1 teaspoon unsalted butter

1 teaspoon flavoring (banana,
      orange, strawberry, or others)
2 to 3 drops food coloring to
      coordinate with flavoring

Combine sugar, corn syrup, water, and salt in 2-quart measure. Microwave on HIGH 8 to 10 minutes, stirring several times, or until mixture reaches soft-crack stage (280° F.). Let mixture stand 2 to 3 minutes, then add butter, flavoring, and coloring. When bubbling subsides, stir candy until well combined. (If you would like to make 2 colors to twist together, pour half the candy into another measure or bowl and mix in first color with a spatula. Add second color to mixture still in measure.)

Pour candy onto oiled marble slab or baking sheet (use 2 sheets for 2 colors) and let stand for about 5 minutes or until cool enough to be handled. With oiled hands, pull and twist taffy about 15 minutes, or until it begins to look dull and becomes too stiff to pull. Twist into long, thin rope and cut into desired lengths with oiled scissors. Individually wrap each piece in plastic wrap and store in a cool place.

- - - - - - - - - - -
If taffy is undercooked, it will not hold its shape. Overcooking produces hard candy.
- - - - - - - - - - -

PULLED BUTTER MINTS

2 cups sugar
1 stick (½ cup) unsalted butter
½ cup water

4 to 5 drops peppermint oil
2 or 3 drops food coloring

MAKES ABOUT 36 CANDIES

.

Combine sugar, butter, and water in 2-quart measure, cover with plastic wrap, and microwave on HIGH 4 to 6 minutes, or until the sugar is dissolved. Stir, then microwave, uncovered, on 70% power 10 to 15 minutes, or until candy reaches soft-crack stage (270° F.). Add flavoring and coloring. Do not beat.

Pour at once onto cold, buttered marble slab or buttered baking sheet. Allow to stand until cool enough to handle.

Butter your hands, pick up all the candy, and start pulling while it is still hot. When the mixture suddenly becomes dull and holds its shape, twist it into a rope about ½ inch in diameter and, with oiled scissors, cut at once into bite-size pieces or sticks. Store tightly covered. Mints will mellow overnight and become creamy.

Smooth and creamy! These candies are almost a lost art, but well worth remembering. Children love to pull them.

- - - - - - - - - - -
It is almost impossible to make pulled mints, as well as many other candies, on a rainy or humid day.
- - - - - - - - - - -

CANDIED APPLES

**MAKES
6 APPLES**

Make candied apples the day you're serving them; moisture from the apples can soften the candy, making it sticky even when tightly wrapped in plastic wrap.

1 cup sugar
¼ cup light corn syrup
⅓ cup water
2 or 3 drops red food coloring

2 or 3 drops cinnamon flavoring
  oil
6 red apples

Combine sugar, corn syrup, and water in 1-quart measure. Microwave on HIGH 8 to 12 minutes, or until the candy reaches hard-crack stage (300° F.), stirring several times. Stir in food coloring and cinnamon flavoring. The syrup should be bright red.

Push a 6- to 9-inch wooden skewer into bottom of each apple. Holding end of skewers, dip apples into hot syrup and twirl to coat apples. Place apples on sheet of foil or an oiled baking sheet and let stand until hardened.

LOLLIPOPS

Prepare coating for Candied Apples, varying flavoring and coloring as desired. Arrange 12 lollipop sticks 4 inches apart on oiled baking sheet. Drop hot syrup from a tablespoon over end of each stick to form a lollipop 2 to 3 inches in diameter. Cool. Lollipop molds are also fun to use, if you have them.

CARAMEL APPLES

**MAKES
5 OR 6
APPLES**

5 or 6 medium apples, washed
1 pound caramel candies
1 tablespoon water

1½ cups finely chopped walnuts
  (optional)

Insert skewer into stem end of each apple (an ice cream stick or chopstick may be used). Microwave caramels and water in 2-quart measure on HIGH 2 to 3 minutes, stirring every minute. Let caramel cool 1 minute. Dip apples, one at a time, into caramel, then roll in chopped walnuts, if desired. (If caramel becomes too stiff before all apples are dipped, microwave on HIGH 2 to 3 minutes to soften again.) Place dipped apples on oiled baking sheet and chill until caramel is firm.

Leftover caramel may be mixed with nuts and poured into candy molds to make small nut brittles.

PEANUT BUTTER APPLES

In 2-cup measure, microwave 6 ounces peanut butter chips on 70% power 2 to 4 minutes, or until softened. Add 1 teaspoon butter and stir to blend. Dip 5 or 6 small apples in mixture completely or partially submerging the apples.

MARSHMALLOWS

3 envelopes unflavored gelatin
½ cup cold water
2 cups granulated sugar
½ cup hot tap water

1 cup light corn syrup
2 teaspoons vanilla extract
¼ cup cornstarch
½ cup sifted confectioners' sugar

MAKES ABOUT 80 MARSH-MALLOWS

•

Fun to make and a versatile treat to keep on hand. Marshmallows were originally made from a jellylike gum taken from the roots of a "marshmallow" plant. They are now made using gelatin.

Combine gelatin and cold water in 2-quart measure and let stand 5 minutes. Stir in granulated sugar and hot water. Cook on HIGH 5 minutes, then on 50% power 4 minutes, or until sugar is completely dissolved.

Combine corn syrup and vanilla in large mixer bowl. Begin beating, then gradually add hot syrup in thin stream. Continue beating 10 to 15 minutes, or until mixture thickens and holds its shape.

Lightly butter 13 × 9-inch baking dish. Combine cornstarch and confectioners' sugar and dust dish with 2 tablespoons of this mixture. Pour marshmallow mixture into dish and let stand 2 to 3 hours to cool and dry.

Sprinkle remaining cornstarch mixture on a working surface and invert marshmallow mixture onto it. Cut into squares and roll each piece in cornstarch mixture. Store in airtight container.

CHOCOLATE MARSHMALLOWS

Add ⅓ to ½ cup Dutch-process cocoa powder to marshmallow mixture during last 5 minutes of beating. To make half chocolate and half plain marshmallows, pour half the plain mixture into 8-inch square dish and mix ¼ cup cocoa with remaining mixture. Add 2 tablespoons cocoa to cornstarch-sugar mixture for chocolate marshmallows.

HAYSTACKS

**MAKES
36 CANDIES**

∎

6 ounces butterscotch chips
1 tablespoon unsalted butter
2 tablespoons milk

2 cups miniature marshmallows
¾ cup roasted peanuts
5 ounces chow mein noodles

In 2-quart measure, microwave butterscotch chips and butter on 50% power 3 to 4 minutes, or until melted. Stir until smooth, then add milk, marshmallows, peanuts, and noodles. Drop by spoonfuls on oiled surface. Let cool and dry. Store in airtight container.

SKEDADDLES

**MAKES
48 TO 60
CANDIES**

∎

1 (10-ounce) package miniature
    marshmallows
2 cups graham cracker crumbs

1 (14-ounce) can condensed milk
3 cups pecan pieces
Confectioners' sugar

In 2-quart measure, microwave marshmallows on HIGH 2 to 3 minutes, or until they are puffed up. Stir in crumbs, condensed milk, and nuts.

Form mixture into 3 rolls, each 1 to 1½ inches in diameter. Chill. Roll in confectioners' sugar, slice, and serve.

ROCKY ROAD

**MAKES
42 CANDIES**

∎

12 ounces milk chocolate chips
2 tablespoons unsalted butter
1 (14-ounce) can condensed milk

1 (10-ounce) package miniature
    marshmallows
2 cups pecan pieces

In 2-quart measure, microwave chocolate chips and butter on 70% power 3 to 4 minutes, or until melted. Stir until smooth. Blend in condensed milk.

Place marshmallows and pecans in bowl, pour chocolate mixture over them, and fold together. Spread candy in oiled 13 × 9-inch dish. Chill and cut into squares. Store candy in airtight container at room temperature.

SNOWBALLS

2 cups graham cracker crumbs
4 cups miniature marshmallows
1 cup chopped nuts

1 cup chopped dates
1 (14-ounce) can condensed milk
14 ounces shredded coconut

**MAKES
60 CANDIES**

▪

Snowballs keep for several weeks stored in airtight containers. They also freeze well.

In 2-quart measure, combine crumbs, marshmallows, nuts, dates, and milk. Microwave on HIGH 2 to 3 minutes to soften marshmallows; they will partially melt. Stir to combine ingredients.

Shape mixture into 1-inch balls and roll in coconut.

S'MORES

2 graham crackers
1 (.3-ounce) milk chocolate bar, or
   1 teaspoon milk chocolate
   chips

1 large marshmallow

1 SERVING

▪

When children of all ages enjoy this sweet treat, they always want s'more.

Place 1 graham cracker square on a paper napkin. Top with chocolate and marshmallow. Microwave on HIGH about 15 to 20 seconds, or just until marshmallow puffs. Lightly press second graham cracker on top.

VARIATION
Spread second graham cracker with peanut butter. Or add a piece of fruit, such as a slice of banana, apple, or peach.

ALMOND ROCA

MAKES
24 TO 36
CANDIES

1 cup milk chocolate chips
1/3 cup slivered blanched almonds,
   toasted (page 441)

1 cup sugar
2 sticks (1 cup) unsalted butter
2 tablespoons light corn syrup

■

Line 8-inch square dish with foil.
Spread chocolate chips and almonds evenly over foil. In 2-quart measure, combine sugar, butter, and corn syrup. Microwave on 70% power 15 to 20 minutes, stirring several times, or until mixture becomes caramel colored and registers 300° F. (hard-crack stage) on candy thermometer.

Spread syrup over chocolate and almonds. As candy begins to harden, score it into squares with a buttered knife. Allow candy to completely cool and harden. Using the foil as an aid, lift candy from dish and break into pieces along scored lines. Store in tightly sealed container for up to 1 week.

SCRUMPTIOUS NUT BRITTLE

MAKES
ABOUT
1 POUND

1 cup sugar
1/2 cup light corn syrup
1/2 stick (1/4 cup) unsalted butter
   (no substitute)
1-inch square (1/2-inch thick) piece
   of paraffin, chopped

2 cups raw nuts (pecan halves,
   peanuts, walnuts, almonds,
   hazelnuts, macadamia nuts,
   coconut, or a combination)
1 teaspoon vanilla extract
2 teaspoons baking soda

■

You can't have a holiday without it! This recipe has long been a favorite because it is so easy to prepare and always brings raves.

In 2-quart measure, microwave sugar, corn syrup, and butter on HIGH 3 minutes. Stir. Stir in the paraffin and nuts. Microwave on HIGH 7 to 12 minutes, or until mixture registers 300° F. on candy thermometer. Syrup will become a light caramel color and nuts will have a roasted aroma. Stir several times during cooking. After first 5 minutes, watch closely to avoid burning nuts.

Stir in vanilla, then add baking soda and quickly stir. While candy is still foaming. pour mixture onto an oiled marble slab, baking sheet, or three 8-inch aluminum pie pans. Let cool and harden. If candy is poured onto marble or a baking pan, it can be stretched thin as soon as it is cool enough to handle. Break into pieces. Store in an airtight container.

BRITTLE PATTIES

To make brittle patties, pour hot syrup into oiled pie pans, and, when cool, remove from pan and wrap in plastic wrap for gift-giving.

DATE-NUT BALLS

1 (8-ounce) package chopped dates
1 cup granulated sugar
1 stick (1/2 cup) unsalted butter

1 cup finely chopped pecans or walnuts
1 1/2 cups Rice Krispies cereal
Confectioners' sugar

MAKES 36 TO 48 CANDIES

In 2-quart measure, combine dates, granulated sugar, and butter. Microwave on HIGH 3 minutes Stir and microwave on HIGH 2 to 3 minutes longer, or until thickened.

Cool until mixture can be handled. Add nuts and cereal and stir well. Shape into 1-inch balls and roll in confectioners' sugar. Store in tightly covered container.

CHOCOLATE RAISIN CLUSTERS

12 ounces semisweet chocolate chips
2 tablespoons unsalted butter

1 (14-ounce can) condensed milk
2 cups raisins

MAKES 24 CANDIES

In 2-quart measure, microwave chocolate on 70% power 3 to 4 minutes, or until glossy and melted. Stir until smooth. Stir in butter, then condensed milk and raisins. Drop by spoonfuls onto wax paper or into paper bonbon cups. Let dry. Store in tightly covered container for up to 2 weeks.

CHOCOLATE PEANUT CLUSTERS

Substitute 2 cups roasted peanuts for raisins.

413

CREOLE PORCUPINES

**MAKES
36 TO 48
CANDIES**

This confection originated in New Orleans.

1 ½ cup chopped pecans
½ stick (¼ cup) unsalted butter
   (no substitute)
1 cup, packed, brown sugar

2 large eggs, well beaten
1 cup chopped dates
3 cups shredded coconut

Place pecans and butter in 2-quart measure and microwave on HIGH 2 minutes. Stir and microwave on HIGH 2 to 4 minutes longer, stirring after each minute of cooking time, or until nuts are slightly toasted.

Combine sugar and eggs until well blended. Add to nuts with dates and 1 ½ cups coconut. Microwave on 70% power 2 to 3 minutes. Shape mixture into balls and roll in remaining coconut. Refrigerate in tightly covered container for up to 2 weeks.

CREAMY PRALINES

**MAKES
24 CANDIES**

Truly a Southern recipe.

2 cups granulated sugar
½ cup, packed, light brown sugar
Pinch of salt
¾ cup buttermilk

2 tablespoons bourbon (optional)
½ stick (¼ cup) unsalted butter
2 cups pecan halves
1 teaspoon baking soda

Combine granulated and brown sugars, salt, buttermilk, and bourbon in 2-quart measure. Microwave on HIGH 8 minutes. Stir and add butter and pecans. Microwave on HIGH 8 to 12 minutes longer, or to soft-ball stage (230° F). Stir in baking soda. Microwave on HIGH 30 seconds. Cool slightly and beat with spoon until creamy and slightly thickened. Working quickly, drop by tablespoonfuls onto wax paper. Cool and store in a tightly covered container.

CARAMEL CANDY

1 cup sugar
1 tablespoon water
1 stick (½ cup) unsalted butter,
   cut into 8 pieces

1 (14-ounce) can condensed milk
1 cup toasted chopped nuts

**MAKES
36 TO 48
CANDIES**

■

In 2-quart measure, microwave sugar and water on HIGH 4 to 6 minutes. Watch carefully after 4 minutes and do not let sugar burn. When sugar turns light golden brown, stir and break hardened sugar from side of dish with wooden spoon. Sugar need not be dissolved at this stage.

Add butter and milk, stir, and cook on HIGH 6 to 8 minutes, or to firm-ball stage (242° F.). Add nuts and pour into buttered 8-inch square dish. Let stand until cool and firm. Cut into bite-size pieces with sharp knife. Store in tightly covered container.

TURTLES

72 pecan halves (about 1½ cups)
24 caramel candies

6 ounces semisweet chocolate
   chips

**MAKES
24 CANDIES**

■

Prepare pecans: Reserve 24 halves for heads. Break each remaining half into 2 vertical pieces for legs.

Unwrap caramel candies and place 8 of them in a circle on an oiled plate. Microwave on HIGH 30 to 60 seconds, or until softened. Lift one softened piece and press a pecan half into bottom to form turtle's head and part of body. Press 4 pecan quarters into bottom to resemble turtle legs. Repeat with remaining caramels and pecans. Place candies on baking sheet and chill until firm.

In cup, microwave chocolate chips on 70% power 3 to 4 minutes, or until melted. Spoon about 1 teaspoon chocolate over each turtle, leaving tips of feet and head showing. Store in tightly covered container.

YOGURT-COVERED NUTS

**MAKES
2 ½ CUPS
CANDY**

2²/₃ cup sugar
½ cup plain low-fat yogurt
Pinch of salt

2 teaspoons vanilla extract
2½ cups pecan halves

■

These confections are delightful. Filberts, walnuts, pecans, or a combination of nuts may be used.

Combine sugar, yogurt, and salt in 2-quart measure and microwave on 70% power 10 to 15 minutes, or to softball stage (236° F.). Stir in vanilla.

Let mixture stand until cool, stirring several times. When candy begins to thicken, place measure in larger bowl of ice water and stir several minutes to cool mixture quickly. Add nuts and stir to coat. Pour out on oiled baking sheet. Quickly separate nuts. Let cool and harden. Store in tightly covered container.

MINTED PECANS
Add 2 to 3 drops of mint extract and a drop of pink or green food coloring, if desired, to yogurt mixture before adding pecans.

SPICED WALNUTS

**MAKES
1 ½ CUPS**

■

1 egg white
½ cup sugar
½ teaspoon grated orange zest
¼ teaspoon cinnamon
⅛ teaspoon ground ginger

⅛ teaspoon ground cloves
Pinch of freshly grated nutmeg
1 to 1½ cups walnut halves
2 tablespoons unsalted butter

In bowl, beat egg white with electric mixer until stiff peaks form. Combine sugar, orange zest, cinnamon, ginger, cloves, and nutmeg and slowly add mixture to egg white, beating constantly. Add nuts and stir gently to coat evenly.

Place butter in large glass pie plate and microwave on HIGH 30 to 60 seconds to melt. Add nut mixture and stir to coat nuts with butter. Spread evenly in pie plate and microwave on HIGH 4 to 8 minutes, or until nuts have a white glaze, stirring several times during cooking. Cool. Nuts will become crisp as they cool. Store in tightly covered container.

CARAMEL CORN

2 sticks (1 cup) unsalted butter
  (no substitute)
1 pound light brown sugar
1/2 cup corn syrup
1/2 teaspoon salt
1 teaspoon vanilla extract

1/2 teaspoon baking soda
6 quarts popped popcorn
2 cups unsalted roasted peanuts
  (optional)
2 cups raisins (optional)

**MAKES
6 QUARTS**

▪

This popcorn treat
melts in your mouth
and is unbelievably
easy to prepare! It's not
at all sticky and makes
a good gift to send by
mail. Prepared conven-
tionally, this recipe
requires 1 hour of
cooking time and stir-
ring every 15 minutes.
It is prepared in the
microwave in less than
15 minutes.

In 2-quart measure, combine butter, brown sugar, corn syrup, and salt. Microwave on HIGH 5 to 6 minutes, or until boiling. Stir and microwave on 70% power 5 to 10 minutes, or to soft-crack stage (270 to 290° F.). Stir in vanilla and baking soda.

Place popped corn in large brown paper grocery bag. Pour hot syrup over corn and toss to coat corn. Roll top of bag loosely and place bag in microwave. Cook on HIGH 1 minute. Shake bag well and continue microwaving on HIGH 1 to 1 1/2 minutes longer. Stir in nuts and raisins, if desired.

Pour caramel corn into large bowl and let cool until crunchy, stirring several times. To speed cooling process, place bowl in freezer.

CARAMEL POPCORN BALLS

With buttered hands, shape hot caramel corn into balls and let cool.

CRUNCH BARS

1 cup butterscotch chips
1/2 cup light corn syrup
1/2 cup peanut butter

4 cups oatbran flakes or corn
  flakes
1/2 cup semisweet chocolate chips

**MAKES
ABOUT 24
BARS**

▪

Satisfy a sweet tooth
with a peanut butter
and oatbran flake con-
fection.

In 2-quart bowl, microwave butterscotch chips on 50% power 2 to 3 minutes, or until shiny and melted. Stir in corn syrup and peanut butter. Add the oatbran flakes and stir to coat.

Press into lightly oiled 11 × 8-inch baking dish. In small bowl, microwave chocolate chips on 70% power 2 to 3 minutes, or until shiny and melted. Spread chocolate over butterscotch mixture. Chill until firm, then cut into bars. Store in tightly covered container.

OPERA CREAMS

MAKES
32 CANDIES

Make instant home-made candies; these belong to the fudge family.

1 stick (¹/₂ cup) unsalted butter
¹/₂ cup milk
2 (3¹/₂-ounce) packages coconut cream pudding mix
¹/₂ teaspoon vanilla extract
1 pound confectioners' sugar, sifted

¹/₂ cup chopped pecans or walnuts
¹/₂ cup shredded coconut (optional)
¹/₂ cup chopped maraschino cherries (optional)

In 2-quart measure, microwave butter on HIGH 1 minute, or until melted. Stir in milk and pudding mix and microwave on HIGH 3 to 4 minutes, stirring after 1 minute. Stir in vanilla, add sugar, and beat until smooth. Stir in walnuts and, if desired, coconut and cherries. Spread in 8-inch square dish. Chill, then cut into squares. Store in refrigerator in tightly covered container.

CHOCOLATE OPERAS
Add 2 ounces unsweetened chocolate to butter and microwave on 70% power 3 to 4 minutes to melt butter and chocolate. Proceed with recipe.

ORANGE BALLS

MAKES
48 PIECES

These taste better if they're kept in a sealed container several days before serving.

6 ounces semisweet chocolate chips
¹/₂ cup plus 2 tablespoons sifted confectioners' sugar
3 tablespoons corn syrup
¹/₄ cup frozen orange juice concentrate

1 (7¹/₄-ounce) package vanilla wafers, finely crushed
1 cup finely chopped pecans
2 tablespoons Dutch-process cocoa powder

Place chocolate in 2-quart measure and microwave on 70% power 2 to 4 minutes, or until melted. Stir in ¹/₂ cup confectioners' sugar, corn syrup, and juice concentrate. Add wafer crumbs and nuts and stir until well blended. Shape into 1-inch balls. Combine remaining 2 tablespoons sugar and cocoa in a plastic bag. Put balls in bag and shake until coated with sugar mixture.

Store in airtight container; these candies also freeze well.

GRANOLA CANDY BARS

6 tablespoons unsalted butter
¼ cup granulated sugar
¼ cup, packed, dark brown sugar
¼ cup dark corn syrup
1 teaspoon vanilla extract
2 cups quick-cooking oats

1 cup chopped nuts, toasted (page 441)
6 ounces semisweet chocolate chips
½ cup peanut butter

MAKES 12 TO 24 BARS

■

If your container is too small for the ingredients, and you see that the candy is about to boil over, simply open the oven door and cooking will stop instantly.

In bowl, microwave butter on HIGH 1 minute, or until melted. Add granulated and brown sugars, corn syrup, and vanilla. Beat until well blended. Stir in oats and nuts. Press evenly in buttered 9-inch square dish and microwave on HIGH 3 minutes.

In 2-cup measure, microwave chocolate on 70% power 2 to 3 minutes to melt. Stir in peanut butter and spread over oatmeal layer. Chill until firm, then cut into bars. Store in tightly covered container.

PECAN LOGS

1 (7-ounce) jar marshmallow cream
1 pound confectioners' sugar, sifted
1 teaspoon vanilla extract

1 (14-ounce) package caramel candies
2 tablespoons heavy cream
1 to 1½ cups chopped pecans

MAKES 36 CANDIES

■

These are easy and yummy.

Combine marshmallow cream, sugar, and vanilla in food processor or mix in by hand. Knead until all sugar is blended in. Shape into 8 rolls about 1 inch in diameter and 3 inches long. Wrap in plastic wrap and freeze.

Unwrap caramels and place in 2-quart measure along with heavy cream. Microwave on HIGH 2 to 3 minutes, or until caramels are softened. Stir to mix and complete melting. Microwave a little longer, if needed.

Holding a frozen candy roll with a fork, dip candy into caramel to coat. Lift out and roll in chopped pecans. Repeat procedure with remaining candy rolls. Store in tightly covered container. Slice rolls for serving. These freeze well.

Beverages

A wide range of drinks can be prepared easily in the microwave, from traditional libations that have been enjoyed since Colonial times to contemporary regional American favorites.

One great advantage of the microwave is that drinks can be prepared individually in the cup or glass without heating a whole kettle of water. Even half a cup of coffee or cocoa can be reheated quickly in the microwave.

Of course, larger quantities can be prepared in the microwave as well, and without any worry about scorching or sticking. For beverages made with fruits or spices, it is not necessary to simmer all the liquid with these flavorings as you would when cooking them conventionally. Instead, microwave only part of the liquid with the fruit or spice until the flavors are blended, then add the remaining liquid and—depending on the recipe— either cool the beverage or microwave it until it is hot.

The most useful vessels for microwaving beverages are 1- and 2-quart glass measures, which are especially convenient because they have handles and pouring spouts. A large heatproof pitcher and individual mugs and glasses are also handy. Do not use a bottle with a narrow neck because pressure can build up in the lower part of the bottle, causing the glass to break where the bottle narrows. When microwaving in mugs and pitchers with glued-on handles, remember that prolonged microwaving can sometimes weaken the holding power of the glue. Do not use metal dishes or dishes with metallic trim.

Beverages are usually microwaved on HIGH.

TIMETABLE FOR HEATING BEVERAGES			
AMOUNT	TIME (HIGH)	AMOUNT	TIME (HIGH)
1 cup	1 to 2 minutes	3 cups	4 to 5 minutes
2 cups	3 to 4 minutes	4 cups	6 to 8 minutes

COFFEE

Coffee tastes best when brewed in a coffeemaker designed for that purpose. The microwave can be used, however, to reheat recently brewed coffee by the pot, by the cup, or even by the half-cup. When reheating coffee, or when making instant coffee, do not allow it to boil or it will taste bitter.

There are coffeemakers manufactured specially for use in the microwave, but unless they can brew one cup at a time they may offer no real advantage.

Cream-filled Miniature Chocolate Cups (page 394) are delicious served with after-dinner coffee. They add a touch of sweetness when no other dessert is being served.

INSTANT COFFEE

Microwave 1 cup water on HIGH 1 to 1½ minutes, or until very hot. Stir in instant coffee powder to taste.

ICED COFFEE

Let strong, flavorful coffee cool to room temperature, then freeze it. Break frozen coffee into chunks and process in food processor to consistency of shaved ice. Spoon into chilled glasses and serve, if desired, with whipped cream (sweetened or not, as you wish) flavored with cocoa, almond extract, or orange juice concentrate. Garnish with sprig of fresh mint or sweet woodruff.

TEA

Many consider tea a beverage, but to some it is a cherished ritual.
To make tea in the microwave, simply pour cold water into a microwavable teapot and microwave, covered, on HIGH until boiling. (See timetable opposite). Then brew the tea according to your favorite method.

Tea for two (or for one) is a snap in the microwave because you can heat the water right in the cups—just be sure they don't have metal trim.

CAFÉ BRÛLOT

8 TO 10 REGULAR SERVINGS; 16 DEMITASSE SERVINGS

■

This New Orleans recipe, a flaming brandied coffee, is a dramatic light ending for an exceptional meal. Serve Café Brûlot with cookies, pastries, or a cheese and fruit tray.

8 whole cloves
1 orange, very thinly sliced
1 lemon, very thinly sliced
12 whole allspice
⅓ cup sugar

2 cinnamon sticks, broken into pieces
1 cup brandy
1 quart strong, hot, freshly brewed coffee

Several hours before serving, press cloves into orange slices. Place orange and lemon slices, allspice, sugar, cinnamon sticks, and ⅔ cup brandy in *brûlot* bowl or chafing dish.

Pour remaining ⅓ cup brandy into small pitcher and microwave on HIGH 30 seconds, or until very warm. Pour brandy into ladle. Light a match, wait a few seconds to let sulfur burn off, then ignite brandy in ladle and pour over citrus mixture in *brûlot* bowl. The brandy will ignite the mixture, so do not lean over bowl. Gently stir fruit with ladle until sugar has melted. Gradually add hot coffee and continue ladling mixture back over itself until flame dies. Ladle into regular coffee cups or demitasse cups and serve immediately.

COFFEE LIQUEUR

MAKES ABOUT 2½ QUARTS

■

4 rounded tablespoons instant coffee powder
4 rounded tablespoons finely ground dark-roast coffee
3 cups vodka

3 cups water
3 cups sugar
1 cup brandy
1 teaspoon vanilla extract

Place instant coffee and ground coffee in coffee filter set over 2-quart measure, pour vodka over coffee, and set aside.

In 1-quart measure, microwave water on HIGH 4 to 5 minutes, or until boiling. Pour boiling water over coffee. When all liquid has filtered through, discard coffee filter and stir sugar into coffee mixture. Microwave on HIGH 10 to 15 minutes, or until slightly thickened. Cool and add brandy and vanilla.

Pour liqueur into bottles, cover, and let stand in cool place 4 to 6 weeks before serving.

ICED TEA

1 quart cold water
5 tea bags

½ to ¾ cup sugar (optional)

**MAKES
2 QUARTS**

Put water and tea bags in ceramic teapot or 2-quart glass measure and microwave, covered, on HIGH 7 minutes, or until just boiling. Add sugar, if desired. Let tea stand, covered, for at least 5 minutes, then remove tea bags.

Pour tea into a pitcher and add enough cold water to make 2 quarts. Chill and serve over ice.

This Southern staple is easy to prepare in the microwave.

ALMOND TEA

2¼ cups water
1 cup sugar
1 quart freshly brewed strong tea

1 (6-ounce) can frozen lemonade
    concentrate
1 teaspoon almond extract

**MAKES
2 QUARTS**

In 2-quart measure, combine water and sugar. Microwave, uncovered, on HIGH 4 to 6 minutes, or until sugar is dissolved. Add tea, lemonade, and almond extract and mix. Serve over ice.

APRICOT-GINGER TEA
Substitute vanilla for almond extract and use apricot nectar instead of water. Measure Apricot Tea, add an equal amount of ginger ale, and serve over cracked ice.

PEPPERMINT TEA
Add 2 or 3 cinnamon sticks to water and sugar before microwaving. Substitute peppermint flavoring for almond extract.

For herbed or fruited ice cubes, freeze boiled and cooled water or other liquid with a sprig, leaf, or flower of an herb that is compatible with the drinks for which the ice is intended. Cherries, citrus peel, strawberries, and raspberries all make delicious fresh fruit ice cubes.

SPICED TEA MIX

**MAKES
3 CUPS MIX**

This mix is convenient to have on hand and, packed in pretty jars, a good gift to share with friends.

½ cup minced orange zest (2 or 3 oranges)
1 tablespoon minced candied ginger

3 cups orange pekoe tea leaves
2 teaspoons whole cloves, coarsely crushed

Spread orange zest on a paper towel and microwave on 50% power 1 to 2 minutes to dry; do not allow to burn. Let stand 1 minute.

Transfer zest to glass pie plate. Add ginger, tea leaves, and cloves and stir to blend. Microwave, uncovered, on HIGH 1 minute. Let mixture stand 5 minutes. Store tea mix at room temperature in an airtight container.

SPICED TEA

1 SERVING

6 to 8 ounces water
1 to 2 teaspoons Spiced Tea Mix (recipe above)

1 cinnamon stick

Pour water into microwavable mug or cup and microwave on HIGH 2 minutes, or until boiling.

Meanwhile, place tea mix in tea ball. When water is boiling, add tea ball and cinnamon stick and let steep 5 minutes. Remove tea ball and cinnamon and microwave again to reheat, if necessary.

To brew Spiced Tea by the pot, microwave a teapot of cold water to boiling. For each 1 cup water, place 1 teaspoon Spiced Tea Mix in a tea ball. Place ball in boiling water and let steep 3 to 5 minutes. To make without a tea ball, add loose tea mix to boiling water, steep, then strain into cups.

GINGER TEA

1 or 2 (¹/₈-inch) slices fresh peeled
* ginger*

Water
1 slice lemon

Place ginger in a mug. Fill mug with cold water and microwave on HIGH 1 to 2 minutes, or until very hot or boiling. Let ginger tea stand 1 minute, then float lemon slice on top and serve.

A refreshing drink that contains neither caffeine nor calories!

VARIATIONS

Add 1 cinnamon stick or fresh mint leaves with the fresh ginger. To make ginger-flavored regular tea, add 1 or 2 slices fresh ginger along with the teabag.

BLACKBERRY ACID

2 quarts very ripe blackberries
2 cups sugar

¹/₂ cup white vinegar

Place blackberries in 3- to 4-quart microwavable mixing bowl and crush with back of large spoon. Stir in sugar. Cover bowl with plastic wrap and microwave on HIGH 10 minutes, or until sugar is dissolved. Let stand at room temperature overnight.

Strain mixture through cheesecloth-lined sieve into a bowl, pressing as much juice from berries as possible. Stir in vinegar. Taste and adjust sweetness, adding more sugar, if desired, and stirring until dissolved. Store in covered containers in refrigerator or freezer, or pour into ice cube trays, freeze, and store in plastic bags.

For a refreshing aperitif, serve Blackberry Acid over ice. Mix it with water or club soda and use as a sauce for sherbet or ice cream. Blackberry Acid makes a delicious daiquiri, too: Just mix 6 ounces each of limeade concentrate, rum, and Blackberry Acid with ice cubes in a blender.

RASPBERRY ACID

Substitute raspberries for blackberries.

HOT COCOA

1 SERVING

■

1 tablespoon cocoa powder,
    preferably Dutch-process
2 tablespoons sugar

Pinch of salt
Milk
Marshmallow (optional)

In a mug or cup, combine cocoa, sugar, salt, and enough milk to form a paste. Mix until smooth. Stir in enough milk to fill cup. Microwave, uncovered, on HIGH 1 to 2 minutes, or until very hot. Add marshmallow during last 15 seconds of cooking, if desired.

HOT MOCHA

Add ½ teaspoon instant coffee powder with cocoa.

COCOA FOR A CROWD

8 TO 10 SERVINGS

■

½ cup cocoa powder, preferably
    Dutch-process
¾ cup sugar

¼ teaspoon salt
2 quarts milk

Place cocoa, sugar, and salt in 3-quart bowl and stir with wire whisk. Add 1 cup milk and whisk to form a paste. Whisk in remaining milk and microwave, uncovered, on HIGH 8 to 12 minutes, or until very hot.

HOT TODDY

1 SERVING

■

Old-fashioned but still effective!

2 teaspoons sugar
1 to 2 ounces whiskey
1 cinnamon stick

Twist of lemon peel, studded with
    2 or 3 whole cloves
Water

Place sugar, whiskey, cinnamon stick, and lemon peel in a mug. Fill mug with water and microwave on HIGH 1 to 2 minutes, or to serving temperature. Stir and serve.

ALABAMA HOT SCOTCH

Substitute Scotch for whiskey.

HOT BUTTERED RUM MIX

1 pound unsalted butter (no substitute)
1 pound dark brown sugar

1 pound confectioners' sugar
1 quart vanilla ice cream

MAKES
2 QUARTS;
50 TO 60
SERVINGS

■

A good combination to store in the freezer.

In large microwavable mixing bowl, microwave butter on 10% power 1 to 2 minutes, or until softened. Add brown sugar and confectioners' sugar and cream mixture with electric beater.

Microwave ice cream in container on 40% power 30 to 45 seconds to soften. Fold ice cream into butter mixture, then spoon mix into containers and freeze.

HOT BUTTERED RUM

To make 1 serving, fill a mug two-thirds full of water, then microwave on HIGH 2 minutes, or until boiling. Stir in 2 to 3 heaping tablespoons Hot Buttered Rum Mix, add 1 jigger of rum, and serve at once.

HOT TOMATO ZIP

2 cups canned tomato-vegetable juice
3 beef bouillon cubes
2 cups water

1 small onion, studded with 5 whole cloves
4 to 6 jiggers vodka (optional)
Lemon wedges or freshly ground black pepper

4 TO 6
SERVINGS

■

Good for a winter brunch or to serve after a day on the ski slopes.

Combine juice, bouillon cubes, water, and onion in 2-quart measure and microwave at 50% power 7 to 8 minutes, or until very hot. Remove onion and stir mixture to dissolve bouillon cubes. Stir in vodka, if desired, and serve in mugs, garnished with lemon wedges or pepper.

If you prefer to serve in stemmed glasses, pour hot tap water into glasses and allow to stand for a few minutes. Pour out water and place sterling silver spoon in glass, then pour in hot drink. (Spoon will conduct heat away from glass.)

MINT LEMONADE

**MAKES
2 QUARTS**

■

2 cups water
12 to 15 fresh mint leaves
1½ cups sugar

Juice of 6 lemons
1½ quarts ginger ale
Mint sprigs

· · · · · · · · · · ·
For clear ice cubes,
use water that has
been boiled and
cooled.
· · · · · · · · · · ·

In 2-quart measure, microwave water on HIGH 5 to 6 minutes, or until boiling. Stir in mint leaves, cover, and let stand 20 minutes. Strain into pitcher.

Add sugar and lemon juice and stir until sugar is dissolved. Refrigerate. To serve, add ginger ale and pour over ice. Garnish each serving with sprig of mint.

LEMONADE SYRUP

**MAKES
2 QUARTS;
64 SERVINGS**

■

Great to have on hand
in the summer to make
fresh lemonade by the
glass. Just pour 2
tablespoons of the
syrup into an 8-ounce
glass, add ice and
water, and stir. The
syrup can be stored in
the refrigerator for
several weeks.

2 cups water
½ cup light corn syrup

5 cups sugar
12 lemons

Combine water, corn syrup, and sugar in 2-quart measure and microwave on HIGH 4 to 7 minutes, or until sugar is dissolved, stirring once. Let syrup cool to room temperature.

Meanwhile, grate zest from 6 to 8 lemons into bowl. Squeeze juice from all lemons into same bowl. When syrup is cool, strain lemon juice into syrup and stir to blend. Store in covered container.

MINTED LEMONADE SYRUP
Add 2 cups fresh mint leaves to syrup mixture before microwaving. Strain cooled syrup before adding lemon juice.

MINT SYRUP

2½ cups water
2 cups sugar
Juice of 6 lemons

2 oranges, thinly sliced
1 to 2 cups, packed, fresh mint
    leaves

MAKES
ABOUT
5 CUPS

Combine water and sugar in 2-quart measure and microwave on HIGH 8 to 10 minutes, stirring to dissolve sugar.

Stir in lemon juice, oranges, and mint leaves. Cover and let steep for several hours. Strain and refrigerate in storage jars.

MINT JULEP

Pour 1 jigger of bourbon over cracked ice in highball glass. Fill with Mint Syrup and fresh mint leaves.

KENTUCKY MINT JULEP

Crush 2 sprigs mint in a highball glass. Add cracked ice. Pour 3 ounces bourbon over ice, then 1 tablespoon Mint Syrup. This version of Mint Julep is cool, refreshing, and dangerous!

This syrup keeps in the refrigerator for weeks and may be used to flavor iced tea, mixed drinks, and fruit juices.

SYLLABUB

2 cups heavy cream
¾ cup confectioners' sugar
1 cup dry white wine, well chilled
2 tablespoons fresh lemon juice
Pinch of salt

2 egg whites
2 tablespoons granulated sugar
1 teaspoon finely shredded lemon
    zest
Freshly grated nutmeg (optional)

8 SERVINGS

In a mixing bowl, whip cream until stiff, gradually adding confectioners' sugar. Fold in wine, lemon juice, and salt. Pour into punch bowl.

In 2-quart microwavable bowl, combine egg whites and granulated sugar and microwave at 10% power 3 minutes. Stir to dissolve sugar. Beat with electric mixer until stiff peaks form. Float dollops of meringue on whipped cream mixture. Sprinkle with lemon zest and, if desired, nutmeg.

This is an Elizabethan drink made with sherry or another red or white wine, or cider. Since it was not made with strong spirits, it was considered appropriate for ladies and even for children on special occasions. "Bub" was Elizabethan slang for "a bubbling drink."

LAMB'S WOOL CIDER

10 SERVINGS

This very old English recipe is called "lamb's wool" because the apple floating in the cider gives it a fleecy appearance.

4 baking apples, peeled, cored, and quartered
2 quarts apple cider

¹/₄ cup, packed, brown sugar
2 teaspoons mixed pickling spice
10 cinnamon sticks

Place apples in shallow 1-quart dish and microwave, covered, on HIGH 6 to 10 minutes, or until soft. Chop or mash apples with fork or puree in food processor. Reserve.

In 3-quart microwavable bowl, combine 2 cups cider, the sugar, and pickling spices. Microwave, covered, on HIGH 5 minutes, or until sugar is dissolved. Stir in remaining cider and microwave, covered, on HIGH 15 to 18 minutes, or until hot. Strain to remove spices. Add apple pulp and serve in mugs with a cinnamon stick in each mug for stirring.

MULLED CIDER
Omit apples.

OLD ENGLISH CIDER

**MAKES
3 QUARTS**

The aroma says "Welcome."

2 quarts apple cider
1 cup, packed, brown sugar
1 teaspoon whole cloves
1 teaspoon whole allspice

3 cinnamon sticks
1 quart unsweetened pineapple juice
1 lemon, thinly sliced

Pour 2 cups cider into 1-quart measure. Add sugar, cloves, all-spice, and cinnamon sticks and microwave on HIGH 5 minutes, or until very hot. Stir to dissolve sugar, then microwave on 50% power 15 minutes.

Strain mixture into microwavable 4-quart serving bowl and add remaining cider, pineapple juice, and lemon slices. Microwave on HIGH until very hot, about 10 to 15 minutes.

Store leftover cider, tightly covered, in refrigerator. For an individual serving, microwave a mug of cider on HIGH 1 to 3 minutes, or until very hot.

MULLED WINE
Microwave 2 cups cider with sugar and spices, as instructed; substitute 6 cups red wine for remaining cider.

RASPBERRY MINT CRUSH

5 cups water
½ cup sugar
1 cup, packed, fresh mint leaves
1 (12-ounce) can frozen raspberry
    juice concentrate

2 (12-ounce) cans frozen
    lemonade concentrate
1 quart club soda

30 SERVINGS

A delightful fruit drink, perfect for a Fourth of July picnic.

In 1-quart measure, combine 1 cup water, the sugar, and mint leaves. Microwave on HIGH 3 to 4 minutes. Let stand until cool. Strain into large pitcher or punch bowl.

Add remaining water, raspberry juice concentrate, and lemonade concentrate, stir well, and chill. Add club soda just before serving.

NOTE

If raspberry juice concentrate is not available, use enough raspberry-flavored sweetened drink powder to make 2 quarts liquid and add 1½ cups more water.

Freeze leftover fruit juices or fruit drinks in ice cube trays to serve in iced tea or other beverages.

CLOVE-STUDDED ORANGE HALVES

Unblemished oranges

Whole cloves

A version of the traditional pomander balls that are used to scent linens or decorate the Christmas tree, these aromatic orange halves can be floated in the wassail or cider bowl, providing perfume and flavor. They can be prepared at your leisure weeks ahead of time and frozen. As a holiday bonus, the used halves can be refrozen and used again.

Cut oranges in half and place cut side down on a plate. Pierce skin with a toothpick to form designs—for instance, flowers or geometric patterns—and insert cloves. Arrange oranges, cut side down, on baking sheet and freeze. Transfer frozen orange halves to a plastic bag and keep frozen until needed.

Before adding to cider bowl, place frozen halves in microwavable casserole and microwave on HIGH 3 to 4 minutes, or until oranges are thawed and warm.

"THE RECIPE"

MAKES
4 TO 5
QUARTS
.

Everyone loves "The Recipe"! It's delightful to have on hand during the holidays. It keeps for weeks and is instantly ready for drop-in company, adults and children alike.

1 quart unsweetened pineapple
   juice
1½ cups sugar
3 cinnamon sticks

½ teaspoon whole cloves
1 quart cranberry juice
2 quarts ginger ale
3 to 6 cups dark rum (optional)

In 2-quart measure, combine 2 cups pineapple juice, the sugar, cinnamon sticks, and cloves. Microwave on HIGH 5 to 6 minutes, or until sugar is dissolved. Let stand 5 minutes. Strain into bowl or pitcher and stir in remaining pineapple juice and cranberry juice. Refrigerate until serving time.

To serve in a punch bowl, pour fruit juice base into punch bowl, then add ginger ale, ice, and, if desired, rum.

To serve by the glass, fill glass with ice cubes, half-fill with fruit juice base, then add ginger ale and 1 jigger rum, if desired.

To serve hot, half-fill microwavable mug with fruit juice base, add enough ginger ale to nearly fill mug, and microwave on HIGH 1 to 2 minutes. Stir in 1 jigger rum, if desired.

STRAWBERRY CHAMPAGNE PUNCH

50 SERVINGS

.

Serve this festive-looking punch for a special occasion.

½ cup fresh lemon juice
1 cup superfine sugar
3 (10-ounce) packages frozen
   unsweetened strawberries
2 (750-ml) bottles champagne,
   chilled

4 (28-ounce) bottles ginger ale,
   chilled
4 lemons, thinly sliced and chilled
3 limes, thinly sliced and chilled
1 pint fresh strawberries, hulled

In 1-quart measure, microwave lemon juice on HIGH 30 to 45 seconds. Add sugar and stir to dissolve completely. Chill.

Remove printed wrapper from frozen strawberries and microwave on HIGH 3 to 4 minutes to soften a little. Place softened strawberries, lemon juice mixture, champagne, ginger ale, lemons, limes, and fresh strawberries in large punch bowl and stir until frozen strawberries are thawed and separated. Serve in punch glasses.

EGGNOG

1½ cups milk
4 large eggs, separated
½ cup sugar
1 cup heavy cream, whipped

1 teaspoon vanilla extract
½ cup bourbon
¼ cup brandy
Freshly grated nutmeg

12 SERVINGS

∎

This American version of an English drink, Posset, uses fewer eggs than the original and is based on a cooked custard. Eggnog, a widely acknowledged sign of gracious hospitality in the Southern colonies, was served with lavish assortments of fruitcakes and other sweets, and, of course, it was made with Kentucky bourbon. This recipe should be made at least one day in advance so that the flavors can mellow.

In 2-quart measure, microwave milk on HIGH 2 to 3 minutes, or until hot. Place egg yolks and sugar in mixing bowl and beat with wire whisk until blended. Gradually add ½ cup hot milk, whisking constantly, then whisk warmed egg mixture into remaining milk. Microwave on HIGH 3 to 6 minutes, or until mixture is thickened, checking 2 or 3 times after first 3 minutes of cooking. Cool custard to room temperature, then cover and chill.

In large mixing bowl, beat egg whites until stiff peaks form. Pour custard into another large mixing bowl and gently fold in egg whites, whipped cream, vanilla, bourbon, and brandy. Cover and refrigerate overnight.

To serve, gently stir eggnog to blend ingredients again, then pour into punch bowl. Sprinkle with nutmeg.

CRANBERRY CORDIAL

3 cups fresh or thawed frozen
    cranberries, coarsely chopped
2 cups sugar

2 cups vodka
1 tablespoon orange zest

**MAKES
3 CUPS**

∎

In 2-quart measure, combine cranberries, sugar, and 1 cup vodka, stirring well. Microwave on HIGH 3 to 6 minutes, or until sugar is dissolved. Stir well, pour mixture into crock or glass storage jar, and add remaining vodka and the orange zest. Cover well and let stand in cool, dark place at least 2 weeks.

Strain cordial through several layers of cheesecloth. Pour cordial into bottle, cork to seal, and store in cool, dark place.

FRUIT CORDIAL

**MAKES
ABOUT
2 QUARTS**

*1 pound dried fruit (apricots,
    peaches, pears, or prunes)*
1 cup sugar

1 quart dry white wine
1 cup brandy

■

This recipe produces a delicate, fruity cordial that is served over the delicious fruit that flavors it. Put up the cordial in pretty glass jars for holiday sharing.

Place dried fruit, sugar, and 2 cups wine in 2-quart measure, and microwave, covered, on HIGH 4 to 5 minutes, stirring several times. Sugar should be almost dissolved.

Gently stir in remaining wine and brandy. Cover well and let mixture stand in a cool, dark place several days, stirring every day.

Ladle cordial into decorative jars, cover well, and let mellow 2 to 3 weeks, or long enough for fruit flavor to fully develop in wine. Wine will keep indefinitely, but fruit will eventually become mushy. When it does, remove it from wine.

To serve, ladle fruit into goblets and pour wine over it. Serve it at room temperature. Fruit is delightful eaten separately over ice cream or used as filling for cookies and cakes.

Potpourri

As a final fillip, we offer an assortment of recipes—from homemade baby food to relishes and preserves to dog biscuits—that are perfect for microwave preparation. A lot of these recipes make wonderful gifts.

Here also are instructions for toasting nuts, and other tasks handled speedily in the microwave.

Enjoy!

TIMETABLE FOR HEATING CONVENIENCE BABY FOOD

Remove cover from jar(s) and microwave on HIGH for minimum amount of time on table below. Stir and check temperature. If microwaving several jars at the same time, check after minimum time. Foods containing sugar or fat will heat faster than vegetables or meats. **Warning: Be sure** to check food temperature before feeding baby; it should be no higher than 80 to 90° F.

AMOUNT	MICROWAVE TIME ON HIGH (SECONDS)
1 (3½- to 4¾-ounce) jar	20 to 30
2 (3½- to 4¾-ounce) jars	30 to 40
3 (3½- to 4¾-ounce) jars	40 to 50

TO WARM BABY FORMULA
- Invert bottle several times to equalize temperature of milk and check to make sure formula is not too hot before feeding the baby.
- Heat 4 ounces on HIGH 10 to 20 seconds if at room temperature, and 20 to 40 seconds if refrigerated.
- Heat 8 ounces on HIGH 25 to 30 seconds if at room temperature, and 40 to 60 seconds if refrigerated.

HOMEMADE BABY FOOD

Preparing homemade baby food in the microwave offers the same convenience and advantages as does regular microwaving. The food is more nutritious, tastes better, and looks more appealing because the fresh color is retained. Homemade baby food can be cooked without salt, sugar, or other additives. Puree cooked food in a blender or food processor and freeze individual servings in ice cube trays. Store cubes in sealed freezer bags for no longer than 5 months.

To defrost homemade baby food, place the cube or cubes in a cup. Microwave 1 cube (2 tablespoons) 25 to 40 seconds on HIGH; microwave 2 cubes (¼ cup) on HIGH 40 to 60 seconds.

COOKING HOMEMADE BABY FOOD FROM FRUITS AND VEGETABLES				
FOOD	**AMOUNT**	**YIELD (IN CUPS)**	**MICROWAVE TIME ON HIGH (MINUTES)**	**COOKING DIRECTIONS**
Apples	4 med	2 to 2½	10 to 12	Peel and core. Place in 1-quart measure, add ½ cup apple juice or water. Cover and cook. Puree.
Carrots	1 lb	2 to 2½	8 to 10	Peel and slice ¼ inch thick. Place in 1-quart measure, add 3 to 4 tablespoons water. Cover and cook, stirring after 5 minutes. Puree.
Beans	1 lb	2 to 2½	13 to 15	Remove strings. Place in 1-quart measure. Add ½ cup water, cover, and cook. Puree.
Sweet potatoes	2 med	2 to 3	7 to 10	Pierce potatoes with a fork. Cook. Turn over after 4 or 5 minutes. Peel, cube, and puree with ½ cup water.

BREAD CRUMBS

**MAKES
5 CUPS**

▪

*1 small loaf stale French or
  Italian bread, broken into
  2-inch pieces.*

Place bread in food processor and process into crumbs.
Transfer crumbs to 13 × 9-inch dish and microwave on
HIGH 6 to 8 minutes, stirring several times. Cool. To make extra-fine
crumbs, process again in food processor.
Transfer crumbs to plastic freezer bags and freeze.

BUTTER·BROWNED CRUMBS

**MAKES
1 CUP**

▪

Use on top of scalloped
dishes.

*½ stick (¼ cup) salted or unsalted
  butter, melted*

*1 cup dry bread crumbs (recipe
  above)*

Combine butter and bread crumbs in pie plate. Microwave on
50% power 2 to 5 minutes, or until browned, stirring several
times. Place crumbs in sieve and drain off butter.

QUICK BREAD CRUMBS

**MAKES
1 CUP**

▪

4 slices bread

Place bread on paper towel in single layer. Microwave on HIGH
1½ to 2 minutes. Cool. Break bread into pieces and process in
food processor.

NUTS AND SEEDS

Use the microwave for making 1 cup or less of blanched or toasted nuts and seeds.

BLANCHED NUTS

To blanch 1 cup shelled almonds, peanuts, or pistachios, place 1 cup of water in 1-quart casserole. Microwave on HIGH 2 to 3 minutes, or until boiling, Add nuts and microwave on HIGH 1 minute. Drain and cool slightly. Slip off skins by pinching them with your fingers. Spread on a paper towel to dry.

TOASTED ALMONDS

Place 1 cup blanched or unblanched almonds in 9-inch pie plate with, if desired, 1 tablespoon unsalted butter. Microwave on HIGH 1 minute, stirring to coat nuts with butter. Cook on HIGH 4 to 6 minutes, or until nuts are light golden brown, stirring several times. Let nuts stand for 5 minutes.

TOASTED PEANUTS, PECANS, OR HAZELNUTS

Place 1 cup nuts in 9-inch pie plate and microwave on HIGH 3 to 6 minutes, stirring several times. Watch carefully after first 3 minutes. (Cooking times vary because of moisture content in nuts.) Add 1 tablespoon salted or unsalted butter and stir to melt, then add salt to taste, if desired.

TOASTED COCONUT

Place 1 cup sweetened coconut in 9-inch pie plate and microwave on HIGH 2 to 4 minutes, or until brown, stirring after each minute. Cook grated fresh coconut 1 to 2 minutes longer. Cool, then store in airtight container.

TOASTED SESAME SEEDS

Place ¼ cup sesame seeds in 2-cup measure and add 1 tablespoon salted or unsalted butter. Cook on HIGH 1 minute. Stir and microwave on HIGH 2 to 4 minutes, or until seeds begin to turn golden brown, stirring after each minute.

CROUTONS

MAKES
7 TO 8
CUPS

■

Good with soups and
salads.

1 stick (¹/₂ cup) salted or unsalted
  butter
15 slices stale white bread, cut
  into ¹/₂-inch cubes

1 to 2 tablespoons garlic powder
¹/₂ cup freshly grated Parmesan
  cheese

In 3- to 4-quart casserole, microwave butter on HIGH 1 minute to melt. Add bread cubes and toss to mix. Sprinkle with garlic powder and cheese. Microwave on HIGH 10 to 15 minutes, or until crisp, stirring several times.

WALNUT OIL

MAKES
1 QUART

■

A delightful addition to
salads, or light chicken
or pasta dishes. Great
as a special gift for
friends who enjoy
cooking.

2 cups shelled walnuts (preferably
  English walnuts)

1 quart corn oil

Spread nuts evenly on 9-inch pie plate. Microwave on HIGH 2 minutes, then stir. Reduce power level to 70% and microwave 3 to 5 minutes. Let cool.

Chop walnuts coarsely in food processor. Transfer nuts to 1¹/₂-quart container and add oil. Cover tightly and store in cool place for 1 week.

Pour walnut oil through a cheesecloth-lined strainer. Drain walnuts on paper towels, then freeze and use for poultry stuffing. Pour walnut oil into jars or bottles and store in a cool place for up to 1 month. Oil will stay fresh longer if stored in refrigerator.

CHILI OIL

1 cup Oriental sesame or vegetable   *²⁄₃ cup crushed red pepper*
    oil

**MAKES
ABOUT 1 CUP**

Pour sesame oil into 2-cup measure and microwave on HIGH 1 to 1½ minutes, or until very hot, but not smoking (about 200° F.). Stir in crushed pepper. Cover and let stand overnight. Strain and store, tightly covered, in refrigerator up to 6 months.

Chili oil is a staple ingredient in Chinese cooking, especially in Szechuan cuisine.

HERBAL VINEGAR

2 to 3 sprigs fresh basil, tarragon,   *2 cups cider or white vinegar*
    or thyme

**MAKES
2 CUPS**

Place herb sprigs in 1-pint jar. Add vinegar and microwave on HIGH 1½ minutes, or until jar is warm to touch. Cap jar while still warm and store in a cool, dark place for 2 weeks.
    Store in refrigerator after opening. Use within 2 months.

CRANBERRY VINEGAR

2 cups raw cranberries   *½ cup sugar*
2 cups cider vinegar

**MAKES
3 CUPS**

Rinse cranberries, remove stems, and drain. Reserve ½ cup cranberries and combine remaining berries, vinegar, and sugar in 2-quart measure. Cook on HIGH 7 to 8 minutes. Stir. Let stand until cool.
    Strain cranberries through a cheesecloth-lined sieve, pressing out as much vinegar as possible. Pour vinegar into bottles, and add several raw cranberries to each jar. Store in refrigerator up to 2 months.

Enjoy on green salads.

RED RASPBERRY VINEGAR

**MAKES
3 TO 4 CUPS**

▪

This delicately flavored vinegar is a welcome gift. Make it in early summer when raspberries are at their peak.

2 pints fresh raspberries   *2 cups white vinegar*

Freeze 1 cup berries to add to finished vinegar.

Crush remaining berries in bowl, then transfer to 1-quart canning jar.* Add vinegar and microwave on HIGH 4 minutes, then cook at 30% power 10 minutes. Let stand until vinegar is cool. Cover tightly and let stand 2 weeks at room temperature, shaking jar daily.

Remove lid from jar and microwave vinegar on HIGH 4 minutes, then on 30% power 10 minutes. Strain vinegar through cheesecloth-lined sieve and transfer to 2 1-pint bottles. Add reserved frozen berries. Store in refrigerator up to 2 months.

* Use only a heat-tempered jar.

PRALINE MUSTARD

**MAKES
1 ½ CUPS**

▪

Use as a glaze for ham, serve with pork, or serve over cream cheese as an appetizer.

2 large eggs, beaten
½ cup dark corn syrup
⅔ cup, packed, dark brown sugar
⅓ cup cider vinegar
3 to 4 tablespoons dry mustard

½ teaspoon vanilla extract
Pinch of freshly grated nutmeg
¼ cup finely chopped pecans,
*   toasted (page 441)*

In 2-quart measure, combine eggs, corn syrup, sugar, vinegar, mustard, vanilla, and nutmeg. Whisk to mix well. Microwave on HIGH 3 to 5 minutes, stirring several times, or until sugar is dissolved and mixture is slightly thickened. Stir in pecans. Cool and store in tightly covered container in refrigerator.

SPICY DILL PICKLES

1 (46-ounce) jar whole kosher dill
  pickles
1 to 1½ teaspoons red pepper
  flakes or 2 to 3 red pepper
  pods

4 cloves garlic, sliced
⅔ cup, packed, light brown sugar

Drain pickle juice (reserve jar) into 2-quart measure. Add pepper, garlic, and brown sugar. Microwave on HIGH 4 to 6 minutes, or until sugar dissolves. Cool.

Cut pickles into quarters lengthwise and place in jar. Pour cooled pickle juice over pickles, cover, and let stand at room temperature 24 hours. Chill before serving.

**MAKES
46 OUNCES**

■

The cucumber, a member of the gourd family, has been cultivated for more than 3,000 years. It is mentioned in the Old Testament as a food eaten in Egypt. Enjoy this modern-day quick pickled version.

CRUDITÉ PICKLES

2 cups cider vinegar
1 cup water
1 cup sugar
2 tablespoons mustard seeds
1 hot red chili pepper or 1
  teaspoon red pepper flakes
2 teaspoons whole black
  peppercorns

3 to 4 cloves garlic
4 to 6 cups leftover raw or
  blanched vegetables (carrots,
  cauliflower, green or red bell
  peppers, or onions), sliced or
  cut into pieces

**MAKES
3 TO 4
PINTS**

■

A good way to use leftover vegetables.

Combine vinegar, water, sugar, mustard seeds, chili pepper, peppercorns, and garlic in 2-quart measure and microwave on HIGH 8 to 10 minutes, or until boiling. Place vegetables in jars or large bowl. While pickling mixture is still hot, pour over vegetables. Cool, cover with caps or plastic wrap, and refrigerate several days before serving.

WATERMELON RIND PICKLES

**MAKES
2 PINTS**

.

2 pounds watermelon rind
1½ cups sugar
1 cup cider vinegar

2 (3-inch) cinnamon sticks
8 whole cloves

Remove dark green outer skin from watermelon rind and discard. Cut rind into 1-inch chunks or uniform shapes and place in 2-quart casserole with sugar. Toss rind to coat with sugar, cover, and let stand overnight.

Add vinegar, cinnamon sticks, and cloves, and stir to mix. Cook, uncovered, on HIGH 10 to 15 minutes, or until rind is translucent, stirring every 3 to 4 minutes.

Spoon pickles into hot sterilized jars, discarding cloves, but putting cinnamon sticks into jars. Cover and store in refrigerator up to 1 month.

CRANBERRY CHUTNEY

**MAKES
3 CUPS**

.

This makes a pretty gift.

½ cup chopped onion
1 medium tart apple, peeled,
    cored, and chopped
⅔ cup, firmly packed, brown
    sugar
¼ cup fresh orange juice
½ teaspoon ground ginger

½ teaspoon ground cloves
½ teaspoon cinnamon
¼ teaspoon salt
⅓ cup cider vinegar
2 cups raw cranberries
½ cup raisins

Combine onion, apple, sugar, and orange juice in 2-quart measure, cover, and microwave on HIGH 5 to 6 minutes. Add ginger, cloves, cinnamon, salt, vinegar, cranberries, and raisins. Cook, uncovered, on HIGH 5 minutes. Cool, then pour into 3 1-cup jars and cap tightly. Store in refrigerator up to 1 month.

SPICED PEACHES

1 (29-ounce) can peach halves,
    undrained
1 tablespoon mixed pickling spices

1 (3-inch) cinnamon stick
1 teaspoon whole cloves
2 tablespoons cider vinegar

6 SERVINGS

▪

Serve with beef, poultry, or ham.

In 1-quart measure, combine peaches, pickling spices, cinnamon stick, cloves, and vinegar. Microwave on HIGH 4 to 6 minutes, then cook on 50% power 5 minutes. Let peaches stand until cool, to blend flavors.

VARIATIONS
Substitute canned pear halves or use half peaches and half pears.

SPICED PRUNES

1 pound dried prunes
1 1/2 cups water
1/2 teaspoon ground cloves

1/4 teaspoon freshly grated nutmeg
1 cinnamon stick
2 tablespoons brown sugar

6 SERVINGS

▪

A good condiment to serve with pork roast.

In 1 quart measure, combine prunes, water, cloves, nutmeg, cinnamon stick, and brown sugar. Cover with plastic wrap and microwave on HIGH 5 to 8 minutes. Let plump until cool.

ONION RELISH

4 cups sliced onions (about 1 1/2
    pounds)
1/2 cup white vinegar

1/2 cup sugar
1/2 teaspoon salt
1/2 teaspoon mustard seeds

MAKES

4 CUPS

▪

Serve with vegetables.

In 2-quart measure, combine onions, vinegar, sugar, salt, and mustard seeds. Cover and microwave on HIGH 7 to 10 minutes, stirring once.

    Spoon into sterilized jars; cover and chill before serving. Store in refrigerator up to 1 month.

CORN RELISH

MAKES

3 CUPS

■

A wonderful condiment to serve with other vegetables.

3 cups fresh or frozen corn kernels
²/₃ cup chopped onion
1 cup chopped celery
¹/₂ cup cider vinegar
¹/₂ cup sugar

1 teaspoon salt
1 tablespoon mustard seeds
1 tablespoon celery seeds
¹/₂ teaspoon turmeric
¹/₂ cup chopped red bell pepper

Place corn in deep 2-quart casserole, cover, and microwave on HIGH 3 to 4 minutes. Add onion, celery, vinegar, sugar, salt, mustard seeds, celery seeds, turmeric, and bell pepper and stir to mix well. Microwave, uncovered, on HIGH 3 to 5 minutes, or until very hot throughout. Cool and store, tightly covered, in refrigerator up to 1 month.

GINGERED ORANGE PEEL

MAKES

ABOUT

2 CUPS

■

Enjoy in a cup of hot tea.

3 large oranges
1 (1-inch) piece fresh ginger,
    peeled and cut into 5 pieces,
    or 1 teaspoon grated fresh
    ginger

1 cup sugar

Peel oranges with a vegetable peeler. Cut zest into ¼-inch strips. Place zest and ginger in 2-quart measure and cover with water. Microwave on HIGH 10 minutes. Drain, return zest and ginger to measure and cover with fresh water. Microwave on HIGH 8 to 10 minutes. Drain.

Combine zest and ¾ cup sugar in 1-quart measure. Microwave on HIGH 2 minutes. Stir and cook on HIGH 8 to 12 minutes, or until mixture reaches 242° F. on a candy thermometer. Remove orange zest from syrup and roll in remaining sugar. Allow to cool and dry before storing in airtight container.

APPLE BUTTER

6 cups peeled, cored, sliced apples
  (about 8 medium)
1 cup apple cider
1 cup sugar or to taste

1 teaspoon cinnamon
1/4 teaspoon ground cloves
1/2 teaspoon freshly grated nutmeg

**MAKES
3 TO 4
CUPS**

■

This old-fashioned favorite is much easier to prepare in the microwave.

Combine apples and cider in 2-quart casserole. Cover and cook on HIGH 12 to 15 minutes. Drain apples, reserving 1 cup juice.

Transfer apples to food processor or blender. Add sugar, cinnamon, cloves, nutmeg, and reserved juice and process until smooth.

Pour apple butter into original casserole and microwave on HIGH 8 to 10 minutes. Pour into sterilized jars. Refrigerate until served. Store no longer than 3 weeks.

PEACH BUTTER

3 pounds ripe peaches, peeled and
  pitted

2 cups sugar

**MAKES
4 CUPS**

■

Prepare extra quick with a food processor.

Place peaches in 2-quart measure. Cover and microwave on HIGH 10 minutes, or until peaches are tender. Drain. Place peaches in food processor and blend until smooth. Add sugar and return to measure. Microwave, uncovered, on HIGH 8 to 10 minutes. Cool. Pour into jars and cover, and refrigerate or freeze until ready to use. Store in refrigerator 3 weeks and up to 6 months in freezer.

SPICED PEACH BUTTER
Add 1 teaspoon ground ginger and 1/4 teaspoon freshly grated nutmeg.

CRANBERRY-ORANGE MARMALADE

**MAKES
4 CUPS
MARMALADE**

•

Especially good served
with turkey.

2 cups raw cranberries
1 (10-ounce) jar orange
　marmalade

⅓ cup fresh orange juice
¼ cup sugar

Combine cranberries, marmalade, orange juice, and sugar in 1-quart measure and microwave on HIGH 5 to 6 minutes. Stir and cook on 70% power 5 minutes. Marmalade will thicken when cool. Serve chilled. Store up to 1 month in refrigerator.

PEPPER JELLY

**MAKES
4 (½-PINT)
JARS**

•

Enjoy with meats or
with cream cheese and
crackers.

4 medium green bell peppers
3 to 4 jalapeño or hot banana
　peppers or 1 to 2 tablespoons
　crushed dried red pepper
　flakes

¾ cup white vinegar
3½ cups sugar
3 ounces liquid pectin
Green food coloring (optional)

Using rubber gloves, cut out stem ends and remove seeds from bell peppers and hot peppers. Cut peppers into chunks and place in a food processor with vinegar. Chop fine.

Transfer pepper mixture to 3-quart casserole and microwave on HIGH 8 to 10 minutes, or until mixture reaches rolling boil, stirring to make sure sugar has dissolved. Add pectin and microwave on HIGH 2 to 4 minutes, or until mixture returns to rolling boil. Boil 1 minute longer.

Pour jelly through strainer into 1-quart measure, skimming foam. Add a few drops of food coloring, if desired, and pour jelly immediately into sterilized jars and seal. Store in refrigerator up to 6 months.

PORT WINE JELLY

1 cup port wine
1 cup dry white wine

3½ cups sugar
3 ounces liquid pectin

MAKES
4 (½-PINT)
JARS

·

Wonderful to include in
a holiday basket.

Combine wines and sugar in 2-quart measure and microwave, uncovered, on HIGH 10 to 12 minutes, or until boiling, stirring after first 5 minutes. Add pectin, stir, and microwave on HIGH 3 to 4 minutes, or until mixture reaches rolling boil. Boil 1 minute. Skim foam with a spoon.

Pour jelly into sterilized jars and seal. When cool, store in refrigerator up to 6 months.

RASPBERRY PRESERVES

1 quart fresh raspberries
2½ cups sugar

4 tablespoons powdered pectin
1 tablespoon fresh lemon juice

MAKES
4 (½-PINT)
JARS

·

Place raspberries in 4-quart casserole and microwave on HIGH 3 minutes. Gradually stir in sugar, pectin, and lemon juice. Cook, uncovered, on HIGH 5 to 7 minutes, or until berries reach rolling boil, stirring every 2 minutes. Boil on HIGH 1 minute longer. Let stand 2 to 3 minutes, then skim foam. Pour into sterilized jelly jars and seal. Cool, then refrigerate and use within 1 month.

VARIATION
Substitute strawberries or pitted cut-up peaches for raspberries.

FRUIT SYRUP

**MAKES
1 PINT**

For pancakes, waffles, ice cream, or cake. The syrup also makes a nice gift.

*1 pint fresh or 16 ounces frozen
    blackberries, blueberries,
    strawberries, or raspberries*

*1 cup sugar
1/2 cup light corn syrup*

Place berries in 2-quart casserole and microwave on HIGH 7 to 10 minutes, stirring several times. Pour fruit into a cheese-cloth-lined strainer placed over 2-quart bowl. Press to extract juices, then discard pulp.

Add sugar and corn syrup to fruit juice. Microwave on HIGH 4 to 6 minutes, or until boiling, stirring every 2 minutes. Boil 1 to 1½ minutes longer. Pour into sterilized 1-pint jar or container. Store in refrigerator up to 2 months.

SIMPLY SCRUMPTIOUS SEASONING MIX

**MAKES
ABOUT
1/3 CUP**

An all-purpose seasoning that contains no salt. Especially good on meats, poultry, and vegetables.

*1 tablespoon dried basil
1 tablespoon dried oregano
1 tablespoon dried parsley
1 tablespoon garlic powder
1/2 teaspoon paprika*

*1/2 teaspoon freshly ground black
    pepper
1/2 teaspoon freshly ground white
    pepper*

In a jar, combine basil, oregano, parsley, garlic powder, paprika, and black and white peppers. Mix well, cover tightly, and store in a cool place.

THREE·PEPPER SEASONING MIX

1 tablespoon freshly ground black
   pepper
1 tablespoon freshly ground white
   pepper
½ to 1 teaspoon cayenne pepper
1 tablespoon dried basil
2 tablespoons onion powder
6 tablespoons garlic powder

2 teaspoons paprika
1 teaspoon filé powder
3 teaspoons dried parsley flakes
2 teaspoons dry mustard
2 teaspoons celery seeds or celery
   powder
4 teaspoons salt or salt substitute
   (optional)

MAKES ABOUT 1 CUP

This is a spicier combination than the preceding recipe. Sprinkle over meats, seafood, and poultry.

In a jar, combine black, white, and cayenne peppers, basil, onion powder, garlic powder, paprika, filé powder, parsley, mustard, celery seeds and, if desired, salt. Mix well, cover tightly, and store in a cool place.

SCHMALTZ

8 ounces chicken fat (reserved
   from chicken cavities and
   frozen)

1 large onion, chopped

MAKES ABOUT ¾ CUP

Schmaltz, rendered chicken fat, is used in Eastern European Jewish cookery either for its own flavor or as a substitute for butter in kosher meat dishes.

Thaw fat and cut into ½-inch pieces. Place fat and onion in 1-quart casserole, cover with paper towels, and microwave on HIGH 10 to 25 minutes, or until fat is rendered and onions are browned but not burned.

Strain fat into bowl, reserving onions and cracklings. Cool fat and freeze in small portions.

Place cracklings in an airtight container and store in refrigerator up to 2 weeks. To reheat, place on paper towels or small plate and microwave on HIGH 30 to 60 seconds. Serve over rye bread or matzos, sprinkled with kosher salt, if desired.

PEANUT POPCORN

MAKES

2 QUARTS

▪

Popcorn is considered the "perfect snack" and a good source of fiber. Kids of all ages like it!

½ cup light corn syrup
½ cup sugar

1 cup smooth or crunchy peanut
    butter
2 quarts hot popped popcorn

Place syrup and sugar in 1-quart measure and microwave on HIGH 2 minutes. Stir and microwave on HIGH 2 minutes longer, or until sugar is dissolved. Stir in peanut butter.

Place popped corn in large paper bag and pour peanut butter mixture over it, shaking bag to coat corn. Serve at once.

PEANUT BUTTER POPCORN BALLS

Immediately after stirring peanut butter mixture into popped corn, wet hands with cold water and press popcorn into balls. Let cool.

SHOW-TIME POPCORN

MAKES

2 QUARTS

▪

You may want to omit salt in this recipe because the cheese and herbs add sufficient flavor. When popping corn in your microwave, follow the instructions that come with your oven or microwave popcorn popper.

½ stick (¼ cup) salted or unsalted
    butter
Pinch of dried herbs (thyme,
    oregano, or fine herbes)*
2 quarts hot popped corn

Freshly grated Parmesan cheese
Cayenne pepper
Salt
Freshly ground pepper

In 1-cup measure, microwave butter on HIGH 1 minute, or until melted. Add herbs. Toss with popped corn. Stir in Parmesan cheese, cayenne, and salt and pepper to taste. Enjoy at once!

* Available at specialty food stores.

Coconut Milk

1 (14-ounce) package unsweetened
    shredded coconut

3 cups milk

MAKES

2 CUPS

Combine coconut and milk in 2-quart measure. Microwave on HIGH 7 to 10 minutes, or until boiling. Strain milk into bowl and reserve coconut. Cool milk and freeze in ½-cup containers.

To toast reserved coconut, spread out in 9-inch pie plate and microwave on HIGH 7 to 10 minutes, or until lightly browned, stirring several times.

■

This coconut is delicious toasted or used as a garnish on desserts.

Dog Biscuits

½ cup all-purpose flour
1 cup whole wheat flour
1 cup dry skim milk
⅓ cup quick-cooking oats
2 tablespoons wheat germ
⅓ cup vegetable oil

1 large egg, beaten
2 beef or chicken bouillon cubes,
    dissolved in 1 tablespoon hot
    water
½ cup milk

MAKES

18 BISCUITS

OR 60

NUGGETS

■

Your pampered pup will love them! Children and adults enjoy making them.

Combine all-purpose and whole wheat flours, milk powder, oats, wheat germ, oil, egg, bouillon, and milk in food processor or mixing bowl and process to mix. Form into a ball and knead for 1 minute.

On a lightly floured surface roll out dough ½ inch thick. Cut with a biscuit cutter. Place 6 biscuits on 9- to 10-inch plate. Cook on 50% power 6 to 9 minutes, until firm. Roll out scraps and continue making biscuits until all dough is used.

Cool biscuits on wire rack. Store in airtight container.

SILVER CLEANER

**MAKES
1 CUP**

■

Remove tarnish from silver flatware in seconds.

1 cup water
1 teaspoon salt
1 teaspoon baking soda

A 4- to 5-inch square piece
    aluminum foil, crumpled

In 2-cup measure, microwave water on HIGH 2 to 2½ minutes, or until boiling. Add salt, baking soda, and aluminum foil.

Dip flatware into mixture and watch tarnish disappear. Wash flatware in soapy water, rinse, and dry.

Tables

TABLE OF EQUIVALENT AMOUNTS (APPROXIMATE)

ITEM	WEIGHTS OR UNITS	UTENSIL MEASUREMENT
Almonds	4 ounces	¾ cup lightly packed
	1 pound in shell	⅔ cup ground
Apples	1 pound (3 medium)	2½ cups pared and sliced;
		1¼ cups applesauce
Bacon	2 ounces, diced raw	⅓ cup
Bananas	1 pound (3 or 4)	2 cups sliced; 1½ cups mashed
Butter	⅛ stick (½ ounce)	1 tablespoon
	¼ stick (1 ounce)	2 tablespoons
	½ stick (2 ounces)	4 tablespoons, ¼ cup
	1 stick, ¼ pound (4 ounces)	8 tablespoons, ½ cup
	2 sticks, ½ pound (8 ounces)	16 tablespoons, 1 cup
	4 sticks, 1 pound (16 ounces)	2 cups
Beans, dry	1 pound, raw	2½ cups raw, 5 to 7 cups cooked
Beets	1 pound (4 medium)	2 cups diced and cooked
Berries	1 pound	2 cups
Bread crumbs	3 to 4 slices oven-dried bread	1 cup fine dry crumbs
	1 slice fresh bread	½ cup fresh crumbs
Cabbage	8 ounces	3 cups shredded
Carrots	1 pound (6 or 7)	3 cups shredded; 3½ cups grated; 2½ cups diced; 1⅓ cups cooked and pureed
Candied fruit & fruit peel	1 pound	3 cups, cut up
Celery	1 large stalk	½ cup diced or sliced
Cheese, cottage	8 ounces	1 cup
cream	3 ounces	6 tablespoons
hard cheese	2 ounces	½ cup
grated	4 ounces	1 cup
Cherries	1 pound	2½ cups pitted
Chestnuts	1½ pounds in shell	2½ cups peeled
	1 pound shelled	
Chicken	3½ pounds raw, cleaned	3 cups cooked and boned
	1 large raw chicken breast	2 cups cooked and diced
Coconut, shredded	3½ ounces	1⅓ cups
Cornmeal	1 cup uncooked	4 cups cooked

TABLE OF EQUIVALENT AMOUNTS (APPROXIMATE)

ITEM	WEIGHTS OR UNITS	UTENSIL MEASUREMENT
Cracker crumbs	15 graham crackers	1 cup fine crumbs
	19 chocolate wafers	1 cup fine crumbs
	22 vanilla wafers	1 cup fine crumbs
	28 saltine crackers	1 cup fine crumbs
Cranberries	1 pound raw	4 cups; 3 to 3½ cups sauce
Dates, pitted	8 ounces	2 cups
Dried fruit	1 pound	about 4 cups, cooked
Eggplant	1½ pounds	2½ cups diced and cooked
Eggs	4 large	1 cup
	1 egg white	1 to 1½ tablespoons
	1 egg yolk	1 tablespoon
	8 large egg whites	1 cup
	12 large egg yolks	1 cup
Figs, dried	1 pound	2¾ to 3 cups chopped
Flour, all-purpose	¼ ounce	1 tablespoon
	1¼ ounces	¼ cup; 4 tablespoons
	5 ounces	1 cup
	1 pound	3½ cups unsifted (4 cups sifted)
Garlic, 1 medium clove	1/16 ounce	⅛ teaspoon
Gelatin, unflavored	¼-ounce envelope	1 tablespoon
Herbs, fresh, leaves only	½ ounce	¼ cup pressed down or 2 tablespoons chopped (1 tablespoon fresh = ⅓ to ½ teaspoon dried)
Lemon or lime	1 medium	2 to 3 tablespoons juice; 1 tablespoon grated zest
Meat	1 pound boneless	2 cups diced
Milk, evaporated	14½-ounce can	1⅔ cups
sweetened condensed	14-ounce can	1¼ cups
Mushrooms	1 pound	4 to 5 cups sliced raw
Noodles	1 cup, uncooked	1¾ to 2 cups cooked
Onion	1 pound (4 or 5 medium yellow)	2½ to 3½ cups sliced or diced
	1 large	½ cup chopped (approx.)

TABLE OF EQUIVALENT AMOUNTS (APPROXIMATE)

ITEM	WEIGHTS OR UNITS	UTENSIL MEASUREMENT
Orange	1 medium zest of 1 medium	1 cup sectioned; ⅓ to ½ cup juice 2 to 3 tablespoons grated zest
Pasta: Macaroni, spaghetti, noodles	8 ounces	4 cups cooked
Peaches	1 pound (4 medium)	2 to 2½ cups sliced
Peanuts	1 pound in shell	2 to 2½ cups nutmeats
Pears	1 pound	2 to 2½ cups sliced
Peas (green)	1 pound in pods	1 cup shelled
Pecans	1 pound in shell	2 to 2¼ cups nutmeats
Peppers (bell)	1 pound (3 to 6)	4 cups chopped
Potatoes	1 pound (3 or 4 medium)	1½ to 2 cups mashed; 3 to 3½ cups sliced or diced
Pumpkin	1 pound raw	1 generous cup cooked and pureed
Raisins (small seedless) and currants	1 pound 4 ounces	3 cups ¾ cup
Rhubarb	1 pound	2 cups cut and cooked
Rice	8 ounces raw	1 cup raw; 3 cups cooked
Shallot	½ ounce (1 large)	1 tablespoon minced
Spinach	1 pound raw 1 pound raw	4 cups raw 1½ cups cooked
Strawberries	1 pint	1½ to 2 cups sliced
Sugar, granulated brown confectioners'	2 ounces 6½ ounces 1 pound 1 pound 1 pound	⅓ cup 1 cup 2¼ to 2½ cups 2⅛ to 2¼ cups firmly packed 4 cups unsifted or 4½ to 5 cups sifted
Tomatoes, fresh canned	1 pound (3 medium) 35-ounce can	1½ cups peeled, seeded, and diced 1¾ cups strained pulp
Walnuts	1 pound in shell	1⅔ cups nutmeats
Zucchini	1 pound	3½ cups sliced; 2 cups grated and squeezed

EMERGENCY SUBSTITUTIONS

INGREDIENT	AMOUNT	EQUIVALENT
Arrowroot	1 tablespoon	2 tablespoons flour, or 1 tablespoon cornstarch or potato flour
Baking powder	1 teaspoon	¼ teaspoon baking soda and ½ teaspoon cream of tartar mixed freshly
Broth, chicken or beef	1 cup	1 bouillon cube or envelope instant broth granules mixed with 1 cup boiling water
Chocolate	1 ounce (1 square) unsweetened	3 tablespoons cocoa plus 1 tablespoon unsalted butter
Cornstarch	1 tablespoon	2 tablespoons flour
Light corn syrup	1 cup	1¼ cups sugar plus ⅓ cup liquid boiled together until syrupy
Cream, light	1 cup	⅞ cup milk plus 3 tablespoons butter (for cooking only)
Egg	1 medium	2 egg yolks plus 1 tablespoon water may be used for 1 egg in baking recipes with flour
Flour	2 tablespoons	1 tablespoon cornstarch, arrowroot, or potato flour for thickening
all-purpose	1 cup (sifted)	1 cup plus 2 tablespoons sifted cake flour
cake	1 cup (sifted)	1 cup minus 2 tablespoons all-purpose
self-rising	1 cup	1 cup sifted all-purpose flour plus 1¼ teaspoons baking powder and a pinch of salt
Hot pepper sauce	Few drops	Pinch ground red pepper (cayenne)
Milk, whole	1 cup	½ cup evaporated milk plus ½ cup water, or 1 cup reconstituted nonfat dry milk plus 2 tablespoons butter, or 1 cup skim milk plus 2 teaspoons melted butter.
light cream	1 cup	¾ cup whole milk plus ¼ cup melted butter

(continued)

EMERGENCY SUBSTITUTIONS

INGREDIENT	AMOUNT	EQUIVALENT
Milk *(cont'd)*		
sour	1 cup	1 cup whole milk plus 1 tablespoon lemon juice or white vinegar, or 1 cup of milk plus 1¼ teaspoons cream of tartar. Let stand 5 to 10 minutes before using.
Potato flour (or starch)	1 tablespoon	2 tablespoons flour or 1 tablespoon cornstarch or arrowroot
Raisins or dried currants (for baking)	1 cup	1 cup finely chopped soft prunes or dates
Sugar, confectioners'	1 cup	⅞ cup granulated sugar processed in the blender with 1 tablespoon cornstarch. (Texture will not be as smooth.)

MEASUREMENT EQUIVALENTS

1 teaspoon = ⅓ tablespoon	1 cup = ½ pint or 8 ounces
1 tablespoon = 3 teaspoons	2 cups = 1 pint
2 tablespoons = 1 fluid ounce	4 cups = 1 quart
4 tablespoons = ¼ cup	1 pint, liquid = 16 ounces
5⅓ tablespoons = ⅓ cup	1 gallon, liquid = 4 quarts
8 tablespoons = ½ cup or 4 ounces	
16 tablespoons = 1 cup or 8 ounces	

Index

About the authors

Rosemary Dunn Stancil and Lorela Nichols Wilkins are the authors of *Simply Scrumptious Microwaving* and *Kids' Simply Scrumptious Microwaving*. Home economists and food professionals involved in the field of microwaving since its inception, both authors are consultants and columnists as well as lecturers. They teach seminars and make presentations for national conventions, professional symposiums, and television shows across the country.

Stancil and Wilkins live in Athens and Atlanta, Georgia.